Platforms, Markets and Innovation

Platforms, Markets and Innovation

Edited by

Annabelle Gawer

Imperial College Business School, London, UK

Edward Elgar

Cheltenham, UK • Northampton, MA, USA

Published by
Edward Elgar Publishing Limited
The Lypiatts
15 Lansdown Road
Cheltenham
Glos GL50 2JA
UK

Edward Elgar Publishing, Inc.
William Pratt House
9 Dewey Court
Northampton
Massachusetts 01060
USA

A catalogue record for this book
is available from the British Library

Library of Congress Control Number: 2009933404

Mixed Sources
Product group from well-managed
forests and other controlled sources
www.fsc.org Cert no. SA-COC-1565
© 1996 Forest Stewardship Council

FSC

ISBN 978 1 84844 070 8 (cased)

Printed and bound by MPG Books Group, UK

Contents

PART III PLATFORMS: MANAGEMENT, DESIGN AND KNOWLEDGE ISSUES

Contributors

Carliss Y. Baldwin is the William L. White Professor of Business Administration at the Harvard Business School. She studies the structure of designs and their impact on the structure of industries over time. She is the co-author of *Design Rules: The Power of Modularity*, the first of a projected two volumes. Recent papers include 'Where do transactions come from? Modularity, transactions and the boundaries of firms' (*Industrial and Corporate Change*, 2008), 'Exploring the structure of complex software designs' (with A. MacCormack and J. Rusnak, *Management Science*, 2006) and 'How user innovations become commercial products' (with C. Hienerth and E. von Hippel, *Research Policy*, 2006). Baldwin received a bachelor's degree from MIT in 1972, and MBA and DBA degrees from Harvard Business School.

Kevin J. Boudreau is an applied microeconomist and strategy researcher studying questions at the intersection of innovation, competition and organization. He teaches Strategy at London Business School. Kevin has a PhD from the Massachusetts Institute of Technology, an MA in Economics from the University of Toronto and a BASc in Engineering from the University of Waterloo.

Stefano Brusoni is Associate Professor of Applied Economics at Bocconi University, Milan. He is Deputy Director of KITeS (Knowledge, Internationalization and Technology Studies) and coordinator of EMIT (MSc in Economics of Innovation and Technology). He obtained his PhD from the University of Sussex (UK) in 2002. His research interests include the division and coordination of innovative labour; the organizational implications of modular design strategies and the analysis of knowledge production and distribution processes within and across firms. He has published his work in leading international journals such as *Administrative Science Quarterly, Organization Science, Research Policy, Organization Studies, Economics of Innovation and New Technology, Industrial and Corporate Change, Journal of Evolutionary Economics, Journal of Management Studies* and many others.

Michael A. Cusumano is the Sloan Management Review Distinguished Professor of Management and Engineering Systems at the Massachusetts

Institute of Technology's Sloan School of Management. He specializes in strategy, product development and entrepreneurship in the software business. He received a BA degree from Princeton in 1976 and a PhD from Harvard in 1984. He consults and speaks widely around the world and is currently a director of Patni Computer Systems, one of the largest IT services and custom software development firms based in India (NYSE: PTI, www.patni.com), and Eliza Corporation, a specialist in speech recognition software applications, focused on healthcare (www.elizacorp.com). Professor Cusumano is also the author or co-author of eight books, including *The Software Business* (2004), *Platform Leadership* (2002, with Annabelle Gawer), *Competing on Internet Time* (1998, with David Yoffie), *Microsoft Secrets* (1995, with Richard Selby), and *Japan's Software Factories* (1991).

Thomas R. Eisenmann is the William J. Abernathy Professor of Business Administration in the Entrepreneurial Management Unit at the Harvard Business School. He studies management challenges in platform-based businesses that exploit network effects. Eisenmann received his DBA (1998), MBA (1983) and BA (1979) from Harvard University. His doctoral thesis examined factors driving consolidation in the US cable television industry. Earlier, Eisenmann worked at McKinsey & Company, where he was co-head of the Media and Entertainment Practice. Eisenmann is a member of the *Strategic Management Journal* editorial board, and is the editor of *Internet Business Models: Text and Cases* (McGraw-Hill/Irwin, 2002). Eisenmann is a member of the Board of Directors of Harvard Student Agencies, the world's largest student-run corporation, and was a Director of OneMain.com, one of the ten largest US Internet service providers prior to its acquisition.

David S. Evans is Executive Director of the Jevons Institute for Competition Law and Economics, and Visiting Professor, University College London and Lecturer, University of Chicago Law School. He is a Managing Director of LECG, where he serves as an expert on antitrust matters in the USA and the European Community. He is also the founder of Market Platform Dynamics, where he serves as a business advisor to a number of pre-IPO (initial public offering) stage platform-based businesses and a strategy consultant to established businesses. He has a PhD in Economics from the University of Chicago. He is the author of more than 90 articles as well as six books, including *Invisible Engines: How Software Platforms Drive Innovation and Transform Industries* (with Andrei Hagiu and Richard Schmalensee, 2006), which won the American Publishers Association Best Business Book of 2006 Award.

Takahiro Fujimoto is a Professor in the Graduate School of Economics at the University of Tokyo, a position he has held since 1998. He has also served as Executive Director of the Manufacturing Management Research Center at the University of Tokyo since 2003. Dr Fujimoto specializes in technology and operations management, as well as business administration. He holds a Bachelors degree in Economics from the University of Tokyo (1979) and a PhD from Harvard Business School (1989), where he served as a Researcher following graduation and later as Visiting Professor (1996–97) and Senior Research Associate (1997). He has also served as Associate Professor on the Faculty of Economics at the University of Tokyo, Visiting Professor at Lyon University and a Visiting Researcher at INSEAD. Dr Fujimoto is the author of numerous publications focused on automobile manufacturing and business management.

Annabelle Gawer is an Assistant Professor in Strategy and Innovation at Imperial College Business School, London. She is a leading scholar in high-tech strategy, and a pioneering contributor to the area of platform research. Her first book, *Platform Leadership: How Intel, Microsoft, and Cisco Drive Industry Innovation* (HBS Press, 2002, with Michael Cusumano), offered a new understanding of the strategy dynamics in high-tech industries, ranging from computers and telecoms to electronics, and became a reference in business and academia. The originator and editor of this collective volume, Annabelle is also extending her work on platforms to service industries. Her research has been published in journals such as the *MIT Sloan Management Review*, the *Journal of Economics and Management Strategy* (with Rebecca Henderson), as well as in the *Wall Street Journal*. She is the Editor-in-Chief of the *Journal of Strategic Management Education*. Annabelle consults with major corporations in the USA and Europe. She has an MSc in Industrial Engineering (1992) from Stanford University and a PhD (2000) from the MIT Sloan School of Management.

Shane Greenstein is the Elinor and Wendell Hobbs Professor of Management and Strategy at the Kellogg School of Management, Northwestern University. He is a leading researcher in the business economics of computing, communications and Internet infrastructure. He has been a regular columnist and essayist for *IEEE Micro* since 1995, where he comments on the economics of microelectronics. He is presently writing a history of the first decade of the commercial Internet in the USA. Greenstein is North American Editor for *Information Economics and Policy*, and Associate Editor for *Economics Bulletin* and the business/economics section of the *Communications of the ACM*. He was administrative head of the Management and Strategy Department from 2002 to 2005. Greenstein received his BA from University of California at Berkeley in

1983, and his PhD from Stanford University in 1989, both in Economics. He also continues to receive a daily education in life from his wife and children.

Andrei Hagiu is an Assistant Professor in the Strategy group at Harvard Business School. Andrei's research focuses on multi-sided markets, which feature platforms serving two or more distinct groups of customers, who value each other's participation. He is studying the business strategies used by such platforms and the structure of the industries in which they operate: payment systems, advertising supported media, personal computers, video-games, mobile devices, shopping malls etc. Andrei graduated from the Ecole Polytechnique and the Ecole Nationale de la Statistique et Administration Economique in France with an MS in Economics and Statistics, before obtaining a PhD in Economics from Princeton University in 2004. Before joining HBS, he spent 18 months in Tokyo as a Fellow at the Research Institute of Economy Trade and Industry, an economic policy think-tank affiliated with the Japanese Ministry of Economy Trade and Industry.

Armand Hatchuel is a Professor and Deputy Director at the Center for Management Science at Mines ParisTech, and was a permanent Guest Professor at the Fenix Center, Chalmers Institute, Gothenburg (1999–2007). His research focuses on the theory and history of management and design, in particular on innovative firms, design processes and collaborative research principles. In 1996, he proposed the C–K design theory, which was further developed with Benoit Weil and Pascal Le Masson. He has published several books and papers and is a member of international journals boards and national scientific boards in France and Sweden. In 1996, he was awarded a prestigious French award for his work in management and in 2003 he received the medal of the Paris School of Arts and Crafts for his work on design theory. He co-chairs the special group on Design Theory of the Design Society and is also a regular columnist on management issues for the French newspaper *Le Monde*.

Pascal Le Masson is an Assistant Professor of Design, Project and Management at Mines ParisTech. His research focuses on the management of innovative design capabilities. This research program is motivated by issues raised by companies striving for growth by intensive innovation and the new theoretical paths opened by the most recent theories of design reasoning (C–K theory, Hatchuel and Weil, 2003). With Armand Hatchuel and Benoit Weil, his research unfolds in three main directions: the analysis of innovation techniques such as creativity, prototyping and user involvement processes; the organization of design-oriented organizations; and models of growth in design-based economies. Pascal has published several papers and his first book, *Les Processus d'Innovation* (2006) co-authored by Armand Hatchuel and Benoit Weil, is soon to be published in English. He is the secretary of the Design Theory Special Interest Group of the Design Society.

Koichi Ogawa is a Professor of Intellectual Asset-based Management, Endorsed Chair, University of Tokyo, Japan. Professor Ogawa holds a doctoral degree in Electronics Engineering. He is the co-author of the paper 'Architecture-based approaches to international standardization and evolution of business models', which received the second-prize Award from the International Electro-technical Commission (IEC) Century Challenge in 2006. He has been in charge of R&D and business development for 30 years at Fujitsu Ltd, Japan. His main fields of research were computer storage technology and, since 2004, the management of technology and the theory of product architecture. His articles have been published in journals such as the *Journal of Applied Physics, Journal of IEEE Transactions, Japan Journal of Applied Physics* and the *Akamon Management Review.* He was one of the Japanese delegates to ISO/JTC1/SC23 as a chairman of a local working group, and contributed to international standardization of the 5.25 inch WORM and the 3.5 inch MO optical disk cartridge.

Geoffrey Parker is an Associate Professor of Economic Sciences at the A.B. Freeman School of Business at Tulane University and serves as Director of the Tulane Energy Institute. Parker has made contributions to the theory of network economics as co-developer of the theory of 'two-sided' networks. Recent research includes multiple studies of the economics of business platform strategy, a cross-industry investigation of outsourced engineering projects, and a study of the performance of electric power markets. Parker's research has been funded by grants from the National Science Foundation, the Department of Energy and multiple corporations. Parker received a BS degree from Princeton University, and MS and PhD degrees from the Massachusetts Institute of Technology. Parker's work has appeared in journals such as *Harvard Business Review,* the *Journal of Economics and Management Strategy, Management Science* and *Production and Operations Management.*

Andrea Prencipe is Full Professor of Management of Enterprise at the Faculty of Economics of the University G. d'Annunzio and Honorary Professor at SPRU (Science Policy Research Unit, University of Sussex). He holds a BA (with honor) in Economics and Commerce from University G. d'Annunzio, an MSc in Innovation Management from Scuola Superiore S. Anna, an MSc in technology Innovation Management and PhD in Technology Strategy from SPRU. He has been visiting scholar at Harvard Business School and Michigan Business School. His research interests encompass strategic management of technological and organizational innovation, organizational learning in project-based organizations, and the implication of modular design strategies on the division and coordination of labor, social capital and innovation processes. Andrea sits on the editorial board of *Long Range Planning, Organization Science* and the *International Journal of Technology and Innovation Management*. His work has been published in such journals as *Administrative Science Quarterly, Industrial and Corporate Change, Journal of Management and Governance, Organization Science* and *Research Policy*.

Mari Sako has been Professor of Management Studies at Saïd Business School, University of Oxford since 1997. From 1987 to 1997 she was Lecturer (then Reader) in Industrial Relations at LSE. Her research focuses on the connections between global strategy, comparative business systems and human resource management. Her books include *Prices, Quality and Trust* (1992), *Japanese Labour and Management in Transition* (1997) and *Shifting Boundaries of the Firm* (2006). She was a principal researcher for the MIT International Motor Vehicle Program (IMVP) during 1993–2006, working on modularization, outsourcing and supplier parks in the global automotive industry. More recently, as a Senior Fellow of the ESRC/EPSRC Advanced Institute of Management Research, her research projects included productivity and performance in business services, the role of lawyers in outsourcing, the impact of outsourcing on professions, and origins of the creation of shared and outsourced services.

Melissa A. Schilling is an Associate Professor of Management at the Stern School of Business, New York University. She received her PhD from University of Washington in Seattle. Her primary research interests are in technological innovation and knowledge creation, with a particular emphasis on how networks and modularity influence the innovative process and outcomes. She is the author of the text *Strategic Management of Technological Innovation* (McGraw-Hill/Irwin, 2004), and her research has been published in journals such as *Academy of Management Review, Academy of Management Journal, Management Science, Organization Science, Creativity Research Journal* and others.

Fernando F. Suarez (PhD, MIT) is a tenured Associate Professor of Management at Boston University and currently serves as the Chair of the Strategy and Innovation Department. His research spans the areas of innovation and technology strategy, standards and dominant designs, information technology and flexibility. His publications have appeared in leading journals such as *Academy of Management Journal, Management Science, Strategic Management Journal, Academy of Management Review,*

Research Policy, Operations Research, Industrial & Corporate Change, Harvard Business Review and *Sloan Management Review*. Professor Suarez is the 2008–09 Program Chair of the Technology and Innovation Management (TIM) Division, Academy of Management, the largest organization of management scholars in the world. He has been a member of the Editorial Board of *Management Research* and a Representative-at-large of the TIM Division. He also serves on the Academic Board of ESE Business School in Santiago and has been active in both institutional and private entrepreneurial activities, having successfully launched an MBA program and a software company.

Hirofumi Tatsumoto is an Associate Professor of International Business Management at University of Hyogo in Japan. He holds an MA in Economics from the University of Tokyo. His main area of research is strategic management, particularly in electronics, software and the semi-conductor industry. He is part of the research project on 'International Standardization' of the New Energy Development Organization (NEDO), Japan. His research was published as chapters in the books *Monodukuri Management, Economic Analysis of the Game Industry* and *Strategic Use of Consensus-based Standards*, and he has published articles in the *SEC Journal* (accepted by IPA the Information-Technology Promotion Agency Japan), *Organizational Science*, the *Journal of the Intellectual Property Association of Japan*, and *Akamon Management Review* (all in Japanese).

Fredrik Tell was awarded his BSc, Lic. Econ. and PhD degrees from Linköping University, Sweden. He is a Professor of Business Administration at the Department of Management and Engineering at Linköping University and is deputy director of the KITE (Knowledge Integration and Innovation in Transnational Enterprise) Research Group. He has previously been a lecturer at the London School of Economics and Political Science, UK, as well as a visiting research fellow at the University of Sussex, UK, and Stanford University, USA. Fredrik Tell's main research interests include management of complex technologies and standards, organizational knowledge, innovation and industry dynamics, history of technology and business history. He has published articles and reviews in journals such as *Business History, Industrial and Corporate Change, Management Learning, Organization, Organization Studies, Research Policy* and *Technology Analysis and Strategic Management*.

Marshall Van Alstyne is an Associate Professor at Boston University and Visiting Professor at MIT. He received a BA from Yale, and MS and PhD degrees from MIT. He has made significant contributions to the field of information economics. He co-authored the first proof that a market mechanism could reduce spam and create more value for users than even a perfect filter. As co-developer of the concept of 'two-sided' networks he has been a major contributor to theories of network effects. He designed and implemented one of the first projects to measure the dollar output of individual information workers. This research has generated multiple patent applications and received numerous awards, including an NSF Career Award and four best paper awards. Articles or commentary have appeared in *Nature, Science, Management Science, Harvard Business Review, The New York Times* and *The Wall Street Journal.*

Benoit Weil is a Professor of Design, Project and Management at Mines ParisTech. His research focuses on the rationalization of collective actions. He has created the Research Program on Design Activities with Professor Armand Hatchuel. Together they proposed a new theory of design reasoning (C–K theory) accounting for the dual expansion of knowledge and concepts characteristic of innovative design. Deepening its foundations, they recently showed striking similarities between C–K design theory and set theory. He is now leading the Research Program on Design Regimes (funded by the French National Research Agency) to study, with Armand Hatchuel, Pascal Le Masson and Blanche Segrestin, the main features of innovative design regimes in several sectors. He has published several papers and books (the most recent one – *Les Processus d'Innovation*, 2006, co-authored with Armand Hatchuel and Benoit Weil – is soon to be published in English).

C. Jason Woodard is an Assistant Professor in the School of Information Systems at Singapore Management University. His research explores the relationship between system architecture and competitive strategy, with a focus on software-intensive systems. He is especially interested in the role of architectural control in shaping the evolution of technology platforms. He studied business, economics and computer science at Harvard University, where he received a PhD in Information, Technology and Management in 2006. Prior to that, he was a technical evangelist for IBM's efforts related to Java, XML and Linux.

Ramsin Yakob was awarded his BSc from the University of North London, UK, his MSc from the School of Business, Economics and Law, Gothenburg, Sweden and his PhD from Linköping University, Sweden. Both degrees were taken within the field of International Business. He is currently an Assistant Professor at Linköping University, Sweden. Ramsin Yakob's main research interests are platform technologies, knowledge management, project organization and innovations. He has also worked as a consultant with the Royal Bank of Scotland, UK and at American Express, UK.

Acknowledgements

It is my pleasure to thank here the many individuals and institutions that helped this book become a reality.

First, I would like to thank Edward Elgar, whose early personal support and commitment to this book project was decisive. Next, I would like to thank the other 23 book contributors who superbly rose to the challenge and created novel, insightful, clear and complementary contributions to this fascinating topic. So, huge thanks to Carliss Baldwin, Kevin Boudreau, Stefano Brusoni, Michael Cusumano, Tom Eisenmann, David Evans, Shane Greenstein, Takahiro Fujimoto, Armand Hatchuel, Andrei Hagiu, Pascal Le Masson, Koichi Ogawa, Geoffrey Parker, Andrea Prencipe, Mari Sako, Fernando Suarez, Melissa Schilling, Hirofumi Tatsumoto, Fredrik Tell, Marshall Van Alstyne, Benoit Weil, Ramsin Yakob and Jason Woodard. This book is a collective endeavour, and I am proud of the end result.

I would like to thank the different institutions that contributed to the completion of this book, through their funding for the organization of the first international conference on Platforms, Markets and Innovation, held at Imperial College London in June 2008: Imperial College Business School, London, and its Innovation Studies Centre; the UK Engineering and Physical Science Research Council; and IBM for a Faculty Award. Additional funding was also provided by the ESRC–AIM (Economic and Social Science Research Council–Advanced Institute of Management) as part of the research grant 'Platforms for innovation: creating replicable product and service components for high-value integrated solutions'. These institutions collectively helped fund the conference, as well as my personal research and my work on this book.

For their personal encouragement and support of this project, I would also like to thank a few Imperial Business School colleagues: David Begg, Principal of the Business School; Dot Griffiths, Deputy Principal of Imperial College Business School; David Gann, Director of the Innovation Studies Centre; Nelson Phillips, Head of the Organization and Management Group; and Andrew Davies, Reader in the Innovation and Entrepreneurship Group, with whom I collaborated on the ESRC–AIM grant mentioned above. Thanks also to research associate Anna Canato, and to my doctoral students Stefano Miraglia and Richard Tee for their editorial assistance on the manuscript. Special thanks to Shelley Meehan, who masterfully helped organize the conference on Platforms.

I would also like to thank the conference panel guest speakers: Mr Alberto Spinelli, Intel Corporation, Director of Strategic Marketing; Dr Robert Berry, IBM, Chief Technology Officer, Messaging Technology; Mr Jose Collazo, British Telecom, President, BT Global Services – Products and Partners; and Mr Simon Brown, Microsoft Corporation, Vice president, Field Evangelism, Developer and Platform Group.

Last but not least, I would like to thank my husband, David Bendor, who thought of this book first, and encouraged me to make it happen. So thanks, David, for your good ideas, steadfast support, and for being the best life partner I could hope for.

Annabelle Gawer
London
24 December 2008

1. Platforms, markets and innovation: an introduction

Annabelle Gawer

INTRODUCTION

The emergence of platforms, whether used inside firms, across supply chains, or as building blocks that act as engines of innovation and redefine industrial architectures, is a novel phenomenon affecting most industries today, from products to services. This book, the first of its kind dedicated to the emerging field of platform research, presents leading-edge contributions from top international scholars from strategy, economics, innovation, organizations and knowledge management.

This book represents a milestone for the vibrant field of platform research. It is the outcome of an ambitious international collaboration, regrouping and making connections between the research work of 24 scholars, affiliated with 19 universities, in seven countries over four continents. The novel insights assembled in the 14 chapters of this volume constitute a fundamental step towards an empirically based, nuanced understanding of the nature of platforms and the implications they hold for the evolution of industrial innovation.

But what exactly are platforms? Why should we care about them? And, why do we need a book about them?

WHY THIS BOOK?

We find platforms in many industries, and certainly in all high-tech industries. Google, the Internet search engine, social networking sites such as Facebook, operating systems in cellular telephony, videogame consoles, but also payment cards, fuel-cell automotive technologies and some genomic technologies are all industry platforms. But perhaps the most media-covered platform (and archetypal example) is Microsoft Windows. Windows is also a great example of just how much we still don't understand about platforms.

The two highly publicized antitrust lawsuits brought against Microsoft by the US Department of Justice and the European Commission have given rise to unprecedented levels of fines, in the hundreds of millions of US dollars, and have revealed profound differences in the opinions held by, on the one hand, the firms involved, and on the other by the regulatory authorities. The disagreements did not stop there: the US and European regulatory authorities upheld very different rulings. In fact, very few experts agreed with each other in the course of these lawsuits, which have been the setting for highly contradictory arguments not only between managers and technologists of opposite camps – which was to be expected – but also between world-class scholars. Leading-edge economists and management scholars, in particular, have publicly taken radically different stands as to whether Microsoft's business practices were anticompetitive.

A central issue addressed in the lawsuits was the potentially adverse effect that certain business practices from Microsoft, a dominant firm in the operating systems market, could have on competition, industry innovation and social welfare. The controversial practices ranged from Microsoft's decision to bundle its Windows software with complementary products to its decision to withhold information on how to connect complementary products to Windows. The theoretical disagreement between economists was particularly noticeable, as, at least in principle, they based their logic on the same economic theory. What was the root of the problem?

Microsoft Windows is an industry platform – a building block, providing an essential function to a technological system – which acts as a foundation upon which other firms can develop complementary products, technologies or services. As a platform, it is subject to so-called network effects, which tend to reinforce in a cumulative manner early gained advantages such as an installed base of users, or the existence of complementary products. In a positive feedback loop, new users get more benefit from using Windows than from using an alternative platform, as it is already installed on many personal computers (PCs) and therefore facilitates exchange of files and interoperability in general. They also benefit from a sizeable pool of existing Windows-compatible software, which makes Windows more useful. Software developers wishing to develop new software applications will find that, when deciding whether to make such new applications compatible with an alternative platform, they will be better off designing for Windows, as most developers have done, since it already has a large installed base of users.

The cumulative nature of these network-fuelled dynamics implies that those platforms that make it past a certain tipping point tend to become really hard to dislodge. In a sense, as platforms' market share grows, so also grow their own barriers to entry. The extreme dominance of firms such as Microsoft, and more recently of Google, is unprecedented. The speed of innovation these firms have conducted, as well as the intensity and speed of innovation conducted in the industries (some prefer the word ecosystem) they operate in, is also unprecedented. And all this is happening, with real-life consequences of enormous proportions, while many observers, managers, regulators or scholars are still coming to terms with the different facets of platforms, and trying to make sense of them. The unresolved differences between the economists mentioned above also invite us to look more deeply into this phenomenon, as it point to the limits of our existing knowledge and understanding. It is the contention of the authors of this book that, with platforms, we are facing a situation where existing theory is reaching its limits. As scholars, we felt that we collectively needed to push our understanding of this multifaceted phenomenon forward, with an inquisitive and open mind, but based on rigorous research and facts.

The emerging phenomenon of platforms affects industrial dynamics, creates new forms of competition, reveals new forms of collaborative innovation across firms and poses a host of new fundamental questions. These new questions include, but are not limited to, social welfare questions, industry dynamics questions and strategy questions. There are also questions about the management and the design of platforms, their impact on international competition, as well as their implications for an economy of services.

Citizens, consumers and regulators care about social welfare questions, such as: how can consumers enjoy the benefits from innovation created by dominant platform firms without letting this dominance get out of control? How can we achieve a more nuanced understanding of the respective impact of competition and of inter-firm collaboration, and particularly of collaborative innovation, on social welfare? For example, how can we assess the possible tradeoffs between benefits from competition and benefits from innovation? How do we evaluate tradeoffs between innovation on the platform, performed by platform owners, and innovation on complements or modules, performed by complementors? What kinds of platform governance should be put in place to ensure the best functioning of platforms and ecoystems?

Then we have a set of industry dynamics questions: under which conditions can we expect industry platforms to emerge? What forms do they take, in what context? And then, there are of course the strategic questions, which are the ones managers and investors care about, as they are linked to firms' performance: how can firms succeed in the new platform game? Which capabilities are needed? When should firms open up their technologies and processes, or when should they adopt proprietary strategies? Is there a continuum between 'open' and 'closed'? How do we know which strategy is best, given our industry's and firm's circumstances?

Last, there are questions related to the management and design of platforms, as well as questions about implications for international competition and division of labour. For example: how to manage the exploratory processes to create a platform? How to manage platform development projects? How to manage the creation of knowledge associated with the collective innovation practices? And, last but not least, what are the implications of all of this for competition and innovation in services? This book uncovers many such questions – and offers some answers.

As the editor of this book, I would say that if there was one idea that I wish readers would take away with them as they start thinking seriously about platforms, and about what is unique about them, it would be the following: platforms invite us to examine carefully the intimate interactions between technology and business, and in particular between the structure of technology and the modalities of business interaction. If this book manages to identify and highlight these interactions, it will have presented a persuasive argument for why we cannot afford to take technology as static, monolithic, exogenous, or as simply the precinct of engineers. That will be a major achievement, as it runs against not only common practice within organizations, but also entrenched intellectual reflexes within academia.

Sometime towards the end of the nineteenth century, the modern industrial firm was born, and with it came a new separation into distinct spheres of the engineers on the one hand, with their instruments, language and knowledge, focusing on creating products, and the business managers on the other, focusing on clients, transactions and markets. As those of us who have worked in firms know from experience, these people talk different languages, and in many organizations don't really talk to each other. Further, the separation of these spheres has also been found in academia. The economists of the twentieth century could relatively safely assume technology away in their models as a mere production function, and many management scholars have done so too. Markets and industries have been assumed to exist, products have been assumed to exist, and their uses were assumed to be known as well: all of these (industries, markets, products and uses) have accustomed us to expect some degree of stability. Therefore questions such as 'Where will market transactions take place?', and 'What will be the nature of these transactions?', had rather obvious answers.

However, when one observes the constantly evolving nature of platforms such as Windows or Google, it seems that their owners are not just part of one industry (computing), but instead able to enter seamlessly into other markets such as cellular telephony or media content. While the content and the uses of the platform product change constantly, one realizes that some of our old assumptions simply don't hold. We shall have to think about what it is in the structure of the technology (which we can also call its architecture) that facilitates or hinders the emergence of new markets and new types of transactions. One of the points of contention of Microsoft and of the economists on its side was to object, on the basis of principle, that no regulator should have the right to intervene in product design.[1] This claim seems obvious and legitimate to many economists: the design of the product should be the prerogative of the firm! However, when product design (which is, precisely, the domain of technology structuring and architecture), in the hands of a dominant firm, affects the sheer possibility of existence of markets, then perhaps the regulator should be allowed to have a look – and a say.

But of course then we enter uncharted territory – where we cannot assume that collaboration between firms is necessarily a price-fixing, colluding endeavour, and where competition and collaboration each play a role less simple than we have been used to. Where the regulator was understood to be the guarantor that competition would be free to play its course, we now face situations when, if unchecked, competition can create adverse conditions for innovation and for consumers. Again, this is uncharted territory, and this is precisely why we need rigorously derived, preferably empirically based, new knowledge that addresses these new issues head on. This book attempts to do just that.

OBJECTIVES OF THIS BOOK AND HOW IT CAME TO EXIST

I conceived of this project because I realized that, over the past ten years or so, since I completed my doctoral work on platform leadership (Gawer, 2000) and published my first book on the topic with Michael Cusumano (Gawer and Cusumano, 2002), many individual researchers had made remarkable progress, each in his or her field, that could contribute towards a better understanding of the multifaceted phenomenon of platforms. It appeared to me that there was an as-yet-unrecognized community of researchers working in different universities and using different approaches, a few of whom knew each other (or each other's work). There were also others who did not know each other, but would certainly benefit if they were put in contact.

I discussed my project with publisher Edward Elgar, and his early personal support and commitment were invaluable. It was most rewarding that the great majority of book contributors I had in mind responded enthusiastically to my invitation to write a chapter either individually or as a team. As my intention was not only to stimulate new research in this field by offering a publication opportunity to these top researchers, but also to contribute as much as possible to the advancement of the field, I thought of a way for these diverse researchers to enrich their own thinking by incorporating each other's insights into their own chapters. I conceived therefore of organizing a conference, to take place roughly mid-course between the time researchers started to work on their chapter and the delivery date of the manuscript, and so, crucially, at a time when they would be actively engaged in the writing process. The objective of this conference was to give each book contributor an opportunity to get feedback from fellow contributors – as well as to learn from their presentations – at a time that was propitious for these insights to be reflected in the end result. As each chapter can be seen as a module of the overall book, this conference aimed to increase the integration of the chapters, to achieve an output whose quality would be better than the sum of its parts.

The first international conference on Platforms, Markets and Innovation took place in June 2008 at Imperial College Business School, London, my home institution, and was a great success. It featured the book contributors, from all over the world, who presented and/or discussed the working chapters to/with each other and to an 80-strong audience of other researchers, managers and students. It also featured a panel discussion between researchers and top executives from IBM, Intel, Microsoft and British Telecom. The conference was also an opportunity for this new community of researchers to meet in one place and get to know each other. Many authors confirmed – and I can testify – that most chapters benefited from this group discussion.

For readers who are familiar with how platforms work, they will have recognized in the vision and the design of this book several themes that are part of platforms thinking, and that are dear to my heart: creating a platform, stimulating others to innovate towards the collective creation of an output that is better through coordination, while preserving individual incentives.

CONTENT OF THIS VOLUME

The book comprises 14 chapters, and is divided into three parts. Part I presents an overview of platforms. Part II focuses on specific questions related to opening or closing platforms, as well as on platform governance issues. Part III focuses on platform management, design and knowledge issues.

Chapter 1, this Introduction, situates the book and summarizes its content.

In Chapter 2, Carliss Y. Baldwin and C. Jason Woodard set an ambitious agenda: to present a unified view of platforms, cutting across the different streams of literature (product development, technology strategy and industrial economics) in which the term has been used. Their chapter aims to shed light on the relationships between platforms and the systems in which they are embedded, in order to better understand firms and industries where platforms play an important role. The authors define a platform as a set of stable components that supports variety and evolvability in a system by constraining the linkages among the other components. Although the term 'platform' is used in diverse ways that seem difficult to reconcile, Baldwin and Woodard find that the fundamental architecture behind all platforms is essentially the same: the system is partitioned into a set of 'core' components with low variety and a complementary set of 'peripheral' components with high variety. The low-variety components constitute the platform. They are the long-lived elements of the system and thus implicitly or explicitly establish the system's interfaces, the rules governing interactions among the different parts. This underlying architectural unity motivates the authors' effort to develop a common set of analytical tools for studying platforms and the industries that produce them. Among the most important tools are representation schemes – in other words, ways to draw pictures of platform architectures. The authors discuss approaches from three different literatures: network graphs from organization theory; design structure matrices from engineering design; and layer maps from technology strategy. The chapter concludes by addressing four questions: first, when is a platform architecture preferable to allowing all components to vary arbitrarily? Second, when can a platform and its peripheral components (complements) remain within the control of a single firm? Third, when should a firm allow or encourage outsiders to develop complements to a platform it controls? And fourth, if a firm does allow – or is forced to accept – external complementors, over which components of the system should it strive to retain control?

In Chapter 3, I aim to answer two research questions: (1) under which conditions can we expect industrial platform dynamics to emerge and unfold? (2) In the context of platform industry dynamics, what kind of platform strategies should firms devise, depending on whether they are incumbents or new entrants? To answer to the first question, I set out to present a new typology of platforms, which identifies the context in which different types of platforms appear. Platforms are designed and used in three main settings: inside firms; across supply chains; or as industry platforms – when they are the building blocks that act as engines of innovation and redefine industrial architectures. I then suggest an 'evolutionary perspective on platform emergence', and identify circumstances under which internal platforms evolve into supply chain platforms, which then evolve further into industry platforms. To answer the second question on platform strategies, I build on Gawer and Cusumano's (2008) concepts of 'coring' and 'tipping', and further specify the combinations of these that should be best suited to new entrants and to incumbents, depending on characteristics of the industry they operate in or wish to enter. I also suggest that firms' 'design capabilities' (i.e. whether a firm's design capability is to be an integrator/system assembler or a specialist/component maker) should have a decisive impact on which strategy to pursue. I conclude with implications and further questions for the study of platforms in services.

In Chapter 4, Fernando F. Suarez and Michael A. Cusumano examine a fascinating but as-yet-understudied aspect of platforms emergence and competition: the role of services. They note that the platform literature has grown out of innovation and new product development studies, which have tended to overlook the role of services. The authors focus on three questions: what is the potential role of services in the outcome of platform battles in product industries? What is the importance of services in platform-mediated markets versus other markets? And which types of firms are more likely to produce services in platform-mediated industries and why? The authors identify several roles that services play: first, they can be used to facilitate adoption, either by lowering adoption risk or through subsidy. Second, delivering services implies a close interaction with consumers, which provides useful feedback for further platform innovation. Third, the authors offer several examples where services enhance the value of the platform through a variety of indirect network effects, and can also act as customer retention mechanisms. In the empirical part of their chapter, Suarez and Cusumano observe that in the software products industry, platform markets such as operating systems, multimedia, and videogames, services revenues do not overtake product revenue – suggesting that this may be caused by the resilience of platform markets to commoditization. Last, the authors discuss circumstances under which the platform firms are likely to provide the services themselves rather than through a network of external service providers.

In Chapter 5, David S. Evans explores how entrepreneurs who start multi-sided platforms must secure enough customers on both sides, and in the right proportions, to provide enough value to each group of customers and to achieve sustainable growth. Evans's chapter, precisely because it focuses on the problem faced by start-up entrepreneurs who have to 'ignite' markets, is an important and welcome contribution to the literature on multi-sided platforms – which have so far tended by and large to assume that the markets on each side of the platform already exist, and have focused almost exclusively on how to price access to the platform to encourage adoption. In Evans's chapter, the entrepreneurs must secure 'critical mass' to ignite the growth of their platforms, otherwise their platform implodes. The chapter details a number of strategies available to entrepreneurs to reach this critical mass. These include the 'zig-zag' – which involves successive accretions of customers on both sides to build up the value to both sides – and the 'two-step' – which involves getting enough members of one side on board first and then members of the other side. These strategies can usefully employ many of the tactics used for new product introductions by non-platform businesses. The relevant strategies depend in large part on whether the nature of the platform requires securing participation by both platform sides at launch, as is the case with dating venues; whether it is possible to acquire one side before approaching the other side, as is the case with search engines; and whether it is necessary to make pre-commitments to one side to induce them to make investments, as is the case with videogames. The chapter concludes with an analysis of two sets of examples: B2B (business-to-business) exchanges, and social networking websites Friendster and Facebook.

Part II focuses on specific questions related to opening or closing platforms, as well as on platform governance issues.

In Chapter 6, Thomas R. Eisenmann, Geoffrey Parker and Marshall Van Alstyne offer a systematic and rigorously derived set of strategies and guidelines for managers on how to make the right choices about opening or closing mature platforms. Selecting optimal levels of openness is crucial for firms that create and maintain platforms. Decisions to open a platform entail tradeoffs between adoption and appropriability. Opening a platform can spur adoption by harnessing network effects, reducing users' concerns about lock-in, and stimulating production of differentiated goods that meet the needs of user segments. At the same time, opening a platform typically reduces users' switching costs and increases competition among platform providers, making it more difficult for them to appropriate rents from the platform. The authors focus on a subset of platforms: those that exploit network effects by mediating transactions between platform users. The conclusions from this chapter are the following: platform openness occurs at multiple levels depending on whether participation is unrestricted at the (1) demand-side-user (end-user), (2) supply-side-user (application developer), (3) platform provider or (4) platform sponsor levels. These distinctions in turn give rise to multiple strategies for managing openness. Horizontal strategies for managing openness entail licensing, joint standard setting and technical interoperability with rival platforms.

Vertical strategies for managing openness entail backward compatibility, platform and category exclusivity, and absorption of complements. Each strategy grants or restricts access for one of the four platform participants. When proprietary platforms mature, they are often opened to encompass new providers. Once network mobilization winds down and free-rider problems are no longer salient, proprietary platform sponsors may find it attractive to license additional providers to serve market segments with diverse needs. Naturally, these new providers will seek a say in the platform's direction: they will try to force a previously proprietary platform to open its governance. Likewise, as shared platforms mature, their renewal may hinge on partners ceding power to a central authority that can set priorities and settle disputes over who will provide next-generation technologies. This closes the governance of a previously open platform. Thus forces tend to push both proprietary and shared platforms over time towards hybrid governance models typified by central control over platform technology and shared responsibility for serving users.

In Chapter 7, Kevin J. Boudreau and Andrei Hagiu make an important contribution to the literature on multi-sided platforms by focusing on the importance and variety of non-price instruments plaform owners use to regulate and govern their platform. Multi-sided platforms (MSPs) are characterized by interactions and interdependence between their multiple sides, and the existence of network effects. The thrust of prior work in the MSP literature has focused on the question of how to get the different sides around an MSP 'on board' in large numbers, while setting up a pricing model that maximizes platform profits. Overall, the MSP literature has emphasized arm's-length pricing as the central strategic instrument used by platform owners to intermediate the ecosystem of users and complementors surrounding an MSP. A number of provocative analyses, however, have suggested a richer picture of the role of MSPs and limitations to arm's-length market interactions. Metaphors of 'open' and 'closed' platforms convey something of how restrictive or liberal a platform may be in its dealings with surrounding constituents. But also, several studies have documented a variety of roles played by platform owners, including ensuring 'coherent' technical development and coordination among contributors to an MSP ecosystem; designing the technical architecture that frames interaction; encouraging complementors to make investments; and generally 'managing' and 'maintaining the health' of the ecosystem, such as by using the non-price levers such as the 'four levers of platform leadership' which include: firm boundaries and internal organization of the platform owner, product technology and relationships with platform participants. The nature of these activities clearly goes beyond governing economic activity solely within the boundaries of platform owners and extends to rule making and regulating the conduct of firms beyond their economic boundaries, as suggested by several authors, who characterize MSPs as a 'licensing authority' that 'regulates connections among ecosystem members' so as to 'increase diversity and productivity'; or go as far as to speculate that 'the monopolist [platform owner] plays a role like that of a "public interest" regulator'. The primary contribution of Boudreau and Hagiu's chapter is to present evidence supporting these notions of a regulatory role of MSPs that goes well beyond price setting and includes imposing rules and constraints, creating inducements and otherwise shaping behaviours. These various non-price instruments essentially solve what would otherwise be (multi-sided) 'market failures'. The authors use four primary case studies to illustrate these points. Two case studies are digital MSPs: Facebook and TopCoder. To emphasize some level of generality of their analysis, they also examine two non-digital platforms: the Roppongi Hills 'mini-city' in Tokyo, Japan, and Harvard Business School.

In Chapter 8, Melissa A. Schilling focuses on the tradeoffs between diffusion and protection of technology platforms. In industries with increasing returns, firms are sometimes encouraged to liberally diffuse their technology platforms (through, for example, open source or liberal licensing arrangements) to increase their likelihood of becoming the dominant design. However, these firms face several dilemmas: if they liberally diffuse the technology to would-be competitors, they relinquish the opportunity to capture monopoly rents when and if their technology emerges as a dominant design. Furthermore, once control of a technology is relinquished, it can be very hard to regain. Finally, liberal diffusion of the technology can result in the fragmentation of the technology platform. These dilemmas raise the following questions: when incompatible technologies compete for the position of dominant design, what factors will determine whether one or more competitors choose to adopt a more 'open' technology strategy? How does a firm decide what level of 'openness' will maximize the technology's chances for survival and the firm's long-term profitability? This chapter systematically examines how either open or closed technologies can rise to the position of dominant design. The conclusions of this chapter help move beyond the appropriability versus open debate by examining the more subtly nuanced benefits of different positions along a 'control continuum', and provide a systematic tool for managers to assess the benefits and costs/risks of adopting a strategy at various points along the control continuum.

In Chapter 9, Shane Greenstein concludes Part II by offering a rich and nuanced essay focusing on the development of commercial Internet, as a unique historical setting allowing in-depth analysis of the relative benefits of open versus closed practices. The structure of the commercial Internet cut against the prevailing opinion of many executives in computing and communications in the mid-1990s, which contended that platform leadership from a commercial organization (*à la* Microsoft and Intel) was necessary for a thriving and growing market. In contrast, the most vocal participants in Internet governance revelled in the freedom of the Internet's development processes, stressing that it placed comparatively fewer restrictions on the flow of technical information. Some even pointed to the PC market as a model of what they were trying to avoid. The debate still persists today about how and why computing platforms thrive with and without commercial leadership. Greenstein's essay illuminates these issues by returning to the first market in which they arose and by re-examining the core issue: what would have been different about the Internet if it had been organized as a proprietary commercial platform? His answer comes in two steps. The first step defines 'open' in the context of the time, namely, comparing Microsoft's development of Windows 95 with similar processes for developing the Internet. The second step examines how three specific features of the Internet might have changed had its processes been less open: the transition from the research-oriented to the commercial Internet; the degree of innovation around the time of the transition; and the events leading to structural change in the commercial Internet market. Greenstein concludes that openness did not do some of the things for which it is often credited, such as make the Internet more innovative. However, he also concludes that openness did play a special role in shaping outcomes in the commercial Internet at this time – in encouraging participation in development of Internet infrastructure and in fostering structural change in the provision of commercial software.

Part III focuses on platform management, design and knowledge issues. It comprises five chapters from authors based in the UK, Italy, France, Sweden and Japan.

In Chapter 10, Mari Sako offers us what will probably become a seminal article on supply chain platforms. Sako's chapter presents an empirically based contribution to the theory of supply chain platforms through an in-depth case study of automotive supplier parks in Brazil. Supplier parks represent a recent template for organizing in the global automotive industry. The template combines outsourcing by automakers and co-location of suppliers on automakers' sites. Sako draws on evidence from three Brazilian supplier parks, Volkswagen Resende, General Motors Gravataí and Ford Camaçari, to analyse the causes and consequences of outsourcing and co-location for the governance of the firm, relations with suppliers, and labour–management relations. She examines three dimensions theoretically and empirically, namely the degree of task outsourcing, the pattern of asset ownership and the nature of relational governance. In theory, task modularity facilitates ownership modularity (that is, asset ownership disintegration). But evidence from three major supplier parks in Brazil reveals a diversity of local arrangements, with a negative correlation between task outsourcing and asset outsourcing. This finding is explained by combining insights from the engineering design literature and the organization economics literature. In particular, asset ownership is one of several ways in which control and incentives may be structured. Moreover, the diversity in arrangements is also explained by different combinations of corporate strategy and state policy, as well as by the emergence of different local labour market institutions.

In Chapter 11, Pascal Le Masson, Benoit Weil and Armand Hatchuel explore how industry platforms can be designed using specific collaborative relationships that also take the form of platforms. In several sectors, the architecture of industry is tending to loosen or even disappear: 'smart grids' in electricity supply, biomaterials and home networking in telecommunications and consumer electronics are all examples of new industrial contexts in search of industry platforms. In such situations, who is the industrial architect, i.e., who provides the industry platform? How do platforms emerge and how do companies contribute to the process? The literature insists on the importance of a platform 'core', performing one essential function or solving one essential problem of the system, without investigating how this core can be identified or designed. The authors explore the issues raised by these collaborations for platform design using a multiple case study in four different industries: biomaterials, microelectronics, aeronautics and biotechnologies. In all four cases, a platform design process was followed longitudinally. The authors suggest that the collaborations for platform design consist not only in delivering an industry platform but in positioning this platform potential into a strategic landscape, characterized by alternative platform strategies, the capabilities enabling these platform strategies and the values of these platform strategies for the partners. They suggest that collaborations for platform design have to manage three main processes: (1) value creation, in order to identify a product platform for the industry, but also to evaluate this platform compared to alternatives, and to integrate all possible alternatives into a strategic mapping process; (2) knowledge production and learning by involving partners, offering support for various experiments and providing specific devices for knowledge production; and (3) the interests of each of the partners by simultaneously creating value at the industry level and increasing the value of the partners' assets.

In Chapter 12, Stefano Brusoni and Andrea Prencipe focus on the process of defining new internal platforms. They observe that it is when platforms are defined that relationships are established among people and units; new bodies of understanding and practice are generated and old ones discarded; information filters are implemented to selectively retain what is defined as relevant information. The process of defining a new platform is, however, a major and highly risky undertaking in which firms engage very rarely. It is difficult to develop routines and heuristics capable of guiding such activities (exactly because they happen so rarely). Yet any wrong decision taken at this time will have long-lasting effects on firm profitability and eventual survival. The authors argue that the successful introduction of new platforms depends on the implementation of consistent changes across the domains of product, organization and knowledge. In a case study in the aeronautics industry, they find that these changes are implemented by organizations that act as cross-domain catalysts through the mediating role of key people who span all three domains. The aircraft engine industry case illustrates the introduction of a new platform architecture in a high-tech setting. The evidence describes radical changes that revolutionized the products and the manufacturing processes. There were 'make-or-break' decisions that implied the definition of a new 'way of doing things'. Brusoni and Prencipe offer some implications for practice: they argue that key individuals play a fundamental role in enacting cross-domain rewirings. Leading figures that played a central role in the connection of the knowledge, organization and product domains were senior engineers with long careers in the industry. It was their involvement in the minutiae of everyday production that enabled them to cumulatively develop a systemic understanding of technologies, products and the overall industry. This is a major point to consider if one notes how easily manufacturing activities are now being outsourced to low-cost countries.

In Chapter 13, Ramsin Yakob and Fredrik Tell investigate possible approaches to problem solving in product platform development. The ability to manage the problem-solving process is a key capability for reduced product development cycle time. The development of platforms is a complex endeavour requiring the organizing and utilization and involvement of a number of different functional areas of a firm and the inclusion of a variety of expertise, usually in cross-functional development projects. Problems and errors are an inherent part of any development work carried out in such projects. As the complexity of the system increases due to the increasing number of components and interdependences, emerging problems and errors become gradually more difficult to solve. The authors envisage that the more complex the hierarchical configuration of product platforms, the more complex the problems and errors encountered in their development will be. Previous research has distinguished between directional and heuristic problem-solving strategies. The authors discuss the appropriateness of these two problem-solving strategies in product platform development projects. The analysis is grounded theoretically as well as in an empirical study of two product platform projects: one in the telecommunications industry and one in the automotive industry. The findings indicate that in developing capabilities for the complex problem solving characteristic of product platform development projects it is paramount to narrow the search process between errors identified and the problem underlying those errors. The successful management of such compression increases the probability of finding remedies for errors, as it reduces the problem landscape in which solutions can be found. For this both heuristic and directional search processes are important.

In Chapter 14, authors Hirofumi Tatsumoto, Koichi Ogawa and Takahiro Fujimoto focus on the effects of technological platforms on the international division of labour. Their chapter focuses on variables such as the characteristics of the platform, the mechanism through which the platform is diffused, and the effect it has on the international division of labour through an architectural analysis of the case of Intel's platform business in Taiwan in the 1990s. The authors define the separation effect of the platform as a mechanism that separates the technologies used in a quasi-modular architecture product into completely modular and integral technologies. The separation effect is derived from the dual nature of the platform: the completely integral architecture inside it and the completely modular architecture outside it. This leads to a difference in the speed of technology diffusion between the finished product level and the platform level, and brings about a production shift of finished products from the developed country to developing countries, while the platform remains in the developed country. With the rapid diffusion of technology, the adoption of a platform leads to a quick expansion of production in developing-country firms. The cost reductions in these firms bring affordable prices and help to create a huge global market, such as the BRIC (Brazil, Russian, India and China) markets. As a result, the platform fundamentally changes the international division of labour by noticeably strengthening the new model of economic collaboration between developing and developed countries. The growth of the platform destroys the advantages of traditional firms in developed countries and encourages entry into the market by new firms in developing countries.

CONCLUDING REMARKS

This book offers a truly multidisciplinary account of the multifaceted phenomenon of platforms, and it has been a privilege to be part of the community of scholars who have contributed to it. This is the outcome of an ambitious programme of international collaboration, but, mostly, all authors join me in hoping that this is just a beginning. We hope this volume will become a reference for students and researchers, and be readable enough for managers who care about the issues of innovation, competition, firms' performance, design and technological development. We hope the insights assembled in this volume will be used as a foundation – dare we say as a platform – for future enquiring minds to improve our responses and uncover new questions. There is much more work to be done. But for now, enjoy your reading!

NOTE

1. In its 2008 *Annual Report* Microsoft stated: 'The European Commission closely scrutinizes the design of high-volume Microsoft products and the terms on which we make certain technologies used in these products, such as file formats, programming interfaces, and protocols, available to other companies. In 2004, the Commission ordered us to create new versions of Windows that do not include certain multimedia technologies and to provide our competitors with specifications for how to implement certain proprietary Windows communications protocols in their own products. *The Commission's impact on product design may limit our ability to innovate* in Windows or other products in the future, diminish the developer appeal of the Windows platform, and increase our product development costs' (emphasis added).

REFERENCES

Gawer, A. (2000), 'The organization of platform leadership: an empirical investigation of Intel's managerial processes aimed at fostering innovation by third parties', PhD dissertation, MIT Sloan School of Management.

Gawer, A. and M.A. Cusumano (2002), *Platform Leadership: How Intel, Microsoft, and Cisco Drive Industry Innovation*, Boston, MA: Harvard Business School Press.

Gawer, A. and M. Cusumano (2008), 'How companies become platform leaders', *MIT Sloan Management Review*, **49** (2), 28–35.

Microsoft (2008), *Annual Report*, available at http://www.microsoft.com/msft/reports/ar08/index.html.

PART I

Platforms: Overview

2. The architecture of platforms: a unified view

Carliss Y. Baldwin and C. Jason Woodard

INTRODUCTION

Product and system designers have long exploited opportunities to create families of complex artifacts by developing and recombining modular components. An especially common design pattern has come to be associated with the concept of a 'platform', which we define as a set of stable components that supports variety and evolvability in a system by constraining the linkages among the other components. Our goal in this chapter is to shed light on the relationships between platforms and the systems in which they are embedded, in order to better understand firms and industries where platforms play an important role.

We begin by reviewing the use of the term 'platform' in three distinct but related fields: product development, technology strategy and industrial economics. Although the term is used in diverse ways that seem difficult to reconcile, we find a number of common threads – most importantly, the conservation or reuse of a core component to achieve economies of scale while reducing the cost of creating a wide variety of complementary components.

This combination of conservation and variety has been harnessed both in product lines within the boundaries of a single firm (for example, the Sony Walkman®) and in large clusters or ecosystems of interdependent firms (as in the computer industry), as well as in the more general setting of multi-sided markets such as credit cards, shopping malls and search engines. We argue that the fundamental architecture behind all platforms is essentially the same: the system is partitioned into a set of 'core' components with low variety and a complementary set of 'peripheral' components with high variety (Tushman and Murmann, 1998). The low-variety components constitute the platform. They are the long-lived elements of the system and thus implicitly or explicitly establish the system's interfaces, the rules governing interactions among the different parts.

This underlying architectural unity motivates our effort to develop a common set of analytical tools for studying platforms and the industries that produce them. Among the most important tools are representation schemes – in other words, ways to draw pictures of platform architectures. We discuss approaches from three different literatures: network graphs from organization theory, design structure matrices from engineering design, and layer maps from technology strategy. Each of these representations has both strengths and limitations, which we describe.

The chapter concludes by addressing what we feel are the most salient questions suggested by a unified view of platform architectures. First, when is a platform architecture preferable to allowing all components to vary arbitrarily? Second, when can a platform and its peripheral components (complements) remain within the control of a single firm? Third, when should a firm allow or encourage outsiders to develop complements to a platform it controls? And fourth, if a firm does allow – or is forced to accept – external complementors, which components of the system should it strive to retain control over?

WHAT IS A PLATFORM, REALLY?

According to the *Oxford English Dictionary*, the word 'platform' has been used since the sixteenth century to denote 'a raised level surface on which people or things can stand, usually a discrete structure intended for a particular activity or operation'. Somewhat surprisingly, the word has been used in an abstract sense for nearly as long. The *Oxford English Dictionary* cites examples from as early as 1574 in which 'platform' refers to 'a design, a concept, an idea; (something serving as) a pattern or model'.

More recently, the concept of a platform has been developed by management scholars in three overlapping waves of research, respectively focused on products, technological systems and transactions. We briefly sketch these waves in the remainder of this section, then examine their common underlying logic in the next. Our citations to this vast literature are merely illustrative; a thorough review would be a substantial and worthwhile project in its own right.

Product development researchers first used the term 'platform' to describe projects that created a new generation or family of products for a particular firm. In their seminal work on product development planning and execution, Wheelwright and Clark (1992a) introduced the term 'platform product' to describe new products that 'meet the needs of a core group of customers but [are designed] *for easy modification* into derivatives through the addition, substitution, or removal of features' (p. 73; emphasis added). This work was followed by research on 'platform investments' (Kogut and Kulatilaka, 1994), 'platform technologies' (Kim and Kogut,

1996), and more generally, 'platform thinking' (Sawhney, 1998), along with rich field studies (e.g. Sanderson and Uzumeri, 1995) and managerial advice on platform-oriented product planning (e.g., Meyer and Lehnerd, 1997; Robertson and Ulrich, 1998).

In the second wave, technology strategists identified platforms as valuable points of control (and rent extraction) in an industry. Competition between platforms thus came to be seen as an important force at the industry level, with the ability to determine both the success and failure of firms and the evolution of product designs. Bresnahan and Greenstein (1999) developed a theory to explain the evolving structure of the computer industry, which remained concentrated around a small number of dominant platforms even as competition intensified within certain market segments. Influential studies of Microsoft and Netscape illustrated contrasting approaches to market leadership, with Microsoft forming a 'Platforms Group' to consolidate its efforts around the Windows operating system (Cusumano and Selby, 1995), and Netscape adopting a 'cross-platform' strategy – in part by creating a new internal platform, the Netscape Portable Runtime, to permit its browser to work with any operating system (Cusumano and Yoffie, 1998). Using Intel, Microsoft and Cisco as major case studies, Gawer and Cusumano (2002) built on this work to articulate a more general framework for 'platform leadership' in rapidly evolving product systems.

Industrial economists subsequently adopted the term 'platform' to characterize products, services, firms or institutions that mediate transactions between two or more groups of agents (Rochet and Tirole, 2003). This literature emphasizes situations in which network externalities across these groups create a 'chicken-and-egg problem', which must be solved by platform owners, typically by cross-subsidizing between groups or even giving away products or services for free (Parker and Van Alstyne, 2005). While this research has built on the previous waves to explain the competitive dynamics of system industries (see, e.g., Evans et al., 2006), its empirical scope is more general, including phenomena as diverse as credit card payment networks, shopping malls and dating services (Eisenmann, 2008; Hagiu, 2008).

In the literatures of product development, technology strategy and industrial economics, many seemingly disparate things have been labeled platforms, including auto-body frames, videogame consoles, software programs, websites, back-office processing systems, shopping malls and credit cards. However, across these literatures, the things called platforms have common roots in engineering design. This shared heritage motivates our effort to identify common structural features, which we call 'the architecture of platforms', and to develop tools for representing and reasoning about platforms in a general way.

PLATFORM ARCHITECTURE AND DESIGN RULES

Most platform definitions focus on the reuse or sharing of common elements across complex products or systems of production. For example, according to Meyer and Lehnerd (1997), 'A product platform is a set of common components, modules, or parts from which a stream of derivative products can be efficiently created and launched' (p. 7). Robertson and Ulrich (1998) defined a platform more broadly as 'the collection of assets that are shared by a set of products' (p. 20), where assets may include components, processes, knowledge and people. Bresnahan and Greenstein (1999) extended the concept to the industry level: 'We define a platform as a bundle of standard components around which buyers and sellers coordinate efforts' (p. 4).

The economic logic of component reuse is simple but powerful. For components that are fixed, it is often possible to realize economies of scale through increased production volume, amortization of fixed costs across product families or generations, and more efficient use of complementary assets (e.g. distribution channels and technical support services). At the same time, economies of scope are created at the system level by reducing the cost of developing product variants that are targeted at different markets or incorporate new technologies. Moreover, decisions to develop these variants frequently take the form of real options, allowing firms to run multiple design experiments and select only the best outcomes without compromising the functioning of the whole system (Baldwin and Clark, 2000).

Although it is a recurring theme across diverse literatures, the reuse and sharing of the core components of a platform is only half the story. Wheelwright and Clark observed that 'a platform project creates products (and processes) that *embed an architecture* for [a] system . . . In fact, *it is the architecture of the system that enables other features to be added or existing features to be removed* in tailoring derivative products to special market niches' (1992b, p. 96; emphasis added). The relationship between platforms and architecture has received little attention up to now, but we think it is crucial to understanding the nature of platforms and hence the dynamics of platform-based innovation and competition.

What is an Architecture?

Product architecture was defined by Ulrich (1995, p. 419) as 'the scheme by which the function of a product is allocated to physical components', including 'the specification of interfaces between interacting components'. Baldwin and Clark (2000) reserved the term 'architecture' for the function-to-component mapping, but included interfaces in the design rules needed to create a modular system. Subsequently, in the engineering systems literature, Whitney et al. (2004) defined architecture more broadly to include: (1) a list of functions; (2) the physical components needed to perform the functions; (3) the detailed arrangement and interfaces between the components; and (4) a description of how the system will operate through time and under different conditions. All complex man-made systems, including all products and processes, have architectures.

The fundamental feature of a platform architecture, in our view, is that certain components remain fixed over the life of the platform, while others are allowed to vary in cross-section or change over time. Thus, either by design or simply because it is the longest-lived component in the system, a platform embodies a set of stable constraints, or design rules, that govern the relationships among components. This view is consistent with the emphasis on reuse and sharing expressed by other authors, but suggests additional implications for the evolution of platform systems over time.

In particular, fixing the interfaces between components creates specific thin crossing points in the network of relationships between the elements of the system (Baldwin, 2008). At these points, the dependencies between the respective components are constrained to obey the interface specification, while other forms of dependency are ruled out. (In contrast, when there is no pre-specified interface governing interactions, designers may introduce any form of dependency that seems beneficial.)

Interfaces in turn establish the boundaries of 'modules' – components of a system whose 'elements are powerfully connected among themselves and relatively weakly connected to elements in other [components]' (Baldwin and Clark, 2000, p. 63). Because they define points of weak linkage (thin crossing points) in a network of relationships, modular interfaces reduce both coordination costs and transaction costs across the module boundary (Baldwin and Clark, 2000; Baldwin, 2008). It follows that the existence of modules and modular interfaces in a large system reduces the costs of splitting design and production across multiple firms (Langlois and Robertson, 1992; Sanchez and Mahoney, 1996). This kind of disaggregation gives rise to 'modular clusters' or 'business ecosystems' of complementary and competing firms (Baldwin and Clark, 1997; Iansiti and Levien, 2004; Baldwin and Woodard, 2007). The modular cluster form of industrial organization tends to be good for consumers and for component and system producers collectively, although it is potentially dangerous for the platform architect, as IBM discovered when it lost control of its personal computer architecture to two of its component suppliers, Intel and Microsoft (Ferguson and Morris, 1993).

Platforms and Evolvability

An important property of platform systems is that they are evolvable, in the sense that they can adapt to unanticipated changes in the external environment. In both biological and economic systems, evolution proceeds via the mechanisms of variation and selective retention of advantageous forms (Campbell, 1965). Darwin himself went to great lengths to establish variation as an empirical fact in biological systems, but he did not consider how such variability arose.

In recent years, biologists have turned their attention to this question. They have theorized that in complex multi-cellular organisms, the huge variety in outward forms is in fact accomplished through the conservation of core metabolic processes at the cellular level. These core processes are conserved precisely because they deconstrain other, complementary processes that support variation, and thus facilitate evolutionary adaptation (Kirschner and Gerhart, 1998). Thus it is the combination of stable core processes and variable complementary processes that generates useful (i.e. non-lethal) variation in complex organisms. Moreover, the conserved processes 'seem designed to minimize the interdependence of processes, [and thus] are flexible and robust mechanisms that support change and variability in other processes' (ibid., p. 8426).

The same arguments can be applied to man-made systems. A platform architecture partitions a system into stable core components and variable peripheral components. By promoting the reuse of core components, such partitioning can reduce the cost of variety and innovation at the system level. The whole system does not have to be invented or rebuilt from scratch to generate a new product, accommodate heterogeneous tastes, or respond to changes in the external environment. In this fashion, the platform system as a whole becomes evolvable: it can be adapted at low cost without losing its identity or continuity of design.

From systems biology we learn when platform architectures are advantageous. Simple systems (like bacteria) can and do vary their core processes (Kirschner and Gerhart, 1998). But there is a limit to the complexity that can be achieved when every subsystem is subject to change. Thus a platform architecture is advantageous when the system as a whole is complex – comprising many interacting parts – but its requirements are heterogeneous, future technological developments are uncertain, and/or the system must adapt to unanticipated environmental changes. The benefits of a platform architecture are variety in the present and evolvability through time. The catch is that the platform architect must know which components should remain stable and which should vary. The architect must also be able to create stable yet versatile interfaces, which can accommodate linkages that are unforeseen at the time the architecture is created.

Different Parts, Same Elephant?

The diversity of the literature on platforms raises the question of whether the various 'platform' concepts are synonymous or simply evocative uses of the same word to mean different things. We subscribe to the former view, arguing that at the level of architecture all platform systems are fundamentally the same. On this view, a platform architecture displays a special type of modularity, in which a product or system is split into a set of components with low variety and high reusability, and another set with high variety and low reusability. The first set is called 'the platform'. The second has no generic name but might be called 'the complements' of the platform. The platform and its complements are distinct modules in the system architecture. Their interoperability is made possible via design rules, i.e. interface specifications binding on both.

To see the fundamental similarity of platform architectures, consider first the distinction between a product platform within a single firm (e.g. the Sony Walkman®, described by Sanderson and Uzumeri, 1995), and a platform whose complements are supplied by many different firms (e.g. Microsoft Windows). While platforms that span firm boundaries raise numerous, wide-ranging strategic concerns – explored by many of the contributors to this volume – at the level of architecture, there is no inherent difference between these 'internal' and 'external' platforms. Both modularize the system in ways that facilitate component reuse and variety in product offerings. Both implicitly or explicitly specify interfaces that mediate interactions among components. Both allocate decision rights (again, at least implicitly) that determine who can interact with or modify which components in what ways.

At first glance, there seems to be a difference between these technology platforms (both within and across firms) and the platforms featured in the literature on multi-sided markets. Although some examples are frequently discussed in both literatures (for example videogames and computer operating systems), others appear to have little in common (for example credit card payment systems, shopping malls and search engines). However, the driving force behind multi-sided markets is the need to induce coordination among two or more groups of agents, and what they 'coordinate on' is precisely a fixed point in the architecture of transactions in which they collectively participate. That fixed point may be a particular component or system, for example the Visa payment-processing system, which both issues cards to consumers and approves transactions on behalf of merchants. Or it may be a physical location, as in the case of a shopping mall or singles bar. Or it may be a convention, such as the use of currency as a medium of exchange (Grewal, 2008) or technical standards for compatibility between systems, such as the TCP/IP Internet protocols (Clark, 1988).

Just as technology platforms provide economies of scale and scope within and across firms, multi-sided market platforms exhibit economies of scale for the platform and economies of scope for the various groups that transact with each other. All platform systems also have the capacity to create low-cost, decentralized options, such as the ability to download new applications onto a mobile device, or to wander into a store in almost any city in the world with credit card in hand.

Finally, all platform systems exhibit tensions between platform owners and complementors. These tensions are variously expressed. For internal platforms, tension arises through the threat of entry by third-party component makers who can hook into the platform at its visible interfaces and create compatible substitutes for the firm's own components. For external platforms and multi-sided markets, the main threat is disintermediation: by replicating or reverse engineering the platform side of these interfaces, rivals may be able to 'clone' the platform itself and compete with it directly.

In summary, platform architectures are united in that they partition a system into low- and high-variety components. The two types of components can be combined into a working system because pre-specified interfaces regulate both sides. The interfaces must be stable relative to the components that depend on them; hence they are, by definition, part of the platform. But the interfaces must also be versatile: they cannot overly constrain the complements or they will reduce the variety and flexibility of the system as a whole. Because interfaces are the main junction points in a platform system, they are a source of strategic tension between platform owners and actual or potential complementors.

In pointing out these similarities we do not intend to minimize the differences between different types of platform. Our goal is simply to be able to talk about platform architectures across different fields in a general way. Having a common language in turn makes it easier to visualize platform architectures using a common set of representation techniques.

PICTURING PLATFORM RELATIONSHIPS

Herbert Simon famously said, 'Every problem-solving effort must begin with creating a representation for the problem' and 'solving a problem simply means representing it so as to make the solution transparent'

(Simon, 1996, pp. 108 and 132). In other words, good representations can help illuminate important dimensions of a problem – in our case, to understand platform behavior and strategy.

However, any representation is an abstraction from reality, highlighting some features while obscuring others. In this section, we describe three ways of representing platforms and their architecture: network graphs, design structure matrices and layer maps. These representations originate in different literatures and draw attention to different aspects of the phenomenon. Below we describe each type, give examples, and discuss the strengths and limitations of each approach.

Network Graphs

Network graphs, which have been used extensively to study social networks and other complex patterns of relationships, are probably the most common way of representing platforms and their complements. In these representations, products or firms are designated as nodes, and relationships between them as links. In a simple platform system, the platform would be the central node (or hub) in the network, with complements (or complementors) radiating outward from that point. For example, Figure 2.1 is a network graph depicting alliances between software firms in 1990. As IBM is the central node in this network, one can surmise that it supplies platforms (both hardware and software) that support a wide variety of complementors.

Network graphs like this are useful when the platform in question has a simple hub-and-spoke structure. In such cases, the graph can show (1) the existence of one or more central elements; (2) the size of the 'cloud' of complements (or complementors); and (3) the evolution of the platform and complements over time. The visualizations are augmented by a host of metrics derived from social network theory and the study of complex systems.

The first limitation of this representation scheme is evident in the encircled subset in the upper right corner. Within the circle, the simple hub-and-spoke structure disappears: many of the complementors have formed alliances with one another. As the number of lateral connections grows, it is more difficult to see what is going on via the network graph.

The second limitation of network graphs is that they are best suited to depicting reciprocal relationships. What is actually shown in Figure 2.1 is the existence of an alliance between two firms. One cannot see whether one firm's software depends *on* the other firm's code. Directional dependencies can be represented in a network graph by drawing the links as one- or two-headed arrows. However, such dependencies are hard for the

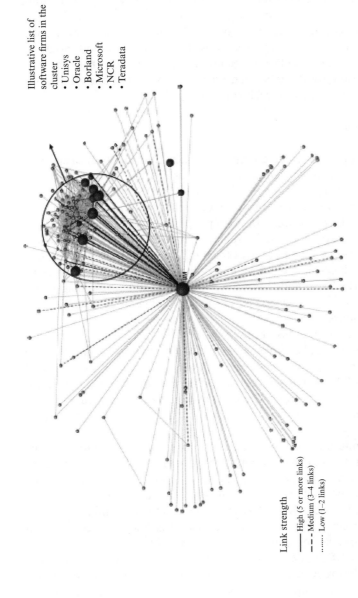

Illustrative list of
software firms in the
cluster
• Unisys
• Oracle
• Borland
• Microsoft
• NCR
• Teradata

Link strength
——— High (5 or more links)
– – – Medium (3–4 links)
········ Low (1–2 links)

Note: The size of each node is proportional to the number of alliances.

Source: Iyer, Lee and Venkatraman (2006). Reproduced by permission.

Figure 2.1   IBM's network in 1990

28

eye to distinguish unless they are very homogeneous (all arrows radiating outward, for example). Design structure matrices, discussed next, are a more powerful way to visualize directional dependencies within a complex system.

Design Structure Matrices

In the design of any artifact, a key relationship between design elements is 'uses' or 'depends on' (Parnas, 1972). Design element B depends on A if a change in A may require a subsequent change in B. For example, if the contents of a particular software file change, the files that call it may need to change as well. The calling files depend on the original file. In a platform architecture, if the platform incorporates interfaces that complementors must use to access the system, the complements depend on the platform.

Directional relationships such as 'depends on' can be visualized using design structure matrices or DSMs (Eppinger, 1991; Baldwin and Clark, 2000). To construct a DSM, one first assigns the design elements – e.g. software files – to the rows and columns of a square matrix. Then if element B depends on A, one puts a mark in the row of B and the column of A. When all dependencies have been accounted for, the result is a square but not symmetric matrix. For example, Figure 2.2 shows a DSM for OpenSolaris, a software project maintained by Sun Microsystems. In this instance, the rows and columns represent the 12 080 files in the codebase, and the marks represent function calls from the row file to the column file.

The main advantages of the matrix view are twofold. First, the matrix easily depicts asymmetric relationships. Second, the matrix can structure a very large amount of information without overwhelming the eye. (Imagine a network graph with 12 000 nodes and 10 million arrows: that is what is being represented by the matrix in Figure 2.2.)

Can we see a platform in this architecture? First, note that Solaris is an operating system, on which complementors can build applications. Thus Solaris *is* a platform, and we are looking inside it. (Indeed, we are focusing on the kernel of Solaris, which is a subset of the whole operating system.) However, by showing this interior view, we can see 'a platform within the platform'. In fact, there are two sets of files on which many others depend. First there are files that are called by many files in the system but do not themselves call others. These appear as a vertical stripe, called a 'bus', at the far left of the matrix. Second, there is a set of approximately 3000 files that are densely interconnected with each other. These appear as a densely shaded square block on the main diagonal. The vast majority of files in the system call into this 'core', as can be seen from the densely

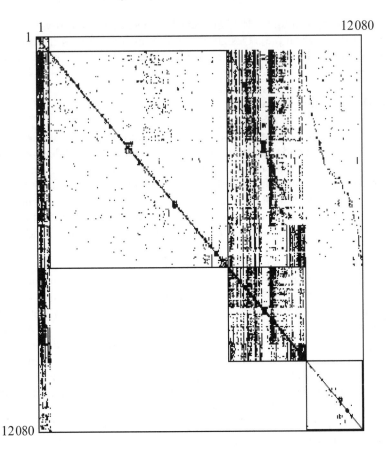

Source: A. MacCormack, J. Rusnak and C. Y. Baldwin, private communication.
Reproduced by permission.

Figure 2.2   Design structure of OpenSolaris

populated columns directly above it. Recent work has shown that a
densely connected core such as this tends to be conserved as the codebase
evolves. One reason for this is that touching any part of the core may have
wide-ranging, unpredictable ramifications, thus such code is 'hard to kill'
(MacCormack et al., 2007).

The DSM view reveals two things about a system. First, it shows
whether there are any 'thin crossing points', i.e. places where the system
might be split apart into modules. In the case of Solaris, the vast majority
of the code is either in the core or calls into the core, hence there are no
natural breakpoints. In contrast, the system shown in Figure 2.3 has two

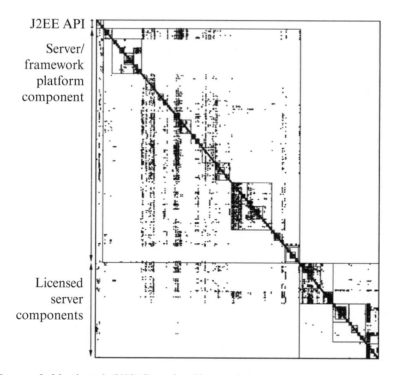

Source: LaMantia et al. (2008). Reproduced by permission.

Figure 2.3   A system with two modules

modules separated by a thin crossing point (LaMantia et al., 2008). In this case, the large upper block of the DSM represents the company's proprietary platform, while the smaller lower block represents licensed-in code. The codebase was designed in this modular fashion to protect the platform from opportunism on the part of the licensor. With this architecture in place, the company could respond to the threat of hold-up by simply splitting the codebase at the thin crossing point, and substituting a new module for the licensed code.

Second, the DSM shows the degree to which the system is evolvable. Again, the kernel of Solaris does not appear very evolvable: the interior of the platform is quite monolithic. In contrast, the system shown in Figure 2.3 *is* evolvable: the platform can be conserved and the complementary, licensed-in code replaced at low cost. (Indeed, shortly after creating this architecture, the company began to offer products that used open-source code in place of the licensed code.)

When one wants to look in detail at the structure of a system, especially the size and boundaries of modules, DSMs are a good alternative to network graphs. However, they too suppress features that are of interest for some types of analysis. For example, it is easier to depict the existence of variants – competing modules that do similar things – in a graphical representation than in matrix form. (One can illustrate substitutes by grouping sets of nodes together, cf. Woodard, 2007.) DSMs also indicate the existence of modular interfaces at thin crossing points, but do not indicate anything about those interfaces. Finally, DSMs usually require some prior knowledge of the system to generate informative clusters.[1]

Layer Maps

The representations discussed thus far can be used to compare and contrast different platform architectures, but they cannot easily comprehend cases where components operate across platforms or different platforms compete. How platform architecture affects competition and complementarity in an industry or ecosystem is hard to see via network graphs or DSMs. In contrast, layer maps are a useful way to visualize 'industry architectures' (Fransman, 2002; Jacobides et al., 2006).

To the best of our knowledge, the first layer map was constructed by Andy Grove, then CEO of Intel Corporation, to depict the changing structure of the computer industry. As he explained:

> 'The computer industry used to be vertically aligned . . . [A] company developed its own chips, its own hardware and its own software, sold and serviced by its own people.
>   Over time . . . a new horizontal industry emerged . . . A consumer could pick a chip from [one vendor], choose an operating system [from another], grab one of several ready-to-use applications off the shelf. . . . (Grove, 1996, pp. 39–42)

Figure 2.4 is an adaptation of Grove's original maps. Although Grove did not use these terms, we have labeled the vertical industry architecture 'vertical silos' and the horizontal architecture a 'modular cluster'.

To construct a layer map for a given industry, one first determines all the complementary components in a particular system. This list can be obtained from technical descriptions of the system. Components are then arranged vertically in separate layers, forming what engineers often call a 'stack'. Then one determines who competes in the product markets defined by the layers. Vertically integrated firms span several layers; specialized component suppliers appear in only one.

Layer maps can easily show changes in industry architecture over time. Usually, such changes occur after and as a consequence of changes in underlying product and process designs. Thus Baldwin and Clark

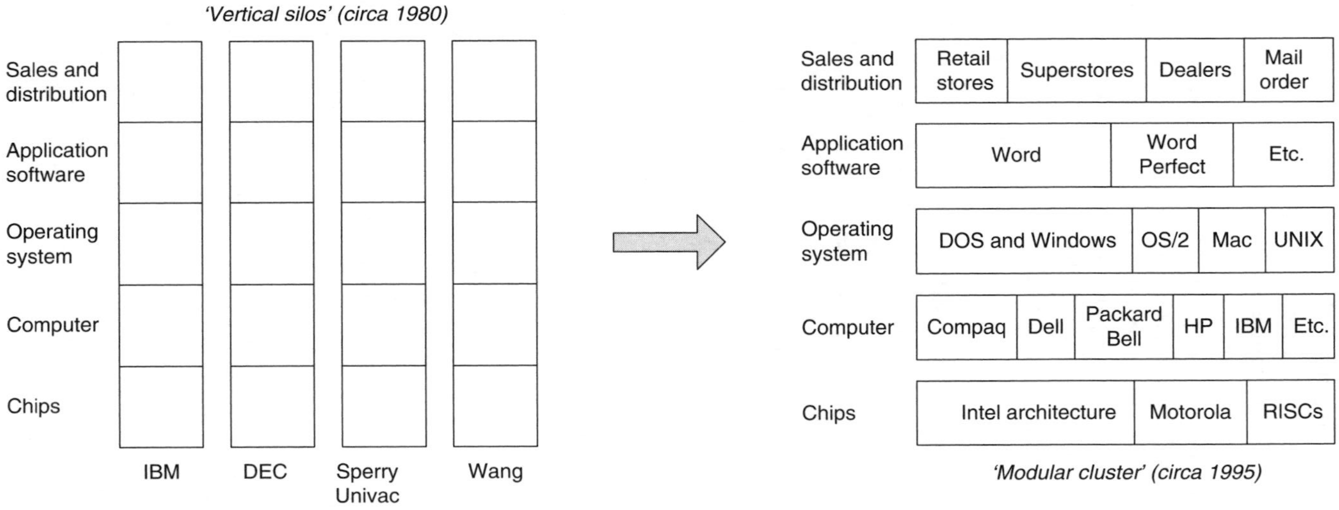

33

'Vertical silos' (circa 1980)

	IBM	DEC	Sperry Univac	Wang
Sales and distribution				
Application software				
Operating system				
Computer				
Chips				

'Modular cluster' (circa 1995)

Sales and distribution	Retail stores	Superstores	Dealers	Mail order
Application software	Word		Word Perfect	Etc.
Operating system	DOS and Windows	OS/2	Mac	UNIX
Computer	Compaq	Dell	Packard Bell	HP	IBM	Etc.
Chips	Intel architecture		Motorola	RISCs

Source: Adapted from Grove (1996, p. 44).

Figure 2.4   The vertical-to-horizontal transition in the computer industry

(2000) found that the computer industry became more vertically disintegrated following the introduction of System/360's modular architecture. Vertical disintegration continued after IBM deployed a modular
architecture and then encouraged external suppliers to provide both
hardware and software for its PC. The change in industry architecture
following the introduction of the PC can be seen in Figure 2.5, which
shows layer maps of the greater computer industry in 1984 and 2005.[2]
Conversely, Fixson and Park (2008) used layer maps and supporting analysis to show how the bicycle drivetrain industry became more
concentrated and vertically integrated following Shimano's successful
introduction of a highly integral (non-modular) product, the Shimano
Index System (SIS).

Simplified layer maps can be used to model 'co-opetition', i.e. the
simultaneous presence of competitors and complementors in an industry
(Brandenburger and Nalebuff, 1996). Most such models consider one or
two firms in each of two layers (e.g. Casadesus-Masanell et al., 2008), or a
two-layer platform structure with one firm (the platform) in one layer and
n firms (the complementors) in the other (for example Hagiu, 2008). In a
departure from these precedents, Baldwin and Woodard (2007) modeled
price competition and complementarity in an industry with an arbitrary
number of layers. For simple platform architectures, they showed that
(1) platform architectures based on open, public interfaces may give rise
to industry clusters that are as profitable, in aggregate, as a system-wide
monopoly; and conversely, (2) competing platforms based on closed,
proprietary interfaces tend to destroy value through ferocious price
competition.

As with all representations, layer maps have their drawbacks. First and
foremost, they assume that the components of a system can be neatly categorized into substitutes and complements, while in reality there are many
shades of gray. For example, is flash memory a substitute or complement
to a disk drive? Is an action game a substitute or complement to a multi-
player game? The neat block structure of a layer map often hides a more
messy underlying reality.

But hiding messy reality is exactly what a good representation is sup-
posed to do. Details and ambiguities are suppressed so that patterns can
be revealed. Each of the representations discussed in this section – network
graphs, design structure matrices and layer maps – highlights some aspects
of a platform architecture while obscuring others. Each can illuminate the
underlying phenomenon; each can inform strategy by suggesting different
risks, threats or opportunities. But no single representation should be used
to the exclusion of others.

CONCLUSION

Our unified view of platform architecture raises questions of interest to both researchers and strategists. We briefly discuss four of these questions below, then conclude with a summary of our basic argument.

1. When is a Platform Architecture Useful?

Platform architectures are useful when the underlying system is complex, but needs to adapt to changing tastes and technologies. Complex systems, by definition, have many parts that must work together to achieve a functioning whole. But tight integration can lead to rigidity. Platform architectures, in contrast, make the system evolvable. Even the core components can evolve – only the interfaces need to be stable.

2. When Will a Platform System 'Spill Over' the Boundaries of a Single Firm? When Can it be Contained?

A platform system consists of a core, its complements, and the interfaces between them. Whether such a system can be contained within the bounds of a single firm and its supply chain depends on both the system design and the appropriability regime of the firm's industry (Teece, 1986). Systems are harder to contain when they have a modular structure with clean interfaces (i.e. very thin crossing points) and the interfaces are weakly appropriable, in the sense that they cannot be protected against duplication or reverse engineering.

The following account from a popular book on PC repair describes how Apple Computer managed to contain the Macintosh platform within its boundaries:

> [T]here are no clones or compatibles of the Apple Macintosh system. It is not that Mac [hardware] can't be duplicated. . . . The real problem is that *Apple owns the Mac OS* as well as the BIOS [Basic Input/Output System], and because Apple has seen fit not to license them, no other company can sell an Apple-compatible system. Also, note that *the Mac BIOS and OS are very tightly integrated*; the Mac BIOS is very large and complex and is essentially part of the OS, unlike the much simpler and more easily duplicated BIOS found on PCs. The greater complexity and integration has allowed both the Mac BIOS and OS to escape any clean-room duplication efforts. This means that without Apple's blessing (in the form of licensing), no Mac clones are likely ever to exist. (Mueller, 2005, p. 28; emphasis added)

In other words, there are two lines of defense for a firm seeking to prevent others from supplying complements to its platform. The first is the

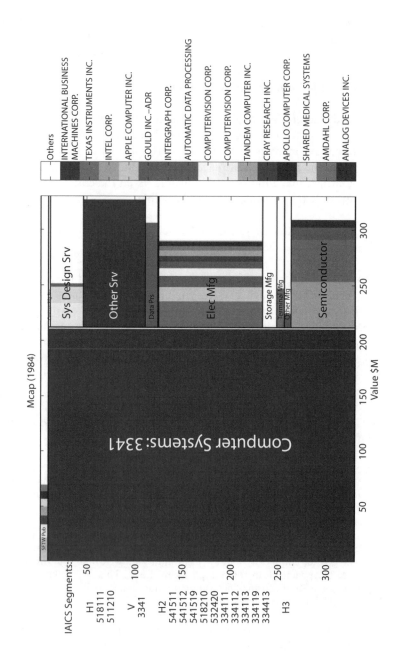

Mcap (1984)

Others
- INTERNATIONAL BUSINESS MACHINES CORP.
- TEXAS INSTRUMENTS INC.
- INTEL CORP.
- APPLE COMPUTER INC.
- GOULD INC.–ADR
- INTERGRAPH CORP.
- AUTOMATIC DATA PROCESSING
- COMPUTERVISION CORP.
- COMPUTERVISION CORP.
- TANDEM COMPUTER INC.
- CRAY RESEARCH INC.
- APOLLO COMPUTER CORP.
- SHARED MEDICAL SYSTEMS
- AMDAHL CORP.
- ANALOG DEVICES INC.

IAICS Segments:

H1
518111
511210

V
3341

H2
541511
541512
541519
518210
532420
334111
334112
334113
334119
334413

H3

Computer Systems: 3341

Sys Design Srv

Other Srv

Data Prs

Elec Mfg

Storage Mfg

Terminal Mfg
Other Mfg

Semiconductor

SFTW Pub

Value $M

50   100   150   200   250   300

50   100   150   200   250   300

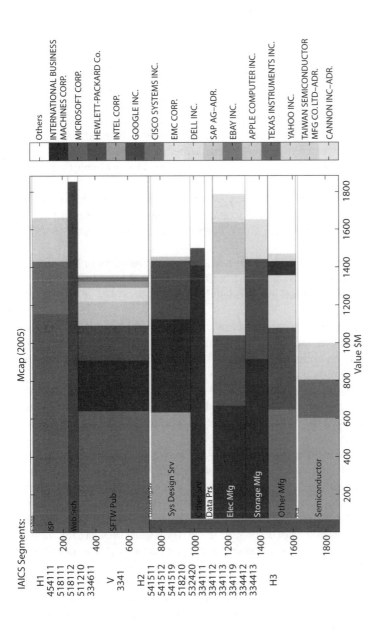

Source: C.Y. Baldwin, M.G. Jacobides and R. Dizaji, private communication. Reproduced by permission.

Figure 2.5   Layer maps of the computer industry in 1984 and 2005

ownership of critical interface components (Apple owns the Mac OS and BIOS and can choose to license them or not). The second line is 'complexity and integration', in other words lack of modularity: the fact that the interface components do not create 'sufficiently thin' crossing points between the different parts of the system. Complexity and integration of the firm's internal platform *design* protect the interfaces from legal duplication via clean-room reverse engineering techniques. But, at the same time, complexity and integration make the overall system less flexible, hence less evolvable. Recalling the Solaris DSM pictured in Figure 2.2, there are few places in this architecture for an outside party to offer a competing subsystem. Hence the Solaris platform would be relatively easy to contain, if Sun wished to do so.[3] By the same token, the interior of Solaris does not appear very evolvable, although it may support evolution in the surrounding system.

The flip side of this question is, when will outsiders try to 'invade' a platform? This is closely related to the next question. The short answer is, whenever they can and there are sufficient financial incentives to do so!

3. When Should the Platform Owner Encourage Outsiders to Develop Complements to the Platform? In Other Words, When Should the Owner Adopt a 'Platform Strategy'?

Outside complementors can be of great value to the system when there is a lot of 'option potential' in the complementary modules. An option is 'the right but not the obligation to take a specific action', in this case, choose one complement over another. Option value is low when consumer tastes are homogeneous and predictable, and designs are on a tightly determined technological trajectory (Dosi, 1982). In such cases, it is usually obvious what will succeed in the market; hence the value of multiple experiments and diverse approaches is low.

Option value is high when consumer tastes are heterogeneous or unpredictable, and technological trajectories are uncertain. In these cases, it is not obvious what will succeed, hence the value of multiple experiments and diverse approaches is high. Outside complementors will be attracted to the platform if there is option value in the complements, provided the platform owner does not expropriate all the value they create. Iansiti and Levien (2004) call the excessive expropriation of value a 'dominator strategy', and argue that such strategies tend to yield unhealthy business ecosystems. Woodard (2008) finds, using computational experiments, that even selfish and fairly myopic platform owners can learn to avoid 'overtaxing' their ecosystem members and find a balance that yields more investment in platforms with higher option value.

Before adopting a platform strategy, however, the architect must ask, what can outside complementors do that the architect's own employees cannot? This question deserves careful consideration. In the first place, outsiders may have skills, capabilities, or an understanding of user needs that those inside the firm do not. Commenting on the possibilities of innovation outside the boundaries of his firm, Bill Joy, a founder of Sun Microsystems, famously said, 'Not all smart people work for you.'[4] The corollary of this observation is 'Smart people are hard to find, but may find you if you open up your platform.'

Second, because they have property rights in their own output, outside complementors experience high-powered incentives that can induce them to greater levels of effort than insiders (Baker et al., 2002). Furthermore, in a world of imperfect capital markets, complementors may be able to provide investment capital that would not be available to the platform owner directly. Accessing this capital in turn makes it possible for a successful platform system to grow faster than its competitors (Baldwin and Clark, 2006). For example, Boudreau (2008) found that, in handheld computing devices, opening up the platform to external developers increased the rate of new device releases by a factor of five. When network externalities are present, such growth can propel the platform to competitive success (see, e.g. Shapiro and Varian, 1999).

Finally, platform complementarity can be a transient relationship that does not warrant employment or any other type of formal contract. This is often the case in multi-sided markets. The buyers and sellers on eBay want to transact with one another, and are willing to pay a fee to the platform if it reduces their transaction costs. The same holds for the merchant and customer in a credit card transaction, and the searchers, searchees and advertisers on Google. For these agents, participation in the platform is a small part of a much larger set of activities. Bringing these complementors 'inside the walls' of the platform owner is simply not a sensible option.

4. In a Platform Strategy with External Complementors, which Components of the Overall System Should be Retained and Developed by the Platform Architect?

In any platform system, there are three types of components: (1) the complements, which exhibit high variety and high rates of change over time; (2) the core components, which remain stable as the complements change; and (3) the interfaces, which are the design rules that allow the core and the complements to operate as one system. Both the core components and the interfaces are relatively long-lived, hence part of 'the platform'.

At first glance, it might appear that the architect should retain control of the core of the system, but this conclusion is not always correct. In man-made systems, the core components of the platform can evolve over time, and hence may be subject to competitive pressures. For example, the core of the first IBM PC was the system board, which contained (among other things) an Intel 8088 CPU. By design, all manner of hardware and software could be connected via the system board and would interoperate. This gave users a wide range of configuration options, and gave complementors rich incentives to develop better hardware devices and new software applications. Not by accident, the core was what IBM chose to sell.

However, in contrast to biological systems in which core processes are conserved through evolutionary change (Kirschner and Gerhart, 1998), the core processes of the original IBM PC were not conserved. The system board of a Lenovo or Dell machine today is very different from that of a 1981 PC. A Pentium processor running at 2.2 GHz is worlds apart from the 8088 processor in the original machine.

What has been conserved are the interfaces that sit between the system board, the hardware and the software. There were three such interfaces: (1) the Basic Input/Output System (BIOS), which insulated software developers from the hardware so that new devices could be added without rewriting programs; (2) the instruction set of the Intel 8088 chip, the basic commands into which all software had to be translated; and (3) the operating system, a set of 'higher-level' services that human programmers could use instead of accessing the BIOS or CPU directly. All of these interfaces have survived to the present day, and thus many programs written and compiled for a 1981 IBM PC will run correctly on a Lenovo or Dell PC in 2008.

This example teaches us that in a man-made platform, the interior of the core – the part hidden behind the interfaces – is not an essential part of the platform. In contrast, the interfaces are essential: the PC interfaces have lasted much longer than their hardware implementations, and their strategic significance has been profound.

What was problematic for IBM in the PC platform architecture was that IBM controlled only one of three critical interfaces, namely the BIOS. This interface, moreover, was simple and not tightly integrated with other parts of the system (cf. Mueller, 2005, quoted above). As is well known, the BIOS was reverse engineered by Compaq and then Phoenix Technologies in the early 1980s (Ferguson and Morris, 1993). At that point, ownership of the true PC platform – those components that would be conserved over the lifetime of the system – devolved onto Intel and Microsoft, where it remains to this day.

SUMMARY OF THE ARGUMENT

We have argued that there is a fundamental unity in the architecture of platforms. In essence, a 'platform architecture' is a modularization that partitions the system into (1) a set of components whose design is stable and (2) a complementary set of components which are allowed – indeed encouraged – to vary. The combination of stability and variety is accomplished via 'stable, yet versatile' interfaces, which govern the interactions of components. The interface specifications are part of the platform; indeed they may be the only components that remain truly stable over long periods of time. The combination of stability and variety in the architecture makes it possible to create novelty without developing a whole new system from scratch. Thus platform systems are evolvable.

Although they display a fundamental unity at the level of architecture, platform systems vary a great deal in construction and appearance. Some are physical (a singles bar), others are virtual (a social networking website). Some platform systems are contained within a single firm or a supply chain, while others are spread over ecosystems consisting of thousands or tens of thousands of firms. Many of these platforms support multi-sided markets.

A benefit of viewing platform architectures in a unified way is that theories and observations of seemingly disparate phenomena in diverse fields can be brought into focus as part of a coherent whole. We hope that this view will in turn serve as a focusing device for new efforts in theory building and empirical analysis.

ACKNOWLEDGMENTS

We are grateful to Annabelle Gawer for conceiving of this project and to the participants of the Platforms, Markets and Innovation conference at Imperial College, London on 2 June 2008 for many thoughtful and productive comments. We are greatly indebted to Alan MacCormack, John Rusnak, Matt LaMantia, Yuanfang Cai, Michael Jacobides, Reza Dizaji, Bala Iyer, Chi-Hyon Lee and Venkat Venkatraman for allowing us to use their graphs, matrices and layer maps. Finally we thank the Harvard Business School Division of Research and the Singapore Management University School of Information Systems for generous financial support.

NOTES

1. In the absence of such knowledge, automatic clustering algorithms can be used, but for matrices of a realistic size, such algorithms have proven to be both computationally intensive and unreliable in the sense that they yield different results from different starting points (Rusnak, 2005).
2. The 'greater' computer industry is defined as all firms in the 17 NAICS industries supplying computer hardware and software. Areas in the layer map are assigned to firms on the basis of market capitalization. When a firm participates in several layers, market capitalization is allocated on the basis of revenue.
3. Sun kept Solaris proprietary for many years, but in 2005 released much of its code under an open-source license. See http://www.sun.com/smi/Press/sunflash/2005-01/sunflash.20050125.1.xml (accessed 26 August 2008).
4. Source: http://www.pbs.org/cringely/nerdtv/transcripts/003.html (accessed 14 August 2008).

REFERENCES

Baker, G., R. Gibbons and K.J. Murphy (2002), 'Relational contracts and the theory of the firm', *Quarterly Journal of Economics*, **117** (1), 39–84.

Baldwin, C.Y. (2008), 'Where do transactions come from? Modularity, transactions, and the boundaries of firms', *Industrial and Corporate Change*, **17** (1), 155–95.

Baldwin, C.Y. and K.B. Clark (2000), *Design Rules, Volume 1: The Power of Modularity*, Cambridge, MA: MIT Press.

Baldwin, C.Y. and K.B. Clark (2006), 'Architectural innovation and dynamic competition: the smaller "footprint" strategy', Harvard Business School Working Paper 07-014, August.

Baldwin, C.Y. and C.J. Woodard (2007), 'Competition in modular clusters', Harvard Business School Working Paper 08-042, December.

Boudreau, K. (2008), 'Opening the platform vs. opening the complementary good? The effect on product innovation in handheld computing', Working Paper, August.

Brandenburger, A.M. and B.J. Nalebuff (1996), *Co-opetition*, New York: Doubleday.

Bresnahan, T.F. and S. Greenstein (1999), 'Technological competition and the structure of the computer industry', *Journal of Industrial Economics*, **47** (1), 1–40.

Campbell, D.T. (1965), 'Variation and selective retention in socio-cultural evolution', in H.R. Barringer, G.I. Blanksten and R.W. Mack (eds), *Social Change in Developing Areas: A Reinterpretation of Evolutionary Theory*, Cambridge, MA: Schenkman, pp. 19–49.

Casadesus-Masanell, R., B. Nalebuff and D.B. Yoffie (2008), 'Competing complements', Harvard Business School Working Paper 09-009, 21 November.

Clark, D.D. (1988), 'The design philosophy of the DARPA Internet protocols', *Computer Communications Review*, **18** (4), 106–14.

Cusumano, M.A. and R.W. Selby (1995), *Microsoft Secrets: How the World's Most Powerful Software Company Creates Technology, Shapes Markets and Manages People*, New York: Free Press.

Cusumano, M.A. and D.B. Yoffie (1998), *Competing on Internet Time: Lessons From Netscape and Its Battle with Microsoft*, New York: Free Press.

Dosi, G. (1982), 'Technological paradigms and technological trajectories: a suggested interpretation of the determinants and directions of technical change', *Research Policy*, **11** (3), 147–62.

Eisenmann, T.R. (2008), 'Managing shared and proprietary platforms', *California Management Review*, **50** (4), 31–53.

Eppinger, S.D. (1991), 'Model-based approaches to managing concurrent engineering', *Journal of Engineering Design*, **2** (4), 283–90.

Evans, D.S., A. Hagiu and R. Schmalensee (2006), *Invisible Engines: How Software Platforms Drive Innovation and Transform Industries*, Cambridge, MA: MIT Press.

Ferguson, C.H. and C.R. Morris (1993), *Computer Wars: How the West Can Win in a Post-IBM World*, New York: Times Books.

Fixson, S.K. and J. Park (2008), 'The power of integrality: linkages between product architecture, innovation, and industry structure', *Research Policy*, **37** (8), 1296–316.

Fransman, M. (2002), 'Mapping the evolving telecoms industry: the uses and shortcomings of the larger model', *Telecommunications Policy*, **26** (9–10), 473–83.

Gawer, A. and M.A. Cusumano (2002), *Platform Leadership: How Intel, Microsoft, and Cisco Drive Industry Innovation*, Boston, MA: Harvard Business School Press.

Grewal, D.S. (2008), *Network Power: The Social Dynamics of Globalization*, New Haven, CT: Yale University Press.

Grove, A.S. (1996), *Only the Paranoid Survive*, New York: Doubleday.

Hagiu, A. (2008), 'Two-sided platforms: product variety and pricing structures', Working Paper, 29 July.

Iansiti, M. and R. Levien (2004), *The Keystone Advantage: What the New Dynamics of Business Ecosystems Mean for Strategy, Innovation, and Sustainability*, Boston, MA: Harvard Business School Press.

Iyer, B., C. Lee and N. Venkatraman (2006), 'Managing in a 'small world ecosystem': lessons from the software sector', *California Management Review*, **48** (3), 28–47.

Jacobides, M.G., T. Knudsen and M. Augier (2006), 'Benefiting from innovation: value creation, value appropriation and the role of industry architectures', *Research Policy*, **35** (8), 1200–221.

Kim, D. and B. Kogut (1996), 'Technological platforms and diversification', *Organization Science*, **7** (3), 283–301.

Kirschner, M. and J. Gerhart (1998), 'Evolvability', *Proceedings of the National Academy of Sciences*, **95**, 8420–27.

Kogut, B. and N. Kulatilaka (1994), 'Options thinking and platform investments: investing in opportunity', *California Management Review*, **36** (2), 52–71.

LaMantia, M.J., Y. Cai, A.D. MacCormack and J. Rusnak (2008), 'Analyzing the evolution of large-scale software systems using design structure matrices and design rule theory: two exploratory cases', *Proceedings of the Seventh Working IEEE/IFIP Conference on Software Architecture (WICSA 2008)*, Washington, DC: IEEE Computer Society, pp. 83–92.

Langlois, R.N. and P.L. Robertson (1992), 'Networks and innovation in a modular system: lessons from the microcomputer and stereo component industries', *Research Policy*, **21** (4), 297–313.

MacCormack, A., J. Rusnak and C. Baldwin (2007), 'The impact of component modularity on design evolution: evidence from the software industry', Harvard Business School Working Paper 08-038.

Meyer, M.H. and A.P. Lehnerd (1997), *The Power of Product Platforms: Building Value and Cost Leadership*, New York: Free Press.

Mueller, S. (2005), *Upgrading and Repairing PCs*, 6th edn, Indianapolis, IN: Que Publishing.

Parker, G.G. and M.W. Van Alstyne (2005), 'Two-sided network effects: a theory of information product design', *Management Science*, **51** (10), 1494–504.

Parnas, D.L. (1972), 'On the criteria for decomposing systems into modules', *Communications of the ACM*, **15** (12), 1053–58.

Robertson, D. and K. Ulrich (1998), 'Planning for product platforms', *Sloan Management Review*, **39** (4), 19–31.

Rochet, J.-C. and J. Tirole (2003), 'Platform competition in two-sided markets', *Journal of the European Economic Association*, **1** (4), 990–1029.

Rusnak, J. (2005), *The Design Structure Analysis System: A Tool to Analyze Software Architecture*, PhD thesis, Harvard University.

Sanchez, R.A. and J.T. Mahoney (1996), 'Modularity, flexibility and knowledge management in product and organizational design', *Strategic Management Journal*, **17** (winter special issue), 63–76.

Sanderson, S. and M. Uzumeri (1995), 'Managing product families: the case of the Sony Walkman', *Research Policy*, **24** (5), 761–82.

Sawhney, M.S. (1998), 'Leveraged high-variety strategies: from portfolio thinking to platform thinking', *Journal of the Academy of Marketing Science*, **26** (1), 54–61.

Shapiro, C. and H.R. Varian (1999), *Information Rules: A Strategic Guide to the Network Economy*, Boston, MA: Harvard Business School Press.

Simon, H.A. (1996), *The Science of the Artificial*, 3rd edn, Cambridge, MA: MIT Press.

Teece, D.J. (1986), 'Profiting from technological innovation: implications for integration, collaboration, licensing and public policy', *Research Policy*, **15** (6), 285–305.

Tushman, M.L. and J.P. Murmann (1998), 'Dominant designs, technology cycles and organizational outcomes', *Research in Organizational Behavior*, **20**, 231–66.

Ulrich, K. (1995), 'The role of product architecture in the manufacturing firm', *Research Policy*, **24** (3), 419–40.

Wheelwright, S.C. and K.B. Clark (1992a), 'Creating project plans to focus product development', *Harvard Business Review*, **70** (2), 67–83.

Wheelwright, S.C. and K.B. Clark (1992b), *Revolutionizing Product Development: Quantum Leaps in Speed, Efficiency, and Quality*, New York: Free Press.

Whitney, D. (chair) and the ESD Architecture Committee (2004), 'The influence of architecture in engineering systems', Engineering Systems Monograph, MIT Engineering Systems Division, March.

Woodard, C.J. (2007), 'Modeling architectural strategy using design structure networks', paper presented at the Second International Conference on Design Science Research in Information Systems and Technology (DESRIST 2007), Pasadena, USA, 13–15 May.

Woodard, C.J. (2008), 'Platform competition in digital systems: Architectural control and value migration', Working Paper, 30 May.

3. Platform dynamics and strategies: from products to services

Annabelle Gawer

INTRODUCTION

The emergence of industry platforms is a novel phenomenon impacting most industries today, from products to services. Industry platforms are building blocks (they can be products, technologies or services) that act as a foundation upon which an array of firms (sometimes called a business ecosystem) can develop complementary products, technologies or services. Platforms exist in a variety of industries, and they certainly exist in all high-tech industries. Google, Microsoft Windows, cellphone operating systems, fuel-cell automotive engines, but also some genomic technologies are all platforms. But while platforms are becoming more and more pervasive, and promising research has been under way (Bresnahan and Greenstein, 1999; Gawer and Cusumano, 2002 and 2008; West, 2003; Rochet and Tirole, 2003 and 2006; Iansiti and Levien, 2004; Eisenmann et al., 2006; Evans et al., 2006; Gawer and Henderson, 2007), important questions remain unanswered. In particular, we don't yet understand the conditions under which industry platforms come to exist, and then to develop. We also don't know much about how firms' capabilities should impact their platform strategies.

The chapter aims to answer two research questions: (1) under which conditions can we expect industrial platform dynamics to emerge and unfold? And (2) in the context of platform industry dynamics, what kind of platform strategies should firms devise, depending on whether they are incumbents or new entrants?

To answer to the first question, I set out to present a new typology of platforms, which identifies the distinct contexts in which different types of platforms appear and summarizes their principal characteristics depending on the context in which they occur. I find that platforms are designed and used in three main settings: inside firms; across supply chains; or as industry platforms. I then suggest an evolutionary perspective on platform emergence, and identify circumstances under which internal platforms evolve into supply chain platforms, which then can evolve further into industry platforms.

To answer the second question on platform strategies, I build on Gawer and Cusumano's (2008) concepts of 'coring' and 'tipping', and specify the combinations of coring and tipping that should be best suited to new entrants and to incumbents, depending on characteristics of the industry they operate in or wish to enter. I also suggest that firms' design capabilities (i.e. whether a firm's design capability is to be an integrator/system assembler or rather a specialist/component maker) should have a decisive impact on which strategy to pursue.

I conclude with some implications and further questions for the study of platforms in services.

A TYPOLOGY OF PLATFORMS

The concept of platform has been used and discussed within distinct streams of academic literature, such as new product development, design, and operations (Meyer and Lehnerd, 1997; Simpson et al., 2005); technology strategy (Gawer and Cusumano, 2002 and 2008, Eisenmann et al., 2006); and industrial economics (Rochet and Tirole, 2003; Evans, 2003; Armstrong, 2006). While the term 'platform' is used across these different literatures, the meaning of the term seems to differ between them. Closer inspection reveals that these different literatures have often focused on different empirical contexts. One could even wonder at first glance if they are discussing the same underlying phenomenon. In the vernacular of business, the term 'platform' can also have different meanings.

To clarify the object of study, I shall create a typology of platforms (see Table 3.1). This typology will organize and categorize the distinct meanings of platforms, and attempt to identify their respective characteristics, as well as the business context in which they usually occur and can be observed. To my knowledge, such a typology has not yet been constructed.

Internal Platforms

The first business setting within which the term 'platform' has been widely used has been within the context of new product development, from the early 1990s. As, in this context, platforms have been observed *within* firms, I call them 'internal platforms'. The corresponding literature predominantly discusses 'product platforms'. First, Wheelwright and Clark (1992, p. 73) define such platforms as products that meet the needs of a core group of customers but are designed for easy modification into derivatives

Table 3.1 Typology of platforms

Type of platform	Internal platforms	Supply chain platforms	Industry platforms	Multi-sided markets or platforms
Context	Within the firm	Within a supply chain	Industry ecosystems	Industries
Number of participants	One firm	Several firms within a supply chain	Several firms who don't necessarily buy or sell from each other, but whose products/services must function together as part of a technological system	Several firms (or groups of firms) who transact with each other, through the intermediary of a double-sided (or multi-sided) market
Platform objectives	• To increase the productive efficiency of the firm • To produce variety at lower costs • To achieve mass customization • To enhance flexibility in the design of new products	• To increase productive efficiency along the supply chain • To produce variety at lower costs • To achieve mass customization • To enhance flexibility in the design of new products	For the platform owner: • To stimulate and capture value from external, complementary innovation For complementors: • To benefit from the installed based of the platform, and from direct and indirect network effects complementary innovation	• To facilitate the transactions between different sides of the platform or market
Design rules	• Re-use of modular components • Stability of system architecture	• Reuse of modular components • Stability of system architecture	• Interfaces around the platform allow plugging-in of, and innovation on, complements	• Not usually addressed in the economics literature*

Table 3.1 (continued)

Type of platform	Internal platforms	Supply chain platforms	Industry platforms	Multi-sided markets or platforms
Context	Within the firm	Within a supply chain	Industry ecosystems	Industries
End-use of the final product, service or technology	• Is known in advance and defined by the firm	• End-use is defined by the assembler/integrator of the supply chain • End-use is known in advance	• Variety of end-uses • End-uses may not be known in advance	• Not usually a variable of interest in the economics literature
Key questions asked in the literature	• How to reconcile low cost and variety within a firm?	• How to reconcile low cost and variety within a supply chain?	• How can a platform owner stimulate complementary innovation while taking advantage of it? • How can incentives to create complementary innovation be embedded in the design of the platform?	• How to price the access to the double-sided (or multi-sided) market to the distinct groups of users, to ensure their adoption of the market as an intermediary?

Note: * With the exception of Parker and Van Alstyne (2005) and Hagiu (2007a), who address questions that are central to the literature on industry platforms.

through the addition, substitution or removal of features. The ensuing literature discussing these product platforms has proposed several definitions around this common theme.

For McGrath (1995), platforms are a collection of the common elements, especially the underlying core technology, implemented across a range of products. Meyer and Lehnerd (1997) define platforms as a set of subsystems and interfaces that form a common structure from which a stream of derivative products can be efficiently developed and produced. Robertson and Ulrich (1998) propose a broader definition, as the collection of assets (i.e. components, processes, knowledge, people and relationships) that are shared by a set of products. Krishnan and Gupta (2001) define platforms simply as component and subsystem assets shared across a family of products, while Muffato and Roveda (2002) add the variant of 'a set of subsystems and interfaces *intentionally planned and developed* to form a common structure from which a stream of derivative products can be efficiently developed and produced' (emphasis added). In the marketing literature, Sawhney (1998) proposes a very broad application of the concept of platforms, by suggesting that firms should move from 'portfolio thinking' to 'platform thinking', which he defines as aiming to understand the common strands that tie the firm's offerings, markets and processes together, and exploiting these commonalities to create leveraged growth and variety.

This literature has identified, with a large degree of consensus, the expected benefits of designing and using product platforms as: fixed-costs saving, gaining efficiency in product development through the reuse of common parts, and in particular the ability to produce a large number of derivative products, as well as gaining flexibility in product design. One key objective of platform-based new product development, as it was extolled to managers, was to provide sufficient product variety to meet diverse customer requirements, business needs and technical advances while maintaining economies of scale and scope within manufacturing processes – an approach that was coined as 'mass customization' (Pine, 1993).

The empirical evidence at hand indicates that, in reality, companies have successfully used product platforms to control the high production and inventory cost, as well as the long time to market induced by product proliferation, to a manageable and competitive level. The empirical evidence is heavily weighted towards durable goods whose production processes involve manufacturing, such as in automotive, aircraft and equipment manufacturing, but also in consumer electronics. Some of the more frequently quoted examples of module-based product families include Sony, Hewlett-Packard, Nippondenso, Boeing, Honda, Rolls-Royce and Black & Decker.

Simpson et al. (2005) distinguish between platforms used to develop module-based product families and platforms used to create scale-based product families. For example, Sony, which has built all of its Walkman® models around key modules and platforms, has used modular design and flexible manufacturing to produce a wide variety of quality products at low cost. This strategy allowed Sony to introduce 250+ models in the USA in the 1980s (Sanderson and Uzumeri, 1997). Hewlett-Packard has successfully developed several of its inkjet and laserjet printers around modular components to gain benefits of postponing the point of differentiation in its manufacturing and assembly processes (Feitzinger and Lee, 1997). Nippondenso Co. Ltd made an array of automotive components for a variety of automotive manufacturers using a combinatorial strategy that involves several different modules with standardized interfaces. For instance, 288 different types of panel meters could be assembled from 17 standardized subassemblies (Whitney, 1993).

Scale-based product families are developed by scaling one or more variables to 'stretch' or 'shrink' the platform and create products whose performance varies accordingly to satisfy a variety of market niches. Platform scaling is a common strategy employed in many industries. For example, Lehnerd (1987) explains how Black & Decker developed a family of universal motors for its power tools in response to a new safety regulation: double insulation. Before that, Black & Decker used different motors in each of their 122 basic tools with hundreds of variations. Rothwell and Gardiner (1990) describe how Rolls-Royce scaled its RTM322 aircraft engine by a factor of 1.8 to realize a family of engines with different shaft horse power and thrust. Sabbagh (1996) relates how Boeing developed many of its commercial airplanes by 'stretching' the aircraft to accommodate more passengers, carry more cargo and/or increase flight range. Naughton et al. (1997) relate how Honda developed an automobile platform – an automobile platform consists of the core framework of cars, including the floor plan, drive train and axle – that can be stretched in both width and length to realize a 'world car' after failing to satisfy Japanese and US markets with a single platform.

As mentioned in Simpson et al. (2005), product platforms also promote better learning across products and can reduce testing and certification of complex products such as aircraft (Sabbagh, 1996), spacecraft (Caffrey et al., 2002) and aircraft engines (Rothwell and Gardiner, 1990). For example, in the automobile industry, platform sharing has become common. Automobile manufacturers often use a common platform for different products, either across models with similar quality levels, or across multiple models with different quality levels. Examples of platform sharing across products with similar quality levels include Mitsubishi, which shares a common platform between its Endeavour and Galant, and Honda, which shares a platform between its CR-V and Civic (Rechtin and Kranz, 2003). Automobile manufacturers can also share a platform across multiple products with different quality levels. For example, Toyota uses a common platform for its Landcruiser and Lexus LX 470, and Honda uses a common platform for its CR-V and Acura RDX (Anonymous, 2006; Rechtin and Kranz, 2003).

Simpson et al. (2005) also report that in the automotive industry, platforms enable greater flexibility between plants and increased plant usage – sharing underbodies between models can yield a 50 per cent reduction in capital investment, especially in welding equipment – and can reduce product lead times by as much as 30 per cent (Muffato, 1999). In the 1990s, firms in the automotive industry that used a platform-based product development approach gained a 5.1 per cent market share per year, while firms that did not lost 2.2 per cent (Cusumano and Nobeoka, 1998). In the late 1990s, Volkswagen saved $1.5 billion per year in development and capital costs using platforms, and they produced three of the six automotive platforms that successfully achieved production volumes over one million in 1999 (Bremmer, 1999; 2000). Their platform group consists of the floor group, drive system, running gear, along with the unseen part of the cockpit – and is shared across 19 models marketed under its four brands Volkswagen, Audi, Seat and Skoda.

Recent research suggests that platform sharing can also benefit consumers. For example, Ghosh and Morita's model (2008) suggests that platform sharing across firms should not only help firms save on fixed costs for platform development, but should also benefit consumers as it intensifies competition in firms' horizontal differentiation as well as increases the quality of the lower-end product in vertical differentiation.

The literature also identifies with a large degree of consensus a few fundamental design principles or 'design rules' (Baldwin and Clark, 2000) that are operating in internal product platforms, in particular the stability of the system architecture, and the systematic reuse of modular components (see Chapter 2 in this book). It also recognizes a fundamental trade-off couched in terms of functionality and performance: the optimization of any particular subsystem may result in the suboptimization of the overall system (Meyer and Lehnerd, 1997). We shall see later that this existing tension will have momentous consequences in other types of platforms.

While most of the product platform literature has traditionally focused on products and its empirical studies have taken place in the context of manufacturing firms, most concepts and variables can be usefully applied to the context of services. The processes involved in the design of services can be broken down into parts that can then be assembled or integrated, and later customized. As several authors (Robertson and Ulrich, 1998) have noticed, there is an important process aspect in the development of platforms. Meyer and DeTore (1999) and Voss and Hsuan (2009) usefully begin to apply the concepts of platforms to services. This is uncharted territory, but one that has promising days ahead.

As we shall attempt to compare some characteristics of platforms across different contexts, we can start to indicate a few limits to this literature. These limits are not so much a criticism of this literature as a framing of the scope of this literature, since the nature of the product platforms observed in their usual empirical settings has led to a few implicit assumptions and unobserved or non-discussed variables. Generally, the literature on product platforms assumes that the firm is a manufacturer, and that it alone is in charge of designing and manufacturing the products. Further, while this literature strives to facilitate the development of variants or derivatives of a product, it still assumes that the manufacturer knows the final use of the product. Lastly, it implicitly assumes that the firm in question has all the capabilities required to develop the new products. As it focuses on platforms occurring inside firms, and with a particular interest in how to manage the development process of such platform projects, this literature does not address the question of tapping into external firms' ability to innovate.

Supply Chain Platforms

A supply chain platform extends the product platform concept to firms within the context of a supply chain.

A supply chain platform is a set of subsystems and interfaces that forms a common structure from which a stream of derivative products can be efficiently developed and produced by partners along a supply chain. It is a similar concept to the internal platform of the previous section, but the difference is that, rather than being designed and manufactured internally, the different elements of the final system are designed and manufactured by different suppliers along a supply chain, or among suppliers and a final assembler. The main difference between internal platforms and supply chain platforms is that the platform is no longer an internal affair. Supply chain platforms can be shared among firms that are part of a formal alliance, often exhibiting some amount of cross-ownership between the firms. Or the platform can be shared between the assembler of a complex product and its suppliers.

Supply chain platforms are common in the automotive industry. For example, Renault and Nissan (as members of the Renault–Nissan alliance) have developed a common platform for the Nissan Micra and the Renault

Clio, and they plan to reduce the number of platforms they use to ten in 2010 from the 34 they had in 2000 (Tierney et al., 2000; Bremner et al., 2004). Szczesny (2003) reports platform sharing between Ford Motor and Mazda. Porsche and Volkswagen use a common platform for Porsche's Cayenne and Volkswagen's Touareg, where the former is more luxurious than the latter. Sako (Chapter 10 in this volume) discusses supply chain platforms in the context of automotive supplier parks in Brazil. Other studies on supply chain platforms include Zirpoli and Becker (2008), Zirpoli and Caputo (2002) (both in the automotive industry), Brusoni (2005), and Brusoni and Prencipe (2006) in aerospace.

The objective of these platforms is similar to that of internal platforms: to improve efficiency and to reduce cost. The benefits of supply chain platforms include reducing the variety of parts to maintain and thus reducing costs across the supply chain. Other objectives are manufacturing efficiency, flexibility in design and increase in product variety.

The main design principles or 'design rules' of supply chain platforms are very similar to those of internal platforms: the systematic reuse of modular components and the stability of the system architecture.

Supply chain platforms can create a specific set of challenges. In particular, divergent incentives between the members of a supply chain, or of an alliance, are not uncommon. Remember that, already present in internal platforms, there was a tradeoff between optimizing the performance of subsystems and optimizing the performance of the overall system. Now that we have several actors, we need to be mindful of possibly divergent objectives and incentives among actors within the supply chain. However, in supply chains there is a clear hierarchy, with the bargaining power resting with the final assembler.

In conclusion, while the architecture is the same for internal platforms and supply chain platforms, the existence of different economic players introduces inter-firm relationships and collaboration/competition dynamics, which create the ground for strategic dynamics.

Examples of interesting insights from recent research include the work of Sako (2003) on modularity and outsourcing, and in particular Sako (Chapter 10, in this volume), who explores the distinction between ownership of assets and ownership of tasks; Doran (2004), who examines the transfer of value-added activities within modular supply chains, and Zirpoli and Becker (2008), who warn of negative consequences in terms of knowledge erosion that comes with extreme forms of outsourcing along a supply chain. But by and large the topic of supply chain platforms is in its infancy, and offers many opportunities for researchers to make valuable contributions. There are potentially interesting links to build with the literature on inter-firm modularity (Staudenmayer et al., 2005), on the limits of modularity (Brusoni and Prencipe, 2001), and the recent literature on industry architecture (Jacobides et al., 2006; Pisano and Teece, 2007).

Industry Platforms

Industry platforms are products, services or technologies that are developed by one or several firms, and that serve as foundations upon which other firms can build complementary products, services or technologies. Microsoft Windows operating system, Linux operating system, Intel microprocessors, Apple's iPod and iPhone, Google the Internet search engine, the Internet itself, social networking sites such as Facebook, operating systems in cellular telephony, videogame consoles, but also payment cards, fuel-cell automotive technologies, and some genomic technologies are all industry platforms. Building on these platforms, a large number of firms, loosely assembled in what are sometimes called industrial ecosystems, develop complementary technologies, products or services. A key distinction between supply chain platforms and industry platforms is that, in the case of industry platforms, the firms developing the complements don't necessarily buy or sell from each other, are not part of the same supply chain, nor do they share patterns of cross-ownership.

The empirical contexts of the first studies of industry platforms have been often set in, but not limited to, computing, telecommunications and other information-technology-intensive industries. Bresnahan and Greenstein (1999), in their study of the emergence of computer platforms, define platforms as a bundle of standard components around which buyers and sellers coordinate efforts. West (2003) defines a computer platform as an architecture of related standards that allow modular substitution of complementary assets such as software and peripheral hardware. Iansiti and Levien (2004) call a 'keystone firm' the equivalent of what Gawer and Cusumano (2002, 2008) call a platform leader, that is a firm that drives industry-wide innovation for an evolving system of separately developed components. Gawer and Henderson (2007) describe a product as a platform when it is one component or subsystem of an evolving technological system, when it is strongly functionally interdependent with most of the other components of this system, and when end-user demand is for the overall system, so that there is no demand for components when they are isolated from the overall system.

From the first studies on industry platforms, a few key characteristics have been observed, in particular with regard to how industry platforms affect competitive dynamics as well as industry innovation. Positions of industrial leadership are often contested and lost when industry platforms emerge, as the balance of power between assemblers and component makers is altered. And, at the same time, industry platforms tend to facilitate and increase the degree of innovation on complementary products and services. The more innovation there is on complements, the more value it creates for the platform and its users via direct and indirect network effects, creating a cumulative advantage for existing platforms: as they grow, they become harder to dislodge by rivals or new entrants, the growing number of complements acting like a barrier to entry. The rise of industry platforms therefore raises complex social welfare questions regarding the tradeoffs between the social benefits of platform-compatible innovation versus the potentially negative effects of preventing competition on overall systems.

Similarly to the first two types of platforms (internal and supply chain), industry platforms tend to be designed and managed strategically to further firms' competitive advantage. However, there are important differences between industry platforms and internal or supply chain platforms. In particular, industry platform leaders (or platform owners) aim to tap into the innovative capabilities of external firms, which are not necessarily part of their supply chain. While there are some obvious links with the work of Chesbrough (2003) on open innovation, research on platforms has highlighted the complex tradeoffs between 'open' and 'closed', as several chapters in this volume indicate (Eisenmann et al. in Chapter 6, Greenstein in Chapter 9 and Schilling in Chapter 8). And beyond the choices about opening or closing intellectual property, platform leaders tend to strategically facilitate and stimulate complementary third-party innovation through the careful and coherent management of their ecosystem relationships as well as decisions on design and intellectual property (Cusumano and Gawer, 2002; Iansiti and Levien, 2004). For example, Gawer and Cusumano (2002) propose that the governance of platforms requires a coherent approach using four distinct levers. The first lever is firm scope: the choice of what activities to perform in house versus what to leave to other firms. This decision is about whether the platform leader should make at least some of its own complements in house. The second lever is technology design and intellectual property: what functionality or features to include in the platform, whether the platform should be modular, and to what degree the platform interfaces should be open to outside complementors and at what price. The third lever covers external relationships with complementors: the process by which the platform leader manages complementors and encourages them to contribute to a vibrant ecosystem. The fourth lever is internal organization: how and to what extent platform leaders should use their organizational structure and internal processes to give assurances to external complementors that they are genuinely working for the overall good of the ecosystem. This last lever often requires the platform leader to create a neutral group inside the company, with no direct profit-and-loss responsibility, as well as a Chinese wall between the platform developers and other groups that are potentially competing with their own complementary products or services. Taken together, and dealt with in a coherent manner, the four levers offer a template for sustaining a position of platform leadership.

The design principles or 'design rules' of industry platforms present some degree of overlap with those for internal and supply chain platforms. In particular, the stability of the architecture of the platform is still essential. However, there are important differences as well. In contrast to what happens for internal and supply chain platforms, in industry platforms, the logic of design is inverted. Instead of a firm being a 'master designer' (and it was always the assembler in previous contexts that conceived of and designed an end product, to later modularize it and dispatch various modular tasks to other groups or firms), here we start with a core component that is part of an encompassing modular structure, and the final result of the assembly is either unknown *ex ante*, or is incomplete. In fact, in industry platforms, the end use of end product or service is not predetermined. This creates unprecedented scope for innovation on complementary products, services and technologies – and in general for innovation on the nature of complementary markets. At the same time it creates the fundamental question of how incentives (for third parties) to innovate can be embedded in the design of platforms. This leads to another design rule for industry platforms: the interfaces around the platform must allow plugging-in of complements, as well as innovation on them.

Specific strategic questions also arise in the context of industry platforms, some of which will be addressed in the latter part of this chapter. For example, which products, services or technologies have the potential to become industry platforms? Gawer and Cusumano (2008) suggest that not all products, services or technologies can become platforms: to have platform potential, they must (1) perform a function that is essential to a technological system and (2) solve a business problem for many firms in the industry. Other questions include: how can firms transform their products, technologies or services into industry platforms – and when should they try? How can a platform owner stimulate complementary innovation while taking advantage of it? How can firms attract ecosystems of complementors, in particular within a context of possible competition between platforms?

One particular challenge that platform leaders or wannabes face is that they must navigate a complex strategic landscape where both competition and collaboration occur, sometimes among the same actors. For example, the question of the effect of a platform owner's entry in complementary markets is a recurrent and critical one. As technology evolves, platform owners often face the opportunity to extend the scope of their platform, and integrate into complementary markets. This creates disincentives for complementors to invest in innovation in complementary markets. The difficulty for platform owners to commit not to squeeze the profit margins of their complementors has been identified by Farrell and Katz (2000), while Gawer and Henderson (2007) show how Intel has used its organizational structure and processes as such commitment mechanisms. Further, Intel's careful choice of which complementary market to enter (the connectors) while giving away corresponding intellectual property allowed the firm to push forward the platform/applications interface, thereby retaining control of the architecture while renewing incentives for complementors to innovate 'on top of' the new extended platform. Another challenge is that, as technology is constantly evolving, the business decisions and the technology/design decisions have to be taken in a coherent manner, which is difficult to achieve as these decisions are often made by different teams within organizations.

The literature on industry platforms is an exciting field, and the 14 chapters of this book are a testimony to its vibrancy. But there is much more work to be done, and many opportunities for researchers.

Double-sided (or Multi-sided) Markets

A section of the literature in industrial organization has started recently to use the term platform to characterize certain kinds of markets, namely double-sided markets or multi-sided markets. In this volume, Baldwin and Woodard (Chapter 2) find common features in the architecture of these multi-sided markets and other kinds of platforms. There are important similarities among the industry platforms and the multi-sided markets. Among the similarities are the existence of indirect network effects that arise between the two sides of the market when they have to affiliate with the platforms in order to be able to transact with one another (Armstrong, 2006; Caillaud and Jullien, 2003; Evans, 2003, Hagiu, 2006; Rochet and Tirole, 2003 and 2006).

However, not all the double-sided or multi-sided markets are industry platforms in the sense described in the previous section (i.e. building blocks that act as a foundation upon which other firms can develop complementary products, technologies or services). In particular, those double-sided markets that are pure exchange or trading platforms, such as dating bars, where the role of the platform is purely to facilitate transactions between different sides of the markets without the possibility for other players to innovate on complementary markets, seem to be a different category. The key distinction I make is whether the multi-sided market facilitates or not innovation in new products, technologies or services. All industry platforms do – but some multi-sided markets don't seem to. Dating bars can certainly be seen as double-sided markets, as they facilitate transactions between two distinct groups of users or customers – but there is no obvious sense of how innovation on the nature of complementary markets is facilitated by the existence of the platform.

The emerging literature on double-sided markets (Rochet and Tirole, 2003 and 2006; Armstrong, 2006; Caillaud and Jullien, 2003; Evans, 2003), while useful for solving the chicken-and-egg problem of how to encourage access to a platform for distinct groups of buyers or sellers, presents some major limitations. As discussed in the introductory chapter to this volume, one such limitation is that this literature has taken for granted the existence of the markets that transact through the platform, without attempting to characterize in depth the distinct roles that platforms play – beyond providing the indirect positive network effects that are assumed to exist by definition in these types of platforms. With the notable exceptions of Parker and Van Alstyne (2005) and Hagiu (2007a and 2007b), this literature has been of limited use for those looking for insights into why platforms come into existence in the first place, how to design platforms, and into the drivers of platform emergence and evolution. Most papers in this literature focus on pricing as the answer to the rather narrow question formulated above (the question of how to encourage access and adoption from a pre-existing population of buyers and sellers, transacting through a platform that already exists).

In contrast, results from the literature on industry platforms (Gawer and Cusumano, 2002, with their four (non-price) levers of platform leadership, and more recently Hagiu in a working paper – 2007b) have indicated that pricing alone cannot be the answer to the fundamental strategic questions that are bound to be present wherever platform dynamics occur, such as how to preserve innovation incentives for complementors, by which mechanisms best to share risks among members of an ecosystem, or how to provide coordination and agreement on fundamental characteristics of complementary markets such as the interfaces that embed rules of interoperability between platforms and complements. In this volume, Evans (Chapter 5), Eisenmann et al. (Chapter 6) and Boudreau and Hagiu (Chapter 7) take the double-sided (or multi-sided) literature to the next level by tackling some of these important issues, and thereby provide a welcome bridge between the strategy and design literature on platforms and the industrial organization literature.

THEORY DEVELOPMENT: AN EVOLUTIONARY PERSPECTIVE ON PLATFORMS

In this section, I propose that the three kinds of platforms (internal, supply chain and industry), having been identified in different contexts and discussed by distinct streams of literature, can be interpreted as different stages of evolution of platform development.

I shall describe as an illustrative and motivating case the development of the computer platform, which started as an internal platform, then became a supply chain platform, and later evolved into an industry platform.

From Internal Platform to Supply Chain Platform

In the 1960s, the computer had become an essential tool for processing, analysing and storing data.[1] The design of computers, however, was becoming very complex and difficult to evolve. Every new computer was to be designed from the ground up. For end users, the decision to invest in new computers meant they would have to write off their investment in so-called 'legacy computers', as well as face the costly process of moving their data to new formats.

At IBM in the early 1960s, designers sought solutions for these problems, and this search led to the creation of System/360, which became the first modular family of computers. The goal was to create a compatible product line. In 1961, a committee named SPREAD (for Systems Programming, Research, Engineering and Development) recommended that IBM develop a new family of compatible processors to replace its entire product line. The report proposed that a set of so-called architectural ground rules be designed and followed, allowing different teams in different locations to design distinct modules –monitored by a central architectural-engineering design office. IBM System/360 not only changed the way computers were designed inside IBM, but became hugely successful in the marketplace.

However, IBM's success in creating an internal platform had unintended consequences, and became, rather quickly, detrimental to IBM. The modular architecture of System/360 offered the possibility for other firms to enter and compete in the computer marketplace, on the basis of providing modules that would 'slot in' or 'plug in' IBM System/360 architecture. Soon after the introduction of System/360, and thanks to the defection from IBM of a number of key designers who went to work for them, a large number of companies started to offer IBM 'plug-compatible' peripherals, including disk drives, tape drives, terminals, printers and memory devices. These new companies offered to consumers modules that were substitutes for the IBM modules.

With the help of these former IBM employees, the 'plug-compatible' firms were able to develop faster-than-IBM, cheaper-than-IBM, plug-compatible disk drives, tape drives and memory devices. In the months and years that followed, a large number of IBM employees left IBM to work with plug-compatible makers, who were soon able to make inroads into IBM's markets.

IBM unsuccessfully attempted to deny these competitors access to its customers. But the clean interfaces and the modular nature of System/360 had in effect created what Baldwin (2008) call 'thin crossing points' for entry, and lowered barriers to entry in the newly created sub-markets. Crucially, it proved difficult for IBM to protect its intellectual property on the modules that the 'plug-compatible' firms created, even if these firms had done so with the help of former IBM employees. IBM attempts to countermove were met with 'plug-compatible' firms starting a series of lawsuits alleging unfair competition from IBM – claims that were eventually rejected. The antitrust lawsuit of the USA versus IBM took a decade to be finally dismissed without merit, but it left IBM weakened, and having lost hundreds of its designers to competing firms.

This story is fascinating, as it highlights the unintended but fundamental effect of IBM's visionary decision of creating an internal platform for its family of computers. IBM's design of an internal platform clearly created an enormous amount of value. Accelerated product development, reuse of components across products, facilitated exploration of design options, and the lowering of costs of design and production are among the noted expressions of the value created in the modularity literature (Baldwin and Clark, 2000; Schilling, 2000). For users, the value stemmed from the lowering of the costs of adoption of new computers by virtue of the fact that their previous investments would not be destroyed.

However, as is always the case when innovation happens, the question of who will be able to capture the value created needs to be answered. And naturally, when value is created and revealed, it excites the interest of observers. Protection of intellectual property linked to the innovation, together with control of complementary assets, is essential to ensure that the innovator will be able to profit from his or her innovation (Teece, 1986). So let's turn to the question of how that newly created value gets captured, and by whom.

A fundamental reason why firms can gain economies thanks to internal platforms is that breaking the system architecture down into a set of modules interrelated through fixed interfaces allows a division of labour between different teams, who can work on different modules without having to know how to build the entire system. Different teams need only to know how to make their own module, as well as to know the rules of interconnection with other parts of the system – these rules being defined by the interface specifications. In the process of modularizing the system architecture, the modules are defined and the rules of interaction between modules are clarified. The interface specifications formalize, codify and therefore reveal the rules of interaction between modules. Once this information is revealed and codified, it becomes easy to transfer – but also becomes hard to protect.

The main point is that precisely because internal platforms create value in a way that allows a facilitated division of labour – at first within the firm – they also allow diffusion and migration of knowledge outside the firm, facilitate imitation of modules by others, and therefore alter the incentives of both outsiders and employees who can be tempted to join the new competition – as they did in the IBM case – or to create their own competing firm.

So an internal platform is a source of economic gains for the firm that designs and uses it, yet it can become a source of losses for that firm as it can facilitate (and indeed create) the conditions for competition to emerge. The ability of a firm to protect its intellectual property on the overall system, combined with the tacit knowledge embedded in its organizational routines, will increase its ability to prevent imitation.

In the case of IBM, the competition that emerged was precisely of a kind that IBM wasn't prepared to face as it had never faced it before. Before the new internal platform, IBM was focusing mostly on competition at the system level, and not at the module level. This is probably one of the reasons IBM was not successful in defending its intellectual property on modules.

Of course, the extent to which the intellectual property on not only the overall system architecture but also its interfaces and modules can be protected is a key determinant of whether a firm that introduces an internal platform will be able to capture the value it has created.

A first hypothesis emerges from the analysis of this part of the IBM story that spans the 1970s and 1980s.

Internal platforms are designed by system makers that are assembler or integrator firms, as a way to achieve efficiency in design, production and innovation. But once they exist, internal platforms make assembler firms more vulnerable to entry and competition on modules from specialist component-maker firms. If the system maker cannot protect its intellectual property on the system, the internal platform then evolves into a supply chain platform.

From Supply Chain Platform to Industry Platform

In the case of the computer industry, IBM was not able to keep control of the architecture of its personal computer (PC), and a large number of firms entered the fast-growing market for PCs (Yu, 1998). As Stigler (1951) pointed out, the division of labour in a given industry is dependent on the size of the overall market, which implies that as markets grow, more specialist makers will emerge and be successful. In the PC industry, two of these specialist component makers, Microsoft and Intel, which were originally part of IBM supply chain, began not only to sell to an array of other firms than IBM, but also developed their innovative capabilities. As the architecture of the PC was no longer protected, a number of firms began commercializing copies of the IBM PC, and an ecosystem of firms grew outside of IBM's supply chain.

As IBM lost control of its supply chain, Intel and Microsoft became less dependent upon IBM to sell their products, and began to challenge the bargaining power of IBM. In particular, Intel and Microsoft firms recognized that in order to steer bargaining power away from IBM, the architecture of the PC had to be further developed to accommodate the increasing performance, as well as technological demands, of Intel's microprocessors and Microsoft's operating system. As IBM gradually lost control over its supply chain, the supply chain platform evolved into an industry platform, with Intel and Microsoft – which had started their life as simple component makers and suppliers to IBM – seizing platform leadership, driving industry innovation and capturing most of the industry profits.

Gawer and Cusumano (2002) describe in detail the rise of Intel to platform leadership in the 1990s, which involved innovating on the architecture of the overall PC system (a task previously reserved to IBM the assembler, and not within the habitual scope of component makers) and creating interfaces allowing faster interconnections between elements of the PC, sharing widely the intellectual property of these interfaces. But Intel was also the undisputed technological leader in microprocessors, able to implement a regular doubling of their performance, exemplifying Moore's Law. Further, a set of coherent decisions across the four levers described above helped Intel gain the support of an ecosystem of firms, stimulate complementary innovation and become a neutral broker of industry initiatives.

IBM, which attempted to regain control of the architecture of the PC by offering an improved, but proprietary, architecture, failed in the face of this new form of competition and innovation – that of the industry platform. As industry platform leaders, Intel and Microsoft had not only succeeded in improving the system's performance, but had established the firm support of a coalition of firms whose business models were tied to the new and open Wintel PC architecture. Further, Intel and Microsoft set up a system of incentives and a set of processes to encourage complementary innovators to keep creating new applications that would be compatible with and optimized for new versions of Intel's microprocessors and Microsoft's operating systems. In particular, Intel refrained from squeezing too much profit from its complementors by avoiding integrating into complementary markets (Gawer and Henderson, 2007).

I now summarize the evolution of the computer platform through its three stages:

- Stage 1: IBM/360 is the modular re-architecture of the mainframe computer. It is a perfect example of an internal platform, and it became the foundation for families of IBM products (late 1960s – early 1970s).
- Stage 2: IBM/360 gives rise to 'plug-compatible' products within a supply chain. It also favours the emergence of specialist firms such as Intel and Microsoft (late 1970s and early 1980s).
- Stage 3: 'emancipation' of these suppliers and emergence of the Wintel industry platform (late 1980s).

In the case of IBM, the transition from supply chain platform to industry platform depends on the system maker losing the control of its supply chain. But how can one predict whether a system maker is likely to lose control over its supply chain? I would suggest, based on the IBM story, that this will happen if three conditions are met: (1) if there exists a pool of external firms with the capability to create significant value in components; (2) if the value to end users provided by the assembler becomes relatively low compared to the value created by the components; and (3) if the component makers can find other markets to sell to than their previous assembler–customer. All these conditions were met in the IBM–Intel–Microsoft story.

A second hypothesis emerges from the analysis of this part of the story of IBM, Intel and Microsoft in the 1990s.

> If system-maker firms lose control of their supply chain, and if component makers can seize the opportunity to innovate on the overall system while preserving incentives for complementors to make profits, then a supply chain platform can evolve into an industry platform.

Figure 3.1 summarizes the hypotheses developed in this section. A set of rigorous empirical studies would be necessary to validate the corresponding hypotheses.

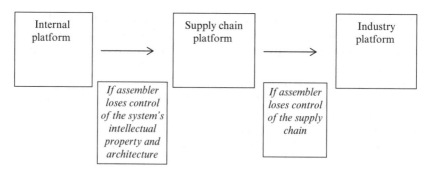

Figure 3.1   An evolutionary perspective on platforms

PLATFORM STRATEGIES

This section aims to answer the second research question: in the context of platform industry dynamics, what kind of platform strategies should firms devise, depending on whether they are incumbents or new entrants? To answer this question, I am building directly on previous research by Gawer and Cusumano (2008), based on a study of a dozen firms in high-tech industries. The main insights from this study are the following.

First, we suggested that not all products, technologies or services can become platforms. We indicated that there are two preconditions for a product, service or technology to have 'platform potential': (1) does it perform a function that is essential to a technological system? and (2) does it solve a business problem for many firms in the industry?

Second, we recommended that firms should make a choice early on between pursuing a platform strategy and what we called a product strategy. This is because the industry conditions and business choices that favour a platform can differ from those that favour a product – creating different incentives for companies that assemble products than for industry platform owners. In particular, industry platform owners benefit from lots of innovation on complements as well as from competition at the overall system level, which would bring its prices down. Gawer and Cusumano (2008) give the example of Microsoft, an industry platform owner, that benefits from competition between PC manufacturers that use its operating system, while these firms, in contrast, would rather see Microsoft face tough competition in computer operating systems so that they could bargain for better prices on the operating system they will load on their PC.

Third, the most important findings from Gawer and Cusumano (2008)

Table 3.2   Coring and tipping

Strategic option	Technology/design actions to consider	Business actions to consider
Coring How to create a new platform when none existed before	• Solve an essential 'system' problem • Facilitate external companies' provision of 'add-ons' • Keep intellectual property closed on the innards of your technology • Maintain strong interdependences between platform and complements	• Solve an essential business problem for many industry players • Create and preserve complementors' business incentives to contribute and innovate • Protect your main source of revenue and profit • Maintain high switching costs to competing platforms
Tipping How to win platform wars by building market momentum	• Try to develop unique, compelling features that are hard to imitate and that attract users • Tip across markets: absorb and bundle technical features from an adjacent market	• Provide more incentives for complementors than your competitors do • Rally competitors to form a coalition • Consider pricing or subsidy mechanisms that attract users to the platform

Source: Adapted from Gawer and Cusumano (2008). Reproduced with permission from *MIT Sloan Management Review.*

are the identification of two generic strategies, 'coring' and 'tipping'. 'Coring' is the answer to the question (1) how to establish a platform when none existed before? And 'tipping' is the answer to: (2) how to win in a platform competition? Coring is the set of activities or strategic moves a firm can use to create a platform when none existed before by identifying or designing an element (a technology, a product or a service) and making it fundamental, or 'core', to a technological system as well as to a market. Tipping is the set of activities or strategic moves firms can use to shape market dynamics and win platform wars when at least two platform candidates compete. These moves cover sales, marketing, pricing, product development and coalition building. Gawer and Cusumano (2008) give detailed examples of coring by Google, Qualcomm and EMC, and tipping by Linux, Microsoft and Nokia. Table 3.2 summarizes what coring and tipping entail.

BOX 3.1   CORING IN SEVEN STEPS

1. Develop a vision of how an alternative, platform-based archi-
    tecture could supplant the current industry architecture
2. Design (or, if necessary, extract and 'un-hide' from an encom-
    passing technological system) an element with platform
    potential (i.e. performing an essential function, and easy to
    connect to)
3. Add connectors or interfaces so that other companies can
    build on the platform and share the intellectual property of
    these connectors
4. Identify third-party firms that could complete the platform for
    different types of finished, integrated products (possibly in dif-
    ferent markets and for different uses)
5. Build a coalition: share the vision by evangelizing the techni-
    cal architecture, but also by articulating a business model for
    different actors in the ecosystem, rally complementors, share
    risks, and facilitate complementary innovation
6. Keep innovating on the core, ensuring that it continues to
    provide an essential (and difficult-to-replace) function to the
    overall system
7. Gradually build up your reputation as a neutral industry
    broker, along with making long-term investments in industry
    coordination activities (whose fruits will create value for the
    whole ecosystem, including end users)

One of the important points of Table 3.2 is that the choices about the
design of the platform are intimately related to choices about structuring
of the business relationships among ecosystem members. To provide more
detail on how firms can successfully perform a 'coring' strategy, I suggest
a seven-step process (see Box 3.1).

We have already seen that not all products, services or technologies
have platform potential. Let us now examine which firms should attempt a
platform strategy, depending on their context. I shall examine first the case
of entrant firms, and then the case of incumbent firms.

Platform Strategies for Entrants

Entrant firms' platform strategies should depend, on the one hand, on
whether the target market already has an industry platform or not, and on

the other hand, on the firm's design capability, i.e. whether it is a system assembler or a specialist component maker. To create a platform where none existed before, and if the firm has the capabilities of a specialist component maker, then it should try to core its market using the seven-step formula. But if, in contrast, its core capability is system integration, it should stay away from a platform strategy and pursue a product strategy instead.

To dislodge an incumbent platform leader, firms should still do market coring, with the caveat that they need to propose an alternative platform to the one already in place. Firms should in this case complement coring with tipping. If a wannabe directly opposes an existing platform, it must identify and rally firms that should have an interest in undermining the existing platform.

In the case of entrants that are not system integrators but component or specialist makers, a combination of coring and tipping, while building an alternative coalition and articulating business models for alternative ecosystem followers, is appropriate. This is what the Linux community and vendors such as Red Hat, as well as Google with search technology, have done. In the case of new entrants who assemble complement products or who are system integrators but enter an industry with an existing platform, it may not be necessary to start with a coring strategy. It may be sufficient to enter with a really good product to tip the market. However, if rivals continue to enter, it is best to encourage developers of complements and pursue coring as well. This is what Apple can do with its iPod and iPhone. Microsoft has also followed this approach with its Xbox video-game console, which challenged the incumbent leaders, Sony and Nintendo (see Figure 3.2).

Platform Strategies for Incumbents

We now turn to strategies for incumbent firms. To protect a firm from new platform threats, it is important to distinguish whether the firm under attack is a focused component provider or a system integrator. If the firm is a component maker (and this can be software, hardware or a service), then, according to Eisenmann et al. (2006), it will be particularly vulnerable to 'envelopment'. This is when an entering platform bundles the specific component as part of a larger platform. These authors rightly suggest that allying with a 'bigger brother' or changing one's business model (change the 'paying side') are good strategies. When the attacked firm is a system integrator, however, the platform leader can attempt to play two games at once: pursue both a product strategy and a platform strategy.

Firms such as SAP and Nokia have made attempts at this counterintuitive

		Target industry	
		Has no dominant platform	**Has a dominant platform**
Entrant's design capability	**Specialist component-maker**	**Coring** Attack the system-based competition with an industry platform • Microsoft • Intel • Qualcomm	**Coring and tipping** Articulate an alternative industry platform business model for those who were left out, or opponents of, the original platform business model. It may be useful to build a coalition of competitors • Google • Linux
	System assembler or integrator	**Do not try a platform strategy** Stay with a product strategy and remain a closed system • Automotive manufacturers	**Product strategy + tipping** Enter with a closed/proprietary system/device, and then bring on complements • Apple iPod, iTV, iPhone • Sony and Nintendo and Microsoft in videogames

Figure 3.2 Platform strategies for new entrants

dual strategy. As explained earlier, the economic logic of systems-based competition runs contrary to what helps a new platform to win. In recent years, however, a few incumbent assemblers, concerned that they could not block an external coring (or platform entry) in their own industry, have attempted to offer an alternative platform themselves. Nokia embraced a dual strategy in the cellphone industry, attempting to ward off Microsoft's entry by backing the creation of a new operating system, Symbian. WCDMA, also backed heavily by Nokia, is a response to Qualcomm's dominance in CDMA technology. This is also what the enterprise software maker, SAP, did when it created a middleware software platform, NetWeaver, that can connect SAP's applications to competitors' applications. These two incumbent product or system firms have become platform wannabes in new markets.

Nokia used to be a pure assembler of cellphones. But when it saw Microsoft aggressively enter the cellphone industry with its operating system, Windows CE/Mobile – a market coring strategy on Microsoft's part – Nokia realized it could very well become the next victim of

Microsoft's entry, akin to what IBM had experienced in the late 1980s. Nokia management did not want to go the way of other PC manufacturers, who, like IBM, cede most of the value in their products to Microsoft's and Intel's core technologies in the Wintel platform. Nokia's retaliation move consisted in sustaining an alternative platform by backing up Symbian's operating system, investing $250 million in 2004 into Symbian's consortium to now owning nearly 50 per cent of the venture. The Symbian OS also powers phones developed by Nokia's competitors, putting Nokia in a position to pursue a dual strategy: maintain the uniqueness of its integrated mobile phones while pushing the operating system component in competitors' phones.

SAP, the German software maker and world leader in enterprise applications, has traditionally developed products for enterprise resource planning, supply chain management and customer relationship management. In general, system integrators such as Accenture, IBM and hundreds of smaller firms implemented and deployed SAP software for their customers. In a departure from its previous strategy of offering integrated solutions, in 2003 SAP started to offer NetWeaver as a 'business process platform' that included predefined enterprise services and integration technology. SAP wanted to create an ecosystem of independent software vendors (ISVs) that would develop applications on top of the SAP NetWeaver platform. Management believed that this platform would also allow customers to modify and reconfigure the building blocks of their SAP systems as well as allow better interoperability of SAP products with non-SAP products. SAP, however, did not intend to abandon its legacy applications business to become a pure platform vendor. This means that SAP has continued to sell applications in competition with the same ISVs it hoped would develop applications using the SAP platform.

Dual strategies are very difficult to implement because the firms must play two different games at the same time and follow two opposing logics: that of the system assembler and that of the platform leader. The challenge lies in that what helps platforms win does not help assemblers make money. We think these strategies are appropriate for threatened firms hedging their bets and preparing themselves for a transition towards a coring strategy. For example, in 2008, Nokia ended up deciding to fully acquire Symbian, and made its code open source, changing its business model, to give itself a better chance to fight Microsoft's mobile operating system (see Figure 3.3).

Not only are these dual strategies difficult to pull off; they also have possible antitrust consequences. Carlton and Waldman (2002) have clarified the use of strategic tying to preserve and create market power in evolving industries. For example, over the years, Microsoft has often played an

		If attacked by an entrant with platform
Firm's design capability	**Specialist component-maker**	**Ally with competitors** But it will be very hard to resist if you are attacked by a monopolist from an adjacent market • Symbian
	System assembler or integrator	**Dual strategy: product and platform** • Nokia • SAP/NetWeaver

Figure 3.3   Platform strategies for incumbents

ambiguous game of openness and closedness – touting the openness of its application programming interfaces but at the same time highlighting the benefits of seamless integration of features across its applications. It has entered many complementary markets and has been accused of extending and leveraging its monopoly power by doing so. It can be tempting for firms that have achieved strong platform-leader positions to attempt to enter complementary markets and compete in systems – in effect, to pursue these two objectives (product and platform) at once. This strategy can make sense if they have the capabilities to develop the complements as well as system integration capabilities because they can exert more control over both the platform and its technologies and over complements. Managers can also justify this strategy as an attempt to hedge their bets in the face of uncertainty, as firms cannot always know in advance which path will yield them most growth or most profit.

Fundamentally, however, dual strategies are very risky. If a platform owner has some market power in its first market, it becomes easy to squeeze profit margins from its complementors' innovations simply by bundling the complements with the platform. Competing with one's complementors too aggressively will eventually ruin a platform owner's reputation for neutrality, weaken complementors' incentives to innovate, and possibly encourage complementors to flee to a competing platform (see Gawer and Henderson, 2007). Microsoft has been accused of doing just that in its landmark antitrust lawsuit, initially brought about by disgruntled competitors and complementors. Monopolistic platform owners thus need to be careful not to commit antitrust violations. Aggressive efforts at market tipping often come too close to violating antitrust law. Intel and Cisco have also come under antitrust investigation.

CONCLUSIONS AND IMPLICATIONS FOR SERVICES

In the context of a profound transformation of our industrial land-scapes and as high technology has become increasingly pervasive, we have observed the emergence of industry platforms. They are associated with new forms of industry collaboration and innovation, as well as new forms of competitive dynamics. This chapter has attempted to answer two questions: (1) under which conditions can we expect industrial plat-form dynamics to emerge and unfold? and (2) in the context of platform industry dynamics, what kind of platform strategies should firms devise, depending on whether they are incumbents or new entrants? I shall now summarize the answers to these questions and draw some implications for further research, in particular on the topic of platforms for services.

To answer the first question, I have presented a new typology of plat-forms, organizing them in three categories: internal platforms, supply chain platforms and industry platforms. This typology is valid for products as well as for services. I have then suggested and motivated an evolutionary hypothesis on the emergence of platforms that states that platforms emerge first within firms as internal platforms, and can then evolve towards supply chain platforms, and finally towards industry platforms. I have indicated circumstances in which such an evolution can occur. Further validation of this hypothesis from rigorous empirical research constitutes an exciting research opportunity.

To answer the second question, I have presented further development on the concepts of 'coring' and 'tipping' initially introduced by Gawer and Cusumano (2008), and I have suggested appropriate platform strate-gies for both new entrants and incumbents, depending on whether their main design capability is to be an assembler/integrator/system maker or a specialist/component maker.

As high technology permeates both manufacturing and services, will we see platform dynamics also emerging and transforming service industries? Platforms are already creating very profound changes in services, but we don't yet fully understand how. A clear example of how services have been affected by platforms can be seen in Internet-based transactions, whether they are facilitated by Google search, or by eBay, Amazon, or other trading platforms. The landscape of retail and of travel services has been fundamentally altered by the emergence of Internet platforms. Another example of a service industry where the impact of platforms is starting to be felt is the financial services industry. For example, financial stock markets are developing as trading platforms, initially driven by cost-cutting and efficiency objectives. This has promoted collaboration and mergers between stock exchanges. But this integration has also brought about more interdependence and vulnerability to external shocks.

But if we want to better understand how service industries will be affected by platforms, further research needs to be done, as there are differences between products and services, and the vast majority of empirical studies on platforms have so far focused on products (see Suarez and Cusumano, Chapter 4 in this volume). Services do not lend themselves to being neatly decomposed as subsystems and component as products do. The division of labour between component makers and assemblers, and the battle of power between them, so crucial to platform dynamics, has therefore to be reinterpreted in the context of services, even if we can observe a tension between specialists and generalists in, say, the financial services industry. The distinction between products and services is itself under much scrutiny. Under which conditions will services platforms emerge? The typology of platforms and the evolutionary hypothesis I presented at the beginning of this chapter can be a starting point, but further research should be grounded in empirical analysis and possibly on in-depth case studies. In terms of platform strategies, we see an abundance of 'tipping' behaviours, and the practice of bundling in particular is quite common within services, as seen in telecom triple play (voice, data, video), tourism package holidays, and with banking accounts and insurance. But so far, except for the case of Internet-based services such as eBay or Amazon built on technology platforms, one cannot see so many 'coring' behaviours. A question of particular interest, still vastly unexplored, is how the ability (or lack of ability) to protect intellectual property in services will affect the possible emergence of industry platforms, and facilitate or hinder cross-firm collaborative innovation. The next frontier of research in platforms will be to explore these topics, as they are of particular importance for advanced economies aiming to create value-added services in the context of increased international competition and globalization.

NOTE

1. Sources for the facts in this section are: Baldwin and Clark (2000), Fisher et al. (1983) and Pugh et al. (1991).

REFERENCES

Anonymous (2006), 'Vehicle profiles: a user's guide', *Consumer Reports*, **71** (April), 39–78.

Armstrong, M. (2006), 'Competition in two-sided markets', *RAND Journal of Economics*, **37**, 668–91.

Baldwin, C.Y. (2008), 'Where do transactions come from? Modularity, transactions, and the boundaries of firms', *Industrial and Corporate Change*, **17** (1), 155–95.

Baldwin, C.Y. and K.B. Clark (2000), *Design Rules: The Power of Modularity*, Cambridge, MA: MIT Press.

Bremmer, R. (1999), 'Cutting-edge platforms', *Financial Times Automotive World*, September, 30–38.

Bremmer, R. (2000), 'Big, bigger, biggest', *Automotive World*, June, 36–44.

Bremner, B., G. Edmondson and C. Dawson (2004), 'Nissan's boss', *Business Week*, 4 October, p. 50.

Bresnahan, T. and S. Greenstein (1999), 'Technological competition and the structure of the computer industry', *Journal of Industrial Economics*, **47**, 1–40.

Brusoni, S. (2005), 'The limits to specialization: problem-solving and coordination in modular networks', *Organization Studies*, **26** (12), 1885–907.

Brusoni, S. and A. Prencipe (2001), 'Unpacking the black box of modularity: Technologies, products and organizations', *Industrial and Corporate Change*, **10** (1), 179–204.

Brusoni, S. and A. Prencipe (2006), 'Making design rules: a multi-domain perspective', *Organization Science*, **17** (2), 179–89.

Caffrey, R.T., T.W. Simpson, R. Henderson and E. Crawley (2002) 'The economic issues with implementing open avionics platforms for spacecraft', *20th AIAA International Communications Satellite Systems Conference and Exhibit*, AIAA-2002-1870, Montreal, Quebec, Canada.

Caillaud, B. and B. Jullien (2003), 'Chicken and egg: competition among intermediation service providers', *RAND Jurnal of Economics*, **34**, 309–28.

Carlton, D. and M. Waldman (2002), 'The strategic use of tying to preserve and create market power in evolving industries', *RAND Journal of Economics*, **33** (2), 194–220.

Chesbrough, H.W. (2003), *Open Innovation; The New Imperative for Creating and Profiting from Technology*, Boston, MA: Harvard Business School Press.

Cusumano, M.A. and A. Gawer (2002), 'The elements of platform leadership', *MIT Sloan Management Review*, **43** (3), 51–58.

Cusumano, M.A. and Nobeoka, K. (1998), *Thinking Beyond Lean*, New York: Free Press.

Doran, D. (2004), 'Rethinking the supply chain: an automotive perspective', *Supply Chain Management: An International Journal*, **9** (1), 102–9.

Eisenmann, T., G. Parker and M. Van Alstyne (2006), 'Strategies for two-sided markets', *Harvard Business Review*, **84** (10), 92–101.

Evans, D.S. (2003), 'The antitrust economics of multi-sided platform markets', *Yale Journal on Regulation*, **20**, 325–82.

Evans, D.S., A. Hagiu and R. Schmalensee (2006), *Invisible Engines: How Software Platforms Drive Innovation and Transform Industries*, Cambridge, MA: MIT Press.

Farrell, J. and M.L. Katz (2000), 'Innovation, rent extraction, and integration in systems markets', *Journal of Industrial Economics*, **97** (4), 413–32.

Feitzinger, E. and H.L. Lee (1997), 'Mass customization at Hewlett-Packard: the power of postponement', *Harvard Business Review*, **75** (1), 116–21.

Fisher, F., J.J. McGowan and J.E. Greenwood (1983), *Folded, Spindled and Mutilated: Economic Analysis and U.S. vs. IBM*, Cambridge, US: MIT Press.

Gawer, A. and M.A. Cusumano (2002), *Platform Leadership: How Intel, Microsoft, and Cisco Drive Industry Innovation*, Boston, MA: Harvard Business School Press.

Gawer, A. and M.A. Cusumano (2008), 'How companies become platform leaders', *MIT Sloan Management Review*, **49** (2), 28–35.

Gawer, A. and R. Henderson (2007), 'Platform owner entry and innovation in complementary markets: evidence from Intel', *Journal of Economics and Management Strategy*, **16** (1), 1–34.

Ghosh, A. and H. Morita (2008), 'An economic analysis of platform-sharing', *Journal of the Japanese and International Economics*, **22** (2), 164–186.

Hagiu, A. (2006), 'Pricing and commitment by two-sided platforms', *RAND Journal of Economics*, **37** (3), 720–37.

Hagiu, A. (2007a), 'Merchant or two-sided platform?', *Review of Network Economics*, **6** (2), 115–33.

Hagiu, A. (2007b), 'Multi-sided platforms: from microfoundations to design and expansion strategies', Harvard Business School, Working Paper No. 07-094, accessed 23 December 2008 at http://www.hbs.edu/research/pdf/07-094.pdf.

Iansiti, M. and R. Levien (2004), *The Keystone Advantage: What the New Dynamics of Business Ecosystems Mean for Strategy, Innovation, and Sustainability*, Boston, MA: Harvard University Press.

Jacobides, M.G., T. Knudsen and M. Augier (2006), 'Benefiting from innovation: value creation, value appropriation and the role of industry architectures', *Research Policy*, **35** (6), 1200–221.

Krishnan, V. and G. Gupta (2001), 'Appropriateness and impact of platform-based product development', *Management Science*, **47**, 52–68.

Lehnerd, A.P. (1987) 'Revitalizing the manufacture and design of mature global products', in B.R. Guile and H. Brooks (eds), *Technology and Global Industry: Companies and Nations in the World Economy*, Washington, DC: National Academy Press, pp. 49–64.

McGrath, M.E. (1995), *Product Strategy for High-Technology Companies*, New York, NY, US: Irwin Professional Publishing.

Meyer, M.H. and A. DeTore (1999), 'Creating platform-based approaches to new services development', *Journal of Product Innovation Management*, **18**, 188–204.

Meyer, M.H. and A.P. Lehnerd (1997), *The Power of Product Platforms: Building Value and Cost Leadership*, New York: Free Press.

Muffato, M. (1999), 'Platform strategies in international new product development', *International Journal of Operations and Production Management*, **19** (5/6), 449–59.

Muffato, M. and M. Roveda (2002), 'Product architecture and platforms: a conceptual framework', *International Journal of Technology Management*, **24** (1), 1–16.

Naughton, K., E. Thornton, K. Kerwin and H. Dawley (1997) 'Can Honda build a world car?', *Business Week*, **100** (7), 8 September, available at http://www.businessweek.com/1997/36/b3543001.htm, accessed 16 June 2009.

Parker, G. and M. Van Alstyne (2005), 'Two-sided network effects: a theory of information product design', *Management Science*, **51**, 1494–504.

Pine, B.J. (1993), *Mass Customization: The New Frontier in Business Competition*, Boston, MA: Harvard Business School Press.

Pisano, G. P. and D.J. Teece (2007), 'How to capture value from innovation: shaping intellectual property and industry architecture', *California Management Review*, **50** (1), 278–96.

Pugh, E.W., L.R. Johnson and J.H. Palmer (1991), *IBM's 360 and Early 370 Systems*, Cambridge, MA: MIT Press.

Rechtin, M. and R. Kranz (2003), 'Japanese step up product charge', *Automotive News*, **77** (18 August), 26–30.

Robertson, D. and K. Ulrich (1998), 'Planning for product platforms', *MIT Sloan Management Review*, **39** (4), 19–31.

Rochet, J.-C. and J. Tirole (2003), 'Platform competition in two-sided markets', *Journal of the European Economic Association*, **1** (4), 990–1029.

Rochet, J.-C. and J. Tirole (2006), 'Two-sided markets: a progress report', *RAND Journal of Economics*, **35**, 645–67.

Rothwell, R. and P. Gardiner (1990), 'Robustness and product design families', in M. Oackley (ed.), *Design Management: A Handbook of Issues and Methods*, Cambridge, MA: Basic Blackwell Inc., pp. 279–92.

Sabbagh, K. (1996) *Twenty-First Century Jet: The Making and Marketing of the Boeing 777*, New York: Scribner.

Sako (2003), 'Modularity and outsourcing: the nature of co-evolution of product architecture in the global automotive industry', in A. Prencipe, A. Davies and M. Hobday (eds), *The Business of Systems Integration*, Oxford: Oxford University Press, pp. 229–53.

Sanderson, S.W. and M. Uzumeri (1997), *Managing Product Families*, Chicago, IL: Irwin.

Sawhney, M.S. (1998), 'Leveraged high-variety strategies: from portfolio thinking to platform thinking', *Journal of the Academy of Marketing Science*, **26** (1), 54–61.

Schilling, M.A. (2000), 'Towards a general modular systems theory and its application to inter-firm product modularity', *Academy of Management Review*, **25** (2), 312–34.

Simpson, T.W., Z. Siddique and J. Jiao (2005), 'Platform-based product family development: introduction and overview', in T.W. Simpson, Z. Siddique and J. Jiao (eds), *Product Platforms and Product Family Design: Methods and Applications*, New York: Springer, pp. 1–16.

Staudenmayer, N., M. Tripsas and C.L. Tucci (2005), 'Interfirm modularity and its implications for product development', *Journal of Product Innovation Management*, **22**, 303–21.

Stigler, G. (1951), 'The division of labor is limited by the extent of the market', *Journal of Political Economy*, **59** (3), 185–93.

Szczesny, J. (2003), 'Mazda ushers in new Ford era: platform sharing across global brands is Ford's new way of doing business', viewed 14 February, 2006, http://www.thecarconnection.com/index.asp?article=6574pf=1.

Teece, D.J. (1986), 'Profiting from technological innovation: implications for integration, collaboration, licensing and public policy', *Research Policy*, **15** (6), 285–305.

Tierney, C., A. Bawden and M. Kunii (2000), 'Dynamic duo', *Business Week* (23 October), p. 26.

Voss, C. and J. Hsuan (2009), 'Service architecture and modularity', *Decision Sciences Journal*, **40** (3), 541–69.

West, J. (2003), 'How open is open enough? Melding proprietary and open source platform strategies', *Research Policy*, **32**, 1259–85.

Wheelwright, S.C. and K.B. Clark (1992), 'Creating project plans to focus product development', *Harvard Business Review*, **70** (2), 67–83.

Whitney, D.E. (1993), 'Nippondenso Co. Ltd: a case study of strategic product design', *Research in Engineering Design*, **5** (1), 1–20.

Yu, A. (1998), *Creating the Digital Future: The Secrets of Consistent Innovation at Intel*, New York: Free Press.

Zirpoli, F. and M.C. Becker (2008), 'The limits of design and engineering outsourcing: performance integration and the unfulfilled promises of modularity', mimeo, presented at the International Workshop on Collaborative Innovation and Design Capabilities, Mines ParisTech, Paris.

Zirpoli, F. and M. Caputo (2002), 'The nature of buyer–supplier relationships in co-design activities: the Italian auto industry case', *International Journal of Operations and Production Management*, **22** (12), 1389–410.

4. The role of services in platform markets

Fernando F. Suarez and Michael A. Cusumano

INTRODUCTION

Numerous factors affect the emergence of a successful platform among competing alternatives. Some of these influences can be very idiosyncratic or platform-specific, although most studies agree on the critical role of the following four factors: (a) adequate pricing strategies to generate momentum behind a platform – e.g. subsidizing one 'side' of the platform as console makers do in the videogames industry (Eisenmann, 2005); (b) having a large set of complementary products that increase the value of a particular platform – for example, a wider array of games for a given console (Gawer and Cusumano, 2002); (c) the strength of 'network effects' that often tilt the balance in favor of platforms that can build their installed base faster than competitors – e.g. the reason why platforms such as VHS as well as MS-DOS and then Windows and Office have been so successful (Katz and Shapiro, 1988); and (d) technological or design advantages – i.e. the possibility that one platform may achieve a high level of differentiation over competitors, for instance due to technological superiority (Suarez and Utterback, 1995). Other factors sometimes mentioned in explaining platform outcomes include the role of market momentum and 'mind share' (e.g. the 'buzz' that Apple or Google generates before the launch of new products) and government regulation (Gawer and Cusumano, 2008). However, these factors seem to be a common denominator in most of the platform studies with which we are familiar.

Most of the research on how platform leaders emerge, however, has neglected another factor: the potential role of services in this process. This chapter attempts to remedy that deficiency in the literature. The question remains, though, as to why researchers have not paid much attention to the role of services in the establishment of new platforms. To answer this question, we need to look briefly at the origins of the platform literature.

The word 'platform' became commonly used in management within studies of product development, particularly in the automobile industry

(Wheelwright and Sasser, 1989; Wheelwright and Clark, 1992; Meyer and Lehnerd, 1997; Nobeoka and Cusumano, 1997; Cusumano and Nobeoka, 1998). In this literature, a platform was considered to be a set of common components and a general design or architectural 'blueprint' that supported product variations and extensions through part substitution and part extension. The auto industry was probably one of the first to adopt a platform strategy, by which products that are apparently very different (such as the Toyota Camry and the Toyota Highlander SUV, in Toyota's current lineup) actually share a common underbody and many other components. In these auto industry studies, a platform typically included elements of the 'chassis' such as the underbody structural components, the suspension type (e.g. McPherson), axle, damper and antiroll mechanism (Nobeoka and Cusumano, 1997; Cusumano and Nobeoka, 1998). These studies, for the most part, had little to say about servicing these components.

The product development literature, in turn, grew largely out of studies of the innovation process and innovation dynamics. As with the platform literature, these studies also tended to ignore the role of services. For instance, von Hippel's work on the sources of innovation focuses on the role of users and, despite this focus, has no major reference to the role of services. Similarly, Abernathy and Utterback (1978) and Klepper (1996) have almost no mention of the role of services in their discussion of the stages of industry life cycle or, in the case of Abernathy and Utterback, in their discussion of the emergence of dominant designs. Later authors, such as Gawer and Cusumano (2002) or Eisenmann et al. (2006), worked more in the domain of technology and innovation strategy. They tend to define platforms more as foundation technologies that become the center of 'ecosystems' driven by complementary products and services produced by a variety of firms, often with strong network effects tying the platform to the complements, such as Windows-based personal computers and Windows-based applications.

Therefore a discussion of the role of services in the emergence of a platform needs to start by pointing out that the platform literature grew out of studies focusing mainly on product industries – research that has tended to overlook the role of services. Although some of the more recent treatments of platforms do include service industries (such as credit cards – see Eisenmann, 2005), there is still a vacuum when it comes to analyzing the role of services in helping to establish product-based platforms. We address this vacuum by focusing on three related questions: what is the potential role of services in the outcome of platform battles in product industries? What is the importance of services in platform-mediated markets versus other markets? And which types of firms are more likely to produce services in platform-mediated industries and why?

SERVICES IN PLATFORM INDUSTRIES

Much of the literature on services is devoted to 'pure service' industries, defined by their output being not a tangible, manufactured good (for example Bell, 1973). This simple definition needs to be expanded for the case of platform-mediated markets built around a product, such as most of the examples found in the literature: game consoles, computers or the Windows operating system (digital goods are no exception and for most purposes here behave like physical goods). Services in product industries have typically been considered a 'complementary activity' to the industry products (Teece, 1986). This approach has generally assumed a one-way relationship between services and products: first there are products and these give rise to services around them, such as for after-sales repair and maintenance. However, in platform markets where services are an essential complement, the availability of the service may need to evolve at least simultaneously with the platform. For instance, the availability of the iTunes digital media service helped Apple dominate the hand-held media device market with the iPod (Eisenmann et al., 2007). Complementors also played a role in the video recorder industry, where the distribution of pre-recorded VHS tapes helped Japan Victor Corporation and Matsushita beat Sony in this market (Cusumano et al., 1992). We can also see services play an important role early on for manufacturing products where the key is to go beyond the traditional image of services as those activities destined to 'repairing and maintaining products'. Although repair and maintenance are still an important component of services in many product industries, they are only a part. Other services include consulting, customization, installation, technical support and training.

SERVICES AND THE EMERGENCE OF PRODUCT-BASED PLATFORMS

The emergence of several competing platforms in early product markets is often characterized by a high degree of uncertainty for customers and firms alike. There is uncertainty as to the extent to which each competing alternative satisfies existing or emerging needs, the reliability and future development of the technology on which the platform is based, possible uses and extensions of the platform, and which of the competing platforms is more likely to remain in the market over the long term. By acting upon each of the key factors for platform dominance identified at the outset of this chapter, services can play an important role in determining the outcome of a platform battle.

Services as a Hedge against Platform Adoption Risk[1]

In platform battles, customers often exhibit a 'wait-and-see' attitude; in other words, users defer their decision to choose a platform until the outcome of the battle is somewhat clear. The reason is that customers may be reluctant to spend resources and commit to platform-specific learning if they cannot reasonably predict who the winners may be (Carpenter and Nakamoto, 1989). Opting for a particular product-based platform often involves significant transition costs from the existing technology or platform to the new one. In such situations, services can help platform firms overcome the natural resistance of customers to adopt.

In these situations, platform leaders and wannabes may offer services to try to minimize customers' platform adoption risk. For instance, by providing consulting services, firms can help customers better understand the differences between competing platforms and assess the potential impact of choosing a platform that does not become the dominant one. It is common for enterprise resource planning (ERP) producers such as SAP and Oracle to offer consulting services to help customers understand the advantages and disadvantages of their products relative to competing alternatives. Likewise, platform firms can provide on-the-job training by stationing training staff on the customer sites, thus lessening the difficulty of transitioning to a new platform. Once customers have a better understanding of the market and the technology, platform companies may encourage adoption by providing easy access to technical support, platform-specific training and implementation services, or special enhancements or customization.

These services can all help minimize potential transition hurdles and may be particularly important for platforms that exhibit high levels of technological and use complexity (use complexity is often defined in terms of the technology requirements and the criteria and effort required to get the product into use – see Leonard-Barton, 1985 and Kahl, 2007). For example, SAP's ERP software has become the equivalent of a 'back office' platform for many large firms around the world, but it has been difficult and expensive to install and use. The global presence of SAP consultants and partners has been essential for SAP to establish its technology. The importance of these service capabilities may be overlooked by researchers, but they can play a very important role in customers' decision of which platforms to adopt.

Situations that combine very high uncertainty and very high technological and use complexity generate the highest reluctance of customers to adopt (Cusumano et al., 2008). In these situations, platform companies may offer services as temporary substitutes for the platform products in order to reduce a customer's adoption risk. A good example of this is provided by the emergence of the mainframe computer platforms. Early computers for business use were complex and expensive machines based on a new, largely unknown technology that required considerable new skills on the part of users – skills that most buyers did not possess. Attewell (1992) reports that, as late as 1982, 70 percent of US businesses under 20 employees had no in-house computer specialist. Consequently, buyers were very reluctant to adopt the new technology. Realizing that the sluggish demand for the new products was due to levels of uncertainty and complexity in their potential customer base, platform competitors such as IBM and Honeywell opened large service units and began to sell not only consulting and training services, but also data-processing services. In other words, they used their (unsold) products to provide services that could demonstrate the benefits of having mainframe computing power for business customers. Once customers saw the benefits and learned more about the technology, many of them started to buy the products. In their detailed study of the history of the mainframe computer, Fisher et al. (1983, p. 172) note that 'the provision of such support services by manufacturers greatly facilitated the marketing of their equipment to users by reducing the users' risks in installing that new, unfamiliar, and expensive object, the computer'.

Services as a Feedback Mechanism for Platform Innovation

As with most technology-driven innovations, platform companies cannot typically anticipate all the uses and applications for their products (von Hippel and Tyre, 1995). This has certainly been true for computers and other software-driven devices such as cellphones. These products today perform an almost unlimited variety of functions, most of which the inventors and pioneers of the technology did not envision. In another example, Tripsas (2008) observed how customers in the typesetting industry began using the technology to print images, which in turn led to subsequent product innovations that the inventors had not envisioned.

The provision of services in early markets gives platform competitors a unique opportunity to learn 'on the job' about emerging customer needs and possible new uses for their offerings. Given that the provision of services entails a close collaboration with users and a thorough understanding of the customer's processes and business model, service professionals are in an enviable position to spot problems with the existing products or learn about the unfulfilled needs that future product versions could tackle. IBM, arguably the best-known example of a products company that has switched much of its business very successfully to services, has used this close connection with customers through services to constantly come up with software and hardware innovations, many of which become platforms in their own right. For instance, IBM Consulting won a job with Norwich Union, a large UK insurance provider, to design a pilot for a new approach to automobile insurance called 'pay as you drive'. IBM designed the system working jointly with the customer, and the success of the new system led to further service and product sales. Other innovations developed by IBM jointly with its customers include: partnering with the US Postal Service to develop software to optimize mail handling; partnering with Boeing to create technologies for network-centric warfare products; partnering with the Mayo Clinic to create systems for gene profiling; and partnering with Bang & Olufsen to develop an electronic pill dispenser. IBM has indeed changed its strategy to focus not only on providing products and services, but also on using its interactions with customers to discover and find solutions to their existing and future problems (Harreld et al., 2007). As reported on IBM's website, CEO Sam Palmisano even declared at the 2005 Annual Shareholders Meeting that IBM was leading 'this shift, this new industry era, "on demand business"'.

Services as Enhancing Platform Value through Complementors

Many platforms can be viewed as what Simon called 'complex artifacts . . . composed by a nested hierarchy of subsystems' (Simon, 1962). In particular, most platforms today require the participation of complementary products or services in order to deliver the expected value to customers. The eBay platform, for instance, requires fast and efficient delivery services and secure payment methods in order to function properly. ERP systems need to 'talk to' (exchange data with) a variety of new and legacy applications in order to be useful. These complementary goods or services are seldom 'plug and play' for the customers. Instead, they require significant integration with other technologies and organizational adaptation (Edmondson et al., 2001).

The ability to integrate seamlessly with complementary goods or systems has long been identified as a key factor in platform adoption (Katz and Shapiro, 1986). By providing integration services between the platform and complementary systems, a platform vendor may be able to increase the appeal of its platform to customers and increase customer loyalty. Achieving platform–complementor integration is often not easy, as it entails solutions that are complementor-specific and cannot be readily found in the open market. For example, Oracle's 'Project Fusion' is a good example of a strategy to increase the value of a platform through services and complementors. Oracle's vision was to offer a comprehensive suite that brought together similar products it had recently acquired (most notably the applications built by PeopleSoft and those by J.D. Edwards, which PeopleSoft had acquired) as well as took advantage of Oracle's own database platform with an open architecture approach (Darrow, 2005; Yoffie and Wagonfeld, 2006). With this in mind, Oracle started developing or acquiring complementary applications (for example Siebel, the CRM firm), beefing up its service offerings and increasing its service staff in order to offer full integration of these complementary systems to the installed base of Oracle databases. Services proved to be an important – and often more stable – source of income for Oracle and many other enterprise software product companies (Cusumano, 2004, 2008). Oracle consulting revenues had already reached 20 percent by 2005, and the percentage of revenues coming from total services at Oracle (including maintenance, training and implementation, in addition to consulting) had reached an impressive 67 percent of sales in 2006.

By increasing the level of services in order to integrate a wide array of working complementary products with their main product, platform firms may also benefit from increased innovation that may emerge from those service encounters related to complementors. Working with complementary products exposes platform firms to a different set of users within the customer organization and therefore new 'solution opportunities' waiting to be addressed. For example, during the 1990s and 2000s, Intel and Microsoft both worked with complementors such as makers of multimedia and telecommunications software, peripheral devices and microprocessor chip sets to add various capabilities to their PC platform, ranging from plug-and-play compatibility to videoconferencing (Gawer and Cusumano, 2002).

Services as the Subsidy Side in Platform Pricing

A growing body of literature has studied the issue of pricing strategies in platform markets. In particular, proponents of 'two-sided networks' stress that, in order to generate a strong adoption rate, platform companies need to subsidize one side of the network – often the side with the lowest willingness to pay (Economides and Katsamakas, 2006, Eisenmann et al., 2007). Each side of the network represents a different type of user, such as bidders and sellers in the eBay system, and platform companies incur costs in serving each group but can potentially collect revenues from each group as well (Eisenmann, 2005). Although not all networks are two-sided, the main concept of subsidizing users in order to foster adoption is common to all platform literature. Faster adoption is particularly critical in platform markets because of the existence of network effects, a phenomenon by which the value of the platform for any user increases with the total number of users of the platform.

So far, the existing literature on platform pricing has focused on subsidizing the product (or part of it), to obtain the desired effect on adoption. For instance, in the videogame industry, console makers subsidize the hardware, i.e. the console itself, in order to generate adoption, and then expect most of the profits to come from the royalties from selling complementary products, that is, videogames, or complementary services such as online game access. (Nintendo's Wii is a notable exception here, as the company has managed to make money out of hardware as well.) A similar pattern can be observed in software products, where Adobe subsidizes a stripped-down version of its Acrobat product – the Acrobat Reader – in order to foster adoption. A free Acrobat Reader (the 'subsidy' side of this network) allows Adobe to generate rapid adoption of its platform in the market, and then the company makes money from selling a full version as well as additional products to those users that need more functionality (the money side). The software business also has many companies such as Red Hat or Google that give away their products for a small fee or for free, and then charge for a variety of services, such as technical support, customization or integration work, or support their products and services by selling advertising (Cusumano, 2004, 2008).

The emphasis in the literature on subsidizing the product as part of a platform pricing strategy is, to some extent, surprising considering the economics behind many platform industries today. For example, services (mainly customization, installation, training and annual maintenance payments) may account for as much as 70 percent of the total lifetime cost of using enterprise software (Cusumano, 2004). Therefore, at least for the case of complex platforms that require extensive support and customization, platform companies could potentially subsidize the services around a platform as opposed to the product itself. There are, of course, issues that managers need to consider when thinking of this option. On the one hand, unlike products, services are not paid for up front but over time (often months or even years), and thus the perception of 'subsidy' may not be the same as in the case of products. The accounting (revenue recognition) is also different. Even if customers pay for services in lump sums in advance, as they would purchase a product, the companies can declare those revenues as sales only as they deliver the services over time. On the other hand, services tend to be quite profitable for platform companies that subsidize their products, and thus any subsidy on the service side may have to be contrasted with the potential savings from not subsidizing (or subsidizing less) the platform product.

The discussion above may imply that services as a sole subsidy side in

Table 4.1   Services and products as the subsidy side in platform pricing

		Side 1 (subsidy side)	Side 2 (money side)
A. Traditional two-sided platform pricing	Product Service	Subsidized Not part of strategic pricing	Not subsidized
B. Services as sole subsidy	Product Service	Not subsidized Subsidized	Not subsidized Not subsidized
C. Services as complementary subsidy	Product Service	Subsidized Subsidized	Not subsidized Not subsidized

a platform market may not always be feasible. Still, in this case, services could be used as a partial subsidy in conjunction with product subsidies. Table 4.1 summarizes the three theoretical alternatives.

Services as a Source of Indirect Network Effects

As discussed above, services have traditionally been considered complementary activities to a product industry. It follows that, by definition, the existence of complementors increases the value of a product platform. Services such as customization and implementation support help customers maximize the benefits of a particular platform. Services such as integration with other products or applications increase the value of a platform by extending its capabilities to other uses and perhaps to other platforms. Services such as repair and maintenance increase the value of the platform by reducing the uncertainty regarding support and continuity of the platform over time.

Therefore a company can increase the value of its platform by creating a powerful array of services and network of service providers. In the computer software and hardware industries, companies ranging from Microsoft and SAP to IBM, Hewlett-Packard, Cisco and Sun Microsystems have all followed this strategy of building up a global network of third-party service providers in addition to their in-house service departments. Automobile manufacturers and other makers of complex products do the same thing by creating networks of certified service technicians. In this way, a large scope and scale of services can be a source of powerful indirect network effects difficult to imitate by competitors. The provision of services entails a two-way knowledge transfer between customer and platform service providers: service providers learn about the customers, actual uses of the platform and potential unfulfilled needs; customers learn about the new technology and intended uses, and learn of the 'best practices' to implement or use the new technology. Much of the knowledge generated is the result of a cumulative process of organizational learning and, in many cases, is platform-specific.

Other things being equal, we should expect customers to prefer platforms with a large and reputed service network, such as products from IBM, SAP and Microsoft, over the offerings of small start-up companies. This case is similar to that of customers in the USA, Europe or Japan preferring products from General Motors, Toyota, and other global automobile companies over a regional automobile producer from, say, Eastern Europe. Customers can expect to get more value out of the more common or globally adopted platform compared to a less popular platform alternative with a weaker services offering. Likewise, once the customer has adopted a particular platform, the service network acts as a retention mechanism, increasing customers' switching costs. A platform company may decide to create this service capability either mostly in house (for example Oracle in enterprise software) or via outsourcing (e.g. SAP, outside of its home country, Germany) – an issue we tackle below. But, in either case, a service network may serve as a source of indirect network effects that favor one platform over another.

SERVICES IN MATURE INDUSTRIES: PLATFORM MARKETS VERSUS OTHER MARKETS

We have suggested that services have a role in early markets and particularly during the emergence of platforms. This is not to say that services are not important in later life-cycle stages. For most researchers, the importance of services for manufacturing firms and product firms in general increases with the age of the industry and firms (Quinn, 1992; Wise and Baumgartner, 1999). As their argument goes, product firms increasingly focus on services because services provide them with a more stable source of revenue than products; in addition, service revenues such as maintenance often outlast the life of the products themselves (Potts, 1988; Quinn, 1992). In many industries, product margins are severely reduced in the late stage as strong pressures for commoditization take place. When product commoditization sets in, firms may retreat to services in order to increase revenue and protect margins, particularly during economic downturns (for example Anderson et al., 1997).

As a result, much of the services literature portrays the movement to more services in product industries as a process resulting from the passing of time and changes in the product industry conditions. Examples of firms such as IBM, Cisco, Hewlett-Packard, Sun Microsystems, Dell and EMC that have successfully placed more emphasis on services during the last decade have helped galvanize the idea that at least some product industries are moving toward services as a major source of revenues or profits or both (Cusumano, 2008). This trend also appears in sectors such as automobiles, where financial services such as loans and leasing, insurance and after-sales repair and maintenance have become increasingly important throughout the industry value chain (Gadiesh and Gilbert, 1998).

Empirical studies tend to support this traditional view. Indeed, in our own studies, this is also the case. Consider Figure 4.1, which plots the percentage of total revenues coming from services from a large sample of software products firms over 16 years (SIC 7372, excluding videogames firms). With the exception of a couple of years, the importance of services has been increasing steadily in this large industry category since 1990. Services surpassed the 50 percent of revenues mark in the early 2000s and have continued to grow in importance since then.

If commoditization dynamics play a key role in the rise of the importance of services in product industries over the long term, then an interesting question arises as to the expected differences in this longitudinal pattern when platform-mediated markets are compared with other markets where platforms do not dominate. Platform theory suggests that, in markets where one platform comes to dominate, the platform leader may enjoy significant market power. This is, for instance, the case of Microsoft in operating systems or Google in online search. Thus, *a priori*, one should expect fewer commoditization pressures – and thus less pressure on product margins – in markets where one platform dominates. This is indeed the case in many of the well-known stories, and certainly in the two mentioned above.

Despite these examples, it is also possible that platform companies, in order to impose their platform as dominant, have to sacrifice profits to a point where they produce or deliver products at a loss or give away proprietary technology for free. However, in most cases, platform companies are able to implement two-sided pricing strategies so as to have at least a 'money side' they can turn to for profits. Therefore we should still expect to find, on average, better product margins over time in platform industries as compared with non-platform industries. It follows that, in industries where one or a few platforms are dominant, we should expect less pressure for firms to retreat into services. In other words, platform dominance

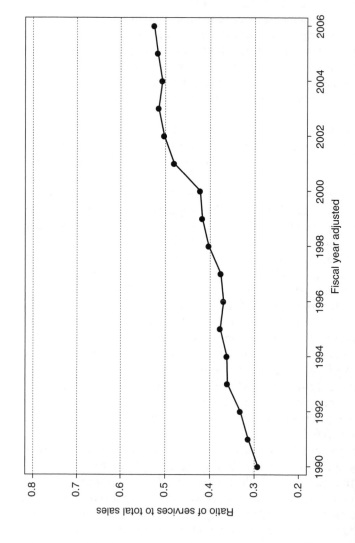

Note: * SIC 7372, excluding videogame producers.

Source: Compiled by authors from 10-K reports and industry publications.

*Figure 4.1 The importance of services in total revenues in the software product industry**

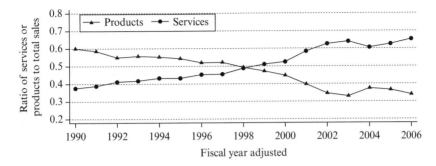

Figure 4.2   Services versus products in total revenues – business applications

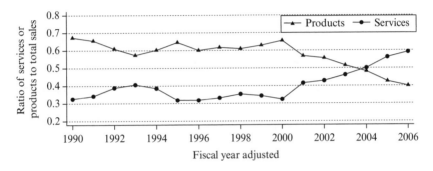

Figure 4.3   Services versus products in total revenues – networking

should help protect product revenues and margins, and therefore should lessen the incentives to move aggressively toward services.

We can offer preliminary evidence for this idea using our data from the software products industry. SIC code 7372 is really a collection of seven different sub-segments, and each of them could be considered a market in its own right: business applications, business intelligence, multimedia, databases, operating systems, networking and videogames. Figures 4.2 to 4.8 show what we call the 'criss-cross' graphs – a visual picture of the relative rise of service versus product sales over time, both measured as a percentage of total revenues. The criss-cross is the point in time at which service revenues match (and then surpass) product revenues in a particular market.

There are several relevant points to make about these the graphs. First, services are indeed on the rise over time in all markets (with the exception of videogames). Second, the extent of the services' inroads on total revenues varies significantly from market to market. Even leaving videogames

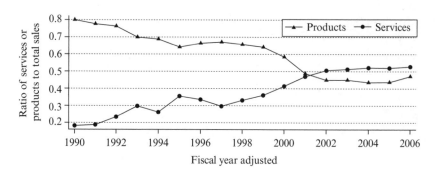

Figure 4.4   Services versus products in total revenues – business intelligence

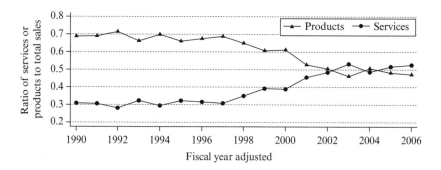

Figure 4.5   Services versus products in total revenues – databases

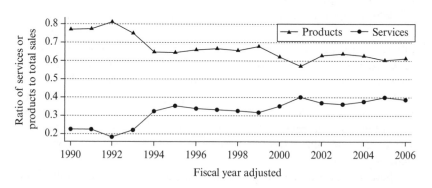

Figure 4.6   Services versus products in total revenues – operating systems

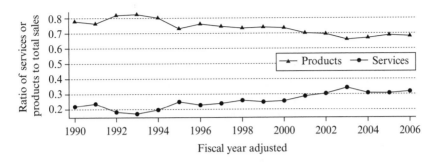

Figure 4.7   Services versus products in total revenues – multimedia

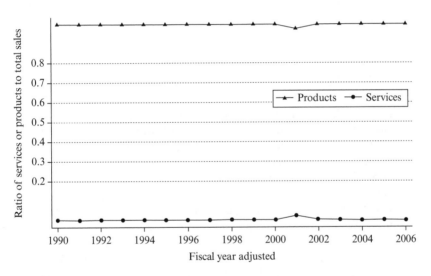

Figure 4.8   Services versus products in total revenues – videogames

aside, the contribution of services varies from less than 30 percent to over 60 percent, depending on the market considered. Overall, as seen earlier in Figure 4.1, service revenues passed product revenues for the whole industry in 2002. Third, as expected, specific markets whose sales are dominated by one or a few platforms tend to show more 'resilient' product revenues. These markets (operating systems, multimedia and videogames – Figures 4.6, 4.7 and 4.8) do not show a criss-cross point during the period of study as do the other markets. Apparently, companies in these sectors have been able to keep 'standardized' or 'packaged' product revenues (or prices) high and thus have felt less pressure to resort to services such as consulting, integration, customization or maintenance. The operating systems market, for example, is highly influenced by the presence of Microsoft, which sells mainly prepackaged software products such as Windows and Office to PC manufacturers and enterprises. Multimedia is influenced by Adobe, which also sells mainly prepackaged software products. The videogames industry is influenced by a few large players such as Electronic Arts and Activision that have produced many of the most successful game packages in the last decade for a few dominant console platforms. All of these firms are predominantly product companies with minimal or no service (including maintenance) revenues for most of their histories, in contrast to companies in segments such as business applications (led by firms such as SAP), networking (for example, Novell and Symantec), business intelligence (for example, Business Objects and Cognos) or databases (for example, Oracle).

THE PROVISION OF SERVICES IN PLATFORM INDUSTRIES

Thus far, we have talked only about levels and types of services within platform industries or markets and have not addressed the question of who actually provides and appropriates the service revenue. This issue is significant because, in many industries, firms other than the product or platform producers also provide services. Moreover, these networks and channels of complementary service providers usually help the product or platform producers sell their products and expand their revenue and profit potential. In the automobile industry, there are many service organizations independent of the automobile manufacturers, ranging from maintenance and repair to driver education as well as financing and insurance. In the computer industry, there are consulting, training, customization, implementation and maintenance firms independent of the computer manufacturers or software product producers. Therefore, in product industries that also have significant service requirements (such as the need for training, customization, repair and maintenance), it is important to understand under what conditions the product (or platform) producer should expect to capture a part or even the majority of the service revenues and profits compared to independent service providers, which may also be important complementors and partners for the product (platform) companies.

We can consider two dimensions of services provision: the level of 'product specificity' and the level of 'industry specificity'. We define the level of 'product specificity' of services as the percentage of total industry services that are exclusively related to the industry's products. Maintenance and repair, for instance, are services that in almost all cases are exclusively related to the given industry's physical product – a high level of product specificity. Similarly, we define the level of 'industry specificity' of services as the percentage of total industry services provided by firms in the product segment of the industry. For example, mainframe computer producers in the 1950s provided most of the hardware and software services required by their customers, until independent firms began to emerge, especially during the 1960s (Campbell-Kelly, 2003; Campbell-Kelly and Aspray, 1996). Even today, telecommunications network equipment providers such as Cisco, Ericsson or Alcatel-Lucent tend to provide a large share of the services in that specialized industry. The automobile industry may represent a case of lower industry specificity, as some services (e.g. insurance) are offered by firms outside the automobile industry, such as insurance companies or other financial institutions.

Product specificity and industry specificity of services do not necessarily go hand in hand. For instance, while financing in the auto industry represents a case of low product and industry specificity (financing not only relates to cars but to many other assets and investments, and car financing is often provided by firms outside the auto industry), other services, such as repair and maintenance, are high in product specificity (almost all services directly relate to autos) but low in industry specificity (independent service providers have a significant share of the market).

The degree of product specificity and industry specificity in services is likely influenced by the location of product-related knowledge. The locus of knowledge, in turn, seems related to the level of complexity of the product platform, and possibly technological or market uncertainty as well. Industry evolution also may affect the location of product-related knowledge in the value chain. For example, the early stage of an industry is often characterized by high product uncertainty and a small market with relatively few buyers and suppliers. In some industries the level of uncertainty regarding the viability of the different alternative platforms does not vanish until the last minute. This was the case with the HD-DVD industry, where Sony's standard emerged as the winner after a long and uncertain battle with Toshiba's.

In situations with high uncertainties and particularly with complex technologies, buyers will tend not to make platform-specific investments. If the prolonged market uncertainty has kept the market small, then potential service company entrepreneurs may not see large enough demand for them to risk creating independent service companies. Firms other than the product producer also may have little incentive to invest in providing complementary products for the new product technology. For a third party, investing in learning about a particular product technology in order to service it or produce complements for it entails several risks, chief among them the risk of choosing a product that will not prevail during the selection and retention process. In these situations, we expect platform companies to develop their own service operations in order to reduce customer uncertainty and encourage customers to purchase and use their products.

We can also anticipate how the provision of services might spread beyond the platform vendors. As markets evolve and grow, and as technological and market uncertainty disappear with the emergence of a dominant platform, there is increasing clarity among users with regard to the possible uses and extensions of the platform. Complementors should emerge, enticed by the growing installed base of industry products, offering related products and services that make the platform product more valuable. This network or positive feedback effect may increase as the market grows because specialization is possible and the industry may 'de-verticalize', encouraging entrepreneurs to create independent services firms (Stigler, 1951).

In the automobile industry, for example, manufacturers routinely set up training and certification programs that transfer product knowledge to maintenance and repair shops. Computer manufacturers such as IBM and DEC followed the same strategy for their platform products during the 1960s and 1970s. In more recent years, Intel, Microsoft, Cisco, Palm and other companies have devised an array of strategies and programs to assist or encourage complementors to offer products and services that increased the utility of the platform products and thus made them more valuable (Gawer and Cusumano, 2002).

Another potential factor is product modularity – the extent to which a product can be decomposed into several subsystems that may be designed independently but work together as a whole system through well-defined interfaces (Sanchez and Mahoney, 1996). Platforms may differ in their degree of modularity. For example, the PC platform has distinct hardware and software layers. A variety of firms provide specific components in these layers in a more or less 'open architecture', with a horizontal or 'de-verticalized' industry structure. Key specifications for how to build components or connect to different layers are available in the public domain or for free or inexpensive licensing fees. In contrast, in most mainframe platforms such as those based on IBM or DEC technology, one company has tended to provide all or most of the hardware and software, and key components such as peripherals, for the entire system. There is much more of a closed integral architecture and 'vertical' industry structure (Campbell-Kelly and Aspray, 1996; Grove, 1996; Farrell et al., 1998).

Modularity can result in simpler designs and reduce the importance of product-specific knowledge possessed by the platform producers, which could then encourage the creation of more independent service providers.

If it has a well-defined core and interfaces, a modular product should interact with other products in a clearer way than in the case of an integral design (Ulrich and Eppinger, 2004). Modularity makes it less crucial for a third-party firm to know exactly how the product works because much of the product knowledge is 'built into' the product's modular design. This in turn means that the platform companies may have less of an advantage in the provision of services if their product simply becomes a 'core module' with well-defined interfaces that link to complementors. With modular platform designs, buyers can even do their own installation and customization, or hire independent service providers.

This is indeed what happened in the computer business. IBM's System/360 mainframe architecture became an industry platform after the mid-1960s. IBM also de-bundled services from its product offerings after 1970. As a result, many other firms around the world began providing maintenance, integration, training and customization services as well as building complementary products (Attewell, 1992). In the PC industry, we can see the role of de-verticalization and modularity even more clearly. Since the mid-1970s, with the exception of Apple, most firms have come to specialize in one horizontal segment (microprocessors, hardware boxes, operating systems, applications software, peripheral devices, integration services, custom software and so on) rather than provide a bundled vertical stack of products and services as IBM and DEC once did. We can also see this in the automobile industry – the more standardized automobile designs and components have become, the easier it became for independent service providers (gasoline stations, repair shops) to provide maintenance and repair services. Thus platform companies are likely to provide a smaller share of platform-specific services in the presence of higher degrees of product modularity.

CONCLUSION: SERVICES AND PLATFORM COMPETITION

We began this chapter by noting that most of the research on platforms, as with innovation and product development in product industries, has not paid much attention to the role of services other than as a complementary activity. We have attempted to fill this gap in the literature by highlighting the potential role of services both in the early or emergent stage of platform completion as well as in the more mature phase. We have also addressed the question of which types of firms are more likely to provide services in platform-mediated industries.

When various platform companies are competing to establish their platforms, the ability to provide services on their own or to line up a network of service providers can serve several functions. Services can reduce the risk to customers of adopting a new platform, provide feedback for further innovation, or enhance the value of the platform through integration with complementary innovations or other platforms. In addition, services can be a tool for platform leaders and wannabes to influence market dynamics. They can act as a type of subsidy for the platform in multi-sided markets (if the companies give the services away or provide them below cost) or increase at least indirect network effects between the platform and complements. Furthermore, in mature markets or product markets particularly vulnerable to price competition and commoditization, services can provide an important source of revenues and profits. Platform firms are likely to dominate the provision of services in early stages of the market, before adoption of the platform has become common, or when the services require special knowledge of the platform architecture and technology, such as when the platform is not highly modularized.

Overall, there are many reasons why platform companies, like product companies in general, should consider the potential role of services as part of their competitive strategy. We are not saying that services will always be important in platform (or product) competition. But services have the potential to make an important difference and possibly cause a market to tip in a particular direction. Services also have become important sources of revenues and profits in many complex high-tech markets where the product alone does not provide much value, such as computers, digital media and telecommunications, as well as in these and other product markets subject to commoditization and other forms of price competition, such as automobiles.

NOTE

1. Steve Kahl assisted in writing portions of this section.

REFERENCES

Abernathy W.J. and J.M. Utterback (1978), 'Patterns of innovation in technology', *Technology Review*, **80** (7), 40–47.

Anderson, E.W., C. Fornell and R.T. Rust (1997), 'Customer satisfaction, productivity, and profitability: differences between goods and services', *Marketing Science*, **16** (2), 129–45.

Attewell, P. (1992), 'Technology diffusion and organizational learning: the case of business computing', *Organization Science*, **3** (1), 1–19.

Bell, D. (1973), *The Coming of Postindustrial Society: A Venture in Social Forecasting*, New York: Basic Books.

Campbell-Kelly, M. (2003), *A History of the Software Industry: From Airline Reservations to Sonic the Hedgehog*, Cambridge, MA: MIT Press.

Campbell-Kelly, M. and W. Aspray (1996), *Computer: A History of the Information Machine*, New York: Basic Books.

Carpenter, G.S. and K. Nakamoto (1989), 'Consumer preference formation and pioneering advantage', *Journal of Marketing Research*, **26** (3), 285–98.

Cusumano, M.A. (2004), *The Business of Software*, New York: Free Press/Simon & Schuster.

Cusumano, M.A. (2008), 'The changing software business: moving from products to services', *IEEE Computer*, **41** (1), 78–85.

Cusumano, M.A., Y. Mylonadis and R. Rosenbloom (1992), 'Strategic maneuvering and mass-market dynamics: the triumph of VHS over Beta', *Business History Review*, **66** (Spring), 51–94.

Cusumano, M.A., S. Kahl and F. Suarez (2008), 'A theory of services in product industries', Working Paper, Cambridge, MA: MIT Sloan School.

Cusumano, M.A. and K. Nobeoka (1998), *Thinking Beyond Lean*, New York: Free Press/Simon & Schuster.

Darrow, B. (2005), 'Oracle "Project Fusion" to converge current Oracle, PeopleSoft, J.D. Edwards functions', *Intelligent Enterprise*, January 18 (www.intelligententerprise.com, accessed September 22, 2008).

Economides, N. and E. Katsamakas (2006), 'Two-sided competition of proprietary vs. open source technology platforms and the implications for the software industry', *Management Science*, **52** (7), 1057–107.

Edmondson, A., R. Bohmer and G. Pisano (2001), 'Disrupted routines: team learning and technology implementation in hospitals', *Administrative Science Quarterly*, **46** (4), 685–71.

Eisenmann, T. (2005), 'Managing networked businesses: course overview for students', Boston, MA: Harvard Business School Note 806-103.

Eisenmann, T., G. Parker and M.W. Van Alstyne (2006), 'Strategies for two-sided markets', *Harvard Business Review*, **84** (10), 92–101.

Eisenmann, T., G. Parker and M.W. Van Alstyne (2007), 'Platform envelopment', Working Paper.

Farrell, J., H. Monroe and G. Saloner (1998), 'The vertical organization of industry: systems competition versus component competition', *Journal of Economics and Management Strategy*, **7** (2), 143–82.

Fisher, F., R. McKie and R. Mancke (1983), *IBM and the U.S. Data Processing Industry: An Economic History*, New York: Praeger.

Gadiesh, O. and J. Gilbert (1998), 'Profit pools: a fresh look at strategy', *Harvard Business Review*, **76** (3), 139–47.

Gawer, A. and M.A. Cusumano (2002), *Platform Leadership: How Intel, Microsoft, and Cisco Drive Industry Innovation*, Boston, MA: Harvard Business School Press.

Gawer, A. and M.A. Cusumano (2008), 'How companies become platform leaders', *MIT Sloan Management Review*, **49** (2), 28–35.

Grove, A. (1996), *Only the Paranoid Survive: How to Exploit the Crisis Points that Challenge Every Company and Career*, New York: Currency Doubleday.

Harreld, J., C. O'Reilly III and M. Tushman (2007), 'Dynamic capabilities at IBM: driving strategy into action', *California Management Review*, **49** (4), 21–43.

Kahl, S. (2007), 'Considering the customer: determinants and impact of using technology on industry evolution', unpublished doctoral thesis, Cambridge, MA: MIT Sloan School of Management.

Katz, M. and C. Shapiro (1986), 'Technology adoption in the presence of network externalities', *Journal of Political Economy*, **94** (4), 822–41.

Klepper, S. (1996), 'Entry, exit, growth and innovation over the industry life cycle', *American Economic Review*, **86** (3), 562–86.

Leonard-Barton, D. (1985), 'Implementation as mutual adoption of technology and organization', *Research Policy*, **17**, 251–67.

Meyer, M. and A. Lehnerd (1997), *Product Platforms: Building Value and Cost Leadership*, New York: Free Press.

Nobeoka, K. and M.A. Cusumano (1997), 'Multiproject strategy and sales growth: The benefits of rapid design transfer in new product development', *Strategic Management Journal*, **18** (3), 168–86.

Potts, G.W. (1988), 'Exploiting your product's service life cycle', *Harvard Business Review*, **68** (5), 58–67.

Quinn, J. B. (1992), *Intelligent Enterprise*, New York: Simon & Schuster.

Sanchez, R. and J. Mahoney (1996), 'Modularity, flexibility, and knowledge management in product and organization design', *Strategic Management Journal*, **17** (Winter Special Issue), 63–76.

Simon, H.A. (1962), 'The architecture of complexity', *Proceedings of the American Philosophical Society*, **106**, 467–82.

Stigler, G. (1951), 'The division of labor is limited by the extent of the market', *Journal of Political Economy*, **59** (3), 185–93.

Suarez, F. and J. Utterback (1995), 'Dominant designs and the survival of firms', *Strategic Management Journal*, **16**, 415–30.

Teece, D. (1986), 'Profiting from technological innovation: implications for integration, collaboration, licensing and public policy', *Research Policy*, **15**, 285–305.

Tripsas, M. (2008), 'Customer preference discontinuities: a trigger for radical technological change', *Managerial and Decision Economics*, **29** (2–3), 79–97.

Ulrich, Karl T. and S.D. Eppinger (2004), *Product Design and Development*, New York: McGraw-Hill.

Von Hippel, E. and M. Tyre (1995), 'How learning by doing is done: problem identification in novel process equipment', *Research Policy*, **24**, 1–12.

Wheelwright, S. and K. Clark (1992), 'Creating project plans to focus product development', *Harvard Business Review*, **70** (2), 70–82.

Wheelwright, S. and W. Sasser (1989), 'The new product development map', *Harvard Business Review*, **67** (3), 112–25.

Wise, R. and P. Baumgartner (1999), 'Go downstream: the new imperative in manufacturing', *Harvard Business Review*, **77** (5), 133–41.

Yoffie, D. and A. Wagonfeld (2006), 'Oracle versus salesforce.com', Boston, MA: Harvard Business School Case Study 705-440.

5. How catalysts ignite: the economics of platform-based start-ups

David S. Evans[1]

1. INTRODUCTION

Starting a business and getting it to the point where it is economically viable is the most difficult problem for all entrepreneurs. Most new businesses fail. In the USA, 61 percent of new businesses that were started in the second quarter of 1998 had ceased business within five years (Knaup and Piazza, 2007). Venture capital firms that invested in new firms do not get any of their money back in 43.7 percent of the first-round investments they make and get less than their initial investment back in 66.7 percent of the first-round investments (Metrik, 2006, exhibit 7-4).

The start-up problem is particularly difficult for firms that are based on multi-sided platforms. In addition to the usual problems faced by new firms, they often must contend with the well-known chicken-and-egg problem. Their firm can deliver value to one side of the platform only if there are participants on the other side of the platform. They have to figure out how to get both sides on board their platform. That problem, which is the subject of this chapter, is very different from that faced by a one-sided start-up whose main challenge is getting just one set of customers to buy its product or service.[2]

The chicken-and-egg problem is central to the study of multi-sided platforms. Yet most of the theoretical and empirical research on two-sided businesses has focused on mature platforms and examined their pricing structures and other properties. Little attention has been given to critical issues that entrepreneurs must solve to create a viable platform business.[3] These include strategies for getting both sides on board, the role of critical mass in establishing the foundations for success, and the particularly thorny issues that arise when both sides must arrive simultaneously.

This introduction provides an overview of multi-sided platforms and the start-up problem. Section 2 then presents some building blocks for solving this problem. A few of these building blocks are similar to those for one-sided businesses, while others are unique to multi-sided ones. Section 3 describes several complementary strategies for solving the chicken-and-egg problem. We then turn to two case studies. Section 4 examines a modern classic in a failed strategy for starting up multi-sided platforms: the *en masse* demise of the B2B (business-to-business) exchanges whose assured success was extolled by many academics and practitioners (Lucking-Reiley and Spulber, 2001; Carr, 2001; Sculley and Woods, 1999). Section 5 considers how social networking sites have started up and considers a successful and unsuccessful one. Section 6 presents some concluding remarks.

The Catalyst Framework

We use the framework developed by Evans and Schmalensee (Evans and Schmalensee, 2007). A business is an 'economic catalyst' if it creates value by bringing two or more groups of customers together and getting them to interact. Catalysts create value by reducing transactions costs faced by multiple distinct economic agents that would benefit from coming together. Catalysts reduce search efforts, facilitate matching, and make it easier for the two groups of economic agents to exchange value between each other. In the traditional literature, a catalyst is referred to as a 'two-sided market' or as a 'multi-sided platform'.[4] In this chapter we use catalyst and multi-sided platform interchangeably.

The economic value created by the catalytic reaction is essential for understanding the feasible set of business strategies that a multi-sided platform can use. That value must be significant enough to warrant the cost and risk of investment in developing the platform. The value also provides the 'pie' that can be split among the distinct groups of economic agents to provide incentives for them to join and interact on the platform, with a portion of the pie going to the platform for performing its role. Some of the pie can be used to subsidize certain groups of economic agents, or members of those groups, to join the platform.

Catalyst innovators are those who discover that it is possible to create economic value by getting two or more groups of economic agents together on a shared platform or develop a more efficient platform for starting and accelerating a catalytic reaction.

Securing Ignition

In chemical catalysis it is necessary to get the catalytic agent and the chemical agents in the right proportions to ignite and accelerate a reaction. The same is true for economic catalysis. Both economic agents have to be present on the platform in the right proportions and levels to create any value at all and to accelerate value creation.

This conundrum is often referred to as the chicken-and-egg problem in the academic and popular literature on platforms. That analogy does not work for many platforms. The problem that platforms face is sometimes sequential, as the riddle suggests – does the platform need to get economic agents *A* on board the platform before economic agents *B*; or *B* before *A*? Other times, though, it is simultaneous – how does the platform secure the participation of economic agents *A* and *B* so that both will be present on the platform when members from each group show up? That typically involves solving a very difficult coordination problem between the platform and these two groups of economic agents.

The problem, however, is not just getting members of the two groups of economic agents to show up at the same time to create value. There have to be enough members of group *A* to make it valuable to members of group *B* to incur the costs of participating in the platform and to return to it in subsequent periods; and vice versa. Strength in numbers arises primarily because economic agents in one group are searching for appropriate value-creating matches among members of the other group. There have to be enough members to make it likely that economic agents will find valuable matches.

In the literature on market microstructure, for example, for financial exchanges a 'liquid' market is one that has enough buy-and-sell orders to facilitate transactions.[5] Markets that are too 'thin', or too illiquid, collapse. There is a critical mass of buy-and-sell orders that allows markets to sustain themselves. We shall see below that the B2Bs failed because they did not achieve a critical mass of buyers and sellers; in particular they did not create enough value to suppliers to entice them to participate in the exchanges.

Catalytic Ignition and Critical Mass

Figure 5.1 shows the basic concept of critical mass and catalytic ignition.[6] There is a range of minimal numbers of customers in each group that, if achieved, provides a 'thick enough market' or a 'sufficiently liquid market' to permit sustainable growth. When the mass of economic agents on either side is insufficient, a catalyst fizzles rather than ignites. Once a catalyst achieves critical mass on C'–C'', for example, it can grow to its profit-maximizing potential of D*; if it does not achieve critical mass on the segment C'–C'' it contracts and fails.

The growth paths to critical mass depend on many factors, including pricing. But the point here is that achieving critical mass is essential. Google Video, for example, failed to achieve critical mass because it did not generate enough content to attract viewers and did not attract enough viewers to attract paid or user-generated content (Johnson, 2006; Pogue, 2006).

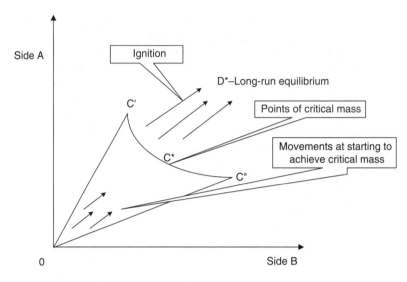

Figure 5.1   Catalytic ignition and critical mass

The optimal growth path to critical mass and to long-run equilibrium is well away from the horizontal and vertical axes in most plausible cases (Evans and Schmalensee, 2009). Relatively balanced growth is necessary. This is reflected in Figure 5.1 in that the equilibrium growth path to critical mass must occur within the triangle 0–C′–C″. Having too many of one side and too few of another side will quickly lead to failure.

The challenge that catalyst entrepreneurs face is how to achieve the critical mass necessary for ignition. That means getting to critical mass over some reasonable space of time. One can think of this phase as the ignition phase of the product launch process, in which customers are trying the platform and assessing its value; these early adopters will stop coming back, and stop recommending it to their friends, if the platform does not grow quickly enough. The entrepreneur must increase the number of customers on each side to a point where there are enough to reach critical mass. That involves horizontal and vertical movements within the cone-shaped area in Figure 5.1. A transaction platform, for example, needs to take actions that increase buyers and sellers.[7] The entrepreneur must also maintain the right proportions of customers on each side so that there are enough participants on each side to interest the participants on the other side. That involves diagonal movements to the north-east in Figure 5.1. An exchange platform needs to make sure there are enough buyers to interest sellers and vice versa.

2.   BASIC CONCEPTS

There is an extensive literature on launching new products.[8] Key tactics involve logistics; advertising, sales and marketing; and pricing. Companies should make sure they have a production and distribution system for getting products and services to consumers. They need to convince consumers of the merits of trying a product through the dissemination of information as well as persuasion. Finally, they need to set prices recognizing both the competition and the fact that consumers may need an incentive to try a new and unproven product. These traditional strategies facilitate obtaining consumers on both sides of a two-sided platform, i.e. in making horizontal and vertical movements.

This section focuses on several aspects of product launch and product design that are likely to be particularly applicable to the ignition problem faced by catalysts. Before we begin, it is useful to clarify some issues concerning the relationships among different platform members that will affect the discussion below.

For some platforms, customer groups are very distinct. Companies such as Electronic Arts that develop and sell videogames for the Sony PlayStation platform are distinct from people who buy and use Sony PlayStations.

For other platforms, the customers appear so similar that the platform may not appear multi-sided at all. A telephone platform connects people who talk to each other. People are people. Closer inspection, though, often reveals that people fall into one of two distinct positions on the platform at any point in time, that they need people in the other positions to connect to, and that it is possible to manipulate the pricing structure to mediate the externalities between these two groups.[9] At any point in time members of a phone network are either calling someone or being called, and carriers can adopt pricing structures to alter the incentives to make or take calls. The same is true for social networking sites that involve inviting and accepting friends and then participating in other interactions that entail initiating or receiving messages.[10]

The fact that customers on the different sides may be the same economic agents clearly facilitates platform ignition. While the catalyst entrepreneur might have to provide incentives for these economic agents to engage in different types of behavior, it can focus on securing the participation of one well-identified group of agents.

Product Diffusion

The original models of product diffusion distinguished between two types of consumers: innovators who would try a product as a result of direct communication with them, and imitators who would try a product as a result of communication with someone else who had tried the product (Mahajan et al., 1990). The innovator might learn about the product through advertisements in the mass media. The imitator might learn about the product either from the innovator or from other people who learned about it directly or indirectly from the imitator. The word-of-mouth aspect to this model gives rise to the well-known S-curve of product diffusion, where there is a convex rise in adoption, an inflection point, and a concave rise that levels off at some saturation point. The population of economic agents is sometimes broken down into innovators, early adopters, early majority, late majority and laggards. Figure 5.2 shows the standard framework (Mahajan et al., 1990).

The literature on social networks provides insights into the process of word-of-mouth communication (Brown and Reingen, 1987; Brown et al., 2007). The social graph describes the relationships among members of a network. It consists of nodes that reflect the agents and lines that show the connection between the agents. The connections can be unidirectional (x communicates with y) or bidirectional (x and y communicate with each other). The nature of the relationships among members of the network can provide insights into the organic workings of the network. There are three key ramifications for product diffusion. Word of mouth will spread more quickly: (1) the more connections innovators have; (2) the more connections friends of the innovators have; and (3) the denser the network is in the sense of there being fewer degrees of separation among members of the network.

Two types of agents facilitate the diffusion information within the network. 'Influencers' – or gregarious members – account for a disproportionate share of communications. They send a lot of messages to a broad range of connections. 'Centers' have connections with many people who are not connected to other agents.[11] They are important because they are the only way to reach isolated agents within the network.

Product diffusion may provide double duty for two-sided businesses in which economic agents have shifting roles in the platform. Individuals who upload photos on the photo-sharing network Flickr may view photos from their friends. People who use eBay's auto exchange may use it for both buying and selling, though some users may specialize in selling, and some may never sell.

Direct Network Effects

Consumers may value a product more if similar consumers use that product as well. This is known as a positive direct network effect (Shapiro and Varian, 1998). It can arise because it is easier to connect to people using the product or because there are knowledge spillovers among them. Consumers may also value a product less if similar consumers use that product. This is known as a negative direct network effect. That might happen because of congestion or because people want to be different. For simplicity, we shall assume that direct network effects are positive unless noted otherwise.

Direct network effects act as an accelerant to a catalytic reaction. Diffusion happens more quickly. The value of the network is higher to each additional member who is contacted. All else equal, direct network effects increase the likelihood that each subsequent agent that is contacted by an earlier adopter will adopt the product also. Figure 5.3 shows how direct network effects modify the S-curve of diffusion.

Social networking theory provides some guidance on how to use direct network effects strategically. I would conjecture that economic agents that are more densely connected in a network have stronger direct network effects among them. Thus using influencers to connect to more densely connected portions of networks will tend to have higher payoffs.

Indirect Network Effects

One type of economic agent may value a product more if more of another group of economic agents uses that product as well. This is known as a positive indirect network effect (Shapiro and Varian, 1998). It can arise because one type of economic agents (e.g. a buyer, a man, cardholder) wants to search for and transact with another type of economic agent (e.g. a seller, a woman, a merchant) and vice versa. It can also arise because one type of economic agent (e.g. a computer user, a videogame user) wants to be able to find complementary products for the platform they use (e.g. applications, videogames) and the maker of those products wants to focus its efforts on platforms that have users who will demand its products. There are also negative indirect network effects: one type of economic agent on the network harms another type of agent. The leading case of this for platform businesses is advertising-supported media. Consumers may dislike the advertisements. The platform solves the externality problem between advertisers and consumers by using content to bribe people into viewing ads.

Indirect network effects are the key aspect of multi-sided platforms. They are the source of the catalytic reaction – and much of the value – created by the platform. A key practical aspect of these indirect network effects is that they require that the platform 'balance' the two sides to maximize the value of the platform to either side. The platform has zero

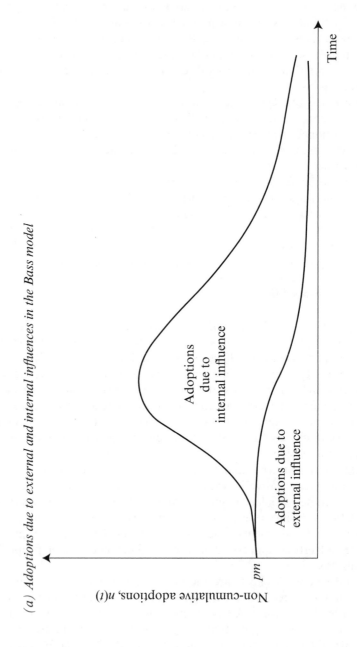

(a) Adoptions due to external and internal influences in the Bass model

Non-cumulative adoptions, $n(t)$

pm

Adoptions due to internal influence

Adoptions due to external influence

Time

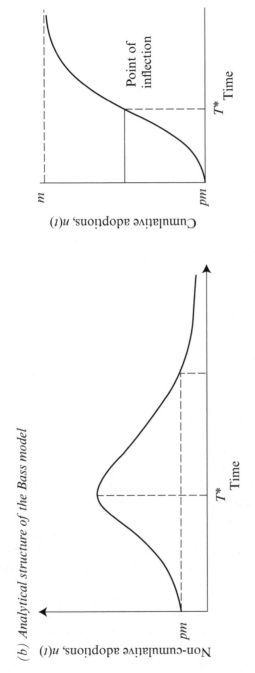

(b) Analytical structure of the Bass model

Source: Reprinted with permission from *Journal of Marketing*, published by the American Marketing Association, Mahajan, Muller and Bass, 'New product diffusion models in marketing: a review and directions for research', *Journal of Marketing*, **54** (1), January 1990, 4.

Figure 5.2   The Bass new product diffusion model

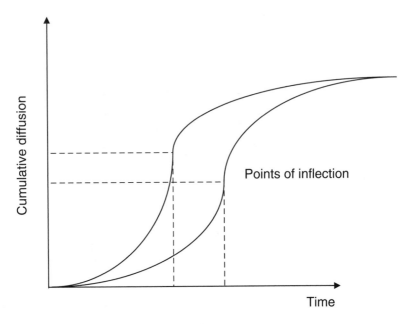

Figure 5.3   Network effects and diffusion

value to either side if the other side is not on board. For many platforms the optimal balance is likely well into the interior and away from the axes as was shown in Figure 5.1 (Evans and Schmalensee, 2009).

The Role of Customer Heterogeneity

The analysis above has already pointed to the fact that not all customers are created equal for multi-sided platforms. It is useful to pull these concepts together here and summarize their implications for platform ignition. There are three major kinds of heterogeneity.

First, some customers value a product or service more than other customers. All else equal, those are the ones to go after initially to grow a business because they involve the lowest cost of sales and marketing. They can then kick off product diffusion. Two-sided platforms sometimes need to recruit these customers on both sides.

Second, some customers on one side are valued more by customers on the other side. The two-sided literature calls these 'marquee' customers (Rochet and Tirole, 2003) while the social networking literature calls them 'prestige' nodes – i.e. nodes that many people want to connect to and therefore receive many messages. All else equal, marquee customers are the most important ones to attract early on. They not only increase the value of the platform but also bring in more customers on the other side who help stimulate product diffusion on that side. Marquee customers may appear on one or both sides.

Third, some customers are more gregarious than others in the sense that they are more likely to influence other customers to join the platform. These 'influencers' are important to attract early on because they will accelerate the vertical or horizontal growth of the platform. To ignite, platforms need to identify and recruit heavy influencers on both sides early on. Prestige and influencer customers both generate significant direct or indirect externalities. It therefore often pays to subsidize their joining the platform.

3. STRATEGIES FOR IGNITING CATALYTIC REACTION BY SOLVING COORDINATION PROBLEMS

This section focuses on diagonal strategies for getting both sides on board in the right proportions. Catalyst entrepreneurs must ultimately solve a coordination problem to get both sets of economic agents to get on board their platforms. The dynamics of this coordination problem can vary considerably depending on the nature of the platform business.

Sequential Entry

In some cases it is possible to get one group of agents on board over time and then make these agents available to the other group of agents later in time. That is the situation with advertising-supported media. One can use content to attract viewers and then bring advertisers on board later. This dynamic works because there are non-positive indirect network effects between the two sides: viewers do not care about advertisers (and may dislike advertising) but come to the platform for the content.

Entry with Significant Pre-commitment Investment

In other cases one group of economic agents need to make investments over time to participate in the platform.[12] That is the case with software-based platforms such as videogame consoles. Game developers must invest in creating games for the next release of a console without knowing how many consumers will be interested in using that platform when their development is done. The videogame console platform must either convince game developers that buyers will show up, provide them with some financial guarantees that buyers will show up, or self-produce games until the platform has proved itself.

Simultaneous Entry of Sides

In some cases the economic agents are making decisions to join the platform around the same time and have both to join around the same time for the platform to provide value. A dating venue demands almost perfect simultaneity. Heterosexual men would quickly leave a new nightclub that had no women and vice versa. Other platforms provide more latitude. Buyers may not desert an exchange platform right away if there are no sellers but they will arrive soon.

In all cases, however, platform growth is not sustainable until the platform reaches critical mass. Therefore the key challenge for new platforms is figuring out ways to reach critical mass quickly.

The Basic Zig-zag

A basic strategy for reaching critical mass is to build participation on the two sides incrementally. The platform starts with a small number of economic agents on both sides. It then persuades agents on either side to join. It also relies on the natural processes of product diffusion. Because of indirect network effects, the platform is more valuable to each successive group of prospective customers. Figure 5.4 shows that basic zig-zag approach to growth.

eBillMe provides an example of this strategy. Consumers who click on the eBillMe sign at the checkout for an e-tailer can pay with their online banking account. They then send an email that contains details for paying from their online banking account. After they enter the information into their online banking account they receive a receipt and the product is shipped. This payment alternative is attractive to people who are either concerned about the security of paying with cards online or do not happen to have a card conveniently available. A small but significant fraction of consumers, as it turns out, like paying this way.

To get started, eBillMe persuaded ToolKing to offer eBillMe at checkout.[13] A small percentage of customers used this payment alternative. eBillMe then went to other online retailers. Each led to eBillMe having more people who were accustomed to using its service. For each subsequent merchant it went to it offered an increasingly valuable offer since it had more users predisposed to use this payment alternative. At the same time it let its users know that they could pay at more places, thereby

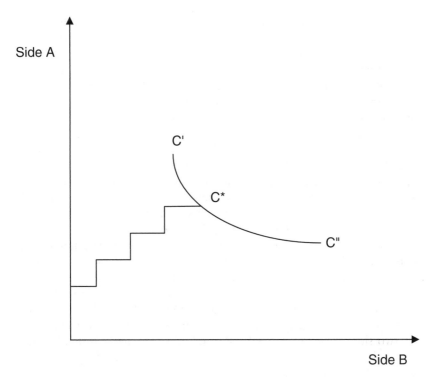

Figure 5.4   Basic zig-zag to critical mass

increasing the value to the merchants. eBillMe grew from one merchant and hundreds of users during its first year of entry in 2005 to hundreds of online stores taking 2 per cent to 10 per cent of the merchant's transaction volume by 2008.

Pre-commitment to Both Sides

Some platforms such as eBillMe are able to start with one member on one side that it uses to attract members on the other side. More commonly, platforms need to have multiple members of both sides to begin the zig-zag process mentioned above. They therefore need to persuade a minimum number of early adopters on both sides to show up at the start of the platform to make it credible. That requires getting both sides to believe that when the platform opens for business there will be members of the other side present.

Diners Club is the classic example of this strategy.[14] Although the precise sequence is lost to history, it persuaded 14 restaurants in Manhattan to accept Diners Club cards for payment. At the same time it persuaded several hundred people in Manhattan to take the Diners Club card. Those commitments were enough to start the platform. Over the next year Diners Club zig-zagged its way to 330 restaurants and 42000 cardholders.[15]

Customers may require more assurance that the other side will in fact show up, especially if they have to invest resources to join. Contingent contracts can be entered into for this purpose. Customers agree to commit to join the platform conditional on other customers on the same and other side also joining. Once these contracts have been entered into, the catalyst needs only to persuade one customer to sign on because that will have a domino effect on all the other customers. MobiTV serves as an example where contingent contracts play an important role for 'catalyzing' the platform (Evans and Schmalensee, 2007, p. 89). Started in 1999, MobiTV planned to offer TV service to customers on their mobile phones for a subscription fee. It needed to persuade TV content providers and mobile operators to join its platform. Neither of the two wanted to embark on the new project unless they were assured that the other side would also join. MobiTV used contingent contracts to ignite the platform. It signed an agreement with Sprint that if TV channels joined, Sprint would offer service and agreements with MSNBC and other TV channels that if Sprint joined, they would broadcast. It was enough for MobiTV to get Sprint to agree and everyone else followed.

The video-console example considered by Hagiu (2006) is an extreme example of this phenomenon. Videogames and other software applications are platforms that connect application developers and videogame players. The latter will not purchase a video console without enough applications and games, and the former will not put in the time to develop them if they are not sure that people will buy their applications. Because game developing is a long process, the vendors have to secure sellers a long time before the new game is launched in order to ensure that developers will provide the applications.

Single- and Double-sided Marquee Strategies

The marquee strategy discussed above is another way to obtain enough members on both sides to begin the zig-zag to critical mass. In a single-sided marquee strategy the platform acquires an 'influential' or 'prestige' member of one side. Announcement of that may attract enough members of the other side at the beginning. The shopping-mall strategy is the classic: the mall gets an anchor tenant that many shoppers want to connect to. In a two-sided marquee strategy the platform acquires 'influential' or 'prestige' members on both sides. They provide value to each other as well as attract other members. Nightclubs are common users of this strategy. They try to get popular men and women to come on opening night. They want to connect to each other and less popular men and women want to connect with them (Evans and Schmalensee, 2007).

The Two-step Strategy

The two-step strategy involves getting enough members of one side on board first and then getting members of the other side on board. As mentioned earlier, this works when the first side does not value access to the second side, which is often the case for advertising-supported media. Search engines followed this strategy. They attracted users who made searches of the World Wide Web. The search results were displayed on a series of pages. Once they obtained enough page views, they sold access to those pages to advertisers. Google, for example, operated its search engine for 23 months (including a beta version) before it opened its search results pages to advertisers.[16] At that time it had more than a billion pages indexed and 18 million user queries per day.

Ziz-zag with Self-supply

Catalysts may be able to jump-start their platforms by providing one of the sides themselves, at least initially. Consider YouTube, which is a three-sided platform: user-generated content attracts viewers; viewers attract content providers who want an audience; and access to viewers can then be sold to advertisers. YouTube started by focusing on users and viewers. Its founders seeded the site with content they generated themselves and started the process of diffusion by suggesting that members of their personal social networks check out the content.[17] They also used various marketing strategies to attract viewers: they posted an ad on Craigslist offering compensation to attractive women for posting videos on the site and promised to give an iPod to a random user every day until the end of the year.

Summary

We have introduced several concepts.

1. Multi-sided platforms often must attain critical mass to ignite a catalytic reaction that leads to organic growth. Platforms that do not reach this critical mass implode.

2. To reach critical mass, platforms can engage in a number of strategies to get 'enough' customers on either side, and in the right proportions, on board. These include the zig-zag and the two-step.
3. These strategies can usefully employ many of the tactics used for new product introductions by non-platform businesses.

We have taken some liberties in explaining the dynamics of platform ignition. As a formal mathematical matter one would have to reach critical mass instantaneously to ignite the reaction. In practice it appears that platforms have some limited time to get to critical mass. Early adopters use a platform. If they come back and if later adopters also find value, then it is possible to reach critical mass. If the platform does not grow quickly enough to critical mass, early adopters lose interest, fewer later adopters come, and word-of-mouth referrals stop or turn negative.

4. B2B EXCHANGES

Entrepreneurs and investors flocked to developing B2B exchanges in the late 1990s.[18] The thesis was simple. Build a better platform for exchange, and buyers and sellers will flock to it. The failure was stark. When the exchanges opened their doors, few sellers showed up. The sellers largely kept staying away.[19] Buyers lost interest. The exchanges could not reach critical mass. They failed *en masse* in the 2001 dot.com bust (see, e.g., Nickerson and Owen, 2001). Despite the great promise many held out for this new way of doing business, few successful B2Bs have emerged in the post-2004 web boom.

The B2B platforms failed to ignite for three related reasons.

First, a new platform must create a significant value as a result of getting two sides together that exceeds what they can do on their own or on alternative platforms. The B2Bs did not provide enough value compared with buyers and sellers connecting without a platform through existing bilateral relationships or an existing offline consortium.

Second, a new platform must allocate that value between the two sides to provide both with a sufficient incentive to join the platform. The B2Bs were not able to offer enough of a value proposition to sellers to get enough of them on board. The sellers saw the B2B exchanges as methods for driving down their prices through auctions. That did not leave them with enough of a long-term return and they therefore stayed away.

Third, a new platform must get enough of both sides on board and in the right proportions to achieve the critical mass that provides a minimum amount of value to both sides. Sellers came on board too slowly. Buyers lost interest. That provided even less motivation for sellers. Platforms that do not achieve critical mass implode and never have the chance to grow.

The Rise and Fall of the B2B Exchanges

B2Bs were viewed as an obvious way in which the Internet could create great value. In the late 1990s and early 2000s, business strategists, economists and others wrote numerous articles on how B2Bs would transform buying and selling. The title of one of the business books on the subject provides a flavor: *B2B Exchanges: The Killer Application in the Business-to-Business Internet Revolution* (Sculley and Woods, 1999). Various researchers forecasted that B2Bs would come to account for a large fraction of commerce. Goldman Sachs predicted in 2000 that B2B e-commerce transactions would equal $4.5 trillion worldwide by 2005. The Gardner Group estimated in 1999 that by 2004 B2B e-commerce would reach $7.3 trillion (Lucking-Reiley and Spulber, 2001). Entrepreneurs and venture capitalists poured into this new industry. Between 1995 and 2001 there were more than 1500 B2B sites. Some of the most prominent ones were Ventro, VerticalNet, Neoforma, Cordiem, CorProcure, Chemdex. Most of them collapsed in the early 2000s as investors realized that they did not have a viable business model and as the expected buyers and sellers failed to turn up.[20] Many of the ones that survived – such as Ariba, which merged with FreeMarkets – shifted their focus from operating true exchanges to offering procurement software that facilitated the normal process of bilateral buyer–seller transactions.

Perhaps the best evidence on what happened not only to B2Bs, but to the idea of B2Bs, is revealed from a simple Google search. News and analyst reports about B2Bs largely end in the early 2000s. The flourishing academic literature on the economics of business of B2Bs appears to have collapsed soon thereafter. Surprisingly, there are few rigorous post mortems on why B2Bs failed to ignite. This chapter does not provide a rigorous study either but places some of the contemporaneous observations about the collapse in the context of the framework presented above.

The Value Proposition

There were well-developed methods that enabled business buyers and suppliers to deal with each other well before the development of the commercial Internet. Buyers had supplier lists to turn to when they had a need. They had sophisticated procurement departments that were experienced in putting the purchase of goods and services out to bid and had knowledge about suppliers. Suppliers also had relationships with companies and had ways to get on the bidding lists. Buyers had the greatest difficulty finding new suppliers, especially for areas where they had few bidders. New suppliers who had not developed relationships also had difficulty. A key question for starting a platform was whether it could provide enough additional value to these two market sides.

The B2Bs were patterned after the successful auction-based B2C (business-to-customer) sites such as eBay. They introduced various types of auction mechanisms that tended to maximize competition among suppliers but mainly based on price. That of course was not attractive to suppliers because it depressed prices and profits, and eliminated the value of other sources of differentiation. As one consultant noted about the proposed B2B exchanges for the airline industry (Odell, 2001, p. 06):

> [Suppliers] continue to be reluctant to sign up to portants and other e-mechanisms created by the prime contractors. The key reason for this is that the primary objective of e-procurement is perceived to be a reduction in the purchase price, therefore forcing pressures on [supplier] margins.

A number of observers of the demise of the B2Bs observed that a major problem was that suppliers were scared, as Kabir puts it, 'of comparison shopping and brand dilution'.[21]

Once we go beyond the perfectly competitive model it is easy to see why exchanges that were built around efficient procurement auctions were not attractive to suppliers. Most businesses have fixed costs that they have to recover. They therefore cannot survive if their prices are competed down to short-run variable costs. Department stores can have sales periodically where merchandise is sold at low margins; they could not survive if they were selling at those prices all the time. B2B auctions will tend to attract suppliers that can offer low prices because they have excess inventories as a result of lack of success.

The B2Bs were not necessarily advantageous to buyers either. Company procurement officers typically learn about the quality of their suppliers. Through interactions over time and discussions with people in the industry they discover the quality of supplier goods and services as well as their reliability for delivery. They can take this information into account in deciding who to put on the bid list, thereby selecting the lowest price from pre-qualified bidders, or they can take non-price features into account in selecting the winning bid. Many of the B2B exchanges focused mainly on price and did not provide companies with significant services for assessing quality. Indeed, the importance of quality and experience was learned the hard way by American toy manufacturers who found suppliers through some of the successful B2Bs that have focused on connecting Chinese suppliers to multinational buyers. Many of these suppliers used lead in their products, which led to significant health risks and product recalls when this was discovered (Barboza, 2007).

Ignition Strategies

Based on the general articles that have been published on the mass demise of the B2Bs, it appears that the B2Bs made several fundamental mistakes in achieving critical mass and in igniting. To begin with, it is not clear that many of these B2Bs could have ignited without modifying their business models to provide sufficient value to the two sides of the platform. That is, it is not clear that the global communication aspect of many of their models, based on the Internet, provided enough value over and above the traditional methods of procurement to justify buyers or suppliers in changing. Therefore there may not have been a pricing structure, and ignition strategy, that could have, under any circumstances, sustained many of these B2Bs.

Some of the B2Bs seem to have adopted the following two-step strategy. They would begin by organizing the buyer side. That could occur by securing the participation of one or more large buyers – a one-sided marquee strategy. For example, Chemdex started with Genentech, which purchased most of the value on the exchange initially. That could also occur as a result of the exchange being started by a cooperative of buyers – as was the case with the automobile exchange, Covisint, which was started by General Motors, Ford Motor Company, DaimlerChrysler, Nissan and Renault. They could then seek suppliers. This strategy would not work for exchanges that were organizing larger groups of smaller buyers. They would have to adopt a simultaneous strategy and secure enough buyers and sellers at the same time.

Many of the B2Bs made the mistake of establishing symmetric pricing structures that sought to earn revenue from both buyers and suppliers.[22] One of the most famous B2B failures – Chemdex – charged suppliers a listing fee for products and charged buyers a commission on transactions (Meyer et al., 2004). It is possible that a symmetric pricing strategy could work if an exchange had enough buyers and suppliers already – at that point suppliers might lack access to a significant market if they refused to pay the fees. But at the start of these exchanges buyers and sellers would have to be persuaded to switch from the widely used bilateral procurement methods.

In any event, it appears that many of the exchanges ended up well off the path to critical mass because they did not offer suppliers with enough of an incentive to join. That could have come in the form of subsidies in cash or kind to suppliers to join the exchange. If the B2Bs could have gotten enough suppliers through what is known as a 'divide and conquer' strategy, they might have gotten enough buyers and then more suppliers (Nickerson and Owen, 2001). Of course, such subsidies could have been large risky investments in the success of the B2Bs, and granting them would have been foolish if, as suggested above, there was no feasible profitable model for the B2B.

5. SOCIAL NETWORKING

Social networks have exploded on the web. By August 2008 there were more than 110 social networking sites, as classified by Alexa,[23] which had more than 580 million active users.[24] In the USA MySpace is the largest one, with more than 68 million active users. The second-largest one, Facebook, has about 32 million active users.[25] These sites generally allow people to construct a public profile, make this profile available to other users to whom they grant permission, and in return obtain the right to see the profiles of these users. The profiles and related technologies provide ways for friends to communicate with each other. For example, Facebook has a place where people can say what they are doing; when a user goes to her profile page on Facebook she will then see what all her friends are doing.

The first social networking site, SixDegrees.com, was started in 1997. But it did not attain critical mass and shut down in 2000. Its founder speculated that this was because people did not have enough friends on line and there was not much to do together once they were on line. The promise of social networking became apparent with the rapid growth of Friendster, which started in 2002. In the USA, it grew to a peak of 1.5 million users in the third quarter of 2003 but then went into decline. MySpace and Facebook have emerged as the two leading global social networking platforms.[26]

Background on Social Networking

Social networking sites are multi-sided platforms with usually at least three sides.

The first two sides are individuals who want to connect with each other. For many social networking sites such as Friendster, these are friends seeking friends. However, people seek friends on social networking sites and are recipients of requests for friendships. This sender–receiver relationship has important consequences for how social networking sites are ignited. The role of gregarious and influential members of the site can have significant effects on the dynamics of growth. The third side consists of advertisers who want to reach these users. Some social network sites have a fourth side that consists of software developers who write applications that work with the social networking site and provide value to users and advertisers.

Social networking sites typically have two sources of revenue. In part they are traditional advertising-supported media. The social networking features and applications attract viewers. Advertisers then pay for the ability to present advertising messages to these viewers. The social networking site earns revenue directly from advertisers or indirectly from application providers who sell advertising. They also earn revenue by selling things that facilitate interactions between the users. These include 'pokes' such as virtual flowers that people can send their friends.

Social networking sites use a variant of a two-step strategy to ignite. They focus on getting a critical mass of 'friends' that generates traffic on their sites. They then earn revenue through selling advertising and pokes. They also persuade developers who want access to their network to write applications that further increase the value of the network as well as provide additional revenue possibilities.

We now turn to the ignition strategies and growth paths for two well-known social networking sites: Friendster and Facebook. Figure 5.5 shows membership on these sites and the growth rates in membership over time.

Friendster

Friendster was the first social networking site to gain wide popularity (Boyd and Ellison, 2007). It attracted users initially by providing a dating venue where people could find romantic partners among friends of friends. That was a different approach than existing online data venues that matched up strangers based on predictions of their likely compatibility. People posted their profile and were able to communicate with other users who were no more than four degrees of separation away. People interested in finding romantic partners liked the fact that there were social connections that not only helped screen people but also helped police bad behavior.

Friendster started with a prototype in 2002. Its founder invited 20 close friends to join.[27] The site launched formally in March 2003. It grew virally from the initial seed of 20 friends and had 835000 registered users by June 2003 and 1.5 million by September. There is no evidence that it focused on influencers or gregarious people – instead it just grew naturally. The growth was not driven entirely by the users looking for people to date. Most people used it to communicate with and expand their network of

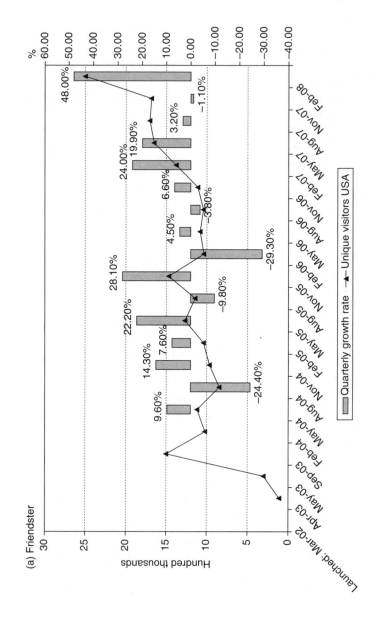

(a) Friendster

Quarterly growth rate ▲ Unique visitors USA

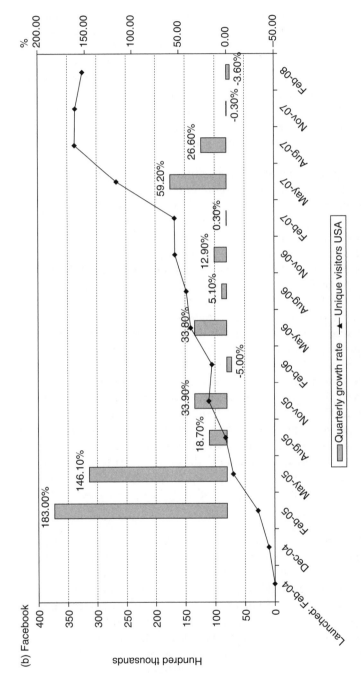

(b) Facebook

Note: Based on ComScore data for the period Feb. 2004–Feb. 2008 and 'Facebook Case Study', Harvard Business School, 2006, for the period Apr. 2003–Feb. 2008.

Figure 5.5   Friendster and Facebook growth

friends. Many people used it as a source of entertainment from looking at the profiles of people that they would not otherwise have contact with.

Although it reached critical mass and grew explosively, Friendster encountered two major problems (Rivlin, 2006). The first was technological. It was not prepared for the upsurge in users, and users started finding that the site was not reliable. The four-degrees-of-separation rule was a major source of the problem. Every time someone signed on to the site the software had to determine who was within the individual's community. As the size of the overall network grew, it took longer and longer to do that calculation.

The second problem involved changes in the community and Friendster's response to those changes. As the community grew, the four-degrees-of-separation rule made people's profiles accessible to people that they did not necessarily want in their social network – for example their bosses. At the same time the rule limited the size of the community that one could acquire. To counter this, people started gaming the system to create more friends. One of these efforts involved creating Fakesters – fake profiles designed to attract a lot of attention and therefore many friends. Friendster banned fake profiles and also dropped the 'most popular' attribute that had encouraged people to engage in some of the bad behavior. As it turns out, the Fakesters were a popular source of entertainment and way to create groups such as alumni of particular universities. Friendster also policed the profiles and kicked users off who did not comply.

The user community became dissatisfied with Friendster. Growth slowed.[28] In the US market, which is the most significant source of advertising revenue, Friendster declined dramatically after the third quarter of 2003 and remained roughly flat for the next three years while other social networking sites grew explosively. Nevertheless, it achieved a critical mass of users in other countries, and remains the third-largest social networking site worldwide[29] and in August 2008, it announced that it had received $20 million of venture capital.[30]

Facebook

Facebook's founders also started with the idea that they would provide a convenient method for dating. As students at Harvard, they thought it would be helpful to have a place where students who saw each other in class and other settings could connect. Within the first month of starting in February 2004, more than 50 percent of Harvard college students had put their profiles on the site.[31] Since Facebook was designed to facilitate communication within a closed community, it was able to obtain critical mass – enough people found it valuable enough to use the site – very quickly and then captured most of the population of potential users.

Shortly thereafter Facebook extended its model to other universities, beginning with Stanford, Columbia and Yale. In each case a significant portion of the undergraduate student body set up profiles. By the end of the year Facebook had almost 1 million active users. All users had to have an '.edu' email extension to verify that they were part of an academic community. Facebook continued to add local networks of students. It had more than 800 college networks by May 2005. It then added international schools and work environments. By August 2006 it had 14782 million registered users.

Facebook opened its doors to everyone in September 2006. However, it offered a very different level of privacy than either the imploding Friendster or the exploding MySpace. When a person creates a profile on Facebook they cannot interact with anyone else at the beginning. That person can build a community of friends either by sending out friend requests, or by being invited by others to be a friend. Users can also 'de-friend' people and have various ways to restrict access to portions of their pages.

Facebook did not have any significant revenue stream for its first 36 months and focused instead on building its user base. In February 2007, when it had 16737 million unique users worldwide,[32] it introduced Facebook Gifts. These are icons such as flowers, hearts and balloons that users can purchase for $1 to send to other friends. In May 2007 it launched Marketplace for classified listings for sales, housing and jobs. In November 2007 the company launched Facebook Ads, an ad system that allows businesses to target their advertising to the precise audience they seek to reach.[33] As of September 2008, it is estimated that Facebook earns $350 million[34] from advertising and $35 million[35] from the sale of gifts.

Facebook's successful ignition was based on a form of the two-step strategy. The first step involved developing the user base. There was a chicken-and-egg problem to be solved there since the network could grow only if there was a reciprocal relationship between enough people. However, by providing an effective vehicle for communication, social networking sites can grow very quickly as friends invite friends who invite more friends.

The second step involved earning revenue from that user base. An important aspect of that was selling access to the user base to advertisers. Facebook and other social networking sites have been disappointed at their ability to secure advertising revenue. Online advertising is sold on the basis of 'cost per thousand' viewers of an advertisement. The average cost per thousand for online advertising is in the range of $10–15. The average for Facebook is reportedly below $0.50. (Of course, although Facebook may not prove as valuable as its founders and investors might have liked, it is likely to be enormously profitable.)

Part of the difficulty that appears not to have been anticipated is that advertising is a bit alien to a social networking community. It is natural to see advertising on publisher websites. It is less natural to see advertising on your own profile page or the profile pages of friends – especially if you have been using Facebook for a while without such advertising. Facebook alienated its customers when as part of its Beacon advertising strategy it started tracking users' purchases from third-party websites. Facebook and other social networking sites are looking for innovative ways to advertise that satisfy the needs of advertisers without reducing the value of the social networking aspects of the sites.

The social networking sites illustrate the power of diffusion in generating web traffic. The successful sites grew very quickly because they provided existing physical networks of friends much more powerful tools for interacting virtually with each other more efficiently. That, however, is only the first step in a sequential entry strategy. The later strategies have required getting advertisers on board the platform.[36]

6. CONCLUDING REMARKS

In this chapter I have raised some of the important issues and provided some preliminary thoughts on them. There is considerable room for further theoretical and empirical research. On the theoretical front we need dynamic models that address the creation of multi-sided platforms, especially in the case in which the platform needs to get both sides on board at the same time. On the empirical front we need research on the successful and unsuccessful launch of platforms. Both econometric studies of platform dynamics and case studies would be informative.

NOTES

1. I have benefited from discussions with and comments from Howard Chang, Annabelle Gawer, Andrei Hagiu, Richard Schmalensee and Karen Webster. I would also like to thank Alina Marinova for exceptional research assistance. E-mail: devans@lecg.com.
2. These comments also pertain to communication platforms in which it is important to distinguish between senders and receivers – even though they are the same people – for both economic analysis and business strategy.
3. There are several notable exceptions to this statement. The role of critical mass in launching exchanges is analyzed in a dynamic model in Fath and Sarvaryi (2003). See also Caillaud and Jullien (2003), who consider platform launch but in a single-period setting. The role of commitment is analyzed in a two-period game in Hagiu (2006). A managerial treatment of the issues is presented in Gawer and Cusumano (2008).
4. I prefer not to use the 'two-sided market' term because the term really refers to a

platform business that provides a matchmaking service in competition with other platform businesses in a market for that service.

5. In financial exchanges liquidity providers (such as market makers) provide buy-and-sell orders. They attract liquidity takers (such as investors who buy and sell through broker–dealers). In other exchange markets there is no institution that plays the role of liquidity providers. However, in these other exchange markets it is essential that the platform attract enough buyers and sellers to make the market liquid. See Harris (2002).

6. For the technical development of this framework see Evans and Schmalensee (2009). We show that in certain plausible cases there is a critical level of liquidity that platforms need to get to in order to evolve towards a stable equilibrium with largest platform size. This framework does not cover the process of getting to critical mass. This chapter uses the framework to motivate an informal analysis of how catalysts can achieve critical liquidity.

7. For most financial exchanges the two sides are liquidity providers who announce prices at which they stand ready to buy or sell and liquidity takers who provide order flow that interacts with those standing orders. See Harris (2002). For non-financial exchanges such as e-commerce the two sides are simply buyers and sellers.

8. See, e.g., Hart and Tzokas (2000); Prasad (1997). For literature summary see Krishnan and Ulrich (2001).

9. The fact that the pricing structure – the relative charges to the two groups – matters makes these a two-sided platform under the definition proposed by Rochet and Tirole (2003). See, e.g., Hausman and Wright (2006). Using data from Australia, they explore the equilibrium prices of fixed-to-mobile calls by taking into account that fixed-line callers might be cellphone users themselves, and thus be from either side of the market. They also point out that it is important to consider whether the mobile receiver pays for the call (as in the USA) or does not (as in most EU countries).

10. The social networking literature distinguishes between senders and receivers, and highlights the important role that gregarious members of a network (i.e. individuals who initiate many interactions) and prestigious members of a network (i.e. individuals who are the recipients of many messages) play. See Wasserman and Faust (1994).

11. The centers are the nodes for 'stars' in which the center is connected to other nodes and the points of the star are connected to the center node.

12. This is the case treated in Hagiu (2006).

13. Interview with Marwan Forzley, founder and chairman of eBillMe.

14. For description and discussion of this example, see Evans and Schmalensee (2007), p. 1.

15. At this point in time credit cards were mainly used in local markets so Diners Club had to secure critical mass in a number of different cities to ignite the platform. The 330 restaurants and 42 000 cardholders refers to the total across these separate markets.

16. Google Milestones: http://www.google.com/corporate/history.html.

17. See YouTube videos: 'The history of YouTube', available at: http://www.youtube.com/watch?v=x2NQiVcdZRY and 'The real history of YouTube in 3 minutes', available at: http://www.youtube.com/watch?v=PazFKj_aIpA.

18. There were over 1600 B2B exchanges by 2001, according to Lucking-Reiley and Spulber (2001).

19. That was the story of Chemdex, one of the first B2B exchanges. Chemdex did not manage to attract enough sellers and buyers in order to secure the automation of the business process. See Nguyen (2001).

20. According to a research study, 'Shakeouts in digital markets: lessons from B2B exchanges', conducted by Wharton School and Pembroke Consulting in November 2002 and reported in Day et al. (2003), of the 1500 independent business exchanges that existed in 2001, fewer than 200 remained at the end of 2003.

21. See Kabir (2003).

22. See the case studies in Engström and Salehi-Sangari (2007). Of the six B2Bs they examined, five started trying to earn revenues from both buyers and suppliers, and one of these moved towards a model in which suppliers obtain services largely for free.

23. 'Top list of social networking sites' (2008).
24. comScore Press Release (2008b)
25. comScore Press Release (2008a).
26. See Boyd and Ellison (2007). In addition to these 'friending' sites there are also professional social networking sites such as Linked In, which in theory help people form professional relationships and in practice help people find jobs and recruiters to find candidates.
27. Chafkin (2007).
28. MySpace picked up a number of Friendster's users. It provided a platform in which people could see anyone's profile and in which people had a great deal of freedom in designing their profiles. An important group that it attracted were indie rock groups, some of whom had been ejected from Friendster, and then musicians more broadly who used the site to connect with their fans.
29. 'Friendster deploys OpenSocial support for benefit of 75 million users, developers and industry', (2008).
30. See Taulli (2008).
31. Phillips (2007),
32. comScore Press Release (2007).
33. 'Facebook company timeline' (2008).
34. Williamson (2007).
35. Rumford (2008) and 'Facebook digital gifts worth around $15m/year' (2008).
36. At this point in time the social networking sites have, as noted above, found it difficult to obtain much interest from advertisers and are charging vastly lower prices for viewers than are other content-oriented sites.

REFERENCES

Barboza, D. (2007), 'Mattel recalls toys made in China', *The New York Times*, http://www.iht.com/articles/2007/08/02/business/toys.5-108444.php, accessed 9 December 2008.

Boyd, D.M. and N. Ellison (2007), 'Social networking sites: definition, history, and scholarship', *Journal of Computer-Mediated Communication*, **13** (1), article 11, http://jcmc.indiana.edu/vol13/issue1/boyd.ellison.html, accessed 27 September 2008.

Brown, J. and P.H. Reingen (1987), 'Social ties and word-of-mouth referral behavior', *Journal of Consumer Research*, **14** (3), 350–62.

Brown, J., A. Broderick and N. Lee (2007), 'Word of mouth communication within online communities: conceptualizing the online social network', *Journal of Interactive Marketing*, **21** (3), 2–20.

Caillaud, B. and B. Jullien (2003), 'Chicken and egg: competition among intermediation service providers', *RAND Journal of Economics*, **34** (2), 309–28.

Carr, N.G. (2001), *The Digital Enterprise: How to Reshape Your Business for a Connected World*, Boston, MA: Harvard Business School Press.

Chafkin, M. (2007), 'How to kill a great idea!', Inc.com, June, available at: http://www.inc.com/magazine/20070601/features-how-to-kill-a-great-idea.html, accessed 9 December 2008.

comScore Press Release (2007), 'Facebook sees flood of new traffic from teenagers and adults', 5 July, available at: http://www.comscore.com/press/release. asp?press=1519, accessed 9 December 2008.

comScore Press Release (2008a), 'comScore Media Metrix releases top 50 web rankings for February', 19 March, available at: http://www.comscore.com/ Press_Events/Press_Release/2008/03/Top_50_US_Web_Sites.

Comscore Press Release (2008b), 'Social networking explodes worldwide as sites increase their focus on cultural relevance', 12 August, available at: http://www. comscore.com/press/release.asp?press=2396, accessed 9 December 2008.

Day, G., A. Fein and G. Roppersberger (2003), 'Shakeouts in digital markets: lessons from B2B exchanges', *California Management Review*, **45** (2), 131–50.

Engström, A. and A. Salehi-Sangari (2007), 'Assessment of business-to-business e-marketplaces' performance', PhD dissertation, Luleå University of Technology, Sweden.

Evans, D.S. and R. Schmalensee (2007), *Catalyst Code: The Strategies Behind the World's Most Dynamic Companies*, Boston, MA: Harvard Business School Press.

Evans, D.S. and R. Schmalensee (2009), 'Failure to launch: critical mass in platform business', 1 March, available at: http://ssrn.com/abstract=1353502.

'Facebook company timeline' (2008), Facebook Website, available at: http://www. facebook.com/press/info.php?timeline, accessed 9 December 2008.

'Facebook digital gifts worth around $15m/year' (2008), WordPress.com, 23 January, available at: http://lsvp.wordpress.com/2008/01/23/facebook-digital-gifts-worth-around-15myear/, accessed 9 December 2008.

Fath, G. and M. Sarvaryi (2003), 'Adoption dynamics in buyer-side exchanges', *Quantitative Marketing and Economics*, **1** (3), 305–35.

'Friendster deploys OpenSocial support for benefit of 75 million users, developers and industry' (2008), PR Newswire, 18 August, available at: http://www. prnewswire.com/cgi-bin/stories.pl?ACCT=109&STORY=/www/story/08-18-2008/0004869579&EDATE=, accessed 9 December 2008.

Gawer, A. and M.A. Cusumano (2008), 'How companies become platform leaders', *MIT Sloan Management Review*, **49** (2), 28–35.

'Google Milestones', http://www.google.com/corporate/history.html, accessed 9 December 2008.

Hagiu, A. (2006), 'Pricing and commitment by two-sided platforms', *RAND Journal of Economics*, **37** (3), 720–37.

Harris, L. (2002), *Trading and Exchanges: Market Microstructure for Practitioners*, Oxford: Oxford University Press.

Hart, S. and N. Tzokas (2000), 'New product launch "mix" in growth and mature product markets', *Benchmarking: An International Journal*, **7** (5), 389–406.

Hausman, J. and J. Wright (2006), 'Two sided markets with substitution: mobile termination revisited', mimeo, http://econ-www.mit.edu/files/1038, accessed 9 December 2008.

Johnson, S. (2006), 'Google Video isn't ready for prime time', *Chicago Tribune*, accessed 9 December 2008.

Kabir, N. (2003), 'E-marketplace: facts and fictions', *WebProNews*, http://www. webpronews.com/topnews/2003/08/20/emarketplace-facts-and-fictions, accessed 9 December 2008.

Knaup, A. and M.C. Piazza (2007), 'Business employment dynamics data: survival and Longevity, II', *Monthly Labor Review Online*, **130** (9), 3–10, http://www.bls. gov/opub/mlr/2007/09/art1full.pdf, accessed 9 December 2008.

Krishnan, V. and K.T. Ulrich (2001), 'Product development decisions: a review of the Literature', *Management Science*, **47** (1), 1–21.

Lucking-Reiley, D. and D.F. Spulber (2001), 'Business-to-business electronic commerce', *Journal of Economic Perspectives*, **15** (1), 55–68.

Mahajan, V., E. Muller and F.M. Bass (1990), 'New product diffusion models in marketing: a review and directions for research', *Journal of Marketing*, **54** (1), 1–26.

Metrik, A. (2006), *Venture Capital and the Finance of Innovation*, New York: Wiley.

Meyer, M.H., N. de Crescenzo and B. Russell (2004), 'Case study: Chemdex: in search of a viable business model', *International Journal for Entrepreneurship Education*, **2** (2), http://web.cba.neu.edu/~mmeyer/cases/Ventro-010105.pdf, accessed 9 December 2008.

Nickerson, J. and H. Owen (2001), 'A theory of B2B exchanges formation', manuscript, http://ssrn.com/abstract=315121, accessed 9 December 2008.

Nguyen, F. (2001), 'The changing face of e-healthcare: is healthcare too complicated for an Internet-based supply-chain solution? Here's what manufacturers should expect in 2001', Medical Device Link, available at: http://www.device-link.com/mx/archive/01/03/0103mx072.html, accessed 9 December 2008.

Odell, M. (2001), 'B2B struggling to achieve take-off', *Financial Times*, London.

Phillips, S. (2007), 'A Brief History of Facebook', *Guardian*, 25 July, available at: http://www.guardian.co.uk/technology/2007/jul/25/media.newmedia, accessed 9 December 2008.

Pogue, D. (2006), 'Google Video: trash mixed with treasure', *The New York Times*, http://www.nytimes.com/2006/01/19/technology/circuits/19pogue.html, accessed 9 December 2008.

Prasad, B. (1997), 'Analysis of pricing strategies for new product introduction', *Pricing Strategies and Practice*, **5** (4), 132–41.

Rivlin, G. (2006), 'Wallflower at the web party', *New York Times*, http://www.nytimes.com/2006/10/15/business/yourmoney/15friend.html, accessed 9 December 2008.

Rochet, J.-C. and J. Tirole (2003), 'Platform competition in two-sided markets', *Journal of European Economic Association*, **1** (4), 990-1029.

Rumford, R. (2008), 'Facebook virtual gifts make big bucks', Facereviews, 2 September, available at: http://facereviews.com/2008/09/02/facebook-virtual-gifts-make-big-bucks/, accessed 9 December 2008.

Sculley, A. and W. Woods (1999), *B2B Exchanges: The Killer Application in the Business-to-Business Internet Revolution*, Toronto: ISI Publications.

Shapiro, C. and H. Varian (1998), *Information Rules: A Strategic Guide to Network Economics*, Boston, MA: Harvard Business School Press.

Taulli, T. (2008), 'Friendster is still alive and well . . . and gets $20 million', Bloggingstocks.com, http://www.bloggingstocks.com/2008/08/05/friendster-is-still-alive-and-well-and-gets-20-million/, accessed 24 September 2008.

'The history of YouTube' (2007), http://www.youtube.com/watch?v=x2NQiVcd ZRY, accessed 9 December 2008.

'The real history of YouTube in 3 minutes' (2007), http://www.youtube.com/watch?v=PazFKj_aIpA, accessed 9 December 2008.

'Top list of social networking sites' (2008), Easy Viral Traffic Blog, http://www.easy-viral-traffic.com/blog/index.php/top-list-of-social-networking-sites/, accessed 9 December 2008.

Wasserman, S. and K. Faust (1994), *Social Network Analysis: Methods and Applications*, Cambridge, UK: Cambridge University Press.

Williamson, D.A. (2007), 'Social Network ad spending keeps rising', eMarketer, 13 August, available at: http://www.emarketer.com/Article.aspx?id=1005257, accessed 9 December 2008.

PART II

Platforms: Open, Closed and Governance Issues

6. Opening platforms: how, when and why?

Thomas R. Eisenmann, Geoffrey Parker and Marshall Van Alstyne

INTRODUCTION

Selecting optimal levels of openness is crucial for firms that create and maintain platforms (Gawer and Cusumano, 2002; West, 2003; Gawer and Henderson, 2007; Boudreau, 2008; Eisenmann, 2008; Parker and Van Alstyne, 2008). Decisions to open a platform entail tradeoffs between adoption and appropriability (West, 2003). Opening a platform can spur adoption by harnessing network effects, reducing users' concerns about lock-in, and stimulating production of differentiated goods that meet the needs of user segments. At the same time, opening a platform typically reduces users' switching costs and increases competition among platform providers, making it more difficult for them to appropriate rents from the platform.

In this chapter, we review research on factors that motivate managers to open or close mature platforms. We focus on a subset of platforms: those that exploit network effects by mediating transactions between platform users (Eisenmann et al., 2006; Evans et al., 2006; Evans and Schmalensee, 2007). Our inquiry excludes platforms that do not mediate network transactions but instead enable a firm to offer product variety by sharing common components (as with Chrysler's K-car or Boeing's 777).

A platform is 'open' to the extent that: (1) restrictions are not placed on participation in its development, commercialization or use; and (2) any restrictions – for example, requirements to conform with technical standards or pay licensing fees – are reasonable and non-discriminatory, that is, they are applied uniformly to all potential platform participants. As described in the next section, platform-mediated networks encompass several distinct roles, including: (1) *demand-side platform users*, commonly called 'end users'; (2) *supply-side platform users*, who offer complements employed by demand-side users in tandem with the core platform; (3) *platform providers*, who serve as users' primary point of

contact with the platform; and (4) *platform sponsors*, who exercise property rights and are responsible for determining who may participate in
a platform-mediated network and for developing its technology. For a
given platform, each of these roles may be open or closed. Consequently,
characterizing a platform as 'open' without referencing relevant roles can
cause confusion.

The Linux platform, for example, is open with respect to all four roles.
Any organization or individual can use Linux (demand-side user role).
Likewise, any party can offer a Linux-compatible software application
(supply-side user role). Any party can bundle the Linux operating system
(OS) with server or personal computer hardware (platform provider role).
Finally, any party can contribute improvements to the Linux OS, subject
to the rules of the open source community that maintains the OS kernel
(platform sponsor role). For Linux and other platforms, openness at the
sponsor level entails greater openness at the user level, as it implies not
only non-discrimination in platform access, but also in the process of
defining platform standards.

By contrast, in 2008 Apple's iPhone was closed with respect to three of
the four roles, and is only open for some prospective demand-side users
under onerous terms. In the USA, only AT&T Wireless subscribers can
use an iPhone. To buy one, other mobile carriers' customers must switch
to AT&T, incurring inconveniences and contract termination fees. Other
roles in the iPhone network are closed. Software applications for the
iPhone are available only through Apple's iTunes Store. Apple reserves
the right to reject third-party applications due to quality or strategic
concerns, and often does so (supply-side user role). Finally, only Apple
manufactures and distributes the iPhone (platform provider role) and
Apple is solely responsible for the iPhone's technology (platform sponsor
role).

Between these extremes, we find platforms that mix open and closed
roles in different patterns (Table 6.1). For instance, Microsoft's Windows
platform is closed at the sponsor level but open with respect to other roles.
Apple's Macintosh platform is closed at the sponsor and provider levels
but open with respect to both user roles. Since all of the platforms in Table
6.1 are successful, it should be clear that without careful definitions, we
cannot make general statements about the attractiveness of open versus
closed platform strategies – notwithstanding enthusiasm about the profu-
sion of open source software and content created in collaborative communities like Wikipedia and Second Life.

This chapter examines decisions to open or close platforms in mature
markets rather than new ones. An extensive body of research analyzes
decisions to pursue compatibility with rivals' technical standards when

Table 6.1   Comparison of openness by role in platform-mediated networks

	Linux	Windows	Macintosh	iPhone
Demand-side user (End user)	Open	Open	Open	Open
Supply-side user (Application developer)	Open	Open	Open	Closed
Platform provider (Hardware/OS bundle)	Open	Open	Closed	Closed
Platform Sponsor (Design and IP rights owner)	Open	Closed	Closed	Closed

launching new products (e.g. Farrell and Saloner, 1985; Katz and Shapiro, 1985; David and Greenstein, 1990; Besen and Farrell, 1994; Shapiro and Varian, 1999). Likewise, a burgeoning literature focuses on competition between open and closed (that is, proprietary) platforms (e.g. Economides and Katsamakas, 2006; Hagiu, 2006; Lee and Mendelson, 2008; Parker and Van Alstyne, 2008). Most of these papers analyze new markets where user mobilization is a priority and network effects are highly salient. However, there has been less research on the relative advantages of open and closed architectures once platforms mature and users are on board (exceptions include Gawer and Cusumano, 2002; West, 2003; Baldwin and Woodard, 2007; Gawer and Henderson, 2007; Boudreau, 2008). By focusing on mature markets, our chapter aims to help fill this gap in the literature.

The chapter is organized into four sections. The first defines our terms and expands on the discussion above of different roles in a platform-mediated network. Section 2 examines horizontal strategies that open or close a platform, encompassing decisions to: (1) interoperate with established rival platforms; (2) license additional platform providers; and (3) broaden a platform's sponsorship. Section 3 considers vertical strategies that open or close the supply-side user role, including choices regarding: (1) backward compatibility with prior platform generations; (2) securing exclusive rights to certain complements; and (3) absorbing complements into the core platform. The final section reviews management challenges confronting closed/proprietary and open/shared platforms in maturity, speculating about forces that push both types of platforms toward hybrid governance models typified by central control over platform technology and shared responsibility for serving users.

1. DEFINITIONS

A 'platform-mediated network' comprises users whose transactions are subject to direct and/or indirect network effects, along with one or more intermediaries that facilitate users' transactions (Rochet and Tirole, 2003; Eisenmann et al., 2006; Evans and Schmalensee, 2007). The 'platform' encompasses the set of components and rules employed in common in most user transactions (Boudreau, 2008). 'Components' include hardware, software and service modules, along with an architecture that specifies how they fit together (Henderson and Clark, 1990). 'Rules' are used to coordinate network participants' activities (Baldwin and Clark, 2000). They include standards that ensure compatibility among different components, protocols that govern information exchange, policies that constrain user behavior, and contracts that specify terms of trade and the rights and responsibilities of network participants.

Platform-mediated networks can be categorized according to the number of distinct user groups they encompass. In some networks, users are homogeneous. For example, although a given stock trade has a buyer and seller, these roles are transient; almost all traders play both roles at different times. Networks with homogeneous users are called 'one-sided' to distinguish them from 'two-sided' networks, which have two distinct user groups whose respective members consistently play a single role in transactions (Rochet and Tirole, 2003; Parker and Van Alstyne, 2000, 2005; Armstrong, 2006). Examples of two-sided networks include credit cards (comprising cardholders and merchants), HMOs (health maintenance organizations – patients and doctors), and videogames (consumers and game developers).

In traditional industries, bilateral exchanges follow a linear path as vendors purchase inputs, transform them, and sell output. By contrast, exchanges in platform-mediated networks have a triangular structure (Eisenmann et al., 2006). Users transact with each other and simultaneously affiliate with platform providers (see Figure 6.1). For example, with Sony's two-sided PlayStation platform, developers on the platform's supply side offer games to consumers on the demand side – the first set of bilateral exchanges. Developers must also contract with the platform's provider, Sony, for permission to publish games and for production support: the second set of exchanges. Finally, consumers must procure a console from Sony: the third set of exchanges.

In a two-sided network, from the perspective of demand-side users, supply-side users like game developers offer complements to the platform. However, such complements are not part of the platform itself: a platform encompasses components used in most user transactions, and

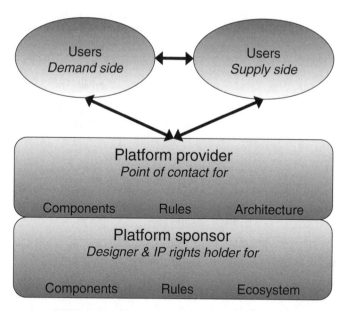

Figure 6.1   Elements of a platform-mediated network

only a fraction of platform use involves any given game. Hence, although games and consoles must be consumed as a system, in the context of the PlayStation platform, the developer is a platform user rather than a platform provider.

Every platform-mediated network has a focal platform at its core, although some complements offered by supply-side users may themselves be platforms nested inside the focal platform (e.g. a multi-player game like Madden NFL 09 with respect to PlayStation), as described below. To create and maintain the focal platform, one or more intermediaries must fulfill two distinct roles: platform provider and platform sponsor. Platform providers mediate users' transactions; they serve as users' primary point of contact with the platform. They supply its components and adhere to its rules. Platform sponsors do not deal directly with users; rather, they hold rights to modify the platform's technology. They design the components and rules, and determine who may participate in the network as platform providers and users.

A platform's sponsor and provider roles may each be filled by one company or shared by multiple firms.[1] These possibilities define a 2×2 matrix depicting four possible structures for platform governance (Figure 6.2). With a proprietary platform such as eBay, the Miami Yellow Pages or Nintendo Wii, a single firm plays both the sponsor and provider role. A

| | | Who provides the platform (*provider role*)? ||
		One firm	**Many firms**
Who controls platform technology (*sponsor role*)?	**One firm**	*Proprietary* • Macintosh • PlayStation • Monster.com • Federal Express	*Licensing* • Palm OS • American Express-branded MBNA cards • Scientific-Atlanta set-tops
	Many firms	*Joint venture* • CareerBuilder (created by three newspaper groups) • Orbitz (created by several major airlines)	*Shared* • Linux • Visa • DVD • UPC barcode

Figure 6.2   Models for organizing platforms

shared platform such as the UPC barcode, DVD, or Wi-Fi has multiple sponsors who collaborate in developing the platform's technology, then compete with each other in providing differentiated but compatible versions of the platform to users. Rival providers of a shared platform employ compatible technologies; hence, users who rely on different providers (e.g Ubuntu Linux versus Red Hat Linux) can access a common set of complements (for example, any Linux-compatible application). If users switch between rival providers of a shared platform, they forfeit neither platform-specific investments in complements nor time spent learning the platform's rules.

By contrast, rival platforms employ incompatible technologies (e.g. PlayStation versus Wii). Platform-mediated markets comprise sets of rival platforms, each serving distinct platform-mediated networks. For example, the console-based videogame market includes the Xbox, PlayStation and Wii networks; the US credit card market includes the Visa, MasterCard and American Express networks. Two platforms are rivals in the same platform-mediated market if they employ incompatible technologies and if changing the price that users pay to affiliate with one platform influences the other's transaction volumes.

Continuing with analysis of the 2 × 2 matrix, some platforms combine proprietary and shared elements in hybrid governance structures. With a joint venture model, several firms jointly sponsor the platform, but a single entity serves as its sole provider. For example, by jointly creating the online recruitment site CareerBuilder, three large newspaper groups shared development expenses and avoided competing with each other.

Finally, with a licensing model, a single company sponsors the platform, then licenses multiple providers. Several factors may motivate licensing. First, licensees may have unique capabilities to create platform varieties that meet users' differentiated needs. For example, licensing Windows has spawned a greater variety of PC designs than are available with the proprietary Macintosh platform. Second, a sponsor can boost platform adoption by harnessing partners' marketing clout – a key ingredient in JVC's success with the VHS videocassette format, which was more widely licensed than Sony's Betamax (Cusumano et al., 1992). Finally, powerful customers may insist upon a second source of supply to reduce vulnerability to hold-up and supply interruptions (Farrell and Gallini, 1988). Scientific-Atlanta, for example, has licensed its cable set-top technologies to a few 'clone makers' in response to demands from large cable system operators (Eisenmann, 2004b).

2.   HORIZONTAL STRATEGY

Horizontal strategies target a firm's existing and prospective rivals, as with horizontal mergers that consolidate a monopoly.[2] In this context, opening a firm's platform means: (1) allowing a rival platform's users to interact with the focal platform's users; (2) allowing additional parties to participate directly in the focal platform's commercialization; or (3) allowing additional parties to participate directly in the focal platform's technical development. Below, we analyze the conditions under which these three strategies for opening mature platforms will be attractive for sponsors.[3]

Interoperability

As markets mature, the sponsors of rival platforms who previously have eschewed compatibility may find it attractive to make technical modifications that allow interoperability, that is, cross-platform transactions between their respective users (Katz and Shapiro, 1985; Farrell and Saloner, 1992). For example, text-messaging services from various US mobile phone carriers were incompatible for many years, until carriers finally agreed in 2002 to allow their subscribers to exchange messages. When two platforms become interoperable, they become more open: users of platform A can interact with platform B's users, including supply-side users who offer complements.

Properties of converters
Interoperability is achieved through the use of converters, which are also known as adapters or gateways (David and Bunn, 1988). For example,

in 2004, RealNetworks created converter software – called 'Harmony' – that allowed iPod owners to use Real's music store instead of iTunes. However, Real's Harmony initiative was not welcomed by Apple, which had designed iPods and iTunes to only work with each other, not with third-party music management software or music players. Apple broke compatibility with Harmony's through subsequent upgrades to iTunes – a tactic often employed when platform providers are targeted for interoperability against their wishes.

Several properties of converters are salient:

- Converters can be costly. Their expense is typically borne by the weaker platform, as with Real's Harmony (Farrell and Saloner, 1992).
- Converters can be one or two way. For example, early Macintosh computers could read DOS-formatted floppy disks, but the reverse was not true. Conversely, Microsoft Word can both read and save files in WordPerfect format.
- Converters may be developed unilaterally – like Real's Harmony – or bilaterally, depending on engineering considerations and intellectual property protection. If a unilateral converter is technically and legally feasible, then an increase in either platform's profitability is sufficient for its introduction. If technical or legal constraints preclude unilateral efforts, then an increase in total industry profits is a sufficient condition for interoperability, assuming the possibility of side-payments between platforms (e.g. licensing fees). Absent side-payments, an increase in both platforms' profitability is necessary for interoperability (Katz and Shapiro, 1985).
- Finally, due to technical compromises and the functional redundancy required to achieve interoperability, cross-platform transactions can suffer quality degradation compared to intra-platform transactions (Farrell and Saloner, 1992; Ulrich, 1995). Also, platforms may deliberately limit the quality of cross-platform transactions to maintain differentiation (Cremer et al., 2000).

Interoperability with established rivals

When a market is young and first-time users are affiliating with platforms in large numbers, a dominant platform is likely to avoid interoperating with smaller rivals. Once platforms are established and user acquisition rates slow, however, it may make sense for rivals to reconsider compatibility policies – especially if their market shares approach parity. These dynamics are evident in the 2005 instant messaging interoperability agreement negotiated between Yahoo! and Microsoft's MSN, which had similar shares of a maturing market. Likewise, after years of operating incompatible automatic teller machine networks, the comparably sized Cirrus and Plus platforms agreed in 1990 to interoperate (Kauffman and Wang, 2002).

The appeal of interoperability to a platform sponsor will depend on the resulting impact on market size and on the sponsor's market share and profit margin.

Market size If network effects are positive and strong, then users' aggregate willingness to pay (WTP) for platform affiliation should increase when interoperability provides access to a larger total user base. However, increased user WTP does not automatically translate into greater industry revenues. As explained below, platform prices may decline due to heightened competition. Also, interoperability may eliminate the motivation for some users to multi-home (i.e. affiliate with multiple platforms), resulting in lower industry unit volumes.

Market share Post-interoperability market shares will depend on several factors, including: (1) the extent to which platforms are differentiated in terms of standalone properties unrelated to network size; (2) switching costs; (3) multi-homing costs; and (4) converter costs.

Margins The impact of interoperability on platform pricing is not clear-cut. With homogeneous platforms and elastic demand, prices may decline (Katz and Shapiro, 1985). However, in a growing market, interoperability may blunt the drive to race for new users. Also, when converter costs are borne by a weaker platform's users, the dominant platform has an ability and incentive to raise prices (Farrell and Saloner, 1992). Finally, a dominant platform provider's margin may improve if it can charge weaker rivals for interoperability rights.

Entry deterrence
An archetypical challenge in industries with strong network effects pits an established platform provider against an entrant with a superior proprietary technology but no installed base. If the market is still young and expected to grow substantially, then prospective users are more likely to favor the entrant's superior proprietary platform (Katz and Shapiro, 1992; Matutes and Regibeau, 1996). Under these conditions, an incumbent's profit in a duopoly with compatibility may exceed profits under an incompatible scenario (Xie and Sirbu, 1995).

By contrast, if the market is mature and little growth is expected, then the entrant will only be viable if the incumbent offers interoperability.

Under these conditions, the incumbent may be able to deter entry through a credible commitment to avoid interoperability. If the incumbent cannot profitably deter entry but it can license its standard, then there should be an optimal royalty rate that causes the entrant to adopt the incumbent's standard, boosting the incumbent's profit relative to an incompatible scenario (Kulatilaka and Lin, 2006).

Licensing New Providers

When a market is young, serving as sole platform provider offers a big advantage: a proprietary provider can mobilize users through subsidization strategies, without fear of free-riding rival providers draining away profits (Katz and Shapiro, 1986; Eisenmann, 2008). This advantage is less salient once users are on board. The proprietary provider of a mature platform may find it attractive to license additional platform providers while preserving control over platform technology. For example, after serving as sole platform provider for several years, Palm licensed its operating system to Sony, Samsung, Handspring, and many other handheld device manufacturers (Yoffie and Kwak, 2001; Gawer and Cusumano, 2002). Likewise, in 2004, after decades of operating as the sole provider of its proprietary platform, American Express agreed to let MBNA issue American-Express-branded affinity cards. Of course, opening the platform in this manner will introduce competition and put downward pressure on platform pricing. The platform's sponsor can limit pricing pressure and guarantee itself a base level of profits by levying license fees on new providers.

Licensing is most attractive when new providers can offer innovative versions of platform products, rather than simply creating clones. As the market grows and matures, user segments with differentiated needs usually emerge. A single firm may be unable to create a sufficiently broad array of products to satisfy increasingly diverse needs. For example, Palm-licensee Sony built advanced photo, video and audio playback into its Clié PDAs. Likewise, Handspring's Palm-powered Visor had an expansion slot that supported modules for games, eBooks, cellular telephones, MP3 players, and digital cameras. In both cases, licensees provided platform extensions that were beyond Palm's in-house engineering capabilities. Arguably, one reason that Apple terminated the license that allowed Motorola and others to sell Macintosh-compatible hardware during the mid-1990s was its licensees' inability to deliver differentiated products. Instead of expanding the market, Apple's licensing strategy created competitors.

Competition with rival platforms may encourage a focal platform's sponsor to license additional providers with the goal of harnessing network effects and attracting additional users. In this way, some of the rents that are competed away by new platform providers can be recovered in the form of increased fees collected from a larger user base (Parker and Van Alstyne, 2008). Verizon, for example, sought to blunt competition from the AT&T/Apple iPhone alliance by opening its mobile communications platform to a wider array of mobile devices.

Sponsors who license additional platform providers should anticipate conflict with new partners over the division of platform rents as well as the platform's technological trajectory and strategic direction. Palm, for example, faced complaints that its control over OS software gave it an unfair advantage over licensees in designing new devices. In response, Palm separated its hardware and software units into separate public companies in 2003.

Broadening Sponsorship

The strategy discussed immediately above, licensing additional platform providers, involves recruiting partners who create and market variants of platform goods and services. In this scenario, the platform's sponsor retains sole responsibility for designing the platform's core technology. Licensees may engineer variations that extend the platform, but they take its core technology as a given.

A more radical option for opening an established platform entails that platform's sole sponsor inviting other parties to jointly develop the platform's core technology. Opening the sponsorship role has several potential advantages. First, assuming that costs incurred in creating and maintaining a platform's core technology are to some extent fixed and independent of the number of firms involved in development, then the original sponsor should be able to reduce its R&D costs by sharing those costs with additional sponsors. Also, competition among sponsors to incorporate their respective technologies into a common standard may result in survival of the fittest proposals. Finally, open processes for jointly developing technologies invite ongoing feedback, which may yield higher quality products (Chesbrough, 2003; West, 2006).

On the negative side for opening the sponsorship role, innovation in formal standards-setting organizations (SSOs) and similar forums may be slowed by political maneuvering and complex coordination processes (Garud et al., 2002; Simcoe, 2006a). Also, 'least common denominator' dynamics in SSOs may yield lower-quality standards due to 'tyranny of the majority' voting (e.g. when most SSO members lack the skills to work with leading-edge technologies) or due to vested interests (e.g. when incumbents reject an entrant's innovations in order to protect their sunk investments). Finally, with a proprietary model, engineering choices are subject to hierarchical direction rather than multilateral negotiation. Especially when core technologies are immature or in flux, proprietary platforms may engineer more tightly integrated systems that outperform those developed through shared platforms.

It is difficult to generalize about conditions under which the various advantages and drawbacks cited above will weigh more heavily. Consequently, the impact of shared sponsorship on rates of innovation is ambiguous, relative to proprietary models. In his study of handheld computing platforms, Boudreau (2008) observed an inverted-'U' relationship between rates of innovation and platform openness. As a platform moved from low to moderate levels of openness, innovation increased as new providers tailored platform variants that leveraged their distinct capabilities. However, in moving from moderate to high levels of openness, disincentives to invest due to excessive competition eventually offset the positive impact on innovation of new providers' diverse capabilities.

The impact of proprietary versus shared sponsorship models on rates of innovation is also difficult to assess because the models seem to favor different types of innovation. Greenstein (1996) argued that a proprietary platform provider will tend to pursue systemic innovation, leveraging its ability to control the pace and direction of concurrent improvements across all a platform's various subsystems. By contrast, according to Greenstein, divided technical leadership under shared sponsorship is more likely to promote a more modular architecture and to yield component-level innovation.

West (2003) concluded, based on his case studies of IBM, Sun Microsystems and Apple, that established platform sponsors will generally prefer the superior rent-capturing regime of proprietary governance models and will only open the sponsorship role when:

- their established platform faces significant pressure either from rival platforms or from users demanding open standards to avoid lock-in;
- commoditizing the platform significantly enhances its appeal, allowing the original platform sponsor to increase its profits from the sale of complementary products and services.

The first motivation is evident in moves by Netscape, RealNetworks and Sun Microsystems to release their respective platforms' software under open source licenses. Each firm was operating under severe competitive duress when it made the decision to open the sponsorship role: Netscape had lost significant browser market share to Microsoft's Internet Explorer; RealNetworks' streaming media platform had been displaced by Microsoft's Windows Media Player; and Sun's Solaris server operating system was facing low-end competition from both Linux-based products and from Windows Server.

West's second motivation is evident in IBM's decision to champion Linux and to transfer intellectual property rights for its Eclipse software development tools to an independent foundation responsible for steward-ship of an open source community (Baldwin et al., 2003; O'Mahony et al., 2005). In this manner, IBM has been able to promote the sale of its proprietary middleware software that leverages the Linux OS and other open source software. IBM also profits from the sales of system integra-tion services to enterprise users who rely on a mix of open source software and in-house applications developed using Eclipse.

3. VERTICAL STRATEGY

Firms that sponsor platforms face familiar decisions about vertical strat-egy. For example, they must decide when to rely on third-party suppliers versus in-house units for platform components. In general, platform spon-sors approach such 'make–buy' choices in the same way as counterparts in traditional industries. Consequently, we focus here on decisions about vertical strategy that are distinctive to platform-mediated networks.

Vertical strategy is especially complex for platforms with supply-side users that offer complements consumed by demand-side users. Sponsors of such platforms must make three sets of choices regarding to the extent to which they open or close the supply-side user role. First, when upgrad-ing their platforms, they must determine whether to extend backward compatibility to complements developed for past platform generations. Second, sponsors must weigh the advantages of granting exclusive access rights to selected complementors. Finally, sponsors must consider the arguments for and against absorbing certain complements into the core platform. Below, we analyze the conditions under which platform spon-sors are likely to pursue these vertical strategies.

Backward Compatibility

When launching next-generation platform products and services, platform sponsors must decide whether to engineer them to be backward compat-ible with complements developed for previous platform generations. Failing to provide backward compatibility can be construed as closing a platform to the extent that it limits existing complementors' access to new versions of the platform.

With generational change, optimal strategy will depend on whether platform providers can price discriminate between existing and new users (Fudenberg and Tirole, 1998). Openness decisions matter less if platforms can price discriminate. With backward compatibility and no price discrimination, existing users will ignore network effects in their adoption decisions. Specifically, they only will adopt the next-generation platform if its price is less than the increase in standalone utility it offers (i.e. utility independent of network effects), compared to the current generation. Consequently, if technical improvements are large, then a platform provider should market an incompatible next-generation platform to both existing users and unaffiliated prospects. If improvements are modest, then the intermediary should offer a backward-compatible next-generation platform at a price that will appeal to new users but will be ignored by existing users (Choi, 1994).

Platform and Category Exclusivity

Agreements between sponsors and third-party complementors that restrict complementors' platform access have two dimensions – platform exclusivity and category exclusivity. First, agreements may dictate whether or not a given complement can also be made available to a rival platform's users (i.e. whether it can be 'ported' across platforms). For example, versions of the non-exclusive videogame 'Spore' are available for all consoles, whereas early versions of the hit game 'Grand Theft Auto' were available only for the PlayStation platform. Second, agreements may specify whether or not a third-party complementor is granted the sole right to offer complements of a given category to the focal platform's demand-side users. For example, the Mozilla Foundation has given Google's search engine an exclusive position on the Firefox browser's menu bar.

For convenience, we refer to the first type of agreement – a sponsor denying a complementor access to rival platforms – as 'platform exclusivity'. Such agreements make a rival's platform less open. We refer to second type of agreement – a sponsor granting privileged platform access to a complementor – as 'category exclusivity'. Such agreements make the focal platform less open. These 'yes/no' options regarding exclusivity and exclusionary agreements define a 2 × 2 matrix with four possible combinations.

Platform exclusivity
When competing against rival platforms, securing the exclusive affiliation of complementors can accelerate a platform's growth. In order to secure exclusive rights when a platform is young and there is uncertainty about

its prospects, sponsors typically must offer economic concessions to third-party complementors.

After users are mobilized, however, the value of exclusive supply agreements to a platform provider typically will decline – unless exclusivity serves to deter platform entrants. In fact, in a mature market with a dominant proprietary platform and several smaller rivals, the dominant provider may be able to demand exclusivity under terms that prove onerous for complementors. If the dominant provider's market share is large enough, it can levy fees for platform access that are so high that they extract almost all the expected rent from supplying complements. If complementors refuse to pay these fees, they may not be able to generate enough sales from smaller platforms to cover their fixed development costs. In that scenario, they will be forced to exit the market or will be unable to afford market entry in the first place.

Such dynamics are evident in the console-based videogame industry, where one platform often garners a large share of sales for a given generation of competing consoles (Eisenmann and Wong, 2004; Lee, 2007). For example, Sony's PS2, which was launched in 2000, had a 75 percent worldwide share of 128-bit generation console sales through 2005. By then, Sony was positioned to easily force platform exclusivity on every third-party videogame title, but it chose not to do so.

In addition to the risk of provoking antitrust litigation (as Nintendo did by aggressively pursuing exclusivity during earlier generations), strategic considerations may explain Sony's restraint. Game developers and console makers play a repeated game. Sony might have been less inclined to exploit its late-cycle dominance because extortionate demands might reduce developers' willingness to support Sony's next-generation console. Also, as shown by Mantena et al. (2007), late in a console generation, a game developer may have increased incentives to negotiate category exclusivity with a small platform. With fewer developers supplying games to a small platform, its more modest market potential is offset by less intense competition within a given game format.

Category exclusivity

Complementors may be reluctant to make platform-specific investments if they will face a serious problem with 'business stealing' by their close rivals. One way for platform sponsors to profit from this situation is to deliberately exclude all but one supply-side user from this category, then charge that sole user high fees for the privilege of trading with the platform's demand-side users. Of course, the platform provider must ensure that sellers granted this privilege do not abuse their monopoly position; otherwise, demand-side users will avoid the platform. Online car buying services like CarPoint, which forwards consumers' queries to a single dealer in any given geographic territory, have succeeded with this strategy (Eisenmann and Morris, 2000).

More generally, Parker and Van Alstyne (2008) and Rey and Salant (2007) have found that platform sponsors can profit by reducing competition among complementors. This stands in contrast to Shapiro and Varian's (1999) analysis showing that platforms may benefit by commoditizing complements. The difference can be traced to assumptions about the ways in which platforms capture value. In Parker and Van Alstyne's analysis, sponsors can charge fees to complementors as well as to end users – a pricing structure that prevails in the videogame industry, among others. With such a pricing structure, platforms benefit directly from the success of complementors. In contrast, Shapiro and Varian consider a case in which platforms profit solely from sales of platform goods and services to demand-side users. With this pricing structure, cheaper complements increase the demand-side user base.

Absorbing Complements

As platforms mature, proprietary providers may absorb complements previously supplied by third parties. For example, the Windows OS has incorporated many functions that began as standalone software applications from third parties, such as web browsing, disk management, streaming media, modem support and fax utilities. Absorption can be construed as closing a platform to the extent that third-party suppliers of standalone complements find it more difficult to compete once the platform provider bundles a variant of their product.

Efficiency gains

When a complement is consumed by a large fraction of a platform's users, bundling its functionality with the platform provider's core offering may be more convenient for users, who can avoid shopping among alternatives, spend less time configuring the complement, and value a single point of contact for customer service.

Likewise, platform providers can improve efficiency in several ways when they bundle complements (Davis et al., 2002; Eisenmann et al., 2007). First, they should realize economies of scope in customer acquisition activities because they can sell a more valuable bundle with a single marketing campaign. Second, integrated designs may yield quality advantages through simplification of interfaces, as with Apple's iPod/iTunes system.

Third, an absorbed complement may be a platform itself, nested – like a Russian matryoshka doll – inside another platform (e.g. a web browser

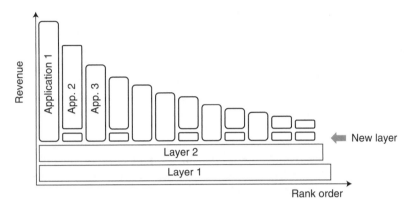

Figure 6.3   Absorbing common complements into new platform layers

vis-à-vis a PC operating system). In such cases, users' willingness-to-pay for the absorbed complement will depend in part, due to indirect network effects, on the availability of additional complements – i.e. a third set of smaller dolls – that leverage the absorbed complement's platform functionality (e.g., 'plug-ins' that extend a browser's capabilities). If bundling results in a dominant share for the platform provider's version of the absorbed complement, then the supply of 'complements to the complement' by third parties should be stimulated by a reduction in their risk of making platform-specific investments (Davis et al., 2002).

Cisco Systems Inc. employs a particularly salient test: absorb complements when competition for a given feature has emerged across multiple industry or category vertical markets (see Figure 6.3). Competitive supply indicates broad demand for the feature, establishes a common standard for downstream development, and harms complementors less since they have already seen their margins erode. Platform firms often extend this test to absorb particularly critical complements. Sorting applications on the basis of popularity, the platform sponsor can choose to own the highest rank order items, as Microsoft has chosen to do for its operating system and game platforms.

Finally, profits can be improved by avoiding double marginalization when bundling complements that otherwise would be supplied by separate monopolists (e.g. Microsoft Windows and Microsoft Office), who each would ignore the externality that their high price imposes upon the other (Nalebuff, 2000; Casadesus-Masanell and Yoffie, 2007).

Other profit improvement opportunities normally available through bundling are less likely to be salient when a platform provider absorbs a complement. Specifically:

Price discrimination   Generally, bundling reduces heterogeneity in consumers' aggregate valuations for a set of items, allowing a firm with market power to extract a larger share of available surplus than it would earn from selling the items separately (Schmalensee, 1984; Bakos and Brynjolfsson, 1999). However, profit gains from price discrimination are weaker to the extent that customers' valuations for bundled items exhibit strong, positive correlation, as is typically the case for complements.

Economies of scope in production   By their nature, complements fulfill different functions, which implies that they will be comprised of different components. This limits opportunities for economies of scope in production and operations from bundling.

Strategic advantages

Beyond the efficiency gains described above, absorbing a complement can also yield strategic advantages. For example, in businesses that entail ongoing customer relationships through subscriptions or upgrades, bundling complements can improve customer retention rates (Eisenmann et al., 2007). To illustrate, assume that a subscriber to a standalone service (i.e. one that is not part of a bundle) is negatively surprised with respect to her initial expectations regarding the utility derived from the service, relative to rival offerings. After factoring in switching costs, if disappointment is big enough, the subscriber may be motivated to change vendors. Now consider the same service consumed as part of a bundle. Assuming that disappointments balance windfalls among bundled elements (i.e. surprises have mean zero and are uncorrelated), then a comparable disappointment with respect to a given feature is less likely to motivate a subscriber to drop the entire bundle. The reason: negative surprises for one bundle element will tend to be offset by positive surprises for another. Even in the absence of positive offsets, a negative deviation for a single component represents a smaller deviation relative to the bundle's value and thus may not exceed the switching threshold.

Under certain conditions, bundling may also allow a monopolist to profitably extend its market power into a complement market (Whinston, 1990; Carlton and Waldman, 2002; Farrell and Weiser, 2003). By foreclosing access to its customers, the monopolist can deny revenue to standalone complement suppliers, weakening them or even forcing their exit (Church and Gandal, 1992 and 2000). Furthermore, using this strategy, a dominant firm may be able to undermine existing rivals or deter entrants in its core market if they are dependent on standalone suppliers for a crucial complement (Nalebuff, 2004).

For example, before acquiring PayPal in 2002, eBay launched its own payment service, Billpoint, in a failed effort to displace PayPal (Eisenmann and Barley, 2006b). Consider a counterfactual in which eBay had banned PayPal and mandated that its auction participants instead use Billpoint. In that scenario, eBay might have caused PayPal's failure, and, in the process, made it more difficult for rival auction sites to serve their users.

Likewise, in 1998, Microsoft launched Windows Media Player (WMP), enveloping RealNetworks' then-dominant streaming media platform (Eisenmann and Carpenter, 2004). Bundled with Windows, WMP rapidly gained share. WMP's compatibility with other PC operating systems was intermittent; for example, new versions did not work with Apple's Macintosh prior to 2000 or after 2003. Hence Microsoft bolstered its Windows OS by effectively closing rivals' access to an important complement.

New market viability
Sometimes a platform sponsor must serve as a supplier in a new applications layer to help build users' confidence that a market will emerge. To resolve 'chicken-and-egg' dilemmas, platform sponsors sometimes step into the user role on one side of their network, producing complements valued by users on the other side. Chicken-and-egg dilemmas become acute when users must make platform-specific investments. Complement suppliers are unlikely to invest without the assurance of access to a critical mass of end users. End users, in turn, are unlikely to affiliate with the platform unless they are confident that complements will be available. For example, when it added contactless integrated circuit technology (called 'FeliCa') to facilitate payments using mobile phones, NTT DoCoMo entered joint ventures to offer electronic money and phone-based credit card services. The availability of these DoCoMo-backed services stimulated consumer adoption of FeliCa, which in turn attracted other payment services to the new application layer (Bradley et al., 2005).

Cross-layer envelopment
Moves like Microsoft's to absorb essential complements play an important role in the evolution of industries that are organized into hierarchical layers. As platforms mature, their providers sometimes embrace modular technologies and cede responsibility for supplying certain complements to partners (Langlois and Robertson, 1992; Suarez and Utterback, 1995; Baldwin and Clark, 2000; Jacobides, 2005; Boudreau, 2008). Reduced integration may result in an industry comprising multiple layers, each with a separate set of suppliers. In the PC industry, for example, the layers consist of semiconductor manufacturing, PC assembly, operating system provision and application software, among others (Grove, 1996; Baldwin

and Clark, 2000). The credit card and telecommunications industries have similarly layered structures (Fransman, 2002; Evans and Schmalensee, 2005).

Over time, dominant players typically emerge within layers that are subject to strong scale economies due to fixed costs and/or network effects. These powerful players will seek to extract a greater share of industry rents and often vie with the focal platform's original sponsor for technical leadership (Fine, 1998; Bresnahan, 1998; Bresnahan and Greenstein, 1999; Gawer and Cusumano, 2002; Iansiti and Levien, 2004; Gawer and Henderson, 2007).

Friction over divided technical leadership is exacerbated as new layers with new leaders emerge. With a modular architecture conducive to experimentation, technological change may yield new, complementary uses for a platform, e.g. browsers or streaming media software *vis-à-vis* PC operating systems. The original platform's sponsor may be slow to integrate the new complement's functionality due to inherent uncertainty about technology and demand. By the time the original platform sponsor absorbs the complement, network effects may have propelled the new complement's pioneering third-party supplier to a dominant position in a new layer, setting the stage for a cross-layer clash between monopolists.

When the absorbed complement is itself a whole platform – as with browsers or streaming media software – a cross-layer attack takes the form of 'platform envelopment' (Eisenmann et al., 2007). Microsoft has enveloped not only RealNetworks' streaming media software but also Netscape's browser (Cusumano and Yoffie, 1998) and Adobe's PDF standard. Likewise, Google has bundled its paid search platform with a new payment service, 'Google Checkout', in a cross-layer envelopment attack on eBay's PayPal unit (Eisenmann and Barley, 2006b). Prospectively, Google is positioned to envelop Microsoft Windows, linking a Linux-based OS to Google's applications (Eisenmann and Herman, 2006).

4.   MANAGING MATURE PLATFORMS

Whether a platform becomes more open or closed as it matures depends on whether it was originally structured as a proprietary or a shared platform. By its nature, a proprietary platform can only become more open. In contrast, a shared platform is already open; the available options are mostly more closed. These dynamics suggest that as proprietary and shared platforms mature, their sponsors and providers will face very different management challenges. Below, we discuss some of these challenges.

Proprietary Platform Priorities: Dealing with Dominance

By definition, a proprietary platform provider is the central participant in its ecosystem. This can be a position of considerable power, especially when the platform is a monopolist in its market. Managers of proprietary platform providers must consider how to leverage their dominance without provoking a damaging response from end users, complementors, regulators and antitrust authorities (Gawer and Cusumano, 2002; Iansiti and Levien, 2004; Yoffie and Kwak, 2006; Gawer and Henderson, 2007).

Successful proprietary platform providers are often able to extract a large share of the economic value generated through platform transactions, leaving little for demand- and supply-side users. When they fully exploit their market power, proprietary platform providers can earn high profits, which may attract entrants who hope to usurp the platform leadership role. If an incumbent has been too aggressive in extracting value, demand- and supply-side users may rally around entrants, as Nintendo learned. When it dominated the console market, Nintendo dealt with third-party game developers in a hard-fisted manner. Consequently, developers were pleased to support Sony when it launched the PlayStation console in 1996.

In the previous section, we explored reasons for platform sponsors to absorb complements, including profit improvement opportunities from price discrimination and economies of scope in production and marketing. Whether or not such absorption is perceived by users to be an abuse of a proprietary sponsor's dominance depends in part on whether the targeted complement was previously produced by just a few third-party suppliers with market power, or in a highly competitive market. In the latter scenario, intense competition will limit the profitability of third-party complementors, so they have less to lose following absorption.

The challenge for managers of proprietary platforms is finding the right balance between behavior that is too timid and too belligerent. Intel and Microsoft executives walk this line every day. Intel's Architecture Lab was deliberately made a cost center in order to promote PC architectural evolution in concert with ecosystem partners (Gawer and Henderson, 2007). Intel's partners might otherwise be deterred from making platform-specific investments if they perceived Intel to be too motivated to maximize profits from each new technology developed by Intel's engineers.

Similarly, with an eye toward the threat of entry, Microsoft has priced Windows below levels that would maximize its short-term profits. Microsoft also deals with emerging threats to its operating system monopoly in an uncompromising manner, as evidenced by Netscape's fate. Microsoft's willingness to move so boldly may be due to lessons learned from IBM.

There are many explanations for IBM's failure to capture a greater share of value from the PC platform it created. One is that IBM worried about structuring coercive contracts with key component suppliers – Microsoft and Intel – that might have been perceived as abusing its monopoly power. According to this view, IBM's managers were too cautious after being hounded by antitrust authorities for decades.

Shared Platform Priorities: Dealing with Stalemates

As a shared platform matures and saturates its market, growth tends to slow and industry profits slide as more providers match 'best-of-breed' features and costs. Attention shifts to the platform's next-generation products and services, which promise renewed growth and higher profits – at least for a while, and at least for some providers. As they did at the platform's inception, firms will strive to incorporate their own technologies into the platform's next-generation standards. By doing so, they can earn license fees, secure a time-to-market lead, or gain an edge in offering proprietary complements (Simcoe, 2006b; Eisenmann, 2008). These are among the few paths to profitability available to a shared platform provider. Absent such advantages, shared platform providers suffer margin pressure because they offer compatible products and their users confront low switching costs.

Competition between sponsors to build their own technologies into next-generation products can lead to the dissolution of a shared platform in two ways. The platform can splinter into incompatible versions. Alternatively, paralysis over the platform's design may retard innovation and expose it to rivals.

Splintering

In designing next-generation platform products, the stakes are sometimes so high that firms would rather wage standards wars than cede technical leadership. For example, since the early 1980s, the Unix operating system has forked into many incompatible variants, each sponsored by a different firm or consortium. Likewise, the recent battle over high-definition DVD formats involved two camps – Blu-ray and HD-DVD – respectively comprising firms that previously had cooperated in offering the original DVD platform.

Stalemates

In other cases, platform participants will prefer the status quo of the current generation's low growth and poor profitability to a full-blown standards war. Stalemates are especially likely when shared platforms rely on established standards-setting organizations (SSOs) with formal voting procedures (Simcoe, 2006a). To attract more members and gain votes, a faction backing a next-generation proposal generally must promise some value to new members, that is, an attractive share of the total profit that platform providers ultimately will earn if the faction's proposal prevails. However, as a faction grows, each member's share of the total profit pool necessarily shrinks. Exploiting this, smaller factions may offer more value and steal some votes. As balloting see-saws, the stalemate festers and the stakes escalate. Month after month, the rival factions spend more on R&D to refine their respective proposals, and the time-to-market gap between eventual winners and losers grows.

Such a stand-off often ends in one of two ways: a 'reset' or a coexistence compromise. With a reset – like the one that ended a recent impasse over next-generation 802.11/Wi-Fi standards (see Box 6.1) – participants merge competing proposals and tweak all technical elements just enough that no player will realize a significant time-to-market advantage. With a coexistence compromise, the SSO simply endorses competing proposals as options under a single umbrella standard, as with the incorporation of both interlaced and progressive scanning in US digital TV standards (Eisenmann, 2004a). As in a classic standards battle, 'coexistence' moves the factional SSO dispute into the marketplace by asking users to choose between competing, incompatible technologies.

Accommodating new platform providers

The management skills needed as a shared platform matures overlap with those required during the platform's early phases. Executives and entrepreneurs must time their proposals carefully, manage intellectual property strategically, practice peer-to-peer diplomacy, and, when necessary, reengineer platform governance arrangements. However, as a shared platform matures, diplomacy is often complicated by the appearance of two types of new players who seek platform leadership roles: start-ups with breakthrough technologies and established firms who leverage platform technologies into new domains.

Start-ups versus incumbents   Start-ups may struggle to gain support for new technologies because their managers lack relationships, experience and clout in standards-setting processes. Logrolling is not a credible option for a newcomer with all its eggs in one basket – especially one that may not survive to fulfill promises. By contrast, diversified incumbents can gain allies for their proposals by lending support elsewhere. Due to the powerful vested interests of incumbents, the next generation of a shared platform may forego a start-up's superior innovations in favor of

BOX 6.1   BRINKSMANSHIP OVER NEXT-GENERATION WI-FI

In 2005, the market for wireless networking equipment built around the Institute of Electrical and Electronics Engineers' (IEEE's) 802.11g (11g) standard – branded as Wi-Fi – was becoming commoditized (Eisenmann and Barley, 2006a). The next generation of Wi-Fi technology, 802.11n (11n), would offer significant improvements over 11g in terms of communications speed and range, and thus had the potential to catalyze industry growth and revitalize flagging prices. However, two competing proposals for 11n had emerged, and neither could garner the 75 percent of IEEE votes required for ratification. After one group pushed for royalty-free licensing, patent-rich companies formed a rival camp. Mobile phone equipment makers (for example, Nokia, Qualcomm) entered the 802.11 standards-setting process for the first time, complicating alliance structures. To make matters worse, a start-up with breakthrough technology – Airgo Networks – was shipping proprietary product based on its interpretation of 11n, hoping to capitalize on the standards stalemate.

Intel, which counted on laptop semiconductor sales for profit growth, worried that more companies would introduce incompatible proprietary solutions. Intel recruited a handful of other large chipmakers from both 11n camps and formed a special interest group, the Enhanced Wireless Consortium (EWC), to forge a compromise 11n proposal. The proposal incorporated technologies from both camps and thus leveled the time-to-market playing field. Since the EWC's organizers collectively sold the lion's share of 11g chips, they could credibly threaten to ship EWC-compliant next-generation products without IEEE ratification. At the same time, Intel's move was risky: working outside the IEEE could provoke a backlash. In the worst case, competitors might gain IEEE approval. Denied access to the trusted 802.11 standard, EWC products would face a tough market battle. However, Intel's gamble paid off: the EWC's proposal eventually secured IEEE approval.

The case of 802.11n illustrates some of the challenges that shared platform providers encounter when they create next-generation products. Firms that incorporate their technologies into new standards gain a big edge. As firms maneuver for this

advantage, an impasse can easily result – especially when platform partners rely on SSOs with democratic voting procedures.
Problems are compounded when new players with new technical
and business priorities – like mobile phone manufacturers – join
the platform. Likewise, start-ups such as Airgo with disruptive
technology and a 'do-or-die' attitude can draw fire from incumbents. In a complex political environment, brinksmanship by a
small, powerful coalition – 'accept our proposal, or else' – is one
way to break the deadlock.

'least common denominator' technology that puts all providers on a level
playing field. Alternatively, slow-moving incumbents with political clout
may deliberately stall standards-setting processes while their engineers try
to match the start-up's innovations.

New demands in new domains As a shared platform evolves, it often
attracts new providers who apply the platform's technology in new
domains. For instance, stock exchanges had to accommodate a surge in
trading through online brokerage firms. Likewise, Wi-Fi technologies are
moving beyond laptops into a range of portable devices including music
players, gaming devices, and mobile phones (Eisenmann and Barley,
2006a). When negotiating over next-generation technologies, established
firms that extend a shared platform into new domains will lobby hard to
ensure that their technical and strategic priorities are met. For example,
when formulating the 802.11n standard for the next generation of Wi-Fi,
mobile phone makers were highly concerned about power management,
since their phones have smaller batteries than laptops. After Motorola,
Nokia and Qualcomm became involved in the 802.11 committees of the
IEEE, an already complex political environment turned into a Byzantine
web of shifting alliances (see Box 6.1).

Centralizing governance

Vertical governance As described above, a mature platform's sponsor
may choose to absorb complements previously supplied by third parties,
especially when the complements are consumed by a large fraction of the
platform's end users. Upon absorption, the functionality of such complements becomes a part of the platform that other complementors can build
upon (e.g. developing location-aware applications that rely on location-
sensing technologies built into smart phones and laptops). In this way and

through other mechanisms described above, absorption may increase the aggregate value realized by participants in a platform-mediated network.

However, not all parties benefit uniformly from a post-absorption increase in platform value. Third-party complementors whose functionality is absorbed will likely see their sales shrink; at the extreme, they may be forced to exit the market. Consequently, in a shared platform lacking a strong sponsor, complementors might rationally choose to withhold their functionality from the platform, profiting instead by selling proprietary goods. Parker and Van Alstyne (2008) explored conditions under which complementors prefer to submit to decisions made by a platform sponsor regarding the timing of complement absorption. A strong sponsor can credibly commit to defer absorption long enough to allow a third-party complementor to earn an acceptable return on platform-specific investments. Under fairly general conditions, complementors prefer that a strong sponsor solve the coordination problem – even at the cost of eventually having their applications folded into the platform.

In related work, Baldwin and Woodard (2007) analyzed the tension between a firm's private incentives and the health of its modular industry cluster. Baldwin and Woodard noted that investors are likely to care more about cluster profits than those of an individual firm. Consequently, investors should prefer that platform leaders not abuse their power by moving into adjacent layers too aggressively, lest the cluster's growth be impeded.

Horizontal governance Reengineering horizontal governance arrangements may also be a priority as a shared platform matures. To prevent splintering and stalemates, platform partners may recognize a need to create or strengthen a central authority that can dictate priorities (Farrell and Saloner, 1988). Likewise, when a shared platform faces an external threat, a strong central authority can rally a response.

The joint sponsors of a shared platform can centralize its governance in at least two different ways. The first approach is to create a 'special interest group' (SIG) – such as the Enhanced Wireless Consortium organized by Intel to end an impasse in the IEEE over 802.11n standards (see Box 6.1). Likewise, to end a stalemate over standards for web services technologies, IBM and Microsoft organized an SIG, the Web Services Interoperability Organization (Eisenmann and Suarez, 2005).

SIGs are often used to exert control over formal standards-setting organizations (SSOs), but they usually do not seek to supplant SSOs. Specifically, SIGs serve as forums where a subset of powerful platform providers can privately negotiate technical specifications and strategic priorities. To facilitate bargaining, SIG membership typically excludes minor players or parties deemed to be 'difficult'. When SIG participants reach agreement on standards and strategy, they present their proposal to the relevant SSO as a *fait accompli*.

A second approach to centralizing governance of a shared platform is available when platform participants coordinate their efforts through a dedicated association rather than an established SSO. Assuming that the association can earn material profits by charging fees to platform providers and users for access to shared infrastructure and services, its members can take the association public. By contrast, an IPO (initial public offering) would not be practical for an SSO such as the IEEE, which earns only modest membership fees and – by charter – is not empowered to collect intellectual property licensing fees or to invest in shared services and infrastructure.

After an association becomes a publicly traded company, its directors and senior managers have a fiduciary duty to advance shareholders' interests. While original association members may retain board seats in the new public company, their ability to veto strategic initiatives solely for self-serving reasons is limited. This can streamline strategic decision-making processes, compared to processes in a private association.

For example, to facilitate a move into computerized trading (among other reasons) the New York Stock Exchange (NYSE) implemented a far-reaching reorganization, culminating in a 2006 IPO. NYSE had previously been owned and controlled by specialists who held seats on the exchange – and whose profits from human-mediated transactions were threatened by a shift to computerized trading. In the same vein, MasterCard completed an IPO in 2006 and Visa followed suit in 2008. With stronger central governance, the credit card associations will be better able to promote the adoption of smart cards and Internet-friendly technologies.

CONCLUSION

Platform openness occurs at multiple levels depending on whether participation is unrestricted at the (1) demand-side user (end user), (2) supply-side user (application developer), (3) platform provider, or (4) platform sponsor levels. These distinctions in turn give rise to multiple strategies for managing openness. Horizontal strategies for managing openness entail licensing, joint standard setting and technical interoperability with rival platforms. Vertical strategies for managing openness entail backward compatibility, platform and category exclusivity, and absorption of complements. Each strategy grants or restricts access for one of the four platform participants.

When proprietary platforms mature, they are opened to encompass new providers. Once network mobilization winds down and free-rider problems are no longer salient, proprietary platform sponsors may find it attractive to license additional providers to serve market segments with diverse needs. Naturally, these new providers will seek a say in the platform's direction: they will try to force a previously proprietary platform to open its governance.

Likewise, as shared platforms mature, their renewal may hinge on partners ceding power to a central authority that can set priorities and settle disputes over who will provide next-generation technologies. This closes the governance of a previously open platform. Thus, forces tend to push both proprietary and shared platforms over time toward hybrid governance models typified by central control over platform technology and shared responsibility for serving users.

NOTES

1. The balance of this section is adapted from Eisenmann (2008).
2. The term 'horizontal strategy' is also used to describe efforts in diversified firms to integrate product offerings and/or functional activities across business units. Such strategies are employed by firms offering multi-platform bundles, but the distinction between 'open' and 'closed' is not relevant in this context. See Eisenmann et al. (2007), for analysis of envelopment strategies encompassing bundles of weak substitutes or functionally unrelated platforms.
3. Portions of the following subsections on interoperability, licensing and backward compatibility are adapted from Eisenmann (2007).

REFERENCES

Armstrong, M. (2006), 'Competition in two-sided markets', *RAND Journal of Economics*, **37** (3), 668–91.

Bakos, Y. and E. Brynjolfsson (1999), 'Bundling information goods: pricing, profits and efficiency', *Management Science*, **45**, 1613–630.

Baldwin, C. and K. Clark (2000), *Design Rules, Vol. 1: The Power of Modularity*, Cambridge, MA: MIT Press.

Baldwin, C. and C. Woodard (2007), 'Competition in modular clusters', Harvard Business School Working Paper 08-042.

Baldwin, C., S. O'Mahony and J. Quinn (2003), 'IBM and Linux (A)', Harvard Business School Case 903-083.

Besen, S. and J. Farrell (1994) 'Choosing how to compete: strategies and tactics in standardization', *Journal of Economic Perspectives*, **8** (2), 117–31.

Boudreau, K. (2008), 'Opening the platform vs. opening the complementary good? The effect on product innovation in handheld computing', HEC Working Paper available on SSRN: abstract = 1251167.

Bradley, S., T. Eisenmann and M. Egawa (2005). 'NTT DoCoMo, Inc.: Mobile FeliCa', Harvard Business School Case 805-124.

Bresnahan, T. (1998), 'New modes of competition: implications for the future structure of the computer industry', in Jeffrey Eisenach and Thomas Lenard (eds), *Competition, Convergence, and the Microsoft Monopoly: Antitrust in the Digital Marketplace*, Boston, MA: Kluwer, pp. 155–208.

Bresnahan, T. and S. Greenstein (1999), 'Technological competition and the structure of the computer industry', *Journal of Industrial Economics*, **47**, 1–40.

Carlton, D. and M. Waldman (2002), 'The strategic use of tying to preserve and create market power in evolving industries', *RAND Journal of Economics*, **33** (2), 194–220.

Casadesus-Masanell, R. and D. Yoffie (2007), 'Wintel: cooperation and conflict', *Management Science*, **53** (4), 584–98.

Chesbrough, H. (2003), *Open Innovation: The New Imperative for Creating and Profiting from Technology*, Boston, MA: Harvard Business School Press.

Choi, J. (1994), 'Network externality, compatibility choice, and planned obsolescence', *Journal of Industrial Economics*, **42**, 167–82.

Church, J. and N. Gandal (1992), 'Network effects, software provision, and standardization', *Journal of Industrial Economics*, **40**, 85–103.

Church, J. and N. Gandal (2000), 'Systems competition, vertical merger, and foreclosure', *Journal of Economics and Management Strategy*, **9**, 25–51.

Cremer, J., P. Rey and J. Tirole (2000), 'Connectivity in the commercial Internet', *Journal of Industrial Economics*, **47**, 433–72.

Cusumano, M.A., Y. Mylonadis and R. Rosenbloom (1992), 'Strategic maneuvering and mass-market dynamics: the triumph of VHS over Beta', *Business History Review*, **66**, 51–94.

Cusumano, M.A. and D. Yoffie (1998), *Competing on Internet Time: Lessons from Netscape and its Battle with Microsoft*, New York: Free Press.

David, P. and J. Bunn (1988), 'The economics of gateway technologies and network evolution: lessons from electricity supply history', *Information Economics and Policy*, **3**, 165–202.

David, P. and S. Greenstein (1990), 'The economics of compatibility standards: an introduction to recent research', *Economics of Innovation and New Technology*, **1**, 3–41.

Davis, S., J. MacCrisken and K. Murphy (2002), 'Economic perspectives on software design: PC operating systems and platforms', in David Evans (ed.), *Microsoft, Antitrust and the New Economy: Selected Essays*, Boston, MA: Kluwer, pp. 361–419.

Economides, N. and E. Katsamakas (2006), 'Two-sided competition of proprietary vs. open source technology platforms and the implications for the software industry', *Management Science*, **52** (7), 1057–71.

Eisenmann, T. (2004a), 'High-definition TV: The Grand Alliance', Harvard Business School Case 804-103.

Eisenmann, T. (2004b), 'Scientific-Atlanta, Inc.', Harvard Business School Case 804-194.

Eisenmann, T. (2007), 'Managing networked businesses: course overview for educators', Harvard Business School Note 807-104.

Eisenmann, T. (2008), 'Managing proprietary and shared platforms', *California Management Review*, **50** (4), 31–53.

Eisenmann, T. and L. Barley (2006a), 'Atheros Communications', Harvard Business School Case 806-093.

Eisenmann, T. and L. Barley (2006b), 'PayPal Merchant Services', Harvard Business School Case 806-188.

Eisenmann, T. and S. Carpenter (2004), 'RealNetworks Rhapsody', Harvard Business School Case 804-142.

Eisenmann, T. and K. Herman (2006), 'Google, Inc.', Harvard Business School Case 806-105.

Eisenmann, T. and G. Morris (2000), 'CarPoint in 1999', Harvard Business School Case 800-328.

Eisenmann, T., G. Parker and M. Van Alstyne (2007), 'Platform envelopment', Harvard Business School Working Paper 07-104.

Eisenmann, T., G. Parker and M. Van Alstyne (2006), 'Strategies for two-sided markets', *Harvard Business Review*, **84** (10), 92–101.

Eisenmann, T. and F. Suarez (2005), 'Sun Microsystems, Inc.: web services strategy', Harvard Business School Case 805-095.

Eisenmann, T. and J. Wong (2004), 'Electronic Arts in online gaming', Harvard Business School Case 804-140.

Evans, D., A. Hagiu and R. Schmalensee (2006), *Invisible Engines: How Software Platforms Drive Innovation and Transform Industries*, Boston, MA: MIT Press.

Evans, D. and R. Schmalensee (2005), *Paying with Plastic: The Digital Revolution in Buying and Borrowing*, Cambridge, MA: MIT Press.

Evans, D. and R. Schmalensee (2007), *The Catalyst Code: The Strategies Behind the World's Most Dynamic Companies*, Boston, MA: Harvard Business School Press.

Farrell, J. and N. Gallini (1988), 'Second sourcing as a commitment: monopoly incentives to attract competition', *Quarterly Journal of Economics*, **103**, 673–94.

Farrell, J. and G. Saloner (1985), 'Standardization, compatibility, and innovation', *RAND Journal of Economics*, **16**, 70–83.

Farrell, J. and G. Saloner (1988), 'Coordination through committees and markets', *RAND Journal of Economics*, **19** (2), 235–52.

Farrell, J. and G. Saloner (1992), 'Converters, compatibility, and the control of interfaces', *Journal of Industrial Economics*, **40** (1), 9–35.

Farrell, J. and P. Weiser (2003), 'Modularity, vertical integration, and open-access policies: Towards a convergence of antitrust and regulation in the Internet age', *Harvard Journal of Law and Technology*, **17**, 86–118.

Fine, C. (1998), *Clockspeed: Winning Industry Control in the Age of Temporary Advantage*, New York: Basic Books.

Fransman, M. (2002), *Telecoms in the Internet Age*, Oxford: Oxford University Press.

Fudenberg, D. and J. Tirole (1998), 'Upgrades, tradeins and buybacks', *RAND Journal of Economics*, **29**, 235–58.

Garud, R., S. Jain and A. Kumaraswamy (2002), 'Institutional entrepreneurship in the sponsorship of common technological standards: the case of Sun Microsystems and Java', *Academy of Management Journal*, **45**, 196–214.

Gawer, A. and M. Cusumano (2002), *Platform Leadership: How Intel, Microsoft, and Cisco Drive Industry Innovation*, Boston, MA: Harvard Business School Press.

Gawer, A. and R. Henderson (2007), 'Platform owner entry and innovation in complementary markets: evidence from Intel', *Journal of Economics and Management Strategy*, **16**, 1–34.

Greenstein, S. (1996), 'Invisible hand versus invisible advisors: coordination mechanisms in economic networks', in Eli Noam and Aine Nishuilleabhain (eds), *Private Networks, Public Objectives*, Amsterdam and New York: North-Holland, pp. 135–61.

Grove, A. (1996), *Only the Paranoid Survive: How to Exploit the Crisis Points that Challenge Every Company and Career*, New York: Doubleday.

Hagiu, A. (2006), 'Proprietary vs. open two-sided platforms and social efficiency', American Enterprise Institute–Brookings Joint Center Working Paper 06-12.

Henderson, R. and K. Clark (1990), 'Architectural innovation: the reconfiguration of existing product technologies and the failure of established firms', *Administrative Science Quarterly*, **35**, 9–30.

Iansiti, M. and R. Levien (2004), *The Keystone Advantage: What the New Dynamics of Business Ecosystems Mean for Strategy, Innovation, and Sustainability*, Boston, MA: Harvard Business School Press.

Jacobides, M. (2005), 'Industry change through vertical disintegration: how and why markets emerged in mortgage banking', *Academy of Management Journal*, **48**, 465–98.

Katz, M. and C. Shapiro (1985), 'Network externalities, competition, and compatibility', *American Economic Review*, **75**, 424–40.

Katz, M. and C. Shapiro (1986), 'Technology adoption in the presence of network externalities', *Journal of Political Economy*, **94**, 822–41.

Katz, M. and C. Shapiro (1992), 'Product introduction with network externalities', *Journal of Industrial Economics*, **40**, 55–83.

Kauffman, R. and Y. Wang (2002), 'The network externalities hypothesis and competitive network growth', *Journal of Organizational Computing*, **12**, 59–83.

Kulatilaka, N. and L. Lin (2006), 'Impact of licensing on investment and financing of technology department', *Management Science*, **52** (12), December, 1824–37.

Langlois, R. and P. Robertson (1992), 'Networks and innovation in a modular system: Lessons from the microcomputer and stereo component industries', *Research Policy*, **21**, 297–313.

Lee, R. (2007), 'Vertical integration and exclusivity in platform and two-sided markets', NET Institute Working Paper 07-39 available at SSRN, abstract = 1022682.

Lee, D. and H. Mendelson (2008), 'Divide and conquer: competing with free technology under network effects', *Production and Operations Management*, **17**, 12–28.

Mantena, R., R. Sankaranarayanan and S. Viswanathan (2007), 'Exclusive licensing in complementary network industries', NET Institute Working Paper 07-04 available at SSRN, abstract = 979330.

Matutes, C. and P. Regibeau (1996), 'A selective review of the economics of standardization: entry deterrence, technological progress and international competition', *European Journal of Political Economy*, **12**, 183–209.

Nalebuff, B. (2000), 'Competing against bundles', in P. Hammond and G. Myles (eds), *Incentives, Organization, and Public Economics*, Oxford: Oxford University Press, pp. 323–36.

Nalebuff, B. (2004), 'Bundling as an entry deterrent', *Quarterly Journal of Economics*, **119**, 159–87.

O'Mahony, S., F. Diaz and E. Mamas (2005), 'IBM and Eclipse (A)', Harvard Business School Case 906-007.

Parker, G. and M. Van Alstyne, (2000), 'Information complements substitutes and strategic product design', Working Paper available at SSRN, abstract = 249585.

Parker, G. and M. Van Alstyne (2005), 'Two-sided network effects: a theory of information product design', *Management Science*, **51**, 1494–504.
Parker, G. and M. Van Alstyne (2008), 'Innovation, openness, and platform control', working paper available at SSRN, abstract = 1079712.
Rey, P. and D. Salant (2007), 'Abuse of dominance and licensing of intellectual property', IDEI Working Paper.
Rochet, J.-C. and J. Tirole (2003), 'Platform competition in two-sided markets', *Journal of the European Economic Association*, **1** (4), 990–1029.
Schmalensee R. (1984), 'Gaussian demand and commodity bundling', *Journal of Business*, **57**, 211–30.
Shapiro, C. and H. Varian (1999), 'The art of standards wars', *California Management Review*, **41** (2), 8–32.
Simcoe T. (2006a), 'Delay and de jure standardization: exploring the slowdown in Internet standards development', in Shane Greenstein and Victor Stango (eds), *Standards and Public Policy*, Cambridge, UK: Cambridge University Press, pp. 260–95.
Simcoe T. (2006b), 'Open standards and intellectual property rights', in H. Chesbrough, W. Vanhaverbeke and J. West (eds), *Open Innovation: Researching a New Paradigm*, Oxford: Oxford University Press, pp. 161–83.
Suarez, F. and J. Utterback (1995), 'Dominant designs and the survival of firms', *Strategic Management Journal*, **16**, 415–30.
Ulrich, K. (1995), 'The role of product architecture in the manufacturing firm', *Research Policy*, **24** (3), 419–40.
West, J. (2003), 'How open is open enough? Melding proprietary and open source platform strategies', *Research Policy*, **32**, 1259–85.
West J. (2006), 'The economic realities of open standards: black, white and many shades of gray', in Shane Greenstein and Victor Stango (eds), *Standards and Public Policy*, Cambridge, UK: Cambridge University Press, pp. 87–122.
Whinston, M. (1990), 'Tying, foreclosure and exclusion', *American Economic Review*, **80**, 837–59.
Xie, J. and M. Sirbu (1995), 'Price competition and compatibility in the presence of positive demand externalities', *Management Science*, **41**, 909–26.
Yoffie, D. and M. Kwak (2001), *Judo Strategy: Turning Your Competitors' Strength to Your Advantage*, Boston, MA: Harvard Business School Press.
Yoffie, D. and M. Kwak (2006), 'With friends like these: the art of managing complementors', *Harvard Business Review*, **84** (9), 88–98.

7. Platform rules: multi-sided platforms as regulators

Kevin J. Boudreau and Andrei Hagiu[1]

INTRODUCTION

In 1983, the videogame market in the USA collapsed, leading to bankruptcy for more than 90 percent of game developers, as well as Atari, manufacturer of the dominant game console at the time. The main reason was a 'lemons' market failure: because it had not developed a technology for locking out unauthorized games, Atari was unable to prevent the entry of opportunistic developers, who flooded the market with poor-quality games. At a time when consumers had few ways to distinguish good from bad games, bad games drove out good ones. The videogame market was resurrected six years later only when Nintendo entered with a set of draconian policies to regulate third-party developers more tightly. Central to Nintendo's strategy was the use of a security chip designed to lock out any game not directly approved by Nintendo.

Twenty-five years later, in the summer of 2008, Apple launched the iPhone store (a digital store of third-party applications for its immensely popular iPhone) at a time when lemons problems had become less of an issue, with widely available reviews and ratings available on the Internet. Even so, Apple reserved the right to verify and exclude any third-party application it did not deem appropriate. And it exerted that right swiftly by taking down an application named 'I Am Rich', which cost $999 (the maximum price allowed by Apple), while doing nothing more than presenting a glowing ruby on the buyer's iPhone screen. Apple also kicked out Podcaster, an application that would allow users to download podcasts without going through iTunes store.

The Atari, Nintendo and Apple examples illustrate instances in which non-price instruments were a critical part of strategy for multi-sided platforms (MSPs) – platforms that enable interactions between multiple groups of surrounding consumers and 'complementors'.[2] This chapter provides a general and basic conceptual framework for interpreting non-price instruments, which analogizes MSPs as private regulators; and provides evidence in support of this view: MSPs regulate access to and interactions around MSPs through nuanced combinations of a long list of legal, technological, informational and other instruments – including price setting.

MSPs are characterized by interactions and interdependence between their multiple sides. For example, more participation on one side attracts more participation on the other side(s) and vice versa, and thus network effects will often emerge (Katz and Shapiro, 1994; Rochet and Tirole, 2006). For this reason, the thrust of prior work has been on the question of how to get the different sides around an MSP 'on board' in large numbers, while setting up a pricing model that maximizes platform profits (e.g. Caillaud and Jullien, 2003; Parker and Van Alstyne, 2005; Rochet and Tirole, 2006; Armstrong, 2006; Eisenmann et al., 2006; Hagiu, 2007). Empirical work on MSPs has largely focused on quantifying network effects and their impact on platform adoption and use (e.g. Nair et al., 2004; Rysman, 2004; Clements and Ohashi, 2005; Lee, 2008). Overall, the literature has emphasized arm's-length pricing as the central strategic instrument used by platform owners to intermediate the ecosystem of users and complementors surrounding an MSP.

A number of provocative analyses, however, have suggested a richer picture of the role of MSPs and limitations to arm's-length market interactions. Perhaps most broadly, metaphors of 'open' and 'closed' platforms convey something of how restrictive or liberal a platform may be in its dealings with surrounding constituents (Shapiro and Varian, 1998; West, 2003; Hagiu, 2007; Boudreau, 2008a; Parker and Van Alstyne, 2008). Several studies have also begun to document a variety of roles played by platform owners, including assuring 'coherent' technical development and coordination among contributors to an MSP ecosystem (Gawer and Cusumano, 2002); designing the technical architecture that frames interactions (Prencipe et al., 2003); encouraging complementors to make investments (Farrell and Katz, 2000; Gawer and Henderson, 2007); and generally 'managing' and 'maintaining the health' of the ecosystem (Iansiti and Levien, 2004). Gawer and Cusumano (2002), in particular, point to several non-price levers, their 'four levers of platform leadership', including: firm boundaries and internal organization of the platform owner; product technology; and relationships with platform participants.

The nature of these activities clearly goes beyond governing economic activity solely within the boundaries of platform owners and extends to rule making and regulating the conduct of firms beyond their economic boundaries, as suggested by several authors. For example, Rochet and Tirole (2004) characterize MSPs as a 'licensing authority'. Iansiti and Levien (2004) suggest that a platform (in their language, 'keystone') 'regulates connections among ecosystem members' so as to 'increase diversity and productivity'. Farrell and Katz (2000, p. 431) go as far as to speculate that 'the monopolist [platform owner] plays a role like that of a "public interest" regulator. The monopolist has some incentives to shape the market for the complementary component efficiently because the firm captures many of the efficiency benefits . . .'

The primary contribution of this chapter is to present evidence supporting these notions of a regulatory role of MSPs that goes well beyond price setting and includes imposing rules and constraints, creating inducements and otherwise shaping behaviors. These various non-price instruments essentially solve what would otherwise be (multi-sided) 'market failures'. We use four primary case studies to illustrate these points. Two case studies are digital MSPs: Facebook and TopCoder. To emphasize some level of generality of our analysis, we also examine two non-digital platforms: the Roppongi Hills 'mini-city' and Harvard Business School.

We find that the scope for market failures in all of these cases is rather extensive, involving externalities, information asymmetries, complexity, non-pecuniary motivations and uncertainty. Thus 'getting the prices right' was not nearly enough to assure the proper functioning of the MSP ecosystem on its own. In the case studies, regulation of access and interactions around MSPs was quite clearly implemented by applying a variety of contractual, technical and informational instruments – rather than simply price setting. Thus it was clear that MSPs were also rather effective in the regulatory role within their ecosystems. We found no conclusive evidence of excessive profit taking or a deadweight loss associated with platform regulation.

Apart from their direct implications for platform strategy, these findings also contribute to the longstanding debate on whether network effects imply externalities and market failures – and a concomitant need for regulation (e.g. Chou and Shy, 1990; Liebowitz and Margolis, 1994; Merges, 2008; Spulber, 2008; Church et al., 2008). The cases here show clear non-pecuniary externalities that could neither be internalized through spontaneous coordination of agents nor through (just) price setting by a central coordinating platform. Further, the potential coordination problems went well beyond just adoption and participation to an endless array of distributed actions and decision making of agents already 'on board' a platform. Unlike this earlier literature, which emphasizes the role of public authorities, our emphasis is on the role the MSP itself plays in regulating the surrounding ecosystem. This chapter also contributes evidence on the precise microeconomic workings of network effects and how these deviate from canonical models (in which network value simply increases with adoption and usage), as have several other contributions (e.g. Suarez, 2005; Boudreau, 2008b; Tucker, 2008).

In the next section we lay out a basic and general conceptual framework for interpreting 'platform regulation' in a large ecosystem. This framework is used to guide and interpret the case studies. The following section contains four case studies to investigate whether the principles highlighted in the conceptual framework regarding platform regulation do in fact appear in practice. Then we discuss the broad insights drawn from the case studies, and conclude.

1.   CONCEPTUAL FRAMEWORK AND HYPOTHESIS DEVELOPMENT

Following the aforementioned accounts and casual observation, the strategies used by MSPs to manage relations in the surrounding ecosystem may involve a long list of instruments beyond just setting prices. In the case of computer platforms, for example, non-price instruments include establishing technical standards and interfaces, rules and procedures, defining the division of tasks, providing support and documentation, sharing information and so on and so forth. Rather than attempt to develop a guiding framework that attempts to contemplate these particulars, we instead lay out a very basic and general set of principles to guide the following empirical analysis.

The gist of our argument, further elaborated in following discussion, is as follows: (1) the markets around MSPs are inherently riddled with externalities and other sources of coordination problems, creating economic scope for regulation; (2) MSPs are in a unique position to be focal, private regulators by virtue of the one-to-many asymmetric relationship between them and the other players; and (3) owners of MSPs have ample instruments, incentives and resources to carry out the task of regulation.

2.   MULTI-SIDED MARKET FAILURE AND THE LIMITS OF 'GETTING THE PRICES RIGHT'

The most fundamental hypothesis that sets forth our analysis is that 'getting the prices right' may not be enough for assuring efficient distributed production and contributions around an MSP. Groups of complementors and consumers around MSPs are, by definition, riddled with externalities. At the very minimum, this is because individual agents do not wholly internalize the effect of their own decisions to participate in a particular MSP on other users and complementors (i.e. network effects). Hence there should be scope, in principle, for a 'central player' to help coordinate other players to achieve a better outcome than would be achieved in ungoverned production. This point has been made in relation to the use of pricing and subsidies in research on 'strategic sponsorship' of ecosystems (Katz and Shapiro, 1986; Shapiro and Varian, 1998), 'internalizing complementary externalities' in multi-component systems (Davis and Murphy, 2000; Farrell and Weiser, 2003), multi-sided markets (see references above) and a stream that focuses on the question of whether network effects are in fact network externalities (Liebowitz and Margolis, 1990, 1994; Clements, 2004; Church et al., 2008).

But price setting may not always be enough. To start with, in the presence of network effects, self-fulfilling expectations can give rise to multiple stable equilibria of participation levels on an MSP for a given set of prices (Katz and Shapiro, 1994; Farrell and Saloner, 1992; Hagiu, 2008). Prices are then clearly insufficient for inducing the desired market outcome. Recent work suggests much more scope for market failures around an MSP that cannot be resolved through price setting alone. For example, detailed descriptive analysis of Intel's role as a platform leader in personal computing, provided by Gawer and Cusumano (2002) and Gawer and Henderson (2007), suggests that profound coordination problems are forever looming. These go well beyond assuring adoption and relate to particular actions taken once complementors and consumers have adopted or entered the ecosystem: investments and design decisions, timing of product introduction and upgrades, etc. Aside from externalities and interdependencies, the complex web of activities going on around an MSP will create a great deal of information asymmetry and strategic uncertainty. Therefore it may be a challenge simply to maintain 'coherence' (Gawer and Cusumano, 2002) of an ecosystem, let alone any sort of optimal behavior. These points lead to our first two hypotheses:

Hypothesis 1: Markets around MSPs are riddled with externalities and other sources of coordination problems.

Hypothesis 2: Price setting and subsidies are insufficient to attain the best possible ecosystem performance from the MSPs' perspective.

3. REGULATING AN ECOSYSTEM

We now turn to outlining essential characteristics of MSP ecosystem production and how this might be governed, to guide the case studies to follow. To interpret a potentially wide array of strategic instruments an MSP might use to shape conduct in the surrounding actors, we analogize the MSP to a private regulator. It proves useful to begin by contrasting 'ecosystem production' by autonomous firms and regulation by a public authority before clarifying what platform regulation should involve.

Basic Terms

In simplest terms, a business ecosystem may be viewed as a collection of (many) firms engaged in joint production, whose choices and actions are interdependent. Let A denote the cumulative set of all payoff-relevant decisions or actions to be taken by all ecosystem participants. Actions might include decisions regarding entry, investments, technology and design choices, pricing, advertising, and a potentially very long list of other decisions taken across the ecosystem. In stressing the governance role of MSPs, we assume that the platform owner does not directly take actions itself. The total value created by the ecosystem, V, is the sum of value created by individual firms, indexed by i, $V = \sum_i v_i$. Value is a function of A. Decision making is distributed: we may think of all actions A as partitioned across firms. The subset of actions performed by firm i is a_i. Interdependence is synonymous with the presence of externalities: a participant's choice of private action(s) a_i impacts the returns to taking other actions, other participants' payoffs, and therefore overall value creation.[3]

Benchmark I: Autonomous, Unregulated Firms in an Ecosystem

Left to make its own choices, an individual firm in an ecosystem will naturally maximize its own private value, v_i, which amounts to choosing actions according to $argmax_{\{ai\}} v_i$.

Obviously, in this context the combination of actions that leads to greatest surplus, the 'first-best' solution, will almost never be attained. The usual problems of colluding, cooperating and coordinating – whether through formal or informal commitments – should only be more difficult in an ecosystem with potentially vast numbers of firms engaging in distributed decision making across a wide body of decisions. Further, where it is the heterogeneity of firms from which the ecosystem largely derives its value, direct transfers of decision rights will likely not be practicable; the inalienability and non-transferability of underlying organizational assets and knowledge should preclude transferring underlying decision rights. Economic outcomes might not even reach the 'second-best' outcome – in which all parties act in a self-interested fashion while strategically anticipating each other's actions – given the aforementioned complexity, strategic uncertainty and asymmetry of information.

Benchmark II: Public Regulator of an Ecosystem

The inability to achieve first- and perhaps even second-best outcomes opens up the possibility of value-enhancing public regulation. A perfect public regulator, with its powers to prohibit, compel and coerce (Stigler, 1971), may set up rules or restrictions. This effectively amounts to directly choosing actions, A, in our framework. In contrast to autonomous firms, the public regulator will therefore – in principle – attempt to implement actions leading yielding the first-best outcome, or $argmax_{\{A\}} V = \sum_i v_i$.

However, there are well-known limitations to regulation by a public authority. Even in the best of circumstances, public regulators tend to have access to just a few blunt instruments. Thus the public regulator will not be able to influence, let alone control, the full set of a_is, A. Typical instruments include regulating entry (often when the public controls a scarce resource, such as radio spectrum), regulating price schedules to customers, setting simple quality and service standards and imposing non-discriminatory trade practices (Kahn, 1988; Laffont and Tirole, 1993; Armstrong and Sappington, 2007). In implementing just a subset of A, the public regulator must also anticipate (many) firms' (many) responses to its imposition of rules and regulations (for the unregulated a_is). This should add considerable complication to the regulatory task.

Public authority governance creates its own challenges. For example, the resources allocated to implementing (costly) regulation may have little correspondence to the returns to doing so. Bureaucracy may stifle incentives and information sharing. There may also be a threat of regulator capture by private interests.

'Platform Regulation'[4]

Where an ecosystem is organized as an MSP with surrounding complementors and consumers, the platform owner effectively controls a 'bottleneck' essential to other players (Rochet and Tirole, 2004; Jacobides et al., 2006).[5] In so far as an MSP represents a scarce, critical asset that facilitates interactions, there will necessarily be an asymmetric one-to-many relationship that emerges between the platform owner and surrounding parties. The usual 'power of exclusion' associated with legal asset ownership is much stronger in this case. MSP ownership conveys 'bouncer's rights' (Strahilovetz, 2006)[6] in the sense that control over the platform also conveys the power to exclude from the ecosystem as a whole. The power to exclude also naturally implies the power to set the terms of access (e.g. through licensing agreements) – and thus to play a role somewhat analogous to the public regulator.

But what might be a platform owner's motivations for regulating their ecosystems? MSP owners' profits are directly tied to the economic value of their ecosystems. This is because the MSP is at the nexus of bilateral relationships with most other parties in the ecosystem and may capture a share of value created via each relationship (e.g. through 'taxing' each party, complementary platform sales etc.) (cf. Jacobides and Billinger, 2006). We denote by σ_i the share of agent i's value extracted by the MSP. Therefore, while the ability to implement rules and regulations across firms should be closely analogous to that of a public regulator, an MSP is attempting to implement actions that maximize its own profits, or $argmax_{\{A\}} \sum_i \sigma_i v_i$.

> **Hypothesis 3**: Platform regulation will be distorted away from pure value creation in the ecosystem, towards actions that lead to higher platform profits.

Given this possible distortion from a pure value-creation orientation, the relative efficiency of platform regulation then depends on how effective the MSP owner is in the regulatory role. While it surely will also not have full control over A (just like the public regulator), the question is whether it has greater control. To begin with, a platform regulator may have superior information and incentives. Unlike a public regulation bureaucracy, the platform regulator will directly derive profits to the extent that its regulation is successful. This should result in 'high-powered incentives' to regulate – something not typically associated with public regulation. These include incentives to acquire and study industry information in order to understand how best to engage in regulation. MSP owners should also have information advantages simply through their position at the nexus of bilateral relations in the ecosystem.

Platform regulators may also have access to a wider menu of regulatory instruments to implement desired actions. Apart from licensing, property rights assignment and other traditional contractual and legal instruments, platform technologies and design are themselves understood as a means of virtually imposing 'laws' (Lessig, 1999) and design 'rules' (Baldwin and Clark, 2000). Accentuating this advantage, MSPs are most often found at the core of the technical design, defining system architecture and technical relationships. The unique position and properties of the platform owner within the ecosystem should also better allow them to be 'leaders' (Gawer and Cusumano, 2002) of other firms by providing access to 'soft' instruments of coordination such as communication, signaling and relational contracting. For example, Intel's implemented 'Moore's Law' simply by declaring it so. These points lead to our final hypothesis:

Hypothesis 4: Platform regulators benefit from extraordinary access to instruments, information and incentives in performing the regulatory role.

4. CASE STUDIES

The remainder of this chapter presents four cases studies intended to investigate the hypotheses developed here. Two case studies – Facebook and TopCoder – are digital platforms; two others – Roppongi Hills and Harvard Business School – are non-digital.

Facebook

In broadest brushstrokes, Facebook[7] can be viewed as following traditional multi-sided platform strategies in its goals of encouraging a critical mass of adoption, while 'monetizing' the installed base. However, platform strategy here is distinctly shaped by idiosyncratic features of network effects acting in this platform. A first challenge is that members care only about their relevant network rather than the aggregate network. Thus growth is about expanding a mosaic of social networks rather than scale *per se*. A second challenge is that Facebook must then activate the 'social graph'. Beyond simply establishing linkages among members, it must keep these linkages active, fresh and compelling. Third, Facebook has the challenge of minimizing negative interactions on its platform, ranging from irrelevant interactions, those that are inappropriate to the context, all the way to 'fraudsters' and illicit activity.

Growth through restricted access
These idiosyncrasies of network effects among members have led to somewhat counter-intuitive interventions by Facebook – including restricting access so as to promote growth. Indeed, in the first two-and-a-half years after launching in February 2004, Facebook was not accessible to all Internet users.

Initially, the social network was accessible just to the Harvard College community. Within just 24 hours of launch, 1200 students had signed up. In just a month, half of Harvard's undergraduates had joined. In March 2004, access was expanded to students at Stanford, Columbia and Yale – then to other Ivy League and Boston-area colleges in April. The Boston College network grew to 2500 members, roughly a fifth of all students, in the first week (Cooke, 2004). In this fashion of adding institutions Facebook membership grew past one million members by year-end 2004. Roughly one thousand institutions were added by 2005. Support was extended to US high schools by September 2005. This new high-school community, however, was designed to be segregated from the main university platform, so as to preserve the integrity of the social milieu while serving distinct groups. The success of this gradual approach revealed that restricting access was a useful means of increasing the likelihood of relevant connections, enhancing word-of-mouth dynamics, and avoiding negative interactions with unknown and potentially undesirable members.

In just about 18 months, the education market for social networking had essentially tipped to Facebook. The market was even becoming saturated by 2005, with as much as 85 percent of students at supported institutions already on board (Arrington, 2005). The imperative to maintain and restore growth pushed Facebook to open more broadly in April 2006 – first to 'work networks' at targeted companies, and then essentially to all comers by September 2006 when Facebook dropped most access restrictions altogether.

Facilitating and imposing member interactions

But opening up the platform wide to all comers created important trade-offs. Incumbent student members might, for example, have preferred to keep the network closed to their own demographic group. When the platform was opened to a wider public, concerns for privacy and undesirable interactions became more prominent. Not surprisingly, then, the opening of the platform to a broader public appeared in combination with the launch of added privacy controls on News Feed, Mini-Feed and other services that most obviously could have led to broadcasted personal information. Privacy controls have since rapidly evolved to provide greater amounts of flexibility and customization, given apparent heterogeneity in users' tastes for privacy. For example, at the time of writing this chapter, there are separate privacy settings for Profile, Search, News Feed and The Wall, and Applications. Each of these categories offers roughly ten adjustable parameters (a relatively large number) to specify individual tastes for privacy.

One key reason for Facebook's incentive to stimulate active usage of the network is monetization through advertising. At the same time, the company also has to make sure that it provides its users with the means to ward off unwanted approaches and protect their privacy. This is a delicate balancing act which has led the company into at least one *faux pas*. In late 2007, Facebook launched a program called Beacon, which aimed to leverage advertising opportunities from a feature that let users know which products and services their friends were buying. This ill-advised foray into 'social marketing' drew a backlash from users, who disliked their invasion of privacy, and in March 2008 CEO Zuckerberg apologized for the program and moved to limit its scope.

Designing a marketplace for widget innovation

The role of Facebook as rule maker and regulator for the ecosystem around its platform is equally seen in its relationship with developers of 'widgets', software applications that can be installed on members' profile pages. A large fraction of widgets are inherently social in nature[8] in the sense that using and sharing widgets will itself lead to building, activating and refreshing the social graph. That the population of over 30 000 widgets has been installed over 900 million times already suggests that they convey considerable value to the platform, both enhancing network effects among members and helping attract new members to the platform.

There are essentially two main challenges to assuring a compelling and regularly refreshed set of applications in Facebook's case: fostering experimentation and encouraging high investments in quality. Wide experimentation is required because unlike in, say, the case of producing 'another' word processor or database, much remains unknown concerning preferences and technical approaches to social applications. To encourage wide experimentation in parallel (cf. Boudreau et al., 2008), Facebook has adopted a strategy of free access and low barriers to entry for widget developers through various measures, including: open and well-documented application programming interfaces (APIs); support for multiple development languages; free tools and test facilities; support for communication among developers within Facebook developer forums and conferences.

Extraordinarily broad entry could, however, result in excessively intense competition, which would then drive down profits and incentives to invest around the Facebook platform (Boudreau, 2008b). This risk is however mitigated by purposeful design choices made by Facebook. Indeed, the company has taken steps to induce a sort of winner-take-all structure in the market for widgets, at the level of application niches (for instance, the niche of chess games includes over 20 widgets but is dominated by just two games – 'Chess' and 'Chess Pro' – which jointly capture 95 percent of all usage). The deliberate encouragement of applications that are social in nature (through the design of APIs and the design on the platform itself, certification programs, funding awards and other means) encourages market concentration by word-of-mouth dynamics and encouraging users to standardize on a particular application to allow interactions. Network effects at the application level then tend to tip niche markets to one or few widgets.

The dissemination of information on Facebook's 'Application Directory' also encourages niche concentration. Although there are thousands of applications, the 'Application Directory' encourages downloads of just the top several dozen applications by displaying titles in a vertical list with only several per page. So important is this dissemination of information that numerous developers reported that they shifted their development attention to higher quality and greater interactivity when Facebook began ranking applications by the (flow of) usage rather than the (stock) of downloads (Naone, 2007).

TopCoder[9]

From the perspective of its clients, TopCoder is a vendor of outsourced software projects. But what sets TopCoder apart is the company's organization as a platform, one that effectively brings together buyers of software on one side of its platform, with a stable of roughly 20000 actively contributing developers spread across 200 countries. Internal TopCoder benchmarking estimates show dramatic efficiency improvements on standard software development practices, with increasing potential savings with increasing project complexity. Lending credence to these claims, the company achieved no. 13 rank on *Inc* magazine's fastest growing software companies in 2008.

TopCoder's 'community' of software developer 'members' compete in regularly scheduled contests to provide solutions to individual software challenges based on software buyer demands. Winners are awarded pre-announced cash prizes for their contributions. Prizes can vary quite widely: most often they are of the order of hundreds or low thousands of dollars but can go all the way up to six figures.[10] Top developers can make hundreds of thousands of dollars per year (Leibs, 2008). Most members, however, are often employees of other firms or students and devote a fraction of their time to TopCoder contests.

Regulation to enhance competition

Let the world compete on your next application.

TopCoder website

A key ambition of TopCoder is to orchestrate an environment of unbridled competition among its developers. While prizes (fundamentally a price instrument) are a clear feature of relationships with the competitor-coders around the platform, this price mechanism is deeply embedded within a rich system of rules and regulated behaviors. A most obvious rule that transforms the price mechanism here from a typical market arrangement is that prizes are presented *ex post* (as opposed to having competitors engage in *ex ante* bidding and selecting a winner prior to the production of the solution). This ensures intensive rivalry throughout the competition, rather than just up to the 'bidding' stage. Furthermore, awarding prizes *ex post* is a means of overcoming uncertainty regarding who in fact is the best supplier of a given software project. Thus, at the crudest level, the price mechanism and the rule of *ex post* rewards is the foundation of TopCoder's selection mechanism.

A range of other non-price instruments is complementary to *ex post* awards. For example, TopCoder actively shares information within contests to heighten rivalry in the pool of competitors. A 'heads-up' display on competitors' computer monitors displays the identity of all competitors, their skill ratings (based on performance in past contests), history of any submissions and competitor performance. TopCoder develops a barrage of formal and objective testing measures for each of its contests and is thus able to assign objective scores on the code that is created by every competitor. What is more, these scores are publicly shared and go into the public record as part of a competitor's skill rating. Thus TopCoder orchestrates a context of cut-throat competition.

Harnessing non-pecuniary incentives

Unbridled competition and *ex post* selection might again raise the concern for quashed investment incentives (as in the Facebook case). Further, *ex post* selection might seem to create enormous wasted and redundant efforts that might translate into reduced efficiency and lower profits for the platform owner. But this sort of analysis fails to recognize that TopCoder is, in effect, harnessing value created by a wide variety of motivations that are typical of coder communities, e.g. intrinsic motivations for doing the work or learning from the work, career concerns, status and recognition in the community or simple affiliation with the community (Lerner and Tirole, 2002; Lakhani and Wolf, 2005). Thus profit opportunities and monetary awards are but one aspect of prizes. Following this logic, 'redundant costs' may in fact be the effort devoted to learning; participation itself may enhance one's affiliation with the broader coder community; posted scores are an opportunity to signal capabilities to prospective employers and to achieve status; objective evaluation can be a useful means of self-improvement. TopCoder has also found that the extreme competition and rivalry (in a behavioral or game-playing sense, rather than an economic sense) is itself a great motivator for coders. Thus the platform is designed to internalize and capture value in non-pecuniary incentives – something a price system on its own would clearly fail to achieve.

Imposing a system of production

TopCoder's basic selection mechanism is able to function as it does by imposing several broader choices around the MSP business model. Most profoundly, TopCoder imposes its control over all interactions with customers: software developers do not interact with final customers. This is clearly a necessary choice in governing the software development process as a set of contests. Thus all communications, transfer of assets, payments and other forms of interactions are effected through the platform itself. Doing so further necessitates that software development be a sequential and planned process in contrast to other popular approaches to programming such as 'extreme' or 'agile' programming, in which developers iterate between experimentation, design and evolving requirements.

Apart from dividing production sequentially and by software modules, TopCoder also divides labor functionally. Apart from contests for software development (the actual creation of modules), individual contests are held for software architecture, software design (i.e. specifications, requirements, functionality of modules), software assembly (creation of applications on the basis of created modules) and testing (creating test scenarios to assess robustness of software). (Bug fixing has been added as a function, but not via a contest mechanism.) Thus more than creating just a 'multi-sided market', TopCoder's platform effectively defines and governs an entire value chain.

Roppongi Hills[11]

Roppongi Hills is a sprawling 12-hectare 'mini-city' shopping center and multi-purpose complex that was opened in April 2003 in the center of Tokyo. It was developed and is managed by Mori Building, one of Japan's most prominent real-estate developers. The center encompasses a large retail space filled with shops ranging from Louis Vuitton, Banana Republic, Diesel and Zara to a range of smaller brands, an eclectic mix of Japanese and foreign restaurants, coffee shops and a cinema. Apart from retail, Roppongi Hills includes an outdoor arena, a television studio, a luxury hotel, commercial office real estate and two residential buildings. Its landmark is the imposing Mori Tower, an elegant 54-story steel-and-glass construction that serves mostly as office space but also contains a library, an observatory and an art museum dedicated to modern art exhibitions on the top floor. The vision for the complex was based on the belief that offices, residences, shopping, entertainment and cultural facilities could not only coexist in close proximity, but also that 'synergies' (in other words, network effects) could be found in such a multi-purpose project.

This mini-city platform has been an unusual success among development projects (and shopping centers, in particular), with over 40 million visitors drawn every year; office and retail space have doubled since opening. While any shopping mall can be viewed as a (at least) two-sided platform between retailers and shoppers (Rochet and Tirole, 2004), Roppongi Hills is exceptional in the extent to which Mori Building actively regulates its mini-city platform.

Enforcing novelty and cultural themes

On the retail side, Roppongi Hills encompasses about 250 retailers (restaurants, shops and various service providers). Each retail tenant paid Mori Building 15 percent, on average, of their sales revenues as rent. Mori Building received a total of about 2000 applications for its desirable 213 locations it had opened initially. However, Mori Building exercised considerable discretion in deciding which retailers they would accept and the positions they would take in the mini-city. This quite clearly deviated from simply always selling to the highest bidder. For example, in Mori Building's quest to ensure that Roppongi Hills remained a novel, fresh and unique environment, they decided to allocate the largest space (3000 square meters) to Estnation, a relatively new and trendy apparel store rather than larger and more prominent brands.

Arguably the boldest space allocation decision regarded the most valuable real estate of the entire mini-city – the top five floors of Mori Tower. On these floors, Mori Building chose to place Academy Hills (a multipurpose education facility), an observatory deck, an art museum (Mori Art Museum) and an art gallery (Mori Arts Center Gallery). The art museum was placed on the top floor – the most prestigious location of all. In so doing, Mori Building was intent on clearly signaling the concept of a 'cultural heart' of its mini-city,[12] thus elevating the cachet of Roppongi Hills as a whole, rather than simply allocating the space to the highest bidder (which would have likely paid a large sum).

Also in the pursuit of novelty and originality, Mori Building believed it was essential to periodically refresh its retail offerings, while tailoring them to the special requirements of the mini-city. To this end, it constantly encouraged retail tenants to renew the designs of their stores. More forcefully, Mori Building actively replaced underperforming stores or those found not to 'fit' with the mini-city environment. For example, by two and a half years after opening already 26 percent of the retail space had changed hands.

Importantly, however, Mori Building has since seen churn reduce to half these levels. The company expects that once features of its platform business model are solidified, it should take less active intervention to achieve its goals. Roppongi Hills' Grand Hyatt's manager further suggested that it will be only after reducing active interventions and allowing the model to stand on its own that true advantages of distributed and autonomous decision making around the platform can take hold: 'I feel that one could improve the attractiveness of such mixed-use developments in the future by allowing them to grow more naturally, instead of designing them as purposefully as they are now.'

'Town Management'

Unlike many real-estate developers, Mori Building did not view its job as ending after the final choice of the tenant mix and their positioning within the mini-city. The company decided that in order to help materialize the 'synergies' – the premise upon which its 'multi-purpose' project had been built, it had to actively manage the complex on an ongoing basis. To do so, it created an internal unit, called 'Town Management' (henceforth TM), whose primary mission was to create a strong, consistent Roppongi Hills brand image and to strengthen the sense of community. In the words of its senior general manager: 'Because there are so many different constituents interacting with each other, effective town management is critical. It is essential to manage Roppongi Hills as a whole. While each constituent has their own agenda, our job is to consolidate, coordinate, and promote a unified image.'

One of the first initiatives of TM was the Community Passport, a loyalty program that allowed subscribers to accumulate points at shops, restaurants and the movie theater, which could be converted to discounts. 'Insiders' (i.e. office and retail employees) were entitled to special advantages through the Community Passport: automatic 10 percent discounts at stores and restaurants within the complex, information about 'secret sales' three days before the sales were opened to the general public etc. TM also regularly came up with initiatives designed to attract traffic and create a stronger sense of community. For instance, it handled certain events for the Tokyo International Film Festival throughout the complex and worked with restaurants and shops to engage them in the selection of themes for the museum's exhibitions.

These policies resulted in tailoring of offerings, even from well-known international brands. For example, the Grand Hyatt hotel was one of the most recognizable brands in Roppongi Hills. The hotel's design and operations were specifically tailored to Roppongi Hills: among other things, its restaurants remained open later than in its other locations in order to attract business customers (which made up 70 percent of the hotel's clientele), it offered discounts to employees of office tenants, and it provided catering for private parties of the Roppongi Hills offices and residents. The hotel even sacrificed some short-term revenues for the larger benefit of the

Roppongi Hills community. For instance, it reserved its banquet rooms for the Tokyo International Film Festival, hosted by Roppongi Hills every year in October, a period that coincided with Japan's biggest wedding season, typically a major source of income for hotels and other establishments, which could easily generate ¥40 million or $340,000 per month.

A key focus for TM was the implementation of the 'only one' policy for retail, consistent with its broader goal of novelty and originality. This policy was introduced in order to differentiate Roppongi Hills from other shopping destinations: not only did Mori Building executives aim for a diverse mix of stores, they went a step further by demanding that retailers produce stores unique to Roppongi Hills. This could take many forms, such as a requirement to stay open late in order to achieve a '24/7' city image, or a requirement to carry different merchandise from other storefronts owned by the same chain in Tokyo. TM worked closely with retailers in order to achieve the 'only one' goal. One of the most noteworthy achievements could be found in the Roppongi Hills Gate Tower. Its main tenant, Japan's largest DVD and CD rental store chain Tsutaya, had agreed to open a store on the lower level of the building and to share the space with a Starbucks coffee shop. This resulted in a popular corner location where residents as well as visitors could browse movies and music, relax with a book or magazine, and drink a cup of coffee. Conversely, the 'only one' policy could also trigger a retailer's exit, such as that of Mikimoto, a world-renowned jewelry retailer, which had to vacate its Roppongi Hills storefront after two years of disappointing sales.

TM was also in charge of monetizing the unique Roppongi Hills complex and brand name by attracting advertisers and sponsors. It sold event sponsorship opportunities and leased the advertising space within the complex – an important source of income. For example, an advertiser (e.g. BMW in 2005) would have to spend ¥50–100 million for a two-week campaign covering the entire mini-city (i.e. monopolizing the publicity channels within the complex).

The strategic use of architecture and design

The aforementioned instruments of control and regulation predominantly rely on outright contracting and traditionally legal mechanisms. This would seem to be in contrast to the heavy reliance on technical design in the earlier case studies of digital platforms that were used to impose rules. However, there are abundant examples in the case of Roppongi Hills where rules embedded in design also played an important role.

For example, the Mori Tower was Tokyo's largest office building in terms of rentable space, with 380 000 available square meters, i.e. roughly one-and-a-half football fields for each floor. This was a daring design decision that specialized this office space to a select set of target tenants, since few companies could use such large floor space. In particular, Mori Building was intent on targeting sectors and firms for which the unique infrastructure would be appealing, particularly foreign financial institutions who were aggressively expanding in Japan, and information technology companies. Indeed, among the first tenants to come on board was Goldman Sachs, which Mori Building had had to persuade to move from its nearby Ark Hills location (an older Mori Building complex). Other tenants included Konami (one of the largest videogame developers in Japan), Livedoor, Rakuten and Yahoo! Japan (the top three Internet companies in Japan in 2003).

Another noteworthy design decision regarded the layout of the complex and the choice of locations of the various uses. To convey a feeling of exploration akin to that found in real, organic cities, the architects opted for a maze-like structure in which visitors and residents could wander around for hours, and 'discover' new shops and restaurants along the way. Thus the layout necessarily guided and increased the likelihood of commercial interactions. The structure was thought to benefit those visitors who enjoyed wandering around and looking at shops and restaurants, although corporate tenants were less pleased with lack of clarity, and some expressed concerns that it might be confusing.

Harvard Business School[13]

Business school education arose as an institution in the early twentieth century. The Wharton School of the University of Pennsylvania was founded as the first American business school within the broader university in 1881. Several European schools of commerce had been opened earlier. Harvard Business School (HBS) was started in 1908 and has since been synonymous with business education and has been particularly successful in fostering a product and reputation to maintain a high ranking.

In the early twentieth century, HBS's education 'platform' was largely 'one-sided' in the sense that it catered to a single group: its students. Graduates received a certificate and were then essentially on their own. When it launched career services decades later it became a two-sided platform that effectively began to internalize the matchmaking process between graduates and recruiters. Today, HBS and the most successful of other business schools are in fact multi-sided platforms. They attract and balance communities of students, faculty, alumni, recruiters, capital providers, community and industry linkages – and enable them to interact in myriad ways. Thus, while the core 'product' of HBS – its teaching delivered in the classroom – remains a key function, the strategy of the institution goes far beyond this.

The central role of HBS's MSP strategy in the overall success of the institution might immediately be understood in remarking that brand name and reputation are widely accepted as the key drivers of business schools' success. But brand and reputation are in turn determined precisely by the participation of the constituents themselves. For instance, an attractive school for students is one that has renowned faculty, a powerful alumni network and that offers access to desirable recruiters. Conversely, recruiters are drawn to the schools with the best students. Capital providers (private donors as well as corporate sponsors) also prefer to bestow their financial support on schools with remarkable students and faculty. Thus the success of a business school hinges on the same sort of chicken-and-egg problems well known to other MSPs. And managing brand and performance can in large part be understood as a matter of managing network effects across different sides of the HBS platform.

Students, alumni and donors on a rather mature and stable MSP

Perhaps the most important and at the same time most difficult aspect of building a business school is the challenge of attracting valuable parties to the platform. HBS solved its chicken-and-egg problem of attracting good students to establish a reputation (and vice versa) some decades ago and has consistently attracted a large number of exceptional students. In the 2008 rankings, for example, HBS and Stanford students tied for top GMAT® (Graduate Management Admission Test®) scores. This is particularly notable given HBS's large class of roughly 900 students (per year). The stable, high quality of HBS applicants over the decades has allowed the institution to develop the other parts of its MSP.

The school was among the earliest and most sophisticated adopters of certain practices now common among leading business schools. This particularly relates to management of the alumni and donor networks. The alumni side of the MSP is of course inevitably populated by intakes of past students and is arguably the most valuable side of the HBS MSP given its sheer size and prominence: it contributes reputation, career opportunities and donations. Since its early history, HBS has focused on training business 'leaders' and has sought to maintain strong relationships with this network (through active communication, mailings, organization of events and local HBS clubs distributed around the world). Similarly, HBS actively pursued large donors from its early history and now maintains an endowment of several billion dollars. Its 2006 capital campaign alone – targeted to fund financial aid, faculty development, global outreach, teaching and technology, campus renewal and other programs – raised $600 million.

HBS publishing: facilitating interactions, imposing rules

Apart from early adoption and small advantages in initiative, HBS made several decisions with multi-sided implications that may have enhanced its network effects. For example, the school's emphasis on training for positions in the highest levels of management may have led to more prosperous careers, a more active and attractive alumni network and more generous donations – at least historically.

Another area was in relation to publishing by another side of the MSP, its professors. While the use of the case study method in the classroom was arguably just another instance of early adoption by HBS, a more fundamental decision was that HBS also became the leading producer of business cases. This deepened relationships with the corporate world (the industry side of the HBS MSP), while also enhancing the classroom experience through more relevant material, presented by the cases' authors (and sometimes protagonists) themselves. Conversely, being the subject of an HBS case started to carry significant value for companies who were attracted to the HBS MSP.

Thus enhanced alumni and industry relations were complementary with superior classroom experience and the advancement of professors' research and careers. A similar logic applied to the creation of a practitioner journal in 1922, the *Harvard Business Review*, which professors could contribute to (the *Review* publishes articles by professors and practitioners from any institution, not just HBS) and alumni could learn from. The wider distribution to a broader management public would also sustain and grow the reputation of HBS in the broader business world. Thus HBS Publishing (which oversaw the publication of cases and the *Harvard Business Review*) was a feature of the HBS MSP business model that intensified network effects among the various sides of the HBS MSP.

One challenge to the HBS model – emphasizing practitioner links and case study writing – that has appeared over the last 30 years is the rise (and now dominance) of academic, research-oriented faculty across business schools. The involvement with practitioners creates opportunity costs for faculty whose careers depend more on research performance. As a result, the positive externality created by case publishing and practitioner links can potentially create a negative externality with the faculty side of the MSP. This negative effect is to some extent mitigated by the fact that case development can be a significant component of tenure and promotion requirements. In fact, it is possible to pursue a tenure track at HBS on the basis of a teaching career. Furthermore, HBS provides ample support to its faculty (e.g. research assistance) in order to minimize the cost (mainly in terms of time) of case writing. Nevertheless, developing cases remains a relationship-specific investment that faculty make in HBS, which has significantly less value if a faculty member has to seek tenure at other institutions.

Restricting and regulating the job market

Another challenge of balancing positive and negative interactions stems from a fundamental tension inherent in managing renowned business schools. HBS and its peers are at the same time education institutions and – to some extent – intermediaries between students, recruiters and faculty. While business schools do recognize the value of matching their students with desirable recruiters, all of them aspire to be much more than mere job matchmakers, in which the most important function would be performed by the implicit certification of the admissions office. Similarly, the collaboration of school faculty with outside companies (in the form of research projects or consulting) is highly desirable, but only to the extent it does not compromise the engagement of faculty with students and research.

It is not surprising, then, that HBS and other business schools have put rules in place in order to regulate these two critical interactions. The faculty–outside companies interaction is simpler to deal with: it is usually regulated by imposing a simple maximal threshold on the amount of hours any faculty member may spend engaging in 'outside activities'. The students–recruiters interaction requires more complicated forms of regulation. First, in order to minimize the potentially negative externalities this matchmaking function may have on the educational function of the institution, business schools typically try to restrict the timing of on-campus recruiting events and ask recruiters to not make interview offers that require students to skip class. And while in principle any employer is free to court any business school's graduates, most business schools offer special opportunities for interacting with students (e.g. through information sessions and various campus events) to a select group of recruiters, usually in exchange for a fee. Not all recruiters have access to such opportunities, and recruiters can lose their privilege if they do not maintain good relations with the school (for example, this may be triggered by overly aggressive recruiting campaigns held on campus and not authorized by the school). Second, business schools also try to ensure that the 'internal' recruiting matchmaking market functions efficiently, which is why most of them impose rules on both recruiters and students regarding timing and deadlines of offers, limited ability to entertain multiple offers etc.

5. DISCUSSION

In Section 2 we hypothesized that the markets around MSPs should often be fraught with externalities and potential coordination problems (Hypothesis 1) that cannot be solved by price setting alone (Hypothesis 2). We argued (Section 3) that the platform owner would itself emerge as a private regulator, invoking an unusually rich set of strategic instruments to influence the behavior of complementors and users around the MSP, while benefiting from privileged information and a privileged position within the ecosystem (Hypothesis 4). The platform owner might then act as an unusually effective regulator of the ecosystem as a whole; however, its goals might be distorted towards capturing profits rather than just increasing value in the ecosystem (Hypothesis 3). The four case studies presented in this chapter provide considerable evidence in support of Hypotheses 1, 2 and 4. The evidence in relation to Hypothesis 3 is less clear and suggests a more nuanced set of issues.

The Limits of 'Getting the Prices Right'

In relation to Hypotheses 1 and 2, the case studies provide clear evidence of coordination problems that would not be solved by pricing alone. For example, Facebook grew its member base by restricting access to certain social groups. This would have been impossible to implement with pricing alone. Using price to encourage particular sorts of interactions on the platform while discouraging others would have been more difficult still. TopCoder did not face this same level of complexity, but instead faced challenges of uncertainty regarding which competitors possessed relevant skills and approach, as well as the need to foster non-pecuniary motivations. In this case, while price (prizes) played an important role, it would have been utterly insufficient without the system of rules, inducements and restrictions built around it. Roppongi Hills used a mixture of subjective selection procedures, imposition of rules and architectural design decisions to foster an overall brand image and 'feel' to its mini-city that would have been impossible to replicate even with the most sophisticated price instruments (e.g. property rights bidding system). Harvard Business School found it necessary to carefully monitor and regulate the interactions between students and recruiters. These and numerous other examples readily convey a range of externalities, complexity, uncertainty, asymmetric information and coordination problems that imposed severe limits on what could be achieved by price instruments on their own.

Regulating Access to the MSP

In relation to Hypothesis 4, we observed clear and extensive interventions above and beyond price setting. These might be thought of as related to either regulating access to platforms or otherwise regulating interactions once on a platform. Fundamentally, the goal of regulating access was to make sure the MSP attracted the 'right' kind of participants on all sides.

For example, Facebook initially restricted user access to the platform based on demographics so as to maximize positive interactions while minimizing negative ones. The implicit assumption was that immediate unrestricted access could have resulted in an overall 'social market breakdown' of the type illustrated by the Atari example in the introduction: undesirable users and connections crowding out desirable ones. Mori Building selected its retailers on its own discretion in accordance with the values of its mini-city. It also reviewed its selections every two years, based on performance and 'fit' with the overall theme of the complex. Harvard Business School selected students and other sides of the platform based on complementary characteristics, among which willingness to pay was not foremost – although the model fostered high willingness to pay among donors. Harvard Business School also restricted access of recruiters to certain times during the year to assure proper functioning of its interactions with students. The concern was a crowding-out of a standalone service (education) by the matchmaking function (recruiting). TopCoder did not outright regulate access, but did regulate interactions with clients *ex post*. Thus we observed rather nuanced regulation of access by number, time, type and even individual identity.

While traditional contractual instruments were clearly invoked to implement access policies, technological instruments were also used. For example, Facebook exploited web addresses as identifiers to bar entry to its platform, in addition to employing contractual user agreements. Roppongi Hills used architectural design as a means of attracting certain types of tenants.

Regulating Interactions on the MSP

Also in relation to Hypothesis 4, considerable rule making and regulation was directed towards achieving desired conduct of – and interactions between – platform participants once they were on board. In order for the potential value from network effects to materialize, MSPs put in place a series of sometimes rather nuanced controls and inducements. There were many examples. For example, Facebook's management of privacy – enabling users to restrict their interactions to trusted contacts – illustrates the most basic function that regulation of interactions serves: minimizing negative network effects. Mori Building's 'Town Management' unit for Roppongi Hills was an explicit attempt to drive positive network effects and synergies. To some extent, the issue there is a public-good investment problem: left to their own devices, individuals (i.e. retailers and tenants) would underinvest in public good provision (i.e. marketing to outside visitors, maximizing complementarities with events throughout the complex).

TopCoder profoundly influenced how its coder–competitors would relate to one another, by carefully designing how they would compete against one another and what they would know about one another. Harvard Business School devoted careful attention to interactions between students, faculty, capital providers, alumni and other groups. The list of precise ways and means of regulating interactions in the case studies was extensive and often extraordinarily nuanced, involving contracting, technology, information provision, investments, tools, inducements, culture and norms. The use of these instruments in concert allowed platform owners to strive to implement rather precise outcomes.

The Objectives and Efficiency of Regulation

In relation to Hypothesis 3, there were limits to what could be concluded on the basis of evidence examined here. Whether platform regulation led to deadweight loss and distortive platform profit seeking was unclear, but the patterns hinted at a more nuanced set of relationships with factors going beyond those in our earlier hypothesis development. Take, for example, Facebook's interest in 'monetizing' its user–members with a platform function (Beacon) that allows the MSP to track and report users' behavior beyond the platform. Or, less controversially, consider Facebook's opening its platform beyond the education segment. Neither move appeared to be in the direct interest of (incumbent) Facebook members. Both appeared to be motivated by Facebook's commercial objectives. But whether or not imposing these changes would have had a net positive or negative effect on economic value created (even for members themselves) is *a priori* ambiguous. On the face of it, continued growth of Facebook would appear to have created enormous value while only slightly inconveniencing student members. It is also conceivable that the tracking service would have created more value for businesses than the value it destroyed for members. Alternatively, it may have even created value for members by bringing richer services. While the evidence is inconclusive, it hints at the possibility that platform regulation is as much about 'pleasing all sides' around an MSP, the outside options of MSP participants, switching costs, ability of participants to coordinate themselves as a group and so on – as much it is about platform profit seeking.

6.   CONCLUSIONS

This chapter presented arguments and evidence that platforms serve as rule-making governance mechanisms – apart from any functional value of the platform itself. 'Platform regulation' involved using a wide range of strategic instruments (well beyond price setting) to regulate economic activity of surrounding platform participants. These instruments were applied in concert, often involving nuanced combinations of legal, technological, informational and other instruments (along with price setting) to implement desired outcomes. This combination of instruments was used to minimize costs associated with a range of externalities, complexity, uncertainty, asymmetric information and coordination problems the multi-sided platform was in a position to address. Perhaps most striking in the analysis was that the regulatory role played in these cases by multi-sided platforms was pervasive and at the core of their business models.

While the choice of disparate case studies should begin to suggest some generality of the findings, clearly wider and more systematic study is warranted. Patterns identified here, moreover, point to deeper questions necessary for understanding the economics of non-price mechanisms used by multi-sided platforms. For example, the findings invite clearer definition of the sorts of multi-sided market failures that can arise – and how particular combinations of platform strategic instruments might attend to these. An obvious starting point for this work might be to understand how price and non-price instruments coexist, interact and should be applied to different sorts of problems. The sheer number and complexity of instruments being used by platform owners (including investments, technology rules, information dissemination, contracting choices and pricing) is also clearly an empirical phenomenon deserving closer attention and clearer explanation. Why so many instruments? The basic terms and analytical framework set forth in the hypothesis development of this chapter also suggest that it may be productive to develop a contingent view of the role of private versus public regulators. The analysis here leaves open the question of whether there was in fact (much of) a deadweight loss associated with platform regulation and pointed to a variety of factors shaping profit taking by platform owners that should be further investigated.

These findings have important managerial implications. First, the scope of strategy for platforms is significantly wider than for normal firms: it is not limited to pricing, product design and technology, but also and critically includes control over interactions that do not happen at your firm's boundaries. Our analytical framework suggests a two-step approach for a platform owner: (1) maximize value created for the entire ecosystem; (2) maximize the value extracted.

Second, our analysis reveals the existence of a wide array of strategic instruments available to implement platform regulation, including contractual, technological and information design. The instruments observed here varied in their effects, whether they were easily reversible or not, and their availability from one context to another. While more detailed analysis of these instruments remains an area of future research, it is useful to emphasize that even non-technology multi-sided platforms can and should use a sophisticated array of regulation instruments (cf. Roppongi Hills).

Third, our analysis begins to suggest that the need for and consequences of platform regulation may evolve over time. Active and early orchestration of the multiple sides of a business has the potential to set powerful network effects and complementarities into motion (cf. HBS). Establishing an MSP regulation model may be most difficult in early stages – particularly if a firm waits while competitors do so. By the same token, once a regulated ecosystem is successfully established, the advantages of distributed innovation and decision making may begin to truly take hold (cf. Roppongi Hills).

NOTES

1. We wish to acknowledge comments and suggestions provided by seminar and conference participants at Imperial College, the 2008 Academy of Management annual meetings and the Paris workshop on digital platforms held at LECG offices. Kevin Boudreau thanks Microsoft for funding that supported this work.
2. Platforms are products, services or technologies that serve as foundations upon which other parties can build complementary products, services or technologies (Gawer and Cusumano, 2002; Gawer, 2009). A 'multi-sided' platform or MSP (e.g. Sony's PlayStation, Visa credit cards, Microsoft's Windows, eBay) is both a platform and a market intermediary (Hagiu 2007). Thus distinct groups of consumers and 'complementors' interact through MSPs.
3. The following discussion focuses on interactions between traditional profit-maximizing agents. We do not in this chapter extend the analysis to highly socialized contexts, as in open source communities (Feller et al., 2007).
4. In setting out basic ideas, we do not consider here how the platform regulator might itself be regulated.
5. For example, Microsoft controls the Windows operating system in the PC ecosystem, eBay controls the information platform that facilitates trade, Visa controls the financial network, and shopping malls control the real estate and infrastructure.
6. We wish to thank Professor Robert Merges for drawing our attention to this useful distinction.
7. Facebook is among the leading social networking platforms, with over 100 million members in 2008. It brings together advertisers, content suppliers, commercial business members, applications software or 'widget' developers and individual 'members', who may display their profiles and link with other members. Here we discuss only facets of the business model that relate to the latter two groups.
8. For example, popular applications include enrichments of the basic social functionality of the platform (e.g. 'SuperWall'), applications intended to initiate interactions (e.g. 'Hug Me'), multi-player games (e.g. 'Texas HoldEm Poker'), means of broadcasting personal information and preferences about oneself (e.g. 'Movies'), means of broadcasting media and content (e.g. 'Slideshow') and other distinctly social applications (e.g. 'Compare People', 'Honesty Box'). See http://www.facebook.com/applications/.
9. This case study builds on insights drawn from research with Karim Lakhani and Nicola Lacetera.

10. This was based on a review of active contests in August 2008 on the TopCoder platform.
11. This case study builds on Elberse et al. (2008).
12. As explained by Minoru Mori, Mori Building's CEO: 'From quite early on, my vision was to create an unprecedented prototypical city. Creating 'a cultural heart for Tokyo' was the main concept for the city-making of Roppongi Hills. This cultural heart for Tokyo would serve as a new platform, new environment or new stage for creative talent who would be attracted to this city from all around the world, as they would benefit from a mix of high-quality residences, work places, shopping, relaxing, studying, and art and design facilities all within an integrated walking distance.'
13. This case study builds on Hagiu and Kester (2008).

BIBLIOGRAPHY

Armstrong, M. (2006), 'Competition in two-sided markets', *RAND Journal of Economics*, **37** (3), 668–91.

Armstrong, M. and J. Wright (2007), 'Two-sided markets, competitive bottlenecks and exclusive contracts', *Economic Theory*, **32** (2), 353–80.

Armstrong, M. and D.E.M. Sappington (2007), 'Recent developments in the theory of regulation', in M. Armstrong and R. Porter (eds), *Handbook of Industrial Organization, Vol. 3*, Amsterdam: North-Holland, Chapter 27.

Arrington, M. (2005), '85% of college students use Facebook', *TechCrunch*, 7 September.

Baldwin, C.Y. and K.B. Clark (2000), *Design Rules, Volume 1, The Power of Modularity*, Cambridge MA: MIT Press.

Boudreau, K. (2008a), 'Opening the platform vs. opening the complementary good? The effect on product innovation in handheld computing', 24 August, Working Paper, available at SSRN: http://ssrn.com/abstract=1251167.

Boudreau, K. (2008b), 'Too many complementors?', 1 January, Working Paper, Available at SSRN: http://ssrn.com/abstract=943088.

Boudreau, K., N. Lacetera and K.R. Lakhani (2008), 'Parallel search, incentives and problem type: revisiting the competition and innovation link', HBS Working Paper.

Caillaud, B. and B. Jullien (2003), 'Chicken and egg: competition among intermediation service providers', *RAND Journal of Economics*, **34** (2), 309–28.

Chou, C. and O. Shy (1990), 'Network effects without network externalities', *International Journal of Industrial Organization*, **8** (2), 259–70.

Church, J., N. Gandal and P. Krause (2008), 'Indirect effects and adoption externalities', *Review of Network Economics*, **7** (3), 337–58.

Clements, M. (2005), 'Inefficient standard adoption: inertia and momentum revisited', *Economic Inquiry*, **43** (3), 507–18.

Clements, M. and H. Ohashi (2005), 'Indirect network effects and the product cycle: U.S. video games, 1994–2002', *Journal of Industrial Economics*, **53** (4), 515–42.

Cooke, M. (2004), 'Facebook expands to BC campus' *The Heights,* April 27th.

Davis, S. J. and K.M. Murphy (2000), 'A competitive perspective on Internet Explorer', *American Economic Review*, **90** (2), 184–7.

Eisenmann, T., G. Parker and M. Van Alstyne (2006), 'Strategies for two-sided markets', *Harvard Business Review*, **84** (10), 92–101.

Elberse, A., A. Hagiu and M. Egawa (2008), 'Roppongi Hills: city within a city', Harvard Business School Case No. 9-707-431.

Evans, D. and R. Schmalensee (2007), *The Catalyst Code: The Strategies Behind the World's Most Dynamic Companies*, Boston, MA: Harvard Business School Press.

Evans, D., A. Hagiu and R. Schmalensee (2006), *Invisible Engines: How Software Platforms Drive Innovation and Transform Industries*, Boston, MA: MIT Press.

Farrell, J. and M.L. Katz (2000), 'Innovation, rent extraction and integration in systems markets', *Journal of Industrial Economics*, **48** (4), 413–32.

Farrell, J. and P. Klemperer (2007), 'Coordination and lock-in: Competition with switching costs and network effects', in M. Armstrong and R. Porter (eds), *Handbook of Industrial Organization, Vol. 3*, Amsterdam, North-Holland, Chapter 31.

Farrell J. and G. Saloner (1992), 'Converters, compatibility, and the control of interfaces', *Journal of Industrial Economics*, **40** (1), 9–35.

Farrell J. and P. Weiser (2003), 'Modularity, vertical integration, open access policies: towards a convergence of antitrust regulation in the Internet age', *Harvard Journal of Law and Technology*, **17** (1), 85–134.

Feller J., B. Fitzgerald, S.A. Hissam and K.R. Lakhani (2007), *Perspectives on Free and Open Source Software*, Boston, MA: MIT Press.

Gawer, A. and M.A. Cusumano (2002), *Platform Leadership: How Intel, Microsoft, and Cisco Drive Industry Innovation*, Boston, MA: Harvard Business School Press.

Gawer A. and R. Henderson (2007), 'Platform owner entry and innovation in complementary markets: evidence from Intel', *Journal of Economics & Management Strategy*, **16** (1), 1–34.

Hagiu, A. (2007), 'Merchant or two-sided platform?' *Review of Network Economics*, **6** (2), 115–33.

Hagiu, A. (2008), 'Two-sided platforms: variety and pricing structures', mimeo, Harvard Business School.

Hagiu, A. and W.C. Kester (2008), 'MBA programs as multi-sided platforms', HBS Working Paper.

Iansiti, M. and R. Levien (2004), *The Keystone Advantage: What the New Dynamics of Business Ecosystems Mean for Strategy, Innovation, and Sustainability*, Boston, MA: Harvard Business School Press.

Jacobides, M.G. and S. Billinger (2006), 'Designing the boundaries of the firm: from "make, buy or ally" to the dynamic benefits of vertical architecture', *Organization Science*, **17** (2), 249–61.

Jacobides, M.G., T. Knudsen and M. Augier (2006), 'Benefiting from innovation: value creation, value appropriation and the role of industry architectures', *Research Policy*, **35** (6), 1200–221.

Kahn, A.E. (1988), *The Economics of Regulation: Principles and Institutions*, Boston, MA: MIT Press.

Katz, M. and C. Shapiro (1986), 'Technology adoption in the presence of network externalities', *Journal of Political Economy*, **94**, 822–41.

Katz, M. and C. Shapiro (1994), 'Systems competition and network effects', *Journal of Economic Perspectives*, **8** (2), 93–115.

Laffont, J.-J. and J. Tirole (1993), *A Theory of Incentives in Procurement and Regulation*, Boston, MA: MIT Press.

Lakhani, K.R. and R.G. Wolf (2005), 'Why hackers do what they do:

understanding motivation effort in free/open source software projects', in J. Feller, B. Fitzgerald, S.A. Hissam and K.R. Lakhani (eds), *Perspectives on Free and Open Source Software*, Cambridge, MA: MIT Press, pp. 3–22.

Lee, R. (2008), 'Vertical integration and exclusivity in platform and two-sided markets', mimeo, New York University Stern School of Business.

Leibs, S. (2008), 'Gaming the system: how a small outsourcing firm uses competition to unite its global community', *CFO*, January, available at: http://www.topcoder.com/i/pressroom/pdfs/cfo_20080103_v2.pdf.

Lerner, J. and J. Tirole (2002), 'Some simple economics of open source', *Journal of Industrial Economics*, **50** (2), 197–234.

Lessig, L. (1999), *Code and other Laws of Cyberspace*, New York: Basic Books.

Liebowitz, S.J. and S.E. Margolis (1990), 'The fable of the keys', *Journal of Law and Economics*, **33** (1), 1–25.

Liebowitz, S.J. and S.E. Margolis (1994), 'Network externality: an uncommon tragedy', *Journal of Economic Perspectives*, **8** (2), 133–50.

Merges, R. (2008), 'IP rights and technological platforms', Working Paper.

Nair, H., P. Chintagunta and J.-P. Dube (2004), 'Empirical analysis of indirect network effects in the market for personal digital assistants', *Quantitative Marketing and Economics*, **2** (1), 23–58.

Naone, E. (2007), 'Refining Facebook's applications', *MIT Technology Review*, 20 September, available at: http://www.technologyreview.com/business/19408.

Parker, G. and M. Van Alstyne (2008), 'Innovation, openness and platform control', mimeo, Tulane University and MIT.

Parker, G. and M. Van Alstyne (2005), 'Two-sided network effects: a theory of information product design', *Management Science*, **51** (10), 1494–1504.

Prencipe, A., A. Davies and M. Hobday (eds) (2003), *The Business of Systems Integration*, Oxford: Oxford University Press.

Rochet, J.-C. and J. Tirole (2004), 'Two-sided markets: an overview', IDEI Working Paper.

Rochet, J.-C. and J. Tirole (2006), 'Two-sided markets: Where we stand', *RAND Journal of Economics*, **37** (3), 645–67.

Rysman, M. (2004), 'Competition between networks: a study of the market for yellow pages', *Review of Economic Studies*, **71**, 483–512.

Shapiro, C. and H. Varian (1998), *Information Rules*, Boston, MA: Harvard Business School Press.

Spulber, D. (2008), 'Unlocking technology: antitrust and innovation', *Journal of Competition Law and Economics*, May, 915–66.

Stigler, G.J. (1971), 'The theory of economic regulation', *The Bell Journal of Economics and Management Science*, **2** (1), 3–21.

Strahilovetz, L. (2006), 'Information asymmetries and the rights to exclude', *Michigan Law Review*, **104** (8), August, 1835–98.

Suarez, F. (2005), 'Network effects revisited: the role of strong ties on technology selection', *Academy of Management Journal*, **48** (4), 710–20.

Tucker, C. (2008), 'Identifying formal and informal influence in technology adoption with network externalities', MIT Working Paper.

West, J. (2003), 'How open is open enough? Melding proprietary and open source platform strategies', *Research Policy*, **32** (7), 1259–85.

8. Protecting or diffusing a technology platform: tradeoffs in appropriability, network externalities, and architectural control

Melissa A. Schilling

INTRODUCTION

In many high-technology markets, there are forces that create strong pressure for the selection of a single technology standard. This standard (or 'dominant design') may be embodied in a product design, the system architecture of a family of products (a 'platform'), or the process by which products or services are provided (Tushman and Anderson, 1986; Utterback and Abernathy, 1975). Although there may have initially been many competing standards on offer, increasing returns to adoption can cause a minor advantage in the number of users to cause a positive feedback effect, resulting in a single technology achieving a nearly insurmountable advantage over all others (Arthur, 1989, 1994; Garud and Kumaraswamy, 1993; Schilling, 1998, 2002). This dynamic can lead to 'winner-take-all' markets that create natural monopolies. A firm that controls the standard can reap monopoly rents, and can exert significant architectural control over both its own and related industries (Ferguson and Morris, 1993; Henderson and Clark, 1990).

This enviable position can be so lucrative that firms may be willing to lose money in the short term in order to improve their technology's chance of rising to the position of dominant design. In fact, firms are sometimes extolled to liberally diffuse their technologies (through, e.g., open source or liberal licensing arrangements) in order to accelerate the technology's proliferation and thereby jump-start the self-reinforcing feedback effect that can lead to the technology's dominance (Lecocq and Demil, 2005). However, the firm often faces a dilemma: if it liberally diffuses the technology to would-be competitors, it relinquishes the opportunity to capture monopoly rents when and if the technology emerges as a dominant design. Furthermore, once control of a technology is relinquished it can be very hard to regain; thus such diffusion may result in the firm losing all hope of architectural control. Finally, liberal diffusion of the technology can result in the fragmentation of the technology platform: as different producers add improvements to the technology that make it fit their needs better, the 'standard' may be split into many non-standardized versions. These dilemmas raise the following questions: when incompatible technologies compete for the position of dominant design, what factors will determine whether one or more competitors choose to adopt a more 'open' technology strategy? How does a firm decide what level of 'openness' will maximize the technology's chances for survival and the firm's long-term profitability? This research addresses these questions by exploring the tradeoffs of protecting versus diffusing a technology, and the conditions that will determine the strategy a firm chooses.

Previous studies have used modeling and empirical approaches to examine the effect of network externalities on the success or failure of a technology (e.g. Farrell and Saloner, 1986; Schilling, 2002; Shankar and Bayus, 2003; Suarez, 2004; Wade, 1995), and the role of firm strategies such as cooperation (Besen and Farrell, 1994), or sponsorship of early users (Katz and Shapiro, 1986).[1] Recent research has also begun to examine the incentives of individuals and firms to contribute development effort to 'open' technologies – most notably 'open-source' software (de Laat, 2005; Hertel et al., 2003; Lakhani and von Hippel, 2003; Lerner and Tirole, 2000). Modeling efforts have also indicated that open technologies might be improved faster (through user modification) than protected technologies, suggesting that in some situations open technologies may outcompete protected technologies (e.g. Dalle and Jullien, 2003; Casadesus-Masanell and Ghemawat, 2003). The current work builds on both of these prior bodies of work by systematically examining how either open or closed technologies can rise to the position of dominant design. Either strategy can be used to increase standalone functionality, installed base and complementary goods (though they do so by different means), but each strategy imposes a different set of tradeoffs upon the firm. For example, while open strategies often require less resource commitment by the developing firm, they also typically relinquish some degree of architectural control. These tradeoffs suggest that firms with different resource bases, objectives and positions in downstream or complementary markets will influence the utility of one strategy versus another.

This work is related to the research that examines voluntary cooperation and compatibility among producers (e.g. Besen and Farrell, 1994; Economides and Woroch, 1992); however, it is also different from this work in a number of important ways. While the work on cooperation has tended to focus on producers that voluntarily cooperate in establishing a standard in order to increase the size of the overall network, the current work focuses on the use of some degree of 'openness' as a competitive lever against other competing technologies. Furthermore, the cooperation among technology producers to jointly create a technology with a large network may or may not extend any benefits of cooperation to downstream producers (e.g. producers of complements or derivative goods). By contrast, relatively 'open' technology strategies are less likely (and in the case of wholly open strategies are unable) to constrain the types of producers that can participate in and benefit from the network.

The chapter begins by discussing how increasing returns influence the emergence of a dominant design. Then it defines wholly proprietary systems, wholly open systems and partially open systems and provides examples of technologies along this continuum of protection and control. By examining the polar cases of wholly proprietary and wholly open systems within a multidimensional framework of technology value, it is possible to trace the different pathways that exist to the emergence of a dominant design. This demonstrates that both protection and diffusion strategies can lead to a dominant design, but they do so by making different tradeoffs. A graphical model depicts this pathway, and a set of hypotheses is constructed about the various paths to the emergence of a dominant design. Finally, from this model it is possible to derive a set of arguments about the factors that influence where a firm should attempt to position itself along the control continuum when choosing among protection and diffusion strategies.

PROTECTION VERSUS DIFFUSION IN INCREASING-RETURNS INDUSTRIES

Complex technologies often exhibit increasing returns to adoption in that the more they are used, the more they are improved (Arthur, 1994). A technology that is adopted usually generates revenue that can be used to further develop and refine the technology. Furthermore, as the technology is used, greater knowledge and understanding of it accrue as byproducts that may then enable improvements both in the technology itself and in its applications. Finally, as a technology becomes more widely adopted, complementary assets are often developed that are specialized to operate with the technology (Katz and Shapiro, 1986). These effects can result in a self-reinforcing mechanism that increases the dominance of a technology regardless of its initial superiority or inferiority to competing technologies.

Increasing returns to adoption can be split into two categories of effects. One category consists of learning-curve advantages. There is ample empirical evidence that as a technology is used, it is further developed and made more effective and efficient (Argote, 1999; Levy, 1965; Yelle, 1979). At the individual-firm level, firms become better skilled at using the technology, and find ways to use it more productively, including developing an organizational context that improves its implementation. At the aggregate level, the more firms that are using the technology and refining it, developing complementary technologies to improve its effectiveness and efficiency, the more attractive the technology becomes to other firms.

The second category of effects is known as network externalities (or positive consumption externalities) (Choi, 1994; Farrell and Saloner, 1985, 1986; Katz and Shapiro, 1985, 1986, 1992). In a market characterized by network externalities, a user's benefit from using a good increases with the number of other users of the same good. The classic examples of markets demonstrating network externality effects are those involving physical networks, such as railroads or telecommunications. Railroads are more valuable as the size of the railroad network (and therefore the number of available destinations) increases. Similarly, a telephone is not much use to you if you can only call a few people with it – the amount of utility the phone provides is directly related to the size of the network.

Network externalities can also arise in markets that do not have physical networks. For example, a user's benefit from using a good may increase with the number of users of the same good when compatibility is important. A user may choose a computer platform based on the number of other users of that platform, rather than on the technological benefits of a particular platform, because it increases the ease of exchanging files. Choosing a platform with the largest installed base increases the number of people with which the user's files will be compatible. Furthermore, the value of the user's training in a particular platform becomes more valuable as the size of the installed base of the platform increases. If the user must invest considerable effort in learning to use a computer platform, he/she will probably choose to invest this effort in learning the format they believe will be most widely used.

Network externalities also arise when complementary goods are important (Choi, 1994; Katz and Shapiro, 1986, 1992; Thum, 1994). Many products are functional or desirable only when there is a set of complementary goods available for them (e.g. videotapes for VCRs, film for cameras etc.). Products that have a large installed base are likely to attract more developers of complementary goods. Since the availability of complementary goods will influence users' choice among competing platforms, the availability of complementary goods in turn influences the size of the installed base. A self-reinforcing cycle ensues that may lead to the dominance of a single-technology platform.

The effect of this cycle is vividly demonstrated by Microsoft's dominance of the operating system and graphical user interface markets. In 1980, IBM approached Gary Kildall, founder of Digital Research and the inventor of CP/M (then the dominant operating system for personal computers), to arrange to have CP/M bundled on the first IBM PC. Kildall, for reasons that are still contested in computer circles, did not sign with IBM. Since IBM was already purchasing other software programs from Microsoft, it called Bill Gates to ask if he could also provide an operating system. That event had a profound impact on the shape of the computer industry as we know it today. Gates provided an operating system, MS-DOS, which rapidly gained a huge installed base as customers clamored for IBM and IBM-compatible PCs. Microsoft was later able to leverage its dominance in operating systems to secure a dominant position with a graphical user interface designed to sit on top of DOS: Windows. Microsoft also worked vigorously to ensure that compatible applications were developed for DOS and Windows, both making applications itself and encouraging third-party developers to support the platform. The network externality benefits of using Windows and Windows-compatible software, which gained an early advantage in installed base and availability of complementary goods, enabled the platform to lock several would-be contenders such as Geoworks and Next completely out of the market.

Proprietary Systems versus 'Open' Systems

There is often considerable ambiguity in the extant literature about what is meant by 'open' systems versus proprietary systems, largely because various domains of management research use the term 'open' in different ways (Gacek and Arief, 2004). Proprietary systems are defined here as those based on technology that is company-owned and protected through patents, secrecy or other mechanisms. A technology may be said to be 'wholly proprietary' when its owner prevents all others from legally producing or augmenting it. Wholly proprietary systems are often not compatible with the products offered by other manufacturers. Because their operation is based on protected technology, other manufacturers are often unable to develop components that may interact with the proprietary system. Because they are protected, proprietary systems typically offer their developers great rent appropriability. However, they may also be less likely to be adopted readily by consumers due to the inability to mix and match components, or customer concerns about the viability of a sole-source technology.

In 'wholly open systems', the technology used in a product is not protected by secrecy or patents; it may be based on available standards or it may be new technology that is openly diffused to other producers. Wholly open systems are usually quickly commoditized, and provide little appropriability of rents to their developers. In the information systems literature, the term 'open standards' does not necessarily mean that the underlying technology is unprotected. For example, the X/Open standard-setting body defines open systems as 'computers and communications environments based on de facto[2] and formal interface standards', but these standards may be proprietary in the sense that they were developed, introduced, and are maintained by vendors (Chau and Tam, 1997). Similarly, Garud et al. (2002) define an 'open systems strategy' as one that allows both rivals and vendors of complementary products easy access to the sponsor's proprietary technology. Since the degree to which rivals or complementary goods producers can access, augment or distribute a proprietary technology varies along a continuum in accordance with the degree of control imposed by the technology's developer, a more precise definition is needed for our purposes here. Anchoring the two ends of the continuum will be wholly proprietary technologies, which are strictly protected and may be accessed, augmented and distributed only by their developers; and wholly open technologies, which may be freely accessed, augmented and distributed by anyone. If a firm grants or sells the right to access, augment or distribute its technology for commercial purposes but retains some degree of control over the technology, this will be termed a 'partially open' technology.

Most technology examples discussed in the literature on standards battles lie somewhere between wholly proprietary and wholly open on the control continuum (see Figure 8.1). For instance, most of the major videogame console producers (Nintendo, Sony and Microsoft) utilize a wholly proprietary strategy for their consoles, but a limited licensing policy for their games. The licensing policies are designed to encourage developers to produce games for the systems, while simultaneously enabling the console producers to retain a great deal of control over the games produced. The console producer must approve all games developed for the consoles before they can be made commercially available. For example, in the case of Microsoft, would-be Xbox games developers must first apply to the Xbox Registered Developer Program (for established games developers) or the Xbox Incubator Program (for smaller or newer games developers). If accepted into one of these two programs, the developer will receive access to development tools, but this does not guarantee the approval of any resulting game titles. The games themselves are subjected to a separate, rigorous approval process.

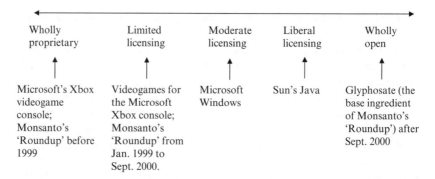

Figure 8.1   Examples on the continuum from wholly proprietary to wholly open

By contrast, the licensing policies for Microsoft's Windows program are more open. Windows is protected by copyright, and Microsoft defends its exclusive right to augment the software; however, it also permits complementary goods providers to access portions of the source code in order to facilitate their development of complementary goods, licenses the rights to such providers to produce complementary applications, and licenses original equipment manufacturers (OEMs) to distribute the software by bundling it with hardware. Those who purchase a license for the software can execute and bundle the software with other goods, but may not augment it. For example, software applications developers may produce and distribute value-added applications for use with Windows so long as those applications do not affect the functionality of the Windows program itself.

Sun's 'community source' (as opposed to 'open source') policy for Java is even more open. Java is a web-oriented software programming language that can be run on any computer, using any operating system (Essner et al., 2001). Sun's 'community source' program allows anyone immediate access to the complete source code for Java, and allows users to develop commercial applications based on the code, or to augment the code for their implementations. These developers pay no license fee to Sun. However, any augmentation to the core infrastructure of Java must be approved by the 'Java community process' (managed by Sun). Sun's 'community source' principle is meant to encourage the broader software community to improve Java and develop complementary applications, but it retains some control over the core platform in order to ensure that the platform does not become fragmented through unmanaged development by the software community.

Many technologies that were once wholly proprietary or partially open become wholly open when their patents or copyrights expire. For instance, Monsanto's highly profitable 'Roundup' herbicide is based on a patented chemical ingredient called glyphosate. This extremely potent herbicide was adopted by farmers in over 100 countries, and accounted for a substantial portion of Monsanto's sales. However, facing impending expiration of its patents, Monsanto began to license the rights to glyphosate production to a few other companies (including Dow Agrosciences, DuPont and Novartis) in 1999. In September 2000 the US patent on glyphosate expired, and any chemical company was free to produce and sell glyphosate-based herbicides in the USA, rendering the technology wholly open.

Incentives for Protection versus Diffusion

In industries characterized by network externalities, it is often argued that the advantages to consumers of adopting open systems (such as increased compatibility with a wider range of complementary products and reduced costs due to greater price competition) outweigh the advantages offered by any of the available proprietary systems. While the greater rent appropriability of a proprietary system might inspire a firm to invest more in technological development (potentially leading to technological advantages), the greater compatibility, flexibility and low costs of open systems can prove very persuasive. However, the relationship between use of open systems versus protected systems and the likelihood of adoption as dominant design is much more complex than this.

Firms that offer products based on open systems usually accrue more rapid adoptions, leading to a larger installed base; however, they do so at the cost of no longer controlling their product technologies. Competitors may easily offer very similar products, and profits may approach those of commodity products. By contrast, protecting the technology not only offers appropriability incentives, but it also can give the firm long-lived advantages in the form of architectural control. First, protecting the technology yields more options for the firm to appropriate rents from its technology. The firm might opt to be the exclusive provider of the technology, enabling it to both control the pricing of the technology and be the sole beneficiary of profits derived from its sales. It could also opt to enter into some restricted licensing or OEM agreements, enabling it to widen the technology's production and distribution while still controlling its diffusion and pricing.

Protecting the technology also gives the developing firm architectural control over the technology (Schilling, 2000). By controlling the technology's architecture, the firm can ensure that the technology is compatible with its own complements, while also restricting its compatibility with the complements produced by others. The firm can also control the rate at which the technology is upgraded or refined, the path it follows in its evolution, and its compatibility with previous generations. If the technology is chosen as a dominant design, the firm with architectural control over the technology can have great influence over the entire industry. Through selective compatibility it can influence which other firms do well and which do not, and it can ensure that it has a number of different avenues from which to profit from the platform.

Microsoft's Windows is the quintessential embodiment of this strategy. Because Windows is the dominant operating system in the PC market, and because it serves as the interface between a computer's hardware and software, Microsoft has considerable market power and architectural control over the evolution of the PC system. Among other things, it has been able to incorporate ever more utility programs into the core program, thereby expanding and taking over the roles of many other software components (Schilling, 2000). Whereas once a user purchased an operating system, uninstaller programs, disk compression programs and memory management programs separately, Windows 95 and 98 integrated all of these products and more into the operating system. This 'feature creep' had a major impact on competition in the industry – many utility producers such as Qualitas, Stac Electronics, Microhelp, Quarterdeck and others, were forced to abandon their once-profitable products.

MULTIPLE PATHWAYS TO THE EMERGENCE OF A DOMINANT DESIGN

The value to consumers of technologies characterized by network externality effects can be divided into (at least) three primary components: (1) standalone functionality and performance; (2) size of the installed base; and (3) availability of complementary goods (Bental and Spiegel, 1995; Schilling, 2003). The importance of each component can vary according to the technology, the market served and individual customer perceptions. For example, customers deciding on a video playing and recording format may place most importance on the availability of complementary goods in the form of prerecorded videos, whereas cellular service customers may place most importance on the size of the installed base and the concomitant network reach. For the customers of videogame consoles, the installed base may be important (because it determines, among other things, the number of other online gamers the individual may play with), and availability of complementary goods may be important (because a console is only as good as the games that may be played on it); however, the technological functionality of the device is also extremely important. Sega was able to take significant share away from Nintendo when it offered a 16-bit system capable of much higher graphics processing (and thus more realistic and fast-paced animation) than Nintendo's 8-bit system. Similarly, Sony and Microsoft were able to break into the videogame console market (despite Nintendo and Sega's installed base and complementary goods advantages) by offering dramatic improvements in technological functionality.

Each of these value components can be managed through different competitive levers of the firm, including the degree to which it protects its technology. For example, a firm can increase its technology's functionality and performance through its own R&D investment (Kristiansen, 1998), or by attracting the development contributions of parties external to the firm (Garud et al., 1998). The firm can increase the size of the technology's installed base and availability of complementary goods through its own investment in penetration pricing or subsidization of installed base, complements or both (Katz and Shapiro, 1986), and through the degree to which it encourages other firms to produce and promote the technology by adopting a relatively 'open' strategy (Hill, 1997). Each of these decisions is necessarily interdependent, and will have implications for the firm's resource needs, its degree of control over the technology and the technology's appropriability.

Standalone Technological Functionality

Both a technology's existing and potential performance can influence its rate of adoption and its likelihood of rising to the position of dominant design (Bental and Spiegel, 1995; Kristiansen, 1998; Schilling, 2003). Although many authors are quick to point out that often it is not the best technology that achieves dominance (Anderson and Tushman, 1991; Arthur, 1989, 1994), a technology's functionality and the rate at which it is improved still play crucial roles in its adoption (Schilling, 2002). Several research studies suggest that for a new technology to displace an entrenched standard, it must provide a significant technological improvement (Gallagher and Park, 2002; Schilling, 1998, 2002; Sheremata, 1999). In each generation of the videogame industry, for example, successful competitors have offered at least three times the clock speed of the fastest system in the previous generation.

If a firm is able to appropriate rents from a technology it has developed, such rents provide both the means and the incentive to invest in further developing the technology. If a technology is 'open', investment in developing the technology by any individual firm results in a positive externality to other firms in the industry, preventing the firm from reaping the full value of its investment. By contrast, if a technology is well protected by its developer, the developing firm will be the primary (or sole) beneficiary of the technology's success, and thus it has greater incentive to invest in further developing the technology. By investing in improving the technology, the firm increases the likelihood that the technology will be adopted by more users and reduces the likelihood that the technology will be displaced by a technology that is perceived as superior. Improving the technology may also enable the firm to charge higher prices for the technology, thus protecting (or improving) its rate of return from its development efforts. The preceding thus suggests that technologies that are protected and controlled by a sponsoring firm are more likely to be improved over time due to investment by the sponsoring firm.

> **Proposition 1a:** Wholly proprietary technologies are more likely to be improved over time through investment by the sponsoring firm than are wholly open technologies.

On the other hand, technologies that are more 'open' may benefit from the collective development efforts of parties external to the sponsoring firm (Dalle and Jullien, 2003; Gawer and Cusumano, 2002). For example, in the software industry, individual programmers may work on an open-source software program because it results in solutions to their own problems, provides an opportunity to interact with peers and improves their reputation as experienced programmers (Bonaccorsi and Rossi, 2003; Ghosh et al., 2002; Lakhani and von Hippel, 2003; Lerner and Tirole, 2000; Perkins, 1999). Apache, Netscape Navigator, Unix and Linux are all technologies that have benefited significantly from external development. Because their source codes were freely available to the vast world of developers that could benefit from them, the technologies were able to reap the advantages of having a much larger pool of talent and resources directed at improving the technologies than could have been rallied by the original developers of the technologies. This suggests that open source provides an alternative path to platform improvement.

> **Proposition 1b:** Wholly open technologies are more likely to be improved over time through the development efforts of parties external to the sponsoring firm.

External development, however, poses some costs and risks. First, while some open-source communities have given rise to a hierarchical organization that helps to govern the development efforts of the community

(Bonaccorsi and Rossi, 2003), it is more common for external development to lack the strong coordination of internal development. External developers may have very diverse objectives for the technology: rather than working together toward some unified vision of what the technology could achieve in the future, they might work in different, possibly even conflicting, directions (Garud et al., 2002). Much of their effort may be redundant, as different external developers work on solving the same problems without communicating with each other. Finally, whether and how these improvements get incorporated into the technology and disseminated to other users of the technology can prove very problematic. Unix provides a stark example of this.

Unix was an operating system first developed by AT&T's Bell Laboratories in 1969. Although a Department of Justice injunction forbade AT&T from selling software commercially, it made the source code for the product available through licensing arrangements. Early licensees (notably University of California at Berkeley) began using and adapting the software for their purposes, causing many incompatible versions of the software to emerge. Although the software community made several attempts to standardize the Unix operating language, their efforts failed. AT&T also challenged the commercialization of several Unix variants, but to no avail. Ultimately AT&T sold the division responsible for Unix to Novell, and Novell in turn handed over the rights to the Unix trademark to the X/Open standards-setting body (Essner et al., 2001).

A firm that protects and controls its technology has both the incentive and the ability to protect the integrity of the technology, and can thus prevent the fragmentation of the platform.

Proposition 1c: Wholly proprietary technologies are less likely to become fragmented than wholly open technologies.

Building Installed Base

As discussed previously, in industries characterized by increasing returns, one of the most important forces driving the emergence of a dominant design is the size of the installed base. A firm that achieves an advantage in installed base will typically reap learning-curve advantages and network externality benefits. A firm that has greater production and sales should be able to drive down unit costs, and reinvest more money into the product design and production process. A technology with a larger installed base typically attracts more users and developers of complementary goods, leading to a self-reinforcing externality effect. Therefore, other things being equal, a firm that can accelerate the adoption of its technology stands a better chance of having that technology become the industry standard.

One method of accelerating the adoption of the technology is to utilize a wholly open technology strategy. If multiple firms are producing, distributing and promoting the technology, the technology's installed base may accumulate much more rapidly than if one firm alone is responsible for such activities. Competition among producers may drive down the price of the technology, making it more attractive to customers. Both customers and complementary goods providers may also perceive the technology as better (or its future more certain) if there are multiple companies backing it. This perception can lead to much more rapid adoption of the technology by customers and complementary goods providers, which further stimulates more companies to back the technology. Thus an open systems strategy can stimulate the growth of the installed base by encouraging collective production, distribution and promotion.

> **Proposition 2a:** A wholly open technology may be produced, distributed and promoted by multiple firms, accelerating the growth of its installed base.

A wholly open technology strategy also, however, dissipates the incentives for firms to promote the technology. If any individual firm's efforts to promote the technology may result in benefits that are distributed among multiple firms, there can be free-rider problems. If firms believe they will benefit from the promotion efforts of others, they have less incentive to invest in promotion themselves. Furthermore, firms may be unwilling to invest in promotion of the technology if they believe other firms will benefit by their activities. Additionally, if competition among multiple producers drives down the price of the technology, the reduced profitability of offering the technology may reduce producers' incentives to either produce or promote it.

By contrast, if a single firm is the primary beneficiary of its technology's success, it has much greater incentive to promote the technology. It may adopt a penetration pricing strategy to rapidly build its installed base, it may spend aggressively on advertising to increase awareness of the technology, and it may even subsidize the production of complementary goods in order to increase the desirability of its technology to customers. A firm may be willing to lose money in the short term in order to secure the technology's position as the standard, because once the technology has emerged as a standard, the payoff can be substantial and enduring. By contrast, when multiple firms can produce a technology, losing money on the technology in the short term in order to promote it as a standard is highly risky since the distribution of the payoffs in the long term is uncertain. This suggests that the installed base of a proprietary technology may grow faster because its sponsor is more likely to invest aggressively in its promotion.

Proposition 2b: A wholly proprietary technology is more likely to be heavily promoted by its sponsor, accelerating the growth of its installed base.

Availability of Complementary Goods

As noted previously, complementary goods can dramatically impact the usefulness or desirability of many technologies. In such a situation, the availability and quality of complementary goods will be a significant force driving the adoption of a dominant design.

If a technology is diffused liberally through an open source strategy, it may attract more developers of complementary goods for a number of reasons. First, if the 'open' strategy results in increased collective production, this may increase the installed base of the technology, making it a more attractive platform for which to develop complements. Second, if multiple companies are backing the technology, then complementary goods producers may perceive the technology as facing a more certain future, reducing any apprehension they might have felt about developing complements for the platform. Third, under an open strategy, complement producers pay little or no licensing fees to the technology's developer, making it very economical for them to build complementary goods. Fourth, the more open the technology, the easier it typically is for complementary goods producers to develop products that are not only compatible with the platform, but fully exploit the platform's capabilities. The preceding thus suggests that using a wholly open strategy to diffuse a technology can lead to greater availability of complementary goods.

Proposition 3a: A wholly open technology strategy can make the development of complementary goods easier, cheaper, less risky and more attractive, thus leading to greater availability of complementary goods.

Carefully controlled proprietary technologies also, however, have certain advantages with respect to complementary goods. First, if a technology is protected, its sponsor can control the proliferation of complementary goods, and can require that complement producers adhere to quality standards that protect the image and integrity of the platform. This can be a significant factor in a technology's success. Consider, for example, the story of Atari. Atari's Pong was tremendously successful, earning over $1 million in revenues in its first year. Its successor, the Atari Video Computer System (VCS, later renamed the 2600) was also very successful, and Atari sold more than $5 billion worth of 2600 systems and products by 1983. However, neither Pong nor the 2600 were well protected. In addition to knock-offs of the consoles (there were 60 Pong console knock-offs on the market by the mid-1970s), there was also a rapid proliferation of unauthorized games designed to run on the VCS/2600. This led to a market glut of games of dubious quality, and many unhappy retailers with videogame inventories they were unable to move. Profits on consoles and games went into a steep decline, and by 1985 many were declaring the videogame industry dead. When Nintendo and Sega resurrected the industry, they were careful to implement very tight security on both the consoles and the games. Nintendo, for example, used a security chip to ensure that non-authorized games could not play on the Nintendo console, and also utilized a very restrictive licensing policy for games developers. Developers were required to submit their game designs to Nintendo, and if they were approved, Nintendo would have the game cartridges manufactured by its own contract manufacturers and then sell the cartridges to the developers. Nintendo could thus carefully control both the quality of games offered for its system and the rate at which they were offered.

Notably, every videogame console manufacturer that has been successful in at least one generation (e.g. Atari, Coleco, Nintendo, Sega, Sony, Microsoft) invested heavily in developing games in house rather than relying solely on external development. Every console manufacturer that relied exclusively on external developers (e.g. NEC, Philips, 3DO) failed (Schilling, 2003). For a videogame console to attract users, it has to arrive on the market with high-quality games already available. This means that console manufacturers must go to whatever lengths are necessary to ensure that quality games are being developed in advance of the launch date, even if this involves considerable effort and expense. More generally, this points to the differential incentives of sponsors of protected technologies versus open technologies with respect to sponsoring the development of complements. If a firm sponsoring a technology stands to gain significantly from its adoption as a dominant design, it has incentives to sponsor the production of complementary goods. The firm may produce the goods themselves (as in the videogame example), or it might find methods of subsidizing their production by other firms. For instance, in the high-stakes battle between Toshiba-backed HD-DVD and Sony's Blu-Ray digital video format, Toshiba agreed to pay Paramount and DreamWorks Animation a total of $150 million to subsidize their production of movie titles in the HD-DVD format. This prompted Sony to commit hundreds of millions of dollars in marketing support if Warner would adopt the Blu-Ray format in place of the HD-DVD format (Grover and Edwards, 2007). Both companies were willing to engage in such aggressive sponsorship because it was clear that the format with the most movie titles would likely be chosen as the dominant platform, and the firm controlling the dominant platform stood to reap significant future profits. Ultimately Warner agreed to back the Blu-Ray format, resulting in Toshiba's concession of defeat and dropping of the HD-DVD platform (Ault, 2008). In sum, a protected technology offers greater incentives for the technology developer to sponsor the production of complementary goods and ensure their quality.

Proposition 3b: A wholly protected technology strategy offers more incentives to its developer to sponsor the production of complementary goods and ensure their quality, thus leading to greater availability of high-quality complementary goods.

These paths (and their concomitant propositions) are summarized in Figure 8.2.

TRADEOFFS, RESOURCES AND INCENTIVES: TUNING CONTROL STRATEGIES

The preceding thus suggests that rather than assuming that open technologies grow faster than protected technologies, we need to think more precisely about the different pathways and incentives that connect technology strategy to outcomes such as technology improvement, growth of the installed base and availability of complementary goods. Doing so reveals the specific nature of the tradeoffs, and can help the firm to assess which protection strategies will work to its best advantage. We begin by considering the tradeoffs between sole production, sponsored production and collective production of both the technology platform and its complements. We then examine the tradeoffs inherent in internal development versus external development. In the last section we consider the role of incentives for architectural control.

Sole Production, Sponsored Production and Collective Production

There are obvious advantages to being the sole producer of a successful technology. The most obvious of these is the ability to earn monopoly rents. Other advantages include control over quality, brand image, control over the development of the technology and so on. However, if being the

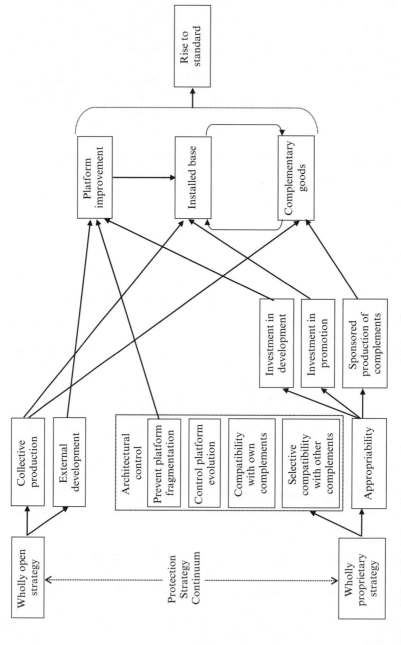

Figure 8.2   Multiple pathways to the emergence of a dominant design

sole producer lessens the technology's chances of being successful, it may be in the firm's best interests to enable production of the technology by others.

Production capabilities, marketing capabilities and capital

If the firm is unable to produce the technology at sufficient volume or quality levels (or market the technology with sufficient intensity), then being the sole provider of the technology may significantly hinder its adoption. For example, when JVC was promoting its VHS standard for video recorders, its management knew that it was at a disadvantage in both manufacturing and marketing capabilities compared to Sony (which was promoting the Beta technology). JVC thus chose to pursue vigorously both licensing and OEM agreements, lining up Hitachi, Matsushita, Mitsubishi and Sharp to boost the technology's production rate (Cusumano et al., 1992).

Similarly, if complementary goods influence the value of the technology to users, then the firm must (a) be able to produce the complements itself in sufficient range and quantity, (b) sponsor their production by other firms, or (c) encourage collective production of the complements through a more open technology strategy. As described previously, the only firms that were successful in the US videogame industry were those that were able to produce games in house (ensuring that a wide range of games would be available at the console's launch) and that also encouraged third-party development of games (to ensure that the number of game titles grew quickly). Both Nintendo and Sega had previous arcade experience, and thus possessed considerable game development expertise in house. Microsoft had long been a producer of PC-based videogames; thus it had some game developing experience, and it also acquired a few small-name developers (e.g. Bungie) to expand its expertise in developing console-type games (Kittner et al., 2002). Sony had no prior game experience, but aggressively acquired in-house developers, licensed external developers, and set up a program with Metrowerks to provide developer tools that would make it easier for external developers to produce Playstation games. Intel pursues a more nuanced strategy to encourage the development of complements for its microprocessor platforms. It provides a partial financial subsidy, combined with a mix of non-financial subsidies such as the sharing of intellectual property, the loan of engineers, and assistance with marketing and commercialization (Gawer and Henderson, 2007).

The preceding thus suggests that if a firm lacks the production capability or expertise to produce and promote the technology at sufficient volume or quality, it should encourage collective production (e.g. limited to aggressive licensing). Similarly, if the firm is unable to provide a sufficient range of high-quality complementary goods, it should encourage collective production of complements through a more open technology strategy (e.g. limited to aggressive licensing), and utilize forms of sponsorship.

> **Proposition 4a**: The degree to which a firm is constrained in production and marketing capabilities or capital will be positively related to the value of adopting an open (any level) technology strategy.

Industry opposition against sole-source technology

Sometimes other industry members are able to exert strong pressure against the adoption of a technology that would give one (or a few) producer(s) undue control and power, causing a technology that is restricted to such production to be rejected or more hotly contested than a more open technology. This was the case with Sony and Philips's Super Audio CD (SACD) audio format. Sony and Philips had jointly created the original compact disk (CD) format, and split the royalties on every CD player ever sold, totaling hundreds of millions of dollars. The rest of the world's leading consumer electronics producers (including Hitachi, JVC, Matsushita, Mitsubishi and Toshiba) and record producers (including Time Warner and Seagram's Universal Music group) banded together to form the Digital Video Disk (DVD) Audio consortium. This consortium's purpose was to promote the DVD Audio standard that was intended to displace the CD and enable royalties to be split among the ten companies that controled the patents (Brinkley, 1999). Industry observers noted that a driving force underlying the formation of the consortium was to prevent Sony and Philips from controlling yet another generation of audio formats. This example illustrates that the degree of industry opposition to a sole source technology needs to be taken into consideration when the firm formulates its technology strategy.

If the industry is able to pose significant opposition, the firm may need to consider a more open technology strategy (e.g. limited to moderate licensing) to improve the technology's likelihood of being chosen as a dominant design.

> **Proposition 4b**: Industry opposition to a sole source technology will increase the value of adopting a limited to moderately open technology strategy.

Internal Development versus External Development

Whether it is optimal for a firm to rely on internal versus external development depends largely on its resources available for internal development, and the importance of controlling the development path of the technology.

Resources for internal development

If a firm does not have significant resources (capital, technological expertise) to invest in the technology's functionality, it may have difficulty producing a technology that has an initial level of performance, and rate of improvement over time, that the market finds attractive. In such instances, it can be valuable to tap the external development efforts of other firms (or individuals) through utilizing a more open technology strategy. For example, when Netscape found itself in a race to match browser capabilities with Microsoft, it was at a tremendous disadvantage in both human resources and capital. Microsoft had legions of internal developers and a lot of money to invest in Explorer; there was no way that Netscape could match those resources internally. Instead, Netscape tapped the external development community by giving them access to its source code and incorporating their improvements into the Navigator product (Garud et al., 1998). This suggests that a firm that lacks the resources to provide sufficient technology quality should employ a more open technology strategy (e.g. limited licensing to an aggressive licensing strategy).

> **Proposition 5a**: The degree to which a firm is constrained in its ability to invest in improving the functionality of its technology will be positively related to the value of adopting an open (any level) technology strategy.

Control over fragmentation

For technologies in which standardization and compatibility are important, maintaining the integrity of the core product is essential, and external development can put it at risk. It is noteworthy that of all the factors influencing the value of the technology, the only one that cannot be reached through a wholly open strategy is the ability to prevent fragmentation of the technology platform. As was illustrated with the example of Unix, if the developing firm relinquishes all control over the development of the technology, the technology will have no 'shepherd' with the ability and authority to direct its trajectory and ensure that a single standard remains intact. This suggests, then, that the developer of any technology that requires standardization and compatibility should retain some degree of control over the technology, or find/establish another governing body with the authority to do so (avoiding a wholly open strategy).

> **Proposition 5b**: The degree to which a technology requires standardization and compatibility will be positively related to the value of adopting a strategy that enables some degree of proprietary control.

Incentives for architectural control

A firm's incentives for architectural control depend heavily on its stake in complements production and a particular development path for the technology. If a firm is a major producer of complements for the technology or its core competencies are tied closely to a particular technology trajectory, then the firm will face greater incentives to control the architecture of the technology (Gawer and Henderson, 2007).

Selective compatibility

Architectural control over the evolution of a technology is always valuable; however, it becomes particularly valuable if a firm is a significant producer of complements to the technology in question. A firm with architectural control can typically design the technology to be compatible with its own complements, and incompatible with those of competitors. If the technology is chosen as the dominant design, this architectural control allows the firm to ensure that it reaps the lion's share of the rewards in complements production. Furthermore, by making the technology selectively compatible with some competitors and not others, the firm can exert great influence over the competitive field (Schilling, 2000). This suggests that if a firm is a significant producer of complements, it should use a strategy that exerts significant control over the technology (e.g. wholly proprietary to moderate licensing).

> **Proposition 6a**: The degree to which a firm competes in markets for complementary products will be positively related to the value of adopting a technology strategy that enables a moderate to high degree of proprietary control.

Controlling the trajectory

Technology trajectories are path-dependent; minor events in their evolution can set them careening off into unexpected directions. A firm that has a significant stake in a particular evolution path (because, for example, it has technological competencies that are much more amenable to one path of evolution than other potential paths) can use architectural control to its advantage. A firm that controls a dominant design can direct the development efforts put into the technology so that it exploits the firm's core competencies (Schilling, 2000). It can co-opt or destroy less favorable development paths by denying their progenitors access to the market. In sum, having architectural control over a dominant design can put the developing firm in the position of puppet master for an entire industry – at least until the dominant design is displaced. The preceding suggests that to the extent that a firm's interests are tied to a particular technology trajectory, the firm should use a strategy that exerts significant control over the technology (e.g. wholly proprietary to moderate licensing).

Proposition 6b: The degree that a firm's capabilities are closely tied to a particular technology trajectory will be positively related to the value of adopting a technology strategy that enables a moderate to high degree of proprietary control.

DISCUSSION AND IMPLICATIONS

This research has developed a model of the tradeoffs inherent in the choice between protection versus diffusion of a technology. Traditionally work in management and economics has emphasized the benefits of strong appropriability. Recent work has challenged this assumption by pointing out the advantages of more open technologies, such as faster technology diffusion in the marketplace. The current research moves beyond the appropriability-versus-open debate by examining the more subtly nuanced benefits of different positions along the control continuum. While either a wholly proprietary or wholly open strategy may offer routes to securing the position of dominant design, the value of either strategy depends on the firm's resources and industry environment. By teasing apart the different levers of competition that determine the success or failure of a particular technology, it is possible to develop a set of propositions about what firm resources and industry conditions will increase the value of particular positions on the control continuum. This analysis also reveals that one key determinant of a technology's success, platform integrity (i.e. a platform that does not become fragmented through uncoordinated development), may be achievable only through a strategy that incorporates some degree of control. This suggests a finding that is likely to be controversial among some researchers: for technologies that require standardization and compatibility, it is possible that a wholly open strategy is never optimal, irrespective of the firm's resources or industry conditions.

The model and propositions developed here have a number of direct implications for management and future research. First, the model provides managers with a systematic tool for assessing the benefits and costs/risks of adopting a strategy at various points along the control continuum. It suggests that one of the first steps managers must take in planning their technology strategy is to assess the relative importance of each of the competitive levers (standalone functionality, installed base and complementary goods) to the technology's likelihood of success. Managers can then analyze their resources and industry environment to determine their best options for achieving desired objectives for that driver – e.g. is the firm capable of achieving necessary performance levels (and rate of improvement) through in-house development? Is there likely to be strong industry opposition to having a sole source? Can the firm ensure that complements are available in sufficient quality and quantity? To what degree are the firm's future profits reliant upon having control over compatibility of complements? And so forth.

The model also reveals the factors likely to influence technology strategy dynamics that play out over time when two or more competitors vie for the position of dominant design. For example, whether a technology offers sufficient standalone utility to attract customers is relative to the utility offered by competing technologies. Furthermore, the sponsors of each of the competing technologies are likely to have different resource profiles that influence their ability to rely on internal versus external development, promotion, complement subsidization and so on. This indicates that when two technologies compete for the position of dominant design, managers must compare not only their technology's relative performance, cost, availability and so on, but also the relative ability of each competitor to increase its position through its own capabilities or through tapping the external production and development community by making the technology more open. For example, the model suggests that if a technology is well positioned according to the competitive levers of standalone utility, installed base and complementary goods, and has greater internal resources than other firms promoting competing technologies, it is unlikely to adopt a strategy that embraces much openness even in response to significant competition. However, if a competitor enters that has far greater internal resources, the originally dominant firm may be forced to utilize some degree of openness to defend its position, even if its technology was initially better positioned according to the competitive levers. This was aptly illustrated in the browser wars case. When Netscape was in a position of having a clearly superior browser on the market (before the entry of Microsoft with Internet Explorer), it did not need to make its technology open. When Microsoft entered, however, not only did its browser imitate many of Netscape's product features (eliminating much of Netscape's performance advantage); it also had far greater resources to invest in improving and promoting the product: Microsoft could spend far more on development; it bundled Internet Explorer with Windows 95, immediately giving the product a large installed base; and it offered the browser for free. It was thus clear that Netscape could not win a standards race relying on internal resources alone, and the firm would be forced to either adopt a more open stance with its technology or to find a way to tap deeper capital resources (through, e.g., courting an acquisition by a much larger firm). By 1998, Netscape had done both – it made the Communicator source code freely available on the Internet and was acquired by AOL.

One of the key contributions of this research is its development of the idea of a control continuum, and identification of factors that influence the value of different firm strategies along this continuum. Future research could greatly extend the value of this model by developing robust measures of degrees of openness that could be used in empirical examinations of firm strategies. The model here also suggests that formal modeling or simulation work may be fruitful in predicting technology outcomes based on initial firm and environment states, and the tactics employed by competing firms. Finally, this research suggests that future research should more vigorously explore firm incentives for architectural control, as these incentives pertain to longer-term (and less easily observable) objectives of firms that can result in outcomes that appear unlikely. Exploration along each of these paths should help us gain greater understanding of how standards battles unfold, and the optimal degree to which a technology should be protected or diffused.

NOTES

1. For good reviews of this work, see Economides (1996) and Quélin et al. (2001).
2. '*De facto* standards' is defined in approximately the same way as 'dominant design' – it is the emergence of a standard through market selection.

REFERENCES

Anderson, P. and M.L. Tushman (1991), 'Managing through cycles of technological change', *Research/Technology Management*, May/June, 26–31.
Argote, L. (1999), *Organizational Learning: Creating, Retaining and Transferring Knowledge*, Boston, MA: Kluwer Academic Publishers.
Arthur, W.B. (1989), 'Competing technologies, increasing returns, and lock-in by historical events', *The Economic Journal*, **99**, 116–31.
Arthur, W.B. (1994), *Increasing Returns and Path Dependency in the Economy*, Ann Arbor, MI: University of Michigan Press.
Ault, S. (2008), 'Stores push out HD DVD', *Video Business*, 25 February, 35.
Bental, B. and M. Spiegel (1995), 'Network competition, product quality, and market coverage in the presence of network externalities', *Journal of Industrial Economics*, **43** (2), 197–208.
Besen, S.M. and J. Farrell (1994), 'Choosing how to compete: strategies and tactics in standardization', *Journal of Economic Perspectives*, **8**, 117–31.
Bonaccorsi, A. and C. Rossi (2003), 'Why open source software can succeed', *Research Policy*, **32**, 1243–58.

Brinkley, J. (1999), 'Disk versus disk: the fight for the ears of America', *New York Times*, 8 August.

Casadesus-Masanell, R. and P. Ghemawat (2003), 'Dynamic mixed duopoly: a model motivated by Linux vs. Windows', Harvard Business School Working Paper Series, No. 04-012.

Chau, P.Y.K. and K.Y. Tam (1997), 'Factors affecting the adoption of open systems: an exploratory study', *MIS Quarterly*, March, 1–24.

Choi, J. (1994), 'Network externalities, compatibility choice, and planned obsolescence', *The Journal of Industrial Economics, 42*, 167–82.

Cusumano, M., Y. Mylonadis and R. Rosenbloom (1992), 'Strategic maneuvering and mass market dynamics: VHS over Beta', *Business History Review*, Spring, 51–94.

Dalle, J.M. and N. Jullien (2003), '"Libre" software: turning fads into institutions?', *Research Policy*, 32, 1–11.

de Laat, P.B. (2005), 'Copyright or copyleft? An analysis of property regimes for software development', *Research Policy*, 34, 1511–32.

Economides, N. (1996), 'The economics of networks', *International Journal of Industrial Organization*, 14, 673–99.

Economides, N. and G.S. Woroch (1992), 'Benefits and pitfalls of network interconnection', Working Paper No. EC-92-31.

Essner, D., P. Liao and M.A. Schilling (2001), 'Sun Microsystems: Establishing the Java standard', Boston University Teaching Case 2001-02.

Farrell, J. and G. Saloner (1985), 'Standardization, compatibility and innovation', *RAND Journal of Economics*, 16, 70–83.

Farrell, J. and G. Saloner (1986), 'Installed base and compatibility: innovation, product preannouncements, and predation', *American Economic Review*, 76, 940–55.

Ferguson, C.H. and C.R. Morris (1993), *Computer Wars*, New York: Random House.

Gacek, C. and B. Arief (2004), 'The many meanings of open source', *IEEE Software*, 21 (1), 34–40.

Gallagher, S. and S.H. Park (2002), 'Innovation and competition in standard-based industries: a historical analysis of the U.S. home video game market', *IEEE Transactions on Engineering Management*, 49 (1), 67–82.

Garud, R. and A. Kumaraswamy (1993), 'Changing competitive dynamics in network industries: an exploration of Sun Microsystems' open systems strategy', *Strategic Management Journal*, 14, 351–69.

Garud, R., S. Jain and A. Kumaraswamy (2002), 'Institutional entrepreneurship in the sponsorship of common technological standards: the case of Sun Microsystems and Java', *Academy of Management Journal*, 45, 196–214.

Garud, R., S. Jain and C. Phelps (1998), 'A tale of two browsers', New York University Teaching Case.

Gawer, A. and M.A. Cusumano (2002), *Platform Leadership: How Intel, Microsoft, and Cisco Drive Industry Innovation*, Boston, MA: Harvard Business School Press.

Gawer, A. and R. Henderson (2007), 'Platform owner entry and innovation in complementary markets: evidence from Intel', *Journal of Economics and Management Strategy*, 16 (1), 1–34.

Ghosh, R.A., R. Glott, B. Krieger and G. Robles (2002), 'Free/libre and open source software: survey and study. Final Report (D18), Part 4, Survey of Developers', International Institute of Infonomics, University of Maastricht,

The Netherlands, available at http://flossproject.org/report/FLOSS_Final4.pdf, accessed 17 June 2005.

Grover, R. and C. Edwards (2007), 'Next-gen DVDs: Advantage, Sony', *BusinessWeek*, **4063**, 28–9.

Henderson, R. and K. Clark (1990), 'Architectural innovation: the reconfiguration of existing product technologies and the failure of established firms', *Administrative Science Quarterly*, **35**, 9–30.

Hertel, G., S. Niedner and S. Hermann (2003), 'Motivation of software developers in open source projects: an internet-based survey of contributors to the Linux kernel', *Research Policy*, **32** (7), 1159–77.

Hill, C.W.L. (1997), 'Establishing a standard: competitive strategy and technological standards in winner-take-all markets', *Academy of Management Executive*, **11**(2), 7–25.

Katz, M.L. and C. Shapiro (1985), 'Network externalities, competition, and compatibility', *American Economic Review*, **75**, 424–40.

Katz, M. and C. Shapiro (1986), 'Technology adoption in the presence of network externalities', *Journal of Political Economy*, **94**, 822–41.

Katz, M. and C. Shapiro (1992), 'Product introduction with network externalities', *Journal of Industrial Economics*, **40** (1), 55–83.

Kittner, J., M.A. Schilling and S. Karl (2002), 'Microsoft's Xbox', New York University Teaching Case.

Kristiansen, E.G. (1998), 'R&D in the presence of network externalities: timing and compatibility', *RAND Journal of Economics*, **29**, 531–47.

Lakhani, K. and E. von Hippel (2003), 'How open source software works: "free" user-to-user assistance', *Research Policy*, **32**, 923–43.

Lecocq, X and B. Demil (2005), 'Open standard: role of externalities and impact on the industry structure', Working Paper, IAE de Lille.

Lerner, J. and J. Tirole (2000), 'The simple economics of Open Source', Working Paper 7600, National Bureau of Economic Research.

Levy, F.K. (1965), 'Adaptation in the production process', *Management Science*, **11**, 136–54.

Perkins, G. (1999), 'Culture clash and the road of word dominance', *IEEE Software*, **16** (1), 80–84.

Quélin, B.V., T. Abdessemed, J.P. Bonardi and R. Durand (2001), 'Standardisation of network technologies: market processes or the result of inter-firm cooperation?', *Journal of Economic Surveys*, **15**, 543–69.

Schilling, M.A. (1998), 'Technological lock out: an integrative model of the economic and strategic factors driving technology success and failure', *Academy of Management Review*, **23**, 267–84.

Schilling, M.A. (2000), 'Towards a general modular systems theory and its application to inter-firm product modularity', *Academy of Management Review*, **25**, 312–34.

Schilling, M.A. (2002), 'Technology success and failure in winner-take-all markets: testing a model of technological lock out', *Academy of Management Journal*, **45**, 387–98.

Schilling, M.A. (2003), 'Technological leapfrogging: lessons from the U.S. videogame industry', *California Management Review*, **45** (3), 6–32.

Shankar, V. and B.L. Bayus (2003), 'Network effects and competition: an empirical analysis of the home video game industry', *Strategic Management Journal*, **24**, 375–84.

Sheremata, W.A. (1999), 'The impact of network effects on strategies of innovation', Panel presentation at the 1997 Strategic Management Conference, Berlin.

Suarez, F.F. (2004), 'Battles for technological dominance: an integrative framework', *Research Policy*, **33** (2), 271–86.

Thum, M. (1994), 'Network externalities, technological progress, and the competition of market contracts', *International Journal of Industrial Organization*, **12**, 269–89.

Tushman, M. and P. Anderson (1986), 'Technological discontinuities and organizational environments', *Administrative Science Quarterly*, **31**, 439–65.

Utterback, J. and W. Abernathy (1975), 'A dynamic model of process and product innovation', *Omega*, **33**, 639–56.

Wade, J. (1995), 'Dynamics of organizational communities and technological bandwagons: an empirical investigation of community evolution in the microprocessor market', *Strategic Management Journal*, **16**, 111–34.

Yelle, L.E. (1979), 'The learning curve: Historical review and comprehensive survey', *Decision Sciences*, **10**, 302–32.

9. Open platform development and the commercial Internet

Shane Greenstein[1]

INTRODUCTION

The structure of the commercial Internet cut against the prevailing opinion of many executives in computing and communications in the mid-1990s. Unlike any successful commercial platform in the recent past, there was no profit-oriented organization providing platform leadership. Platform leadership was thought to be necessary for a thriving and growing market. For example, both Intel and Microsoft claimed that their actions helped move the PC market forward and helped make it more prosperous.

The most vocal participants in Internet governance did not apologize for their unusual structure. Rather, they crowed about their independence. They reveled in the freedom of the Internet's development processes and stressed that it placed comparatively fewer restrictions on the flow of technical information. Some even pointed to the PC market as a model of what they were trying to avoid.

That difference of opinion has not declined with time. A debate persists today about how and why computing platforms thrive with and without commercial leadership. This chapter illuminates these issues by returning to the first market in which they arose and by re-examining the core issue: what would have been different about the Internet if it had been organized as a proprietary commercial platform?

The answer comes in two steps. The first part of the chapter defines 'open' in the context of the time, namely, comparing Microsoft's development of Windows 95 with similar processes for developing the Internet. While many of Microsoft's practices as a proprietary software maker were not appreciably different from those found at other firms (such as Oracle, Apple, SAP or IBM), Microsoft's practices serve as a useful benchmark. Its managers knew how to reach the organizational frontier for production of large scale software in a way few others did.[2]

The comparison focuses attention on one key difference between open and proprietary processes, namely, in the policies governing information about pervasive standards embedded in the platform. Open processes employed documented standards and did not restrict access to these documents or their use. In contrast, proprietary processes resulted in more limited rights for market participants other than the platform leader. Only the platform leaders had unrestricted access to information.

The second step in this chapter examines how three specific features of the Internet might have changed had its processes been less open: the transition from the research-oriented to the commercial Internet; the degree of innovation around the time of the transition; and the events leading to structural change in the commercial Internet market. I shall conclude that openness did not do some of the things for which it is often credited, like make the Internet more innovative. However, I shall also conclude that openness did play a special role in shaping outcomes in the commercial Internet at this time – in encouraging participation in development of Internet infrastructure and in fostering structural change in the provision of commercial software.

The chapter contrasts with prior examinations of open processes aimed at potential participants in those processes or potential imitators.[3] It places more emphasis on showing how Internet processes shaped commercial outcomes, if at all.[4] This will make the chapter similar to studies of participation in open source projects, which often stress that many participants in the commercial Internet favored no restrictions (on information and participation) for reasons that had little to do with their commercial consequences.[5] However, rather than just assuming restriction mattered for market outcomes, this study examines how and why.

This chapter brings the analysis of openness closer to the literature on platform leadership. This is rarely done because the two literatures draw on very distinct and disparate sets of institutional facts and circumstances. Interesting and useful exceptions are West and Dedrick (2000, 2001).[6] Those essays use some of the same platform concepts to illuminate events in the Japanese PC market and the Linux market. In contrast, here those concepts are used to illuminate the processes for shaping the Internet's protocols.[7] That yields insights that differ from prior studies of Internet governance,[8] and about the commercial Internet's economic development.[9] In particular, this chapter's analysis circumscribes some common claims for the benefits of openness – such as whether openness led to more innovation. This analysis also makes more precise how and why openness mattered for commercial outcomes – such as how openness fostered structural change in the commercial Internet.

COMPUTING PLATFORMS AND THE INTERNET

How can the openness of the commercial Internet be compared with other platforms, such as personal computing? In 1995, the commercial Internet was quite young while the PC market was almost two decades old. Yet they had many economic similarities.

Both the Internet and the PC were platforms. That should not be a surprise, since any widely deployed computing technology cannot function efficiently without employing a platform, namely, a standard bundle of components that users employ together as a system to regularly deliver services.[10]

They shared another feature. In both platforms, users had discretion to make modifications after purchase. The IBM PC (and its descendants) had allowed for user modification ever since its introduction, through user additions of electronic cards, peripherals or software applications. The Internet also gave considerable discretion to users. If any administrators or users found existing code unsatisfactory, they were at liberty to propose a new retrofit. They also had the option of proposing a new protocol if they had the running code for it.

In North America the Internet and the PC also both drew on a similar knowledge base and similar pools of programming talent who shared lessons with one another, sometimes reluctantly. The most talented developers and programmers moved between multiple platforms, whether it was a Unix-oriented network software or C++ for a PC.[11]

Despite all those similarities, the commercial Internet of early 1995 and the personal computing platform differed in two key aspects. First, the PC came as a box with peripherals. In contrast, the Internet was not a corporal good. The Internet could not be touched, unpacked or shipped in a turnkey form. Despite the efforts of some enterprising vendors, a user could not simply purchase 'the Internet in a box'.[12] That rendered the business proposition for the Internet rather inchoate in comparison to the PC.

The second difference received considerable attention from contemporaries. The PC bundle was developed and sold in a proprietary environment. In contrast, developers called the Internet more 'open'. There was only one problem with that label. 'Open' was inherently vague. To a contemporary, it elicited about as many definitions in trade discussions as Eskimos had for snow.[13] In the context of comparing development in a proprietary and open source environment, DiBona et al. (2006, p. 22) sums up the blending of similarities and differences when he remarks that 'they come from the same people, and they're using a lot of the same methods and tools. It is the licenses and ideals behind open source programs that make them remarkable, different and revolutionary.'

There was a third difference, and it served as another source of confusion. Each platform employed distinct processes for decision making. That is, two commercial firms, Microsoft and Intel, retained and guarded their right to make unilateral decisions about the pervasive standards embedded within the platform. The Internet, in contrast, employed a consensus process for determining the design of pervasive standards and protocols.[14]

To disentangle the consequences of restricting information, it is essential to view the functions of platform leadership broadly. A platform leader performs four functions:

- designing a standard bundle of technical implementations that others used in their applications;
- operating processes to alter those standards and inform others about those alterations;
- establishing targets and roadmaps to coordinate developer and user investments;
- providing tools and alternative forms of assistance to others who wanted to build applications using their technical standards.

As we shall see, unilateral and consensus processes perform these functions in very different ways. In addition, each process employed distinct policies for releasing information. This is best illustrated by examining each process in some detail.

The Proprietary Side: Windows 95

In early 1995 the PC platform was in the midst of an upgrade to Windows 95, which was due in the summer of that year. The upgrade was a culmination of a major transition away from DOS as the predominant compatible system for IBM PCs. As a text-based operating system, DOS – along with several upgrades – had been the operating system since 1981.

Yet getting from blackboard conceptions into mass-market products had vexed many firms. By early 1995 it was apparent that Microsoft had found a way to make that transition for the IBM PC, and simultaneously keep the Redmond-based firm at the center of it.[15] What had Microsoft done? In short, Windows 3.0 had been an addition, residing on top of DOS, and later improved in Windows 3.1. Microsoft also had lined up every major application firm around a new development, later to be named Windows 95. The new operating system would resemble Windows 3.1 in its user interface, but include many improvements. In addition, it would reside at the core of the operating system, which would yield numerous technical benefits and functional improvements.[16]

The project imposed a set of rules and policies on application developers. Microsoft defined a technical layer, invented on one side of it, and then enabled peripheral developments at the other side of the layer. These boundaries between the layers were called APIs (application programmer interfaces). The use of APIs was typical for a proprietary platform. Other proprietary software firms (e.g. Apple, Oracle and SAP) used similar practices to organize a community of others. If anything was novel, it was the scale of the community involved in Windows 95. The number of participants in the PC community in the mid-1990s exceeded anything ever organized by Apple, IBM or SUN, for example, or by Microsoft, for that matter.

This strategy came with many challenges in execution. Microsoft's employees worked hard to provide inviting pervasive standards on which others built their applications. This required good designs that supported a developer's needs and which had to be backed up with technical support staff. The firm also considered subsidizing the costs of tools for developers.

None of this arose solely through altruism. Helping many developers also helped Microsoft. If a tool helped many developers, then the costs of its development were defrayed over a large base. The development of more applications for Windows 95 also would help Microsoft through its sales.

More generally, financial motives stood at the center of Microsoft's actions. It gave away tools if it thought it recouped the investment with more developer actions or more valuable applications. It invested in designs if the returns looked financially strong. It invested in an organization to provide technical support because developers made the operating system more valuable for a greater range of applications.

The resulting operating system was both a mundane and quite astonishing combination of old and new. Windows 95 was backward-compatible with many applications from Windows 3.0, but the system included many features that were bigger, faster, more varied, more complex, and more efficient for many tasks. That embodied a promise for a high payoff. Most developers anticipated selling more applications, and Microsoft anticipated selling more operating systems. For that reason alone, virtually every vendor acquiesced to Microsoft's design choices for most of the key standards.

That experience, along with related actions from Intel that had industry-wide benefits, fueled the view that platform leadership helped computing markets grow.[17] Yet holding the enthusiasm in check was a sense of *quid pro quo* embodied by less accessible information and more restrictions on the use of technology.

A Strategy for Pervasive Standards

Microsoft did not aspire to control all frontier technologies. Rather, its strategy stressed having an exclusive position as the provider of pervasive technologies on which applications were built. That exclusive commercial position was valuable to Microsoft for several reasons.

Obviously, it made life easier for Microsoft's own employees. Microsoft's own application designers could contact another Microsoft employee to have their needs addressed. Microsoft also could retain the right to change any feature if it yielded strategic benefits. Indeed, outsiders frequently accused Microsoft of using its position to make its own life easier – such as documenting for Microsoft's use, but not necessarily for any others, or not documenting code so they could alter it to their advantage.[18]

While Microsoft's technological leadership position also reinforced the value of the PC, its actions also shaped its ability to capture a larger fraction of the value from each PC sold if it reinforced the lack of substitutes for its operating system. For example, it contributed value to the PC through supporting new applications, growing user demand or motivating more frequent purchases. It also enhanced its ability to capture a larger fraction of value by enhancing its bargaining position with developers, often through the inclusion of features into the operating system that substituted for another firm's, and for which the other firm had charged users.[19]

Microsoft owned or developed assets important to making the standards by using intellectual property, such as patents, copyright or trade secrets and excluding others from imitating their actions. Microsoft also prevented others from gaining information about a standard's features, how it operated, and how it would change, necessitating that others negotiate with Microsoft to gain access to that information.[20] These actions could and did bring about conflicts.[21]

As a practical matter, most application firms liked the improvements but objected to how the governance of the platform had changed around them. They perceived the use of too many carrots and sticks by Microsoft. One set of carrots was the tools provided to developers to make Windows 95 easier to use. One set of sticks was the actions, such as withholding information about near-term changes from 'unfriendly' developers. An alternative carrot/stick involved offering/withholding lucrative marketing deals/discounts to 'friendly/unfriendly' firms. In settings where speed to market was valuable or margins were tight, offering relevant information sooner or withholding it could be a very effective incentive/punishment to inducing cooperation.[22]

Many vendors could perceive that they had become dependent on

Microsoft's proprietary standards. Microsoft's technical staff held important information about how the APIs worked inside the operating system. These needs arose at the beginning of product development, in the middle, and sometimes even just prior to launching a new product. It left developers vulnerable to getting held up at crucial moments in an urgent development process. Microsoft's management recognized the situation too, and increasingly the use of technical support came along with reminders that only developers with friendly relationships with Microsoft got the best service.[23]

Dependency also came with a danger in the near future. Many software executives wondered if they could trust ambitious Microsoft employees with sensitive information. Executives at application firms who had seen the innovative features of prior software show up as features in later versions of Microsoft's products wondered if their employees' conversations with Microsoft's technical staff would contribute to seeding a future competitor.[24] Years earlier the danger had seemed to be an exaggeration, but by early 1995 it did not because the experience was quite common and well documented.

In addition to pressure in bargaining and distrust over sensitive information, Microsoft seemed to be able to expand its actions in ubiquitous ways. For instance, it could expand into a software market if its ambitious executives thought it was profitable to do. By the mid-1990s Microsoft had entered a wide range of product areas, such as network software, games, encyclopedias (Encarta), and online services (MSN), as well as announcing its intent to produce a wider range of application software – most typically through self-development, but potentially also through purchase of others. In fact, only the opposition of the antitrust division at the Department of Justice stopped Microsoft from buying Intuit.

The public discussion had become heated over these practices. SUN's CEO, Scott McNealy, for example, relished making public remarks using sharp language that denigrated Microsoft's lack of openness in comparison to his firm's. For example: 'We had openness. In other words, nobody should own the written and spoken language of computing. In the same, nobody owns English, French, or German. Now, Microsoft might disagree and think they ought to own the written and spoken language of computing and charge us all a $250 right-to-use license to speak English or Windows or what they happen to own.'[25]

In summary, by 1995 virtually all computer industry participants were familiar with these practices. Microsoft retained control over information about the standards that comprised its platform as part of a broader strategy to enhance its bargaining position with others, to deter entry, and to support its ability to generate revenue.

Standards and the Commercial Internet

Viewed broadly, the commercial Internet had comparable processes in place for making a standard bundle of protocols and altering those standards, but the details were quite different. Whereas Microsoft unilaterally made decisions about standards, all such decisions in Internet standards emerged from consensus. In addition, the processes were much looser regarding establishing roadmaps and targets, and providing tools and assistance for others.

For making standards and altering them, the bulk of activity took place in the Internet Engineering Task Force, or IETF, which had descended from the pre-commercial Internet and had assumed responsibility for standardizing protocols for the Internet.[26] The IETF inherited a process for designing and endorsing protocol standards, still called request for comments (RFCs) from the earlier days.[27] While the privatization efforts of the early 1990s altered the financial support and legal status of the organization, it did not alter the standards-making processes at the IETF, nor the composition of those involved in working groups.[28]

However, it had altered the assignment of authority at the top, devolving it from its older hierarchy in which the members of IAB had the final say over approval of proposals for standards. By the mid-1990s such authority rested with the members of the Internet Engineering Steering Group (IESG), which was a larger group comprising different area heads. The area heads appointed/coordinated with working groups, and tried to keep a semblance of structure to an otherwise unstructured activity. In the mid-1990s many of the members of the IESG had been appointed by the very members of the IAB who had previously held authority. Uncertainty about the transition was largely gone by late 1994 and early 1995. Routines had emerged.[29]

In contrast to Microsoft, the IETF produced non-proprietary standards. Like efforts in other standard-setting organizations, the IETF asked workshop leaders to develop protocols and standards that did not use patents or other forms of proprietary technology, if possible.[30] Workshop leaders were discouraged from endorsing proprietary technologies unless the owner agreed to license those at reasonable and non-discriminatory rates.[31]

Nothing in the commercial Internet contained subsidies after the NSF (National Science Foundation) withdrew its support. Yet the IETF leadership did its best to invest in several actions to aid the process it governed. First, it tried to provide editorial guidance and support for the entire process. That resulted in remarkably clear and comprehensive documentation (particularly from some contributors who were not practiced at clarity and thoroughness). It also helped coordinate and sponsor 'plugfests',

where vendors could test their interoperab...
In principle, these fests were used to verify
before advancing a proposal for an RFC to

The Internet did not lack tools and librari...
of years of development with widespread un...
the IETF leadership and many participant...
protocols.

The situation for roadmaps and targets di...
norms in the least. That was obviously so sin...
parable to Bill Gates at the center of the com...
executive vision and discipline, but it was true i...
commercialization this function had not resen...
there was active resistance to changing it after c...
as if there had never been any planning under
intents and purposes, the decisions about the dire...
made and implemented in 1993 and 1994.[32] By t...
computing, that left a void in planning as of 1994

I next explain why this void was only partially
also illustrates the role of open processes in the c...
of policies.

Why so Little Centralization?

It would not have been odd to embed some coordina...
building Internet protocols. After all, that was the m...
ful commercial platforms. Yet the IETF faced a bro...
what processes best coordinated distributed user-dri...
setting with enormous heterogeneity in the ultimate c...
network? There was no obvious solution. Indeed, in thi...
chial tugs and pulls inherited from the pre-commercial
a unique set of processes and policies.

First and broadly, lack of centralization – and loose...
maps and targets – was consistent with many other decisi...
privatization. Beginning with the earliest conversations i...
quent legislation, and the final drafts of the NSF privatizati...
had been plenty of opportunities to establish central instit...
rare cases, such as the establishment of a single entity to m...
base for all the domain names, were those opportunities u...
tion, centralization was not viewed favorably by many part...
pre-commercial Internet. For example, the establishment c...
name system in the early 1990s was not widely viewed by i...
participants as a good model for any other decision.[36]

The
govern...
is, virt...
contri...
words...
prop...

An...
devel...
cally...
the t...
cont...
men...
revie...
end-...
cou...
pot...

wa...
it g...
aca...
un...
th...
al...
th...
re...

p...
a...
f...

looseness about roadmaps also arose, in part, from the norms
ing academic debate, which were the origins of the Internet. That
ually any argument remained unsettled (in principle) so that some
utor could make a proposal and generate consensus. In other
, there was a preference for 'open-ended' debate that accommodated
sals from many corners.

open-ended process was thought to accommodate the realities of
ping a communications technology whose user base was geographi-
dispersed, where there were many administrators or intense users of
chnology, and each had a different experience that informed their
ibution. It accumulated incremental advances in publicly docu-
ed ways, which far-flung contributors could independently access and
w. That had worked well in evolving applications that coordinated
to-end processes with many contributors, such as email.[37] It also
d accommodate a 'swarm of standards', that is, multiple proposals for
ntial solving the same problem.[38]

While documenting decision making at intermediate and final stages
s necessary to support open-ended debate, it also had another benefit:
ave public credit for individual effort.[39] The IETF's RFC process gave
demics concrete results to which they could point for credit within their
iversities. It was useful in the era when NSF funded improvements and
e academics needed to document their contributions for NSF. It was
o useful because so many tools and contributions came voluntarily, and
ose contributors needed to establish their historical credentials or gain
wards from prior accomplishments.

As in any large organization, there were multiple motives behind each
ractice. In this case, some participants did not care about the efficacy of
practice. Instead, there was a strong distaste among many participants
or insular bureaucratic hierarchies that had historically shaped the flow
of information and decision making in communications markets. While
rough consensus and running code' had become part of the identity of the
IETF, the first part of David Clark's 1992 phrase was well remembered
too. It said: 'We reject kings, presidents and voting.'[40] That remark was
a not-so-veiled reference to AT&T and the other local telephone firms,
whose corporate hierarchical practices were held in low esteem by many
participants. Indeed, by early 1995, the norm of open-endedness was
deeply embedded in the identity of the community, frequently referenced
as a top priority and often expressed as a norm not to restrict decision
making to a club of experts.[41] The IETF leaders drew explicit attention
to that difference with other standard-setting organizations in their own
materials.[42]

The importance of preferences for open-endedness came with a potential risk and large cost, namely, lack of coordination between the technical proposals of distinct groups. No participant wanted to see the growth of families of mutually incompatible protocols from distinct subgroups within the IETF. Yet such an outcome was not only technically possible, but it was likely as the commercial Internet grew and participation at the IETF grew with it.

Rather than abandon the bottom-up processes for the sake of coordination, however, the IETF adopted a structure to accommodate it. The costs of this process were explicitly placed on the shoulders of the heads of working groups and their area coordinators within the IESG. They were charged with the responsibility for identifying and coordinating development across distinct working groups with overlapping agendas, even requiring area coordinators to do so before assessing whether rough consensus had emerged for a proposal.[43]

Hence the IETF did not lack a planning process or *de facto* roadmap at a broad level, but it was rather open-ended in its details at any point in time, by definition. The collective efforts of the IESG at planning and assigning work between working groups provided the guidance for developments in the short run. They could only do that job if working groups documented their work at every stage of decision making. Then a conversation with one of the members of the IESG could serve the same function as a roadmap, providing a member with a sense of where their efforts fit into the broader collection of ongoing work.

That solution worked as long as the community of researchers would share information about their technical inventions with each other – through email, postings in RFCs, and conversations at meetings. In other words, making accessible all documentation of decision making supported other principles of importance to the community.

In summary, by early 1995 the IETF had its most distinctive features. It involved many developers and administrators who had worked together for years, and who shared the goal of building a national TCP/IP network.[44] It was neither an open source project nor a staid standard-setting organization with restricted participation. It remained unrestricted in its participation, with most of its progress documented on line, even at intermediate stages of development. In addition, it placed no restrictions on use of that information after publication.

ALTERNATIVES TO OPENNESS

The comparison of Microsoft's development of Windows 95 with similar processes for developing the Internet highlights several key differences – in ownership over the rights of leaders to design and alter standards, in use of unilateral decision-making instead of consensus processes, and in policies governing release of information about decision-making processes and outcomes. In particular, open processes employed documented standards and did not restrict access to these documents or their use, while proprietary platform leaders had options not to make information available.

Before considering the consequences of this policy, one might reasonably ask a question that always arises in counterfactual history. How would the alternative have operated in practice? That is, how would the Internet have employed a less open process?

My answer is simple: the Internet's design might have had a more proprietary flavor by the mid-1990s if one firm had dominated development of standards. For example, that one firm could have been IBM. Lest that sound implausible in retrospect, recall that contemporaries considered such an outcome plausible in the early 1990s. Indeed, concerns about IBM's dominance over the Internet were expressed in Congressional hearings regarding favoritism in the privatization of the NSFNet. These concerns ultimately shaped policy over the design of the privatization plan.[45] Those hearings support the speculation that, had policy been different, IBM would have been in a position to shape standards and protocols in a more proprietary technical direction.[46]

That said, the next step in the analysis does not focus on IBM's behavior in its specifics, nor consider how IBM would have or could have executed platform leadership as efficiently as Microsoft. Instead, it considers issues in more general terms, pointing towards the likely direction of change had the alternative been a less open process.

The Value Chain for the Commercial Internet

Did the openness of the IETF contribute to establishing the value chain for the commercial Internet as the Internet made its transition from being predominantly a research-oriented network to a commercial network with mass-market use? In an earlier stage it surely had. Open processes had played a role in facilitating some entrepreneurial entry among carriers – e.g. at PSINet or Netcom – as well as a plethora of equipment firms. By early 1995, however, we shall see that openness did not play much of role in encouraging growth in the value chain for the commercial Internet, at least among major firms. By the mid-1990s the value chain had taken on its predominant features and openness did not contribute to resolving open questions.

A value chain is a set of interrelated activities that produces a final product of value greater than the incremental value of each part. All mature industries have a value chain.

For example, the value chain for the PC distributed revenue to a wide set of firms. The typical PC used a microprocessor (usually from Intel or AMD), a motherboard design that resembled IBM's 1981 design with several standard upgrades to the memory and bus, an operating system (often from Microsoft), an internal memory device (from one of several hard-drive firms), as well as many other parts. These were assembled together by one of several firms (Compaq, Dell, Gateway, IBM etc.) and distributed to users along with other compatible peripheral components, such as printers (most often from Hewlett-Packard, but also from many other companies), either directly by the assembler (Dell, Gateway) or by a third-party retailer (BestBuy, Circuit City). Standard software applications included office-oriented applications (from Microsoft, Intuit), games (from a variety of firms), numerous utilities (Norton, Macafee), and potentially thousands of niche applications.

In comparison, by early 1995, the commercial Internet's value chain was more than a kernel, but it still needed to resolve some open questions. The best-laid plans at NSF had come to fruition. Not only had the commercial Internet survived its transition from public funding to privatization, but a regular routine for exchanging data and settling accounts between private parties had also continued and made a transition into a marketplace. With the release of the commercial web, the prospects for growth looked promising. The market prospects for Internet services were improving, and awareness was growing outside of the *cognoscenti* into a mass market.[47]

What were the insiders observing in late 1994 and early 1995? While Internet equipment firms and networking equipment firms had been developing new equipment and protocols for quite a few years, the activity had tended to be aimed at business and technical users. A mass market, one outside of business and technical users, was only just emerging.

For one, Netscape had just released its first commercial product and claimed to be at the forefront of a revolution; and the CEOs at firms such as Cisco, MCI and PSINet observed the eye-opening commercial prototype and began reassessing the Internet's market potential. They came to the tentative conclusion that existing investments in the Internet by carriers and equipment firms might turn out to be more valuable than the earliest most optimistic projections. Aside from an abundance of web pages from researchers and university users, they also noticed several small web start-ups and provocative initiatives, such as the beginnings of Excite, eBay[48] and *Encyclopedia Britannica*'s web-compatible version of its text.[49] The buzz in Silicon Valley was palpable. Perhaps new investments might be called for by many others, not just a few engineering-led start-ups, as had been the norm for Internet equipment until then.

How much investment and by whom? This was the new feature of the brave new commercial Internet world. Nobody knew the answer. Nobody was in charge of coordinating the operations of the Internet or its investments.

What a contrast with the recent past! In the pre-commercial Internet platform, the NSF had coordinated large-scale investment activity. For example, as recently as 1991 and 1992, the NSF had upgraded the Internet backbone bandwidth. That upgrade had shaped the performance of virtually every university installation, allowing a greater scale of traffic at any point in time without degradation in user experience.[50] In response, administrators at many installations then upgraded their facilities to support a large user base. In contrast, in early 1995, the discretion to make such upgrades sat with private parties.

Market relations between firms that had newly become competitors were functioning well, as data managed to find their way across all the networks without incident. That resolved what had been considered a big open question. As market competitors, these firms were no longer required to work with one another – nonetheless they found ways to exchange traffic. Routines for exchanging data and settling accounts had emerged between 1992 and 1994, and by early 1995 were taken for granted.[51]

Similarly, the market relationships between equipment manufacturers and carriers also emerged without a 'midwife'. Experienced router firms and network equipment firms existed prior to privatization (e.g. Cisco, IBM, 3Com and many smaller firms). With commercialization, each of these firms began to develop distribution channels for further sales to large enterprises, cable carriers and entrepreneurial ventures.

On the whole, the commercial Internet contained a healthy set of operations built around TCP/IP-compatible parts. Long-distance data carriers used compatible processes, so too did data-exchange carriers, equipment providers of routers, such as Cisco. Looking to develop efficient services and enhance revenue-generating activities, every provider of carrier services from the research-oriented Internet had remained in the market.[52] Units from MCI, Sprint, BBN and IBM, as well as entrepreneurial spin-offs such as UUNet and PSINet had operations and provided service. Although less surprising, every regional carrier had stayed, and some of the managers at these organizations were beginning to discuss privatizing their operations as well.

These facts alone tell us that mundane economics factors were playing a role by early 1995. Existing firms stayed in the market after NSF withdrew support because they had sunk entry costs and they continued to see a market opportunity. Those were comparatively straightforward business calculations.

Open Questions about the Value Chain

Despite the propitious start, the value for the Internet was still a work in progress in 1995. Many open questions concerned the 'last mile'. Although in late 1994 some carriers had decent Internet businesses, such as IBM, PSINet, UUNet and the entrepreneurial ISP Netcom,[53] and although a number of smaller entrepreneurial ISPs also had begun to spring up and advertise in *Boardwatch Magazine*, the trade magazine for bulletin boards, all in all, there was not a mature supply for the mass market. The supply of Internet services for households and businesses was found primarily in major cities and was aimed at business users and technically adept households. It was still too small to support a mass-market service.

Household service for novice users was the biggest question mark. Some of the existing bulletin board firms, such as Genie, had adopted plans to offer Internet service, but others, such as AOL (America On-Line) had not. No norm had emerged for how services for households should operate. For example, there were open questions about whether to charge per time period, per traffic flow in bits, or simply for the connection. There were also unanswered questions about how to charge a premium for increasing the quality of services.

Norms for providing Internet service to the business enterprise market were not settled either. The servers were usually Unix-based, and these offered the technically most straightforward route to TCP/IP compatibility.[54] Using them, however, also required hiring technically oriented staff, which only the largest installations tended to do.

In addition, the software issues were complex. Because local area network (LAN) equipment had to be made more usable, some standard retrofits had emerged, but better software upgrades were anticipated. Novell's Netware, the most commonly employed network and server software, did not blend with TCP/IP-based networking very easily.[55] In addition, Microsoft's server software, Windows NT, was slated to have TCP/IP compatibility, but that product release was still half a year away.

Similarly, the workstation was the most common client for accessing the Internet, but Internet connection software was not easy enough for a novice user.[56] As with the servers, TCP/IP-based traffic and web-based traffic worked easily on Unix-based computers in a client role, but that appealed only to technically adept users. Many participants awaited the arrival of Windows 95 for the PC, which promised better compatibility with the core plumbing of TCP/IP, and appeal to mass-market users.

Question marks also hung over the optimism for the World Wide Web. By early 1995, Tim Berners-Lee's inventions had diffused throughout the research and university user community. That working prototype had not yet turned into a recognizable commercial industry of web services, but the prospects looked better with Netscape's recent advances.[57]

In addition, by early 1995, it appeared the Internet was no longer a USA-only networking technology. Many other developed countries had their own networking technologies (e.g. France, Germany). Some countries had oriented themselves to international efforts (such as those at OSI – Open Systems Interconnection), but these had not grown into viable services and were considered unviable by everyone in the Internet community. In comparison, the working prototypes of the TCP/IP Internet had more attraction for networking functions because everything worked now, worked robustly, and allowed for vendor and user participation.

Did openness play a role in resolving these key open questions? If anything, openness was a potential disadvantage. Use of non-proprietary standards eliminated points of differentiation, potentially turning data-carrier services and equipment design into a commodity service or product. Lack of coordination also cast uncertainty over the plans of every participant.

Other key events – such as those policies and events that contributed to the emergence of a competitive backbone market – were of much more importance than openness.[58] Moreover, as noted, more mundane economic factors were playing a key role. Existing firms stayed in the market because it was a good business decision to do so. Openness did not have much to do with those business calculations.

OPENNESS AND INNOVATION

The discussion so far begs the question of how the Internet's form of openness affected innovation. As it turned out, the answer depended on where one looked.

In many respects, openness did not contribute to innovation. The questions that arose from an open environment propelled parties to invest in the Internet to protect their own interests. The absence of the NSF had left a planning void for all the commercial firms in the equipment and carrier businesses. It left many open questions about the future structure of operations. It also raised budgetary uncertainty about long-term revenues from research and university clients. None of that encouraged innovation from private firms.

Would a less open process have encouraged more innovation in the commercial Internet? In comparison, Microsoft's process of using incentives and subsidies to encourage incremental innovative applications had an advantage over the openness of the Internet. The commercial Internet did not encourage anything with subsidies. But did this difference matter in practice? Probably not much, if at all. As it turned out, the commercial Internet did not lack supplies of tools and libraries for sharing, often coming from university contributors and researchers with a wide variety of settings. The IETF also could accommodate an innovative commercial application, just as any platform leader would have.

There was one other way in which an organized platform had an innovative advantage over an open one. A large platform leader, such as Microsoft, had skills at organizing an upgrade requiring a 'big push', one that simultaneously altered the programming environment for many applications and that supported it with technical help. The upgrade to Windows 95 was an illustration of that innovative advantage. Nothing equivalent took place at the IETF, which tended to focus on incremental improvements on existing protocols, as developed by small teams of contributors to a working group.

All in all, the open processes seem to be no worse at encouraging incremental innovative applications from commercial application firms, and arguably worse at encouraging big ones. That was offset, at least partly and possibly wholly, by the superior ability of the open process to generate more enthusiasm from its widely dispersed participants, who came from a variety of backgrounds and had a variety of ideas for how to improve operations. Also, the open Internet was able to take advantage of innovative tools from university contributors.

How the Web Grew

Openness turned out to have one important consequence for structural change, but this was not obvious until circumstances exposed it. The lack of restriction on the development of new protocols could enable an unanticipated innovation of a pervasive standard that reduced the value of incumbent firm properties. Tim Berners-Lee's experience illustrates this argument.

The World Wide Web was first diffused through the initiatives of Tim Berners-Lee on shareware sites, starting in the early 1990s.[59] Initially, Berners-Lee expected an individual installation to adopt software to support the three components of the Web – the hypertext markup language (html), the hypertext transfer protocol (http), and what eventually would be called the uniform resource locator (or URL), which Berners-Lee preferred to call the universal resource identifier (or URI).[60] Berners-Lee also diffused a browser, but very quickly the online community began to put forward better versions throughout 1992 and 1993.

Even before the Web began to explode into large-scale use, Berners-Lee worried about standardizing his creation. By 1992, numerous installations had experience using the core technologies. In the summer of 1992, Berners-Lee took the initiative to start standardizing several aspects of the Web within an IETF-sponsored subgroup.

To Berners-Lee a standards process had several benefits. It would permit the Web to evolve, that is, add new functionality, without fragmenting into versions that could not interoperate. He also believed such standardization would contribute to making the Web more pervasive, if users perceived less uncertainty about the management of its future.[61]

Berners-Lee assumed his experience at the IETF would go well. He had 'running code' for a problem that had vexed others. As he learned to his disappointment, however, the existence of his running code did not imply the emergence of a rapid consensus.

The topic led to a contentious debate at the IETF. Problems in developing hypertext had generated intellectual interest for decades in computer science. Numerous camps for distinct theoretical points and philosophical viewpoints had formed long ago. The deliberations of the IETF became mired in many philosophical and theoretical debates.[62]

By Berners-Lee's account, the debate became often focused on issues he did not consider important, such as the meaning of 'universal' when it is used as a label for a protocol. He gave in on several of these issues in the hope of realizing resolution, but he did not give in on anything to do with his design.

Almost certainly the debates partly reflected the social strains taking place at the IETF at the time. Berners-Lee was one of hundreds of new participants, and one with a particularly ambitious agenda. While he also had the confidence that came with partial success, his status as a comparatively new participant was bound to cause misunderstandings and interfere with achieving his goals quickly.

Another issue also clouded the debate. In 1992, Berners-Lee's employer, CERN, still retained rights to the code. Participants at the IETF clearly were concerned about that, and Berners-Lee could appreciate why. That issue was not settled until CERN renounced all claims to intellectual property rights in Web technologies in April 1993, and Berners-Lee pressed ahead. Yet, once again, consensus eluded the working group.

Eventually, in mid-1994, Berners-Lee followed two paths simultaneously – he both worked with the IETF and followed an ambition to establish another institution to support the Web's standards. He decided to issue an informational RFC (RFC 1630) about what he had already designed, but he concluded that this RFC left too many issues unresolved to serve as an effective standard.

At the same time Berners-Lee was already working to establish the

World Wide Web Consortium (W3C). In February of 1994, he had a meeting of minds with Michael Dertouzos at MIT. It altered Berners-Lee's vision for what type of institutional support for the Web would help him achieve his goals. Berners-Lee established his consortium in mid-1994. By early 1995, his consortium was set up at MIT and Europe,[63] and he was able to elicit cooperation from many firms in the industry – in terms of both eliciting financial contributions and representation at consortium discussions. Through this path Berners-Lee started on his way to bypassing existing processes at the IETF.

A brief comparison between the processes at the IETF and those adopted by Berners-Lee at the W3C shows what Berners-Lee took with him from his experience at the IETF. Berners-Lee stated that he had wanted a standardization process that worked more rapidly than the IETF, but otherwise shared many of its features, such as full documentation. In contrast to the IETF, however, the W3C would not be a bottom-up organization with independent initiatives, nor would it have unrestricted participation. Berners-Lee would act in a capacity to initiate and coordinate activities. To afford some of these, his consortium would charge companies for participating in efforts and for the right to keep up to date on developments.

While there were misunderstandings with others at the IETF, Berners-Lee also continued to have cordial relationships with many active Internet pioneers and participants. That cordiality stood in contrast to the rivalry and strained relationships between many IETF participants and other organizations that claimed to design networking standards in the pre-commercial Internet, such as the OSI.[64]

Why was cordiality noteworthy? The establishment of the W3C removed the IETF from a position of technological leadership in the development of important new infrastructure for users and developers. Yet it rendered concrete what was commonly stated: IETF's leaders remained open to a variety of proposals to improve the Internet. They did not presume to be the exclusive institutional progenitor of technological source for all Internet-related activities.

To be sure, most initiatives ended up coming back to the IETF processes in one form or another because it was useful for them to do so. Protocol writers found it useful to use and reuse existing processes. Indeed, Berners-Lee also returned to the IETF. He eventually got the RFCs he had sought all along, just much later than he had initially aspired to.[65] Eventually the primary dispute between two groups would be over minor issues, such as the boundaries of expertise between the two groups for niche topics.

This experience illustrates the role of lack of restriction on use of information. The participants at the IETF treated the ideas behind the Web as an object for philosophical debate, and (initially) the leaders treated the

W3C with benign neglect, particularly in 1994. Neither action was helpful to the Web, but none stopped it. More to the point, in spite of that unhelpful experience, lack of control over the IETF standards effectively gave discretion to other individuals or organizations – in this case, Berners-Lee and the W3C – that were entrepreneurial enough to build on existing Internet protocols, even in ways that bypassed the existing process for making protocols and established new ones.

The Commercial Web and the PC

Tim Berners-Lee's experience with the IETF would contrast with events in the PC market, although that was not apparent at the outset. Though often forgotten due to later events, the invention of the Web was greeted with a shrug at Microsoft. Microsoft's managers acted much like everyone else, incorrectly forecasting little technological and commercial success for the World Wide Web.

Events got more interesting in the fall of 1994. The activity around Netscape's founding had generated considerable publicity, if not actual products, and that had started a number of reassessments among the *cognoscenti*, both inside and outside Redmond. Bill Gates was late to appreciate the importance of these events, however. He would not state that he had changed his opinion until May of 1995, when he wrote an internal memo titled 'The Internet Tidal Wave'.[66] The memo is eight pages long and single spaced, so it hardly deserves the label 'memo'. It is useful here because it provides an honest window into the change in Gates's view.

When Netscape first began to develop its commercial browser in the summer and fall of 1994, it was treated like any other application firm meeting a niche need. Even in early 1995, Netscape was viewed as a firm making an application that helped raise demand for the platform. It was given access to software tools and to the usual technical information, Windows 3.0 and 3.1, as well as Windows 95.

Gates's memo no longer catalogues Netscape as an application. Instead, he states, 'A competitor was born on the Internet',[67] that is, a competitor to Microsoft. He goes on to outline why he interprets a browser company as a threat. It was not the company, *per se*, that posed any threat, but the potential for their standards to be pervasive on virtually every PC was a step towards reducing revenue at Microsoft.[68]

Gates worried about two scenarios in which Microsoft's operating system could become 'commoditized'. One scenario involves Netscape directly, where Gates asserts, 'They are pursuing a multi-platform strategy where they move the key API into the client to commoditize the underlying operating system.' Translation: Netscape helps to coordinate developers whom Microsoft would have been coordinating, and so Netscape's browser substitutes for Microsoft's operating system as the point of access to those applications, which reduces the value of Microsoft's operating system.

The other scenario is less specific about who will take the action, but is given the label 'scary' by Gates. It involves the combination of several component firms developing a new device. In this vein he says, 'One scary possibility being discussed by Internet fans is whether they should get together and create something far less expensive than a PC which is powerful enough for Web browsing.'[69] Indeed, this forecast did come to pass shortly after Gates predicted it, although the trial largely failed in the market place.[70]

Not long after writing this memo, Gates tried to have Microsoft buy a stake in Netscape and gain a board seat. Those negotiations did not get very far.[71] After further talks, the executives in Redmond concluded that Netscape would not cooperate on their terms, which led Microsoft to treat Netscape in as unfriendly a manner as it could in the summer of 1995, by denying it access to technical information and other marketing deals. Coming as late as they did for a product that had already been released, these actions only slowed Netscape down a little bit but came nowhere close to crippling it.

The confrontation escalated from there. Over the next few years, Gates went to enormous and deliberate lengths to prevent Netscape's browser from becoming pervasive, particularly with new users.[72] Microsoft put forward its own browser and undertook numerous defensive actions, such as making deals to prevent Netscape's browser from becoming a default setting at ISPs or in the products PC assemblers shipped. Microsoft's attempt to limit Netscape's access to distribution channels led to a major federal antitrust case.

Comparing the Web in Two Settings

Historical circumstances rarely provide a clean comparison of the consequences from distinct market structures, but in 1995 circumstances did. Here were two markets that provided just such a comparison – in this case, about the receptiveness of existing organizations to structural change.

Only a few months apart, the same technology, the Web, diffused into two settings with distinct processes for documenting decision making. One was open while the other was less open. In both cases, the Web received little help from established platforms leaders. In both cases, the leadership eventually recognized the error and began to take action. There the similarities end. The IETF eventually came to an understanding with the W3C where both could coexist. In contrast, the first firm to develop a product for the Web, Netscape, met with active resistance from Microsoft, the firm providing proprietary technological leadership.

The difference arose for an obvious reason. By publishing its proceedings and decisions and giving unrestricted access to anyone, the IETF had committed itself to not restricting use of Internet protocols. Microsoft had no such commitment, nor is that a surprise. Microsoft was intent on protecting its position as the exclusive firm to support pervasive standards. It had strong incentives to slow the diffusion of the pervasive software coming from any other provider.

OVERVIEW

It is time to look back and summarize. Did openness matter for the commercial Internet – did openness shape the transition to commercialization, the amount of innovativeness, and/or the tendency to experience structural change? Maybe, probably not, and yes.

Maybe: many long-time participants in development processes preferred openness for its own sake. Openness kept them involved, which helped with the transition to the commercial era. Beyond that, however, openness played little role in helping firms establish operations in the young network. If anything, it was discouraging.

Probably not: if anything, open processes made the commercial Internet less inviting for some incremental innovation than it might have been. This structure also was not well suited for a 'big push'. Encouraging enthusiastic participation and incremental innovation from a wide variety of contributors made up for some of that disadvantage.

Yes: in the commercial Internet, the creator of the World Wide Web, Tim Berners-Lee, tried to standardize his protocols; and though he met with misunderstanding and questions, for the most part, he was treated like anyone else. No institutions prevented him from taking initiative. In contrast, the emergence of the World Wide Web was not greeted with glee by the leaders of the personal computing market. Microsoft, by actively trying to gain exclusive ownership and control over the deployment of pervasive standards, slowed the diffusion of a commercial Web it could not control.

Later events also illustrate the themes. In a short time some participants would step in with potential roadmaps and related tools. For example, the W3C would bid to provide targets and organize tools for others. So too did the group that established Apache, which also stepped into this setting with tools for Web server software. In 1995 and 1996, these attempts were quite effective. In due time, of course, both Microsoft and Netscape sought to provide those tools and have their provision serve competitive goals.

Moreover, by mid-1995 the potential for growth in the commercial Web soon began to motivate an extraordinarily large amount of entrepreneurial entry in equipment markets, access markets, hosting markets and web design/maintenance. It grew rapidly from there. Readily available information facilitated that activity by making technical information accessible to any entrant. Once again, lack of restrictions on information played a role.

I conclude that openness played a very specific role in early 1995, in fostering participation in the development of Internet infrastructure and in fostering structural change in the provision of commercial software. Because those were very important for commercial outcomes, I conclude that openness played a significant role in a watershed moment for the commercial Internet.

NOTES

1. I thank Tim Bresnahan, Dave Crocker, Michael Cusumano, Rebecca Henderson, Annabelle Gawer, Andrew Russell, Alicia Shems, Tim Simcoe, Scott Stern and Joel West for useful conversations. The Searle Foundation and the Kaufman Foundation provided funding. All errors are mine.
2. See, e.g., Cusumano and Selby (1995).
3. See, e.g., ibid.
4. See, e.g., Abbate (1999), Segaller (1998), Shah and Kesan (2001), and Greenstein (2008) for analyses of legal and technical aspects of privatization.
5. For a well-known programmer's view, see Raymond (1998). Among the many collections, see, e.g., the two books edited by the O'Reilly group, DiBona et al. (1999) and DiBona et al. (2006), or Feller (2005). For an emphasis on the user's contribution, see, e.g., von Hippel (2002). For the similarities and differences between open standards and open innovation, see e.g., West (2007).
6. Another related set of papers, West (2002, 2007) and West and O'Mahoney (2008), focus on whether it is feasible for commercial firms to establish platforms that meld open and proprietary norms. Those are more focused on explaining managerial challenges in the context of many recent examples, not on this case.
7. I particularly build on insights about platform leadership of Intel's and Microsoft's platform strategies, as found in Cusumano and Selby (1995), Gawer and Cusumano (2002), Casadesus-Masanell and Yoffie (2007), Bresnahan and Greenstein (1999), and Gawer and Henderson (2007), among others.
8. This essay builds on Greenstein (2007), Aspray and Ceruzzi (2007), Partridge (2008), Mueller (2004), and Russell (2006).
9. See, e.g., the work of Simcoe (2006, 2007) and Fleming and Waguespack (2005, 2008). Each of these studies focuses on understanding why firms participate in developing new standards for the Internet, and why the process works well (or not).
10. Bresnahan and Greenstein (1997) state: 'A computing platform is a reconfigurable base of compatible components on which users build applications. Platforms are most readily identified with their technical standards, i.e., engineering specifications for compatible hardware and software.'
11. For more on moving between the Unix and Windows programming environment, see, e.g., DiBona et al. (2006).
12. When the Internet first commercialized, Spry networks developed a product called

'Internet-in-a-box' and sold it. In fact, this was nothing more than a CD for download-ing a program on a PC to generate an Internet connection to a dial-up ISP. It did not sell well.

13. For an analysis of the wide range of meanings, see, e.g., West (2007).
14. For more on the theory of consensus decision making in standards, see Farrell and Simcoe (2008).
15. This is a long story. The account in the text provides the basic outline, but does not provide much information about the alternatives, such as OS2, DR-DOS, and so on. For some of the history, with an emphasis on the effects it had on IBM, see Carroll (1994) or Lowe and Sherburne (2008).
16. This is a cursory explanation for a complex set of technical events. See, e.g., Cusumano and Selby (1995).
17. See, e.g., the discussion in Gawer and Cusumano (2002) about 'growing the pie', which features Intel's sponsorship prominently. See also Gawer and Henderson (2007), who discuss why Intel invests in some projects that lead to advancing standards on which others build.
18. These accusations also could be exaggerated. See the discussion in Allison (2006), who takes a developer's perspective and sees the merits of both sides. For example, when discussing why Microsoft did not document one part of the internal subsystems for Win32, he states,

> Why do this, one might ask? Well, the official reasoning is that it allows Microsoft to tune and modify the system call layer at will, improving performance and adding features without being forced to provide backward compatibility application binary interfaces . . . The more nefarious reasoning is that it allows Microsoft applications to cheat, and call directly into the undocumented Win32 subsystem call interface to provide services that competing applications cannot. Several Microsoft applications were subsequently discovered to be doing just that, of course . . . .These days this is less of a problem, as there are several books that document this system call layer . . . .But it left a nasty taste in the mouths of many early Windows NT developers (myself included). (Ibid., p. 47)

19. See Bresnahan (2004) and Henderson (2000).
20. These strategies could become quite complex. For a related set of arguments about Intel's comparable strategies, see Gawer and Henderson (2007) or Shapiro (2001).
21. Perhaps the best known was Microsoft's fight with Stac over compression software. Both parties won part of the legal victory and they eventually settled for just over $80 million (from Microsoft to Stac). See http://www.vaxxine.com/lawyers/articles/stac.html for a copy of the original suit.
22. See discussions in Gawer and Cusumano (2002), Bresnahan and Greenstein (1999), Gawer and Henderson (2007), Bresnahan (2004), and Henderson (2000) for illustra-tions of the range of such actions.
23. Henderson (2000) stresses that this action was typically taken in context, as one of many ways for Microsoft to discourage other firms from taking action it deemed undesirable.
24. A similar dilemma for Intel is discussed at length in Gawer and Cusumano (2002).
25. Segaller (1998), p. 235
26. The IETF was founded in 1986 and descended from earlier efforts to organize the devel-opment of protocols for the research-oriented Internet. In 1992 the Internet Society was founded to provide a superstructure for the IETF's activities and other matters. By early 1995, these institutions were well established. See, e.g., Abbate (1999), Bradner (1999), Russell (2006), Simcoe (2007), or Fleming and Waguespack (2005).
27. For a review of the process and how it has changed, documented as RFCs, see http://www.ietf.org/IETF-Standards-Process.html. Other places that explain drafting stand-ards are RFC 2026 or RFC 1602.

28. The IETF appoints working groups, and those have grown considerably over time. See, e.g., Abbate (1999), Russell (2006) or Simcoe (2006).
29. See Russell (2006) or Simcoe (2006).
30. Participants were also required to disclose such positions. For the present general guidelines, see https://datatracker.ietf.org/ipr/about/ and RFC 3979. Prior policies are largely spelled out in RFC 2026, and the anticipated processes and policies that pertained to the mid-1990s can be found in RFCs 1602 and 1310 (especially sections 5 and 6).
31. The IETF leadership chose a position that allowed it to retain its inherited functioning processes. It also continued to do as many other standards organizations: it did not close the door on adopting a protocol that covered a private firm's patent, as long as that firm agreed to license at a reasonable and non-discriminatory rate.
32. Technical roadmaps had partially emerged from the NSF's efforts to establish the Internet backbone and exchange points, as well as its efforts to subsidize diffusion of the Internet to many universities. Ultimately NSF's privatization plan also served as a partial roadmap for the near term in the 1990s, although private firms would and did depart from it a few years later.
33. Many of the earliest studies from these earliest meetings were published in Kahin (1992).
34. For details about this process, see, e.g., Abbate (1999), or Shah and Kesan (2001).
35. For a description of how this was done, see, e.g., Mueller (2004).
36. The control over the domain name system was effectively handed to a single firm. Many participants objected to the appointment of a firm into a monopoly position without many safeguards put in place. These concerns eventually escalated into a continuous and extraordinary policy soap opera. See Shah and Kesan (2001) for some of the early events, and Mueller (2004) for that and many later incidents.
37. See, e.g., Partridge (2008), who stresses that contributions came from many.
38. The term 'swarm of standards' is due to Updegrove (2007).
39. See Crocker (1993), Bradner (1999) or Simcoe (2006) for explanations of the roles of 'informational' RFCs, which often served as public documentation about a discussion for a new protocol or standard at an intermediate stage.
40. See the account of Russell (2006). This phrase harks back to a 1992 address. See Clark (1992), whose slides refer to events in New Jersey without naming AT&T by name.
41. See the account of Russell (2006).
42. This comes out clearly in Bradner (1999), for example. After summarizing many of the processes, he states, 'In brief, the IETF operates in a bottom-up task creation mode and believes in "fly before you buy"' (p. 51).
43. Once again, the leadership at the IETF was aware of these requirements, and area directors (ADs) from the Internet Engineering Steering Group (IESG) were to have frequent contact with working group chairmen. As stated in RFC 4677 (titled, 'The Tao of the IETF: A novice's guide to the Internet Engineering Task Force'),

> The IETF is run by rough consensus, and it is the IESG that judges whether a WG has come up with a result that has community consensus . . . Because of this, one of the main reasons that the IESG might block something that was produced in a WG is that the result did not really gain consensus in the IETF as a whole, that is, among all of the Working Groups in all areas. For instance, the result of one WG might clash with a technology developed in a different Working Group. An important job of the IESG is to watch over the output of all the WGs to help prevent IETF protocols that are at odds with each other. This is why ADs are supposed to review the drafts coming out of areas other than their own.

44. To be sure, this statement needs qualification in light of the growth the IETF started to experience at this time. Bradner (1999) states there were 500 participants in the March 1992 meeting, 750 in the March 1994 meeting, 1000 in December 1994 meeting, and

2000 by the December 1996 meeting. Such growth in participation would have placed strain on establishing a new, shared set of norms but it also might have interfered with operating under the assumption that all present understood the same set of references.

45. See, e.g., Shah and Kesan (2001) and Greenstein (2008).
46. This is the position taken by Shah and Kesan (2001).
47. No Wall Street firm had yet catalogued the value chain in a standardized format, and none would until early 1996. Meeker and Dupuy (1996) performed their first analyses of Internet firms in 1995.
48. Segaller (1998) has a good description of this atmosphere and some of the antics of these early initiatives.
49. This initiative received high-profile news coverage, but actually emerged from a skunk works for the firm, which subsequently had great difficulty integrating it into regular operations. See Devereaux and Greenstein (2009).
50. This upgrade was funded by the 1991 High Performance Computing Act, sponsored by then Senator Al Gore. For a cogent history of these policies and their later misinterpretation, see Wiggins (2000).
51. There were two key innovations, one involved technical issues and the other involved business processes. The technical innovation concerned the design of an exchange point for a router that exchanged data between all firms. See Hussain (2003). The business innovation concerned the compensation one firm gave to another for carrying each other's traffic. See Greenstein (2008) for details.
52. For an examination of the technical and business issues developing services in this period, see, e.g., Marcus (1999).
53. This transition is described in Greenstein (2007).
54. Virtually all Unix designs were TCP/IP-compatible long before early 1995. In part this arose because the DOD required the feature for any vendor bidding for military contracts. As a result, TCP/IP had become a routine feature of Unix designs years earlier than for any major manufacturer or designer.
55. Forman (2005) describes these issues and offers statistical evidence about their consequences for how fast enterprises adopted the Internet.
56. Numerous retrofits and add-ons had enabled users of Windows and DOS-based machines to get functional service over dial-up networks and local area networks, but these technical solutions were *ad hoc*.
57. The new browser from Netscape was freely downloadable and seemed poised to threaten Mosaic's place (and, indeed, it soon would replace it as dominant browser in use). See Cusumano and Yoffie (1998) and Bresnahan and Yin (2007).
58. These events are described at length in Greenstein (2008).
59. For lengthy description of the challenges and difficulties, see Berners-Lee with Fischetti (1999) and Gillies and Cailliau (2000).
60. The URL is the term that emerged from the IETF deliberations. Berners-Lee preferred URI because it came closer to what he was trying to accomplish philosophically. See Berners-Lee and Fischetti (1999), p. 62.
61. This is a frequent theme in the first few chapters of Berners-Lee and Fischetti (1999), especially before the formation of the W3C.
62. See Berners-Lee and Fischetti (1999), p. 62, for a description of meetings in 1992 through 1994.

> Progress in the URI working group was slow, partly due to the number of endless philosophical rat holes down which technical conversations would disappear. When years later the URI working group had met twelve times and still failed to agree on a nine-page document, John Klensis, the then IETF Applications Area director, was to angrily disband it.

63. As it turned out, CERN did not become the European home for the World Wide Web. Management considered such activity too far outside the scope of their mission. Both

Berners-Lee and Fischetti (1999) and Gillies and Cailliau (2000) discuss the scope of activity at CERN during the development of the Web.

64. Just as many participants did not want to model the IETF after AT&T, they also did not want to imitate the practices of the ITU or ISO. See Drake (1993) and Russell (2006) for analyses of these rivalries.

65. Berners-Lee did return to the IETF for further refinements and upgrades. This included RFC 1738 in December of 1994 (a proposal for URL), RFC 1866 in 1995 (a standard for html), RFC 1945 in May 1996 (informational about http), RFC 2068 in January 1997 (a proposal about http), RFC 2396 in August 1998 (a draft standard about URIs), RFC 2616 in June 1999 (a draft standard for http), and RFC 3986 in January 2005 (a standard for URIs).

66. See Gates (1995).

67. Ibid., p. 4.

68. See Bresnahan (2004).

69. Gates (1995), p. 4.

70. See Bresnahan (1999).

71. Cusumano and Yoffie (1998) provide a timeline of these events and an analysis of the changing strategies of those involved. These meetings have been interpreted in numerous ways, in part because different interpretations served distinct legal arguments in the antitrust trial that followed later.

72. See Bresnahan and Yin (2007) for an analysis of the behavior of new users during the initial diffusion of the commercial browser, and how that shaped firm strategies to establish a pervasive standard in this episode.

REFERENCES

Abbate, J. (1999), *Inventing the Internet*, Cambridge, MA: MIT Press.

Allison, J. (2006), 'A tale of two standards', in C. DiBona, D. Cooper and M. Stone (eds), *Open Sources 2.0: The Continuing Revolution*, Sebastopol, CA: O'Reilly Media Inc., pp. 37–56.

Aspray, W. and P.E. Ceruzzi (2007), *The Internet and American Business*, Cambridge, MA: MIT Press.

Berners-Lee, T., with M. Fischetti (1999), *Weaving the Web: The Original Design and Ultimate Destiny of the World Wide Web by its Inventor*, New York: HarperCollins.

Boardwatch (1996–99), *Directory of Internet Service Providers*, Littleton, CO.

Bradner, S. (1999), 'The Internet engineering task force', in C. DiBona, S. Ockman and M. Stone (eds), *Open Sources: Voices From the Open Source Revolution*, Sebastopol, CA: O'Reilly Media Inc., pp. 47–52

Bresnahan, T. (1999), 'The changing structure of innovation in computing', in J.A. Eisenach and T.M. Lenard (eds), *Competition, Convergence and the Microsoft Monopoly: Antitrust in the Digital Marketplace*, Boston, MA: Kluwer Academic Publishers, pp. 155–208.

Bresnahan, T. (2004), 'The economics of the Microsoft case', Working Paper, accessed at http://www.stanford.edu/~tbres/research.htm.

Bresnahan, T. and S. Greenstein (1997), 'Technical progress and co-invention in computing and in the use of computers', *Brookings Papers on Economics Activity: Microeconomics*, 1–78.

Bresnahan, T. and S. Greenstein (1999), 'Technological competition and the structure of the computer industry', *Journal of Industrial Economics*, March, 1–40.

Bresnahan, T. and P.-L. Yin (2007). 'Setting standards in markets: browser wars', in S. Greenstein and V. Stango (eds), *Standards and Public Policy*, Cambridge, UK: Cambridge University Press, pp. 18–59.

Carroll, P. (1994), *Big Blues: the Unmaking of IBM*, New York: Crown Publishers.

Casadesus-Masanell, R. and D.B. Yoffie (2007), 'Wintel: cooperation and conflict', *Management Science*, **53** (4), 584–98.

Clark, D.D. (1992), 'A cloudy crystal ball: visions of the future', Delivered to the 24th IETF, July 1992, http://ieft20.isoc.org/videos/future_ietf_92.pdf.

Crocker, D. (1993), 'Making standards the IETF Way', *Standards View*, **1** (1), 1–15, also available at http://www.bbiw.net/musings.html.

Cusumano, M.A. and R. Selby (1995), *Microsoft Secrets: How the World's Most Powerful Software Company Creates Technology, Shapes Markets and Manages People*, New York: Simon & Schuster.

Cusumano, M.A. and D.B. Yoffie (1998), *Competing on Internet time: Lessons from Netscape and its Battle with Microsoft*, New York: Free Press.

Devereaux, M. and S. Greenstein (2009), 'The Crisis at Encyclopedia Britannica', Kellogg Case Collection 5-306-504.

DiBona, C., S. Ockman and M. Stone (eds) (1999), *Open Sources: Voices from the Open Source Revolution*, Sebastopol, CA: O'Reilly Media Inc.

DiBona, C., D. Cooper and M. Stone (eds) (2006), *Open Sources 2.0: The Continuing Revolution*, Sebastopol, CA: O'Reilly Media Inc.

Drake, W. (1993) 'The Internet religious war', *Telecommunications Policy*, December, 643.

Farrell, J. and T. Simcoe (2008), 'Choosing the rules for formal standardization', mimeo, University of Toronto.

Feller, J. (2005), *Perspectives on Free and Open Source Software*, Cambridge, MA: MIT Press.

Fleming, L. and D. Waguespack (2005), 'Penguins, camels, and other birds of a feather: Brokerage, boundary spanning, and leadership in open innovation communities', 8 April, available at SSRN: http://ssrn.com/abstract=710641.

Fleming, L. and D.Waguespack (2008), 'Startup strategies for participating in open standards communities', mimeo.

Forman, C. (2005), 'The corporate digital divide: determinants of Internet adoption', *Management Science*, **51** (4), 641–54.

Gates, W. (1995), 'The Internet tidal wave', 20 May, Internal Microsoft memo, Redmond, WA, http://www.usdoj.gov/atr/cases/ms_exhibits.htm, exhibit 20.

Gawer, A. and M.A. Cusumano (2002), *Platform Leadership: How Intel, Microsoft and Cisco Drive Industry Innovation*, Boston, MA: Harvard Business School Press.

Gawer, A. and R. Henderson (2007), 'Platform owner entry and innovation in complementary markets: evidence from Intel', *Journal of Economics and Management Strategy*, **16** (1), 1–34.

Gillies, J. and R. Cailliau (2000), *How the Web Was Born: The Story of the World Wide Web*, Oxford: Oxford University Press.

Greenstein, S. (2007), 'The evolution of market structure for Internet access in the United States', in W. Aspray and P.E. Ceruzzi (eds), *The Internet and American Business*, Cambridge, MA: MIT Press, pp. 47–104.

Greenstein, S. (2008), 'A man, a plan, a stick, a carrot', mimeo, Northwestern University.

Henderson, R. (2000), 'Declaration of Rebecca Henderson', *United States of America v. Microsoft*, http://www.usdoj.gov/atr/cases/f219100/219129.htm.

Hussain, F. (2003), 'Historic role of the commercial Internet eXchange router and its impact on the development of the Internet eXchange points [IXCs]', http://www.farooqhussain.org/projects/cixrouter19912001/index_html, accessed July 2007.

Kahin, B. (1992), *Building Information Infrastructure: Issues in the Development of the National Research and Education Network*, Cambridge, MA: McGraw-Hill Primis.

Lowe, W.C. and C. Sherburne (2008), *Pragmatic Innovation: Business Strategies for Success in the Twenty-First Century*, New York: Morgan James Publishing.

Marcus, J.S. (1999), *Designing Wide Area Networks and Internetworks: A Practical Guide*, Reading, MA: Addison Wesley.

Meeker, M. and C. Dupuy (1996), *The Internet Report*, New York: HarperCollins.

Mueller, M. (2004), *Ruling the Root: Internet Governance and the Taming of Cyberspace*, Cambridge, MA: MIT Press.

Partridge, C. (2008), 'The technical development of Internet email', *IEEE Annals of the History of Computing*, April, 3–29.

Raymond, E.S. (1998), 'The cathedral and the bazaar', *First Monday*, **3** (2), March, http://www.firstmonday.org.

Russell, A.L. (2006), 'Rough consensus and running code and the Internet–OSI standards war', *IEEE Annals of the History of Computing*, July–September, 48–61.

Segaller, S. (1998), *Nerds: A Brief History of the Internet*, New York: TV Books LLC.

Shah, R.C. and J.P. Kesan (2001), 'Fool us once, shame on you – fool us twice, shame on us: what we can learn from the privatizations of the Internet backbone network and the Domain Name System', *Washington University Law Quarterly*, **79**, 89–220.

Shapiro, C. (2001), 'Navigating the patent thicket: cross licenses, patent pools, and standard setting', in A. Jaffe, J. Lerner and S. Stern (eds), *NBER Innovation Policy and the Economy*, vol. 1, Cambridge, MA: MIT Press, pp. 119–50.

Simcoe, T. (2006), 'Standard setting committees', Working Paper, University of Toronto, http://www.rotman.utoronto.ca/timothy.simcoe/papers/Simcoe_SSOCommittes.pdf, accessed May 2008.

Simcoe, T. (2007), 'Delay and de jure standardization: exploring the slowdown in Internet standards development', in S. Greenstein and V. Stango (eds), *Standards and Public Policy*, Cambridge, UK: Cambridge University Press, pp. 260–95.

Updegrove, A. (2007), 'Product evolution and standards swarms', http://consortiuminfo.org/blog/blog.php?ID=45, 31 January.

von Hippel, E. (2002), 'Innovation by user communities: learning from Open-Source software', in Edward B. Roberts (ed.), *Innovation: Driving Product, Process, and Market Change*, San Francisco, CA: Jossey-Bass, pp. 299–310.

West, J. (2002), 'How open is open enough? Melding proprietary and open source platform strategies', *Research Policy*, **32** (7), 1259–85.

West, J. (2007), 'The economic realities of open standards: black, white, and many shades of gray', in S. Greenstein and V. Stango (eds), *Standards and Public Policy*, Cambridge, UK: Cambridge University Press, pp. 260–95.

West, J. and J. Dedrick (2000), 'Innovation and control in standards architectures: the rise and fall of Japan's PC-98', *Information Systems Research*, **11** (2), 197–216.

West, J. and J. Dedrick (2001), 'Open Source standardization: the rise of Linux in the network era', *Knowledge, Technology and Policy*, **14** (2), 88–112.

West, J. and S. O'Mahony (2008), 'The role of participation architectures in growing sponsored Open Source communities', *Industry and Innovation*, **15** (2), 145–68.

Wiggins, R. (2000), 'Al Gore and the creation of the Internet', *First Monday*, http://www.firstmonday.org/issues/issue5_10/wiggins/.

PART III

Platforms: Management, Design and
Knowledge Issues

10. Outsourcing of tasks and outsourcing of assets: evidence from automotive supplier parks in Brazil

Mari Sako[1]

1. INTRODUCTION

Supplier parks represent a recent template for organizing in the global automotive industry in the last decade. The template combines outsourcing and co-location of suppliers on automakers' sites. Its implementation began in Brazil, with Volkswagen's modular consortium in Resende in 1996, followed closely by other greenfield sites, including General Motors in Gravataí in 2000 and Ford in Camaçari in 2002. This chapter draws on evidence from these three sites to analyze supplier parks as an example of what Gawer (Chapter 3 in this volume) calls supply chain platforms.

Supplier parks consist of multiple firms that develop modules and systems that fit the product platform designed by the automaker. As such, the use and maintenance of the product platform becomes an inter-firm (rather than an intra-firm) affair, requiring attention not only to product design performance but also to supply-chain design performance. Because suppliers with divergent interests come together in a competitive–cooperative ecosystem, the performance of supply chain design depends on the development of site-specific norms and the structuring of incentives to enhance site-wide performance. This chapter considers three design parameters in supply chain platforms, namely the degree of task outsourcing, the pattern of asset ownership, and the nature of relational governance.

The key contribution of this chapter lies in systematically comparing the three supplier parks with theoretical perspectives that combine engineering design, organization economics and economic sociology. In particular, outsourcing of tasks (a focus of engineering analysis) facilitates the disintegration of asset ownership (a focus of economic analysis), although the two are conceptually distinct. Evidence from the three major supplier parks in Brazil reveals a diversity of local arrangements, with a negative correlation between task outsourcing and asset outsourcing. This finding is explained by the fact that asset ownership is one of several ways in which incentives may be structured, other mechanisms being reputation and social norms (Holmstrom and Roberts, 1998; Baker, Gibbons et al., 2002). The diversity in arrangements is explained also by different combinations of corporate strategy and state policy, and the emergence of different local labor market institutions.

The remainder of this chapter is structured as follows. Section 2 presents a framework for comparing different configurations of supplier parks. Section 3 analyzes the three Brazilian supplier parks using this framework. Section 4 discusses the reasons behind the differences and similarities amongst the three sites before concluding.

2. A FRAMEWORK FOR ANALYZING SUPPLY CHAIN PLATFORMS: OUTSOURCING OF TASKS AND OUTSOURCING OF ASSETS

An automotive supplier park is variously called industrial park, supplier campus or modular consortium, with a cluster of co-located suppliers, i.e. those located adjacent to, or inside, automakers' final assembly plants (Sako, 2003, 2004). Such supplier parks became a template for organizing production for some automakers as they outsourced more and more tasks, increasingly parcelled out in big chunks called modules. Thus the fundamental concepts useful for analyzing supplier parks are outsourcing and co-location.

Outsourcing is about the redrawing of the boundary of the firm. In theory, economists and engineers are both concerned with the division of labor inside and outside the firm. But they approach this issue from different starting points. Economists focus on asset ownership as a key to defining the boundary of the firm. For example, General Motors hiving off Delphi implies outsourcing, in the sense that assets are transferred to an independent supplier, and the right to direct how tasks are performed using those assets is also transferred. Engineers, by contrast, focus on the reallocation of tasks from one unit of production to another, regardless of ownership of these two units. So Ford may move seat production from within its assembly area to a seat-making plant, but it is not the engineer's concern whether or not the plant is owned by Ford. In effect, economists assume that the underlying task structure when asset ownership alters remains unchanged, whilst engineers are oblivious to changes in incentives to perform tasks when ownership passes hands. This section explores theoretically the consequences of combining the engineering design and organization economics perspectives on outsourcing.

Outsourcing of Tasks

In considering outsourcing, engineering design scholars focus on the allocation of tasks derived from the design of product architecture (Ulrich and Eppinger, 1999; Baldwin and Clark, 2000). In any production system, a whole series of tasks is carried out, from design and development, parts fabrication, assembly and testing. These tasks may be represented by a design structure matrix (DSM), which visually presents the extent of information flows, interactions and feedbacks necessary to carry out the tasks in sequence (www.dsmweb.org).

A number of methods is available to reduce interactions and feedbacks in a DSM. One such method is partitioning, so that tasks are reordered in time and space to enable a complex system to be decomposed into relatively independent 'chunks' or modules. Thus two chunks of tasks may be carried out independently of each other, and therefore in parallel, if each concerns the development of a distinct module with well-defined interfaces. The partitioning of a set of tasks from other tasks, in this way, is the basis for theorizing about the effect of product architecture on organization architecture and ultimately the boundary of the firm (Sanchez and Mahoney, 1996; Galunic and Eisenhardt, 2001; Schilling and Steensma, 2001).

Baldwin and Clark (2003) make advances in this literature by building their theory on DSM. They develop an analytical framework called the task and transfer (T&T) network, in which a transfer is the flow of information, materials and energy from one task to another, or one chunk of tasks to the next chunk. A transfer becomes a market transaction when a transfer can be standardized (i.e. when an object of transfer is mutually recognized by parties to a transaction), counted and valued (Baldwin and Clark, 2003). Thus, whilst this framework goes a long way to specify under what circumstances partitioned tasks can be carried out by a separate organizational entity, it cannot address whether the separate organization unit should be independently owned or not. Thus the engineering design perspective does not distinguish between integrated and disintegrated ownership structure. Moreover, it assumes that tasks are always clearly defined, leading to clearly prescribed performance levels. There is no multi-tasking with alternative use value, and no possibility of incentives or bonus affecting the level or quality of task performance.

Outsourcing of Assets

Organization economists define outsourcing as the divestment of assets, so the firm boundary is identified by asset ownership patterns (Williamson, 1985; Baker, Gibbons et al., 2002). For example, Henry Ford's Rouge factory was highly vertically integrated in the sense that Ford owned its own steel mill and component factories. The 100-year history of Ford has been marked by divestment of the ownership of various component operations.

Contracts govern relations between the buyer and the supplier. These contracts are typically relational, in the sense that they are incomplete and informal (i.e. cannot be enforced by a third party). Non-contractible elements in contracts arise from the fact that tasks are observable but non-verifiable. In this setting, the decision on whether or not to own assets is taken with a view to aligning incentives between the parties ('as an instrument in the service of the parties' relational contracts'). Thus the firm disintegrates if the supplier can be correctly incentivized via a bonus, and if there is a small chance that it can enhance alternative use value of the asset it owns. By contrast, the firm integrates asset ownership if the supplier cannot be incentivized via a bonus, and if there is a large chance of being able to enhance the alternative use value of the asset in question.

Economists are thus good at noting that asset ownership structure influences supplier incentives to carry out the prescribed tasks. But they are not so good at examining the underlying task structures that may give rise to non-contractibility. This study suggests that the DSM (and its derivative, the T&T network) provide one framework for analyzing non-contractibility. For example, 'observable but non-verifiable' tasks are more likely to occur when tasks are non-partitioned, and therefore interdependent, than when they are partitioned.

Combining the Two Perspectives

Combining the two perspectives of engineering design and organization economics gives rise to the following specific insights. First, as noted above, engineers know that partitioning tasks facilitates the outsourcing of tasks, but they ignore the fact that if partitioning is accompanied by the outsourcing of assets, incentives to perform those tasks may alter when asset ownership changes hands. Second, economists know that the outsourcing of assets is one mechanism for aligning incentives between parties in relational contracting, but they have little to say about the underlying task structure that gives rise to non-contractibility.

Third, by separating the notion of task outsourcing from the notion of

		Asset ownership pattern	
		Integrated	Disintegrated
Task structure	Partitioned	**Some supplier parks e.g. VW Resende**	**Outsourcing**
	Not partitioned	**Insourcing**	**Engineering design-in**

Figure 10.1   Typology of outsourcing: combining engineering design and organization economics

asset outsourcing, the combined perspective indicates that off-diagonals (in Figure 10.1) are not necessarily misalignments or mismatches. One off-diagonal is combining task outsourcing with asset integration (top left box in Figure 10.1). For example, a modular product architecture enables certain partitionable tasks to be outsourced from the automaker to suppliers. But such task outsourcing is combined with asset ownership integration at Volkswagen Resende (see next section for details). The extent of task outsourcing depends on automakers' corporate strategies on whether or not to outsource capacity only or knowledge as well (Fine, 1998; Brusoni, Prencipe et al., 2001). By contrast, the extent of asset outsourcing may depend on a different set of criteria, including financial strategy, to improve return on asset through divestment (Sako, 2003), and government financial incentives for attracting investment into specific locations. Asset integration makes sense to the extent that suppliers cannot be incentivized via a bonus, and there is a large chance that they can enhance alternative use value of the asset had they owned it.

The other off-diagonal is a combination of asset outsourcing with non-partitioned tasks (bottom right box in Figure 10.1). A good example of this is engineering design-in, in which supplier engineers work as part of a team with automaker engineers to develop a car. Design and development tasks are not clearly partitioned into two teams, so that necessary interactions are thick and complex. In this case, relational contracting between the automaker and the supplier is serviced by mechanisms other than asset ownership (Holmstrom and Roberts, 1998).

One such mechanism is co-location (i.e. the proximity of suppliers' operations to the automaker's), which not only lowers monitoring costs, but also facilitates the development of local norms and institutions that influence the social relations between firms and employees. In his seminal article, Granovetter (1985) makes the point that a systematic attention to actual patterns of personal relations on which economic transactions are based 'threads its way between the oversocialized approach of generalized morality and the undersocialized one of impersonal, institutional arrangements' (p. 493). Since the supplier parks studied here are greenfield sites, they provide an opportunity to study how actors have invoked larger political and social institutions, alongside creating new norms, in which to embed their transactions. These institutions include those that regulate the labor market, government policies and industry associations. One aim of this chapter is to study the evolution of concrete patterns of social relations in which economic transactions are embedded. This factor may explain the unique configuration at each supplier park.

To summarize, the framework presented here pays explicit attention to (a) the extent of task outsourcing, (b) the extent of asset outsourcing, and (c) relational governance, i.e. the concrete patterns of social relations with suppliers and employees, underpinned by specific local norms and institutions. There are already many studies on Brazilian supplier parks (Lung et al., 1999; Abreu et al., 2000; Salerno, 2001; Ramalho and Santana, 2002), but none systematically examines these three dimensions explicitly.

3. EVIDENCE FROM BRAZIL: VW RESENDE, GM GRAVATAÍ AND FORD CAMAÇARI

The Brazilian supplier parks have received much global attention because of their dual significance. First, they are part of a new phenomenon in the Brazilian auto industry, associated with policies for regional industrial development (Zilbovicius, Marx et al., 2002). State governments and private business have engaged in 'bidding wars' to create new opportunities for value-adding activities and employment in regions that are not traditionally renowned for industrial development (Rodriguez-Pose and Arbix, 2001). Second, Brazil is seen by global automotive companies as an experimental ground for new ideas and practices in integrated manufacturing and logistics. As such, what is happening in Brazil has significance well beyond Brazil's own industrial development, in potentially transforming 'best practice' in the global auto industry. This study keeps the second dimension within the scope of analysis, while demonstrating the diversity in local arrangements to pursue the first dimension.

I visited Volkswagen in Resende, General Motors in Gravataí, and Ford in Camaçari in late November and early December 2004. At this time the Brazilian automobile industry was growing rapidly, with capacity utilization well above the global industry average. Each visit lasted between half a day and two whole days. Interviews were with plant managers and various functions of the automakers, such as purchasing, logistics, quality control, human resources and finance. At each visit, key suppliers on site and labor representatives were also interviewed.

Empirical work presented in this chapter is restricted to three supplier parks from a single country, Brazil, in order to control for configurational variations that result from differences in national institutions.[2] However, even with a comparison of only three supplier parks within Brazil, diversity, rather than similarity, is striking. The key similarity is that all three sites are greenfield, built from scratch on land provided to the automakers with heavy government subsidies. Differences are as follows. First, the type of products made differ, ranging from trucks in the case of Volkswagen Resende to small passenger cars in the case of Ford Camaçari and GM Gravataí. Second, the number of suppliers on site varies from only seven at Volkswagen Resende to 21 at Ford Camaçari (see Table 10.1). Third, the degrees of asset outsourcing and task outsourcing vary considerably from site to site. Last, but not least, the density of social relations among suppliers and employees appears higher at Resende and Camaçari, and somewhat lower at Gravataí.

In order to make some sense out of this diversity, I now describe the configurations at Volkswagen Resende, GM Gravataí, and Ford Camaçari, following the order in which they were established. This enables us to examine the extent to which an early site was used as a benchmark for later sites.

Volkswagen Resende

Set in the hills of Paraiba Valley in the state of Rio de Janeiro in Brazil, the VW Resende truck plant is a modular consortium in its pure form. It opened with much fanfare and publicity on a greenfield site in 1996, well before many of the new assembly plants outside the traditionally industrial ABC region started their operation.[3] VW Resende therefore represented the earliest implementation of an experimental production system that had existed only as an idea. As with most early experiments, however, the formal production arrangements may be evident to all participants, but the mode of cooperation and social norms – i.e. the relational contracts – required within the consortium emerged only through a process of trial and error. Whilst much has been written about this model factory (Lung et al., 1999; Abreu et al., 2000; Salerno, 2001; Ramalho and Santana, 2002), our discussion will focus on the following three aspects: (a) the modular consortium concept in its essence; (b) the underlying asset ownership pattern; and (c) the emergent relational contracts within the consortium.

The modular consortium concept at Volkswagen is attributed in part to Ignacio Lopez, who moved from GM to Volkswagen to find a receptive

Table 10.1 Key characteristics of three Brazilian supplier parks at the end of 2004

Automaker	VW Resende	GM Gravataí	Ford Camaçari
Models	Versao, Titan	Corsa	Fiesta, EcoSport
Start of production	1996	2000	2002
Annual production in 2004	38000	120000	250000
Employment: automaker/ total (ratio)	477/2118 (0.225)	1699/2441 (0.696)	3372/7753 (0.435)
Number of suppliers on site	7 (of which 5 under the same roof)	16	21 (of which 11 under the same roof)
Chassis	Maxion (chassis) Remon (tire, wheel) ArvinMeritor (suspension, axles)	Goodyear (tire, wheel) Delphi (suspension, axle)	Benteler (suspension) Pirelli (tire)
Drivetrain/electrical	Powertrain (powertrain)	Valeo (cooling) ArvinMeritor (exhaust) Arteb (lighting) TI Bundy (fuel line) IPA Soplast (fuel tank)	ArvinMeritor (exhaust) Cooper Standard (fluid tubes) Kautex (fuel tank)
Exterior	Delga (body shop) Carese (paint)	Santa Marina (glass) Polyprom (stampings)	DDOC (paint) Ferrolene (blanks for stamping) Colauto/Powercoat (painting) Pilkington (glass) DuPont (paint) Faurecia (door module) Sodecia (stamping) Valeo (front-end module)

Interior	Siemens VDO (seat, cockpit)	Lear (seats, headliner) Siemens VDO (cockpit) Borsal-Gerobras (toolkit) Pelzer (plastic parts) Inylbra (carpet) Sogefi (air filter) FSM-Fanaupe (fastner)	Autometal (plastic injection) DOW (plastic injection, painting) Intertrim (headliner) Lear (seat) Mapri-Textron (fastner) Pelzer (soft trim) SaarGummi (rubber parts) Visteon (cockpit)
Services outsourced	Logistics	Personnel services (transport, cafeteria, site protection, medical centre, recruitment and selection)	Maintenance, logistics, product development
Asset ownership by automakers	High: land, buildings, machinery and equipment, inventories owned by VW	Low: suppliers own land, buildings, machinery and equipment	Medium: Ford owns land and buildings; suppliers own machinery and equipment
Union presence	Força Sindical	Força Sindical	CUT
Summary ranking			
Task outsourcing	1	3	2
Asset outsourcing	3	1	2
Uniformity of HR system	3	2	1

Source: Author's site visit and interviews.

home for his ideas, and in part to the failure of Autolatina, a joint venture with Ford that had expertise in designing and developing truck components. Left with no such in-house expertise, Volkswagen had to rely on suppliers that can design modules. Volkswagen was to focus on strategic functions such as the overall vehicle architectural design and customer satisfaction, and decided to ask suppliers not only to manufacture components but also to participate in final assembly of the trucks. The modular consortium at Resende is therefore unusual in the vehicle manufacturing industry for its practice of totally outsourcing final assembly.

Seven 'partner' supplier entities are involved in the production process. First, Delga welds body panels, which are then passed on to Carese (owned by Eisenmann) for painting. Separate buildings exist for the body shop and the paint shop, but all other partner suppliers are under one roof in the final assembly area. The final assembly line starts with Maxion assembling the chassis. Remon (a consortium of Pirelli, Bridgestone and Michelin) fixes the assembled tires and wheels on to the chassis. Powertrain (a consortium of Cummins and MWM) operates a sub-assembly area for engines and transmissions, but also delivers and fixes them at the final assembly line. Lastly, Siemens/VDO installs seats and cockpits inside the cabin, before Volkswagen conducts final inspection of the completed truck.

On the surface, the above production arrangement might appear to resemble that of a 'manufacturer without factories' such as Nike, whose main asset is the product brand in a buyer-driven global commodity chain (Gereffi and Korzeniewicz, 1994). However, a closer examination of the asset ownership pattern at Resende defies this logic. Volkswagen is said to have made an initial investment of $250 million in 1996, in order to construct the modular consortium on a one million square meter area that used to be a sugar-cane field. Much of the funds went to construct the 90000 square meter buildings and shared facilities, and to purchase machinery and equipment. Consequently, Volkswagen owns and controls more or less every factor of production, except labor. Specifically:

1. The land is owned by VW, and partner suppliers pay no rent.
2. The buildings are also all owned by VW, and suppliers pay no rent.
3. Machinery and equipment, including those in the paint shop and the body shop, are designed by, paid for and, therefore, owned by VW.
4. Condominium facilities are owned by VW, and suppliers pay for the use of the canteen, medical care facilities etc. However, suppliers are not charged for the use of energy and water.
5. Inventories of materials and components on site are also all owned by VW. Typically, an external logistics company (Binotto) delivers parts to a consolidation center, and another logistics company (Union

Manten) records the delivery on behalf of VW and delivers parts to the lineside. Since the partner suppliers use only materials and components 'on consignment', they do not pay for the material inputs they work on, and therefore have no scope for earning profit on their price. Also, since the inventories are owned by VW, the suppliers would have no incentive to lower the cost of holding inventories.

In all, the suppliers' hands are tied, as VW owns every input except labor. This ownership structure gives suppliers limited incentives beyond the management of labor. Based on the asset ownership pattern, therefore, VW Resende is an integrated firm that has outsourced the management of labor. It does not engage in production activities but has retained full ownership of the physical assets of production.

It is possible that VW's ownership of physical assets emerged out of necessity rather than choice. In theory, the modular consortium idea seems to have involved suppliers as partners in the financing of the factory as much as in the production and assembly on site (Abreu et al., 2000). In reality, VW did not find many suppliers with financial resources or incentives to invest in machinery and equipment, when real interest rates were running high at 40 percent in the mid-1990s. Moreover, with relatively low labor costs, the Resende plant ended up being much less automated than its counterparts in Europe, with nearly 100 percent manual welding and painting operations. However, by late 2004, at the time of my field visit, VW had a plan to adopt a new supplier that will pay for the construction of a new body shop with welding robots.

The labor-intensive nature of the operations suggests that the management of labor is central to the success of the Resende plant. However, in contrast to the attention that was given to the innovative configuration of the supply chain – with suppliers brought inside the factory as assemblers – there is nothing innovative about the management of labor. The management of all direct workers is outsourced to suppliers, so VW employs only 477 indirect staff out of a total of 2118 employees on the Resende site. These VW staff work in functional offices overlooking the main assembly line, responsible for product development, purchasing, and process engineering in order to tightly control process engineering in its body shop, paint shop and final assembly. By contrast, in Delga's body shop, 100 percent of welding is manual, and the hammering din was unbearably high even with ear protection.

The outsourcing of the management of labor nevertheless did not lead to each supplier acting separately on its own accord. Given the physical proximity of suppliers housed under one roof, it is not surprising that some sort of social norm has to emerge to govern labor–management relations for the whole site. In particular, there is a common wage and benefits agreement with the union (Força Sindical), to pre-empt any dispute that might arise from pay differentials between suppliers. Workers all came from the same labor pool trained by SENAI; once hired to work inside the Resende plant, shopfloor supervisors – leaders in each assembly area – were given a general orientation about the VW vision, its culture and common values. It is therefore not surprising that workers have developed an identity as *de facto* employees of the German multinational (Abreu et al., 2000).

If the wage is the same whether workers are employed by suppliers or directly by VW, and since there is much coordination associated with working with partner suppliers, why doesn't VW do its own final assembly? According to an HR manager:

> The new concept was for VW to do the start and the finish of the assembly line. This was partly for cost reasons and there was also an advantage to not getting involved in managing labor. VW's main interest is to focus on product design and on marketing and managing client relations. We are not all that interested in managing the assembly process itself nor in managing labor.

To summarize, VW Resende is a 'pure' case of a modular consortium, in which even the final assembly is outsourced to the partner suppliers on site. However, all productive assets are owned by VW, giving these suppliers a very narrow scope for discretionary action, even in matters of inventory control. The key area in which suppliers could have exercised discretion is the management of labor. But even here, VW ended up taking a lead in imposing a uniform norm, so that pay and conditions are identical for all workers at VW and 'partner' suppliers.

VW Resende has been a success story, judging from the sale of its main product, the Titan. Production volumes increased very rapidly, growing threefold in seven years, from 35 per day in 1997 to 112 in 2003. In late 2004, a second shift was introduced with 400 new hires (temporaries placed via labor agencies), and plans are under way for expansion, including an automated body shop. More flexible labor and a higher degree of automation are challenges for VW, whose stance in outsourcing the management of labor has to be reconciled with maintaining the social fabric of the Resende site.

GM Gravataí

VW Resende has an integrated asset ownership structure with a uniform human resource system on the site, except that task outsourcing is taken to its extreme with VW undertaking no final assembly. At GM's supplier park in Gravataí, in the state of Rio Grande do Sul, the degrees of outsourcing of asset ownership and tasks are both less than at Resende. That is, suppliers purchased their own piece of land and constructed their own separate factory building. GM has also retained final assembly in house. Despite a more dispersed physical layout and disintegrated ownership patterns, GM Gravataí has come to insist on a similarly uniform HR system as at VW Resende.

The Blue Macaw project started in 1996, in order to develop a small subcompact car, with a modular product architecture based on the Corsa platform. Its vision also included (a) full participation of suppliers who would co-design, co-validate and co-locate, (b) the implementation of lean manufacturing concepts, and (c) a high degree of de-proliferation (i.e. a base car for which only a small option variety is offered).

The production of a Corsa derivative, called Celta, started in 2000 with 16 *sistemistas*, as the suppliers are known, which came to locate on the Gravataí site (see Table 10.1). The whole site was initially bought by the state government, which in turn sold allotment by allotment at a subsidized rate to GM and the suppliers. Thereafter, each company erected its own factory building, and purchased its own machinery and equipment. The only exception is Polyprom, which does small stampings within GM's stamping shop. There are no other suppliers inside the stamping shop, body shop, paint shop or the final assembly area. Suppliers' ownership of assets was considered unproblematic by GM, whose manager expected suppliers to stay around for a long time, like the Blue Macaw birds which, once mated, stay together for ever. This expectation is reinforced by the fact that model cycle tends to be rather long in Brazil, lessening the chance of supplier turnover. At the same time, there is a formal contractual safeguard, prohibiting suppliers from supplying to other automakers from the Gravataí site.

Whilst respecting supplier autonomy in matters of asset ownership, GM at Gravataí takes a lead in instituting a uniform human resource system in a manner similar to VW's at Resende and Ford's at Camaçari. At the time of my visit in November 2004, the Gravataí site employed a total of 2441 workers, of whom a majority – 1699 – were on GM's payroll. The Personnel Policy Committee (PPC), consisting of HR managers from GM and the 16 suppliers, meets once a month to discuss matters concerning personnel services, labor relations and the human resource system. Each of these three areas has a sub-committee that meets more frequently. First, personnel services consist of transport, cafeteria, site protection and medical center, and are all outsourced to one single company. Second, labor relations on site are governed by a five-year collective works contract, signed between the Força Sindical union and the Gravataí Industrial Complex (i.e. GM and supplier managements all put together), to implement a common system of flexible work hours, disciplinary steps and conflict resolution procedure. Lastly, there is a common wage scale that applies to all companies on the site.

The common way of doing things can emerge only over time, even if 'the intention is to commonize everything', according to GM's HR manager. 'The challenge is to work with 16 different ways of working and of managing people. This has been a problem with us at the beginning.' Compromises had to be made in some cases. For example, GM wanted the *sistemistas* to use the same recruitment and selection process (involving tests, assessment center and interviews), but acquiesced to suppliers using their different ways when they claimed that the GM way was too expensive. Similarly, initial training at GM consists of a five-day 'lean orientation week' to learn and practise the lean production principles. Every new recruit at GM gets this training, but suppliers thus far have argued, despite numerous attempts by GM, that they cannot afford to let their workers go for a week-long training. Nevertheless, GM thinks that it can establish a progressive labor relations philosophy in Gravataí, where GM is in a monopsonistic position, compared to their positions at their older sites in the ABC region. Thus a powerful labor market position compensates for fragmented ownership structure in attempts to impose a uniform HR system for the supplier park.

GM's hands-on approach to establishing a local social norm for Gravataí is also evident in the following view by one of the on-site suppliers:

> Here at Gravataí, GM wants to participate in everything on the condominium. Suppliers have security, and GM is committed to developing the suppliers. Compared to other GM sites, there is a good culture at Gravataí; people at the top, like the plant manager, are very accessible; you can stop them for a chat on the street.

Ford Camaçari

Ford Industrial Complex at Camaçari, in the state of Bahia in Brazil, is a condominium with suppliers, some of which are under a single roof with Ford. As at VW Resende, the land and buildings are owned by the automaker. As at GM Gravataí and VW Resende, all employees on the Camaçari site are on an identical human resource system. But unlike at VW Resende, Ford controls final assembly.[4]

The so-called Amazon project involved the development of an economical B-platform car using Ford's product architecture with 19 modules. The New Fiesta started its production at Camaçari in 2002, and the EcoSport was subsequently launched in 2003. From the start, the Amazon project idea was to push outsourcing to its limit, and to economize on overhead and fixed costs by sharing them with suppliers. Therefore the target agreement signed by suppliers at the time of program approval (when design was frozen) included a requirement that they locate on Ford's site.

Whilst Ford retains control over the final assembly process, 21 component suppliers and four service providers (in maintenance, logistics and product development) are located on the site. Eight further component suppliers are located outside, but close to, the site. Of the 21 component suppliers, 11 are in the final assembly area 'under one roof'. They are Faurecia (door module), Visteon (cockpit), Pelzer (soft trim), Intertrim (headliner), Lear (seats), Mapri-Textron (fasteners), Valeo (front-end module), Benteler (suspension), ArvinMeritor (exhaust), Cooper (fluid tube), and Pirelli (tire assembly).[5] These suppliers are not responsible for fitting their modules on the final assembly line, but some of them employ a quality-check person at the point of fit, indicating the need for seamless coordination of assembly tasks that cross the boundary of the firm. Moreover, compared to VW Resende and even GM Gravataí, Ford Camaçari is a much bigger site in which significant value-adding manufacturing processes other than assembly are carried out.

All the suppliers for the Amazon project were selected by the time the site was originally chosen at Guaiba in Rio Grande do Sul. After discovering that the new RS governor was not going to honor all aspects of the agreement signed with the previous state government, Ford was lured away to the state of Bahia, 2000 km north of the industrial south. All but one of the suppliers followed Ford at its new location, as it was a prerequisite for winning a contract for suppliers to locate on site. Both federal and state incentives made the Camaçari location attractive, and the package included improving the road infrastructure and the promise to build a new port nearby.

Although the state subsidies and tax benefits lowered considerably the cost of setting up a greenfield site in Bahia as in Rio Grande do Sul, the asset ownership pattern at the Ford Industrial Complex came to be different from the one at GM's Gravataí site, giving rise to different supplier incentives. In the Ford Industrial Complex, land and buildings are owned by Ford, whilst the machinery and equipment that suppliers use are owned by suppliers themselves. This means that for suppliers, 'Bahianization' – bringing more value-adding manufacturing activities to Bahia – involves a calculation of financial tradeoff. The distance between the industrial south and Bahia is equivalent to three days in transit, tying a high level of inventory. However, the logistics savings if processes are brought on site to Camaçari have to be traded off against the need for upfront new equipment investment, because sourcing from local suppliers in Bahia with no history of industrial production is ruled out in most cases.

With the launch of the EcoSport and the hiring of 2100 new employees in August 2004 to cope with the expansion, the Camaçari site employs 7753, of whom 3372 are on Ford's payroll. Ford is very much in charge, to create a uniform human resource system that applies to all employees on the Camaçari site regardless of their employer. New recruits are trained by SENAI, which provides 900 hours of training over six months, 450 hours before hiring and 450 hours after hiring. A labor pool created via SENAI is subdivided and allocated to Ford and suppliers, who conduct their own selection process based on interviews. Once selected, all workers are put through an identical training programme, using Ford's on-site technical center which houses a mock paint shop, body shop and final assembly line: 'no short cuts for suppliers', says Ford's HR manager. This uniformity of training for all supplier employees is in contrast to the more decentralized mode of training at the GM Gravataí complex.

Apart from recruitment and training, there is a comprehensive list of facilities that are shared among Ford and its suppliers, including the restaurant, medical services, banking, maintenance and logistics, health and safety procedures, plant security, fire protection and cleaning services. The Camaçari site also has a common wage structure for operators (but not for managers and engineers) that apply to Ford and its suppliers on site, negotiated with the union, Central Unica dos Trabalhadores (CUT). Ford management regards CUT to have a tougher negotiating stance than FS, for example, over flexible work hours. But according to a Ford HR manager, 'CUT is tough but will implement an agreement. By contrast, FS often agrees to something but doesn't have the power to implement it.'

A Human Resource Management Committee exists in order to develop and monitor such a common system so as to avoid labor conflict. The idea is to create a consensus, even if it means forcing a common solution through the committee structure. G7 consists of seven key companies (Ford, Benteler, Visteon, ABB, Lear, Exel, Faurecia), each representing other suppliers. Every Thursday, the G7 plant managers and HR managers meet to discuss various issues. Ford's HR manager reflected on the process of arriving at a consensus:

> It's a challenge, but after three years, we're aligned with our partners to do this. Sometimes, one supplier wants to do things differently – e.g. pay their workers more – but we lean on the supplier to stick to the common rule.

Thus, compared to GM Gravataí, Ford Camaçari is characterized by a more unified asset ownership structure and a tighter control over establishing a uniform HR system for the whole site. But the degree of task outsourcing is greater at Ford than at GM, leading to Ford's view that no further tasks can be outsourced. Because of the sheer nature of its distant location, Ford Camaçari has more suppliers who are undertaking processing and manufacturing on site than mere assembly and sequencing. Moreover, Ford Camaçari's physical layout of the final assembly area, that houses 11 suppliers under the same roof, is closer to VW Resende's modular consortium than to GM Gravataí. The tightly knit co-location and unified asset ownership are both conducive to establishing a unified HR system.

4. COMPARISONS AND DISCUSSION

Each of the three parameters of the supply-chain platform design – task outsourcing, asset outsourcing and relational governance – gives a different ranking for the three supplier parks studied above (see the bottom of Table 10.1 for a summary of the rankings). This section provides an explanation of how these rankings fit together.

On task outsourcing, VW Resende (78 percent) lies at one extreme, outsourcing all final assembly, followed by Ford Camaçari (57 percent) and GM Gravataí (30 percent) in that order. The figures in brackets are the ratios of supplier employees to total employees on site, a proxy measure for the degree of task outsourcing. Some observers might consider task outsourcing to be more prevalent in trucks than in passenger car assembly. However, within the passenger car market, there are also cases in which final assembly is outsourced, for example to Magna Steyr in Graaz, which undertakes final assembly for BMW. Thus, GM's and Ford's retention of final assembly is a matter of strategic choice.

On asset outsourcing, GM is most disintegrated as it expects suppliers to own land, buildings, and machinery and equipment. Ford Camaçari is in the middle, with suppliers owning machinery and equipment which they operate on land and buildings owned by Ford. VW is most integrated as it owns all types of capital, including inventory. All three automakers benefited from significant sums of state and federal subsidies, making land purchase not a major part of initial investment. Nevertheless, the emergent asset ownership patterns came to differ, due to a combination of state policies and corporate strategy. More importantly, these different asset ownership patterns have given rise to different supplier incentives, with VW suppliers having the least incentive to economize on inventory holdings, and GM suppliers having the most incentive to maximize returns from their assets.

On the uniformity of HR systems as one form of relational governance, all three sites had coordination efforts of varying kinds, characterized

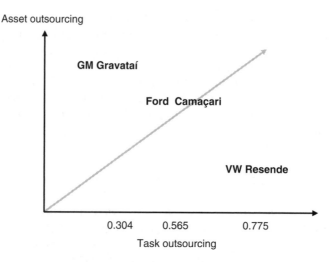

Asset outsourcing

GM Gravataí

Ford Camaçari

VW Resende

0.304   0.565   0.775

Task outsourcing

Note: The horizontal axis is an index of supplier employees as a percentage of total employees on site.

Figure 10.2   Correlation between task outsourcing and asset outsourcing

at a minimum by an identical wage system for all direct employees on site. However, the devil is in the detail, and Ford Camaçari continued to recruit, select and train all Ford and supplier employees through a single channel, whilst VW recruited its recent cohort of temporary workers via a separate channel of labor placement agencies. Although GM attempts to be like Ford, its recruitment, selection and training are conducted separately by suppliers. Thus Ford is most uniform, GM in-between, and VW least uniform.

These rankings are summarized in Table 10.1. Each dimension is ranked differently, underpinning the notion that each configuration of supplier parks is unique. As shown in Figure 10.2, the degree of asset outsourcing is negatively correlated with the degree of task outsourcing, but the third dimension of relational governance does not map neatly onto either of the other two dimensions. There therefore appears to be no single 'Brazilian model' in this field, revealing an element of experimentation. Nevertheless, the framework developed in this chapter provides at least three reasons why diversity in local configurations within a country like Brazil is possible. They are (a) corporate policy combined with state policy; (b) asset ownership as one of several ways to deal with control and incentives; and (c) the emergence of varied labor market institutions.

One reason for diversity is different automakers' financial strategy, combined with diversity in state policy. The empirical cases of VW, GM and Ford demonstrate that modular product architecture is indeed associated with greater outsourcing of tasks, but task outsourcing is not necessarily associated with asset outsourcing. The decision on the latter – how much asset to outsource – is made on the basis of a combination of reasons, such as return on assets and other financial targets, which are different from those for task outsourcing. In Brazil, automakers' decision to outsource assets was influenced not only by their budget for developing a greenfield site, but also by Brazilian state policies on allocating subsidized land, either as a single plot to the automaker in the case of the states of Rio de Janeiro for Volkswagen and Bahia for Ford, or plot by plot in the case of Rio Grande do Sul for General Motors. Moreover, as we saw at Resende, asset ownership appears to have been influenced also by the financial capacity and willingness of suppliers to invest in machinery and equipment on site.

Second, automakers may use asset ownership as one of several ways in which they can structure incentives for suppliers on site (Holmstrom and Roberts, 1998). Thus, at Gravataí, although GM does not own assets used by suppliers, it has enhanced its control over suppliers on site by contractually limiting suppliers' decision rights to deploy their assets for competitors to GM. Also GM's hands-on approach to developing a local norm for standardizing everything on human resource management provides an alternative control mechanism to asset ownership. Moreover, co-location itself may be regarded as a control mechanism, as such extreme proximity reduces automakers' cost of monitoring suppliers' behavior.

The third reason for diversity is the path dependence in the evolution of local social norms and institutions at specific supplier parks. Common Brazilian pressures are present in all three sites we studied. Outsourcing has always been associated with the automaker's motive to access low-cost labor in emerging markets or in non-unionized workplaces. The location choice for many of the greenfield supplier parks reflects this motive. In Brazil, automakers have chosen locations away from the traditionally industrialized ABC region in the southeast with the presence of strong metalworking unions, to justify paying lower wages.[6] Moreover, the corporatist legacy in the Brazilian labor law dictates that one union is to be recognized for a specific industrial sector in a given geographical region. There is also the general pressure towards a uniform human resource management system on each site due to the physical proximity of suppliers to the automaker.

Nevertheless, different local institutions, notably in the labor market, also led to diversity. At the time of my visits, the VW and GM managements dealt with the more conservative Força Sindical (FS) metalworkers'

union, whereas the Ford management dealt with the metal union affiliated to the more left-oriented Central Unica dos Trabalhadores (CUT).
However, there was a varying degree of contest between FS and CUT,
with CUT taking recognition cases to the labor courts and simultaneously
attempting to win grass-roots support from workers through the creation
of factory commissions (non-mandated works council-like bodies) within
supplier parks. The key issue for the Brazilian unions is not the closing of
wage gaps between automakers and suppliers, as in the USA, but differentials between the industrial south and the new greenfield locations. Within
this broad framework, different unions have entertained varying degrees
of willingness to acquiesce to flexible work hours (in the form of hour
banks) and the use of temporary workers. Volkswagen Resende made use
of such flexibility much more than the other two sites.

5.   CONCLUSIONS

This chapter developed a framework for analyzing supplier parks, which
represent a template for organizing in the automobile industry since the
1990s. Supplier parks were treated as an example of what Gawer calls
supply chain platforms. This study focused on examining three parameters
in designing these platforms, namely the degree of task outsourcing, the
extent of asset outsourcing, and the nature of relational governance manifested for example in a site-wide human resource management system.
This framework enables us to unpack the ecosystem of each supplier park
in Brazil, an important level of analysis that complements a more macro
perspective on the use of the Brazilian automobile sector for regional
industrial development (Rodriguez-Pose and Arbix, 2001) or for transforming national labor–management relations (Anner, 2003).

   This study provided empirical support for the following theoretical
insights. First, task outsourcing may not necessarily lead to asset outsourcing, so that a discussion of the boundary of an organizational unit
should clearly be separated from a discussion of the boundary of the firm
as a legal entity. Second, asset outsourcing may occur for reasons other
than those for task outsourcing. Corporate financial strategy and state
policy affect asset outsourcing directly, whilst product architecture and
the underlying task structure affect task outsourcing. Third, asset outsourcing is one of several ways in which control and incentives may be
structured, other ways being contracts that limit suppliers' decision rights
and the development of local social norms.

   In conclusion, this study developed a framework for analyzing the
governance of supplier parks as supply chain platforms. Moreover, the

insights from this study might enrich our understanding not only of such platforms but also of platforms in general. For example, the distinction made between task ownership and asset ownership is still a topic worthy of further exploration in the area of industry platforms. The results of this study also suggest the importance of incorporating the notion of governance of platforms and human resource practices in particular into the study of platforms, their performance, stability and evolution.

NOTES

1. I thank the MIT International Motor Vehicle Program (IMVP) for funding this research. I am particularly grateful to Jose Ricardo Ramalho, who facilitated access to the supplier parks, and to Mahrukh Doctor, who acted as co-researcher and interpreter on our company visits.
2. This was part of a larger international study of supplier parks, in which I also visited 14 sites in the USA and Europe (Germany, France, Spain).
3. The ABC region is an industrial region southeast of the city of São Paulo where the largest auto plants are concentrated. It is made up of Santo André (A), São Bernardo (B) and São Caetano (C).
4. This was despite sensational media reporting that Ford would outsource key parts of its final assembly operations, which 'could signal the company's gradual withdrawal from final assembly as a core activity – transforming Ford from a carmaker into a global consumer products and services group' (*Financial Times*, 4 August 1999).
5. Other significant suppliers include Forrrolene and Sodecia in the stamping shop, DDOC undertaking body painting, Dow and Autometal doing plastics injection, ABB in maintenance, and Exel providing logistics service.
6. In 2001, the average monthly wage at newer auto plants was US$477, just over half the average of US$907 prevailing in the traditional auto plants (Anner, 2003).

REFERENCES

Abreu, A.R. de P., H. Beynon and J.R. Ramalho (2000), '"The Dream Factory": VW's Modular Production System in Resende, Brazil', *Work, Employment & Society*, **14** (2), 265–82.

Anner, M. (2003), 'Industrial structure, the state, and ideology: shaping labor transnationalism in the Brazilian auto industry', *Social Science History*, **27**(4), 603–34.

Baker, G., R. Gibbons et al. (2002), 'Relational contracts and the theory of the firm', *Quarterly Journal of Economics*, **117** (1), 39–84.

Baldwin, C.Y. and K.B. Clark (2000), *Design Rules: The Power of Modularity*, Cambridge, MA: MIT Press.

Baldwin, C.Y. and K.B. Clark (2003), 'Where do transactions come from? A perspective from engineering design', Saint-Gobain Centre for Economic Research, Paris, France.

Brusoni, S., A. Prencipe et al. (2001), 'Knowledge specialization, organizational coupling, and the boundaries of the firm: why do firms know more than they make?', *Administrative Science Quarterly*, **46**, 597–621.

Fine, C.H. (1998), *Clockspeed: Winning Industry Control in the Age of Temporary Advantage*, Reading, MA: Perseus Books.

Galunic, D.C. and K.M. Eisenhardt (2001), 'Architectural innovation and modular corporate forms', *Academy of Management Journal*, **44** (6), 1229–49.

Gereffi, G. and M. Korzeniewicz (1994), *Commodity Chains and Global Capitalism*, New York: Praeger.

Granovetter, M. (1985), 'Economic action and social structure: the problem of embeddedness', *American Journal of Sociology*, **91** (3), 481–510.

Holmstrom, B. and J. Roberts (1998), 'The boundaries of the firm revisited', *Journal of Economic Perspectives*, **12** (4), 73–94.

Lung, Y. et al. (1999), 'Flexibility through modularity: experimentations with fractal production in Brazil and in Europe', in Y. Lung et al. (eds), *Coping with Variety*, Aldershot, UK: Ashgate, pp. 224–57.

Ramalho, J.R. and M.A. Santana (2002), 'VW's modular system and workers' organization in Resende, Brazil', *International Journal of Urban and Regional Research*, **26** (4), 756–766.

Rodriguez-Pose, A. and G. Arbix (2001), 'Strategies of waste: bidding wars in the Brazilian automobile sector', *International Journal of Urban and Regional Research*, **25** (1), 134–54.

Sako, M. (2003), 'Modularity and outsourcing: the nature of coevolution of product architecture and organisation architecture in the global automotive industry', in A. Prencipe, A. Davies and M. Hobday (eds), *The Business of Systems Integration*, Oxford: Oxford University Press, pp. 229–53.

Sako, M. (2004), 'Governing supplier parks: implications for firm boundaries and clusters', in H. Dumez (ed.), *Gouverner les Organisations*, Paris: L'Harmattan, pp. 215–53.

Salerno, M.S. (2001), 'The characteristics and the role of modularity in the automotive business', *International Journal of Automotive Technology and Management*, **1** (1), 92–107.

Sanchez, R. and J.T. Mahoney (1996), 'Modularity, flexibility, and knowledge management in product and organization design', *Strategic Management Journal*, **17** (10), 63–76.

Schilling, M.A. and H.K. Steensma (2001), 'The use of modular organizational forms: an industry-level analysis', *Academy of Management Journal*, **44** (6), 1149–68.

Ulrich, K. and S. Eppinger (1999), *Product Design and Development*, New York: McGraw-Hill.

Williamson, O.E. (1985), *The Economic Institutions of Capitalism*, New York: Free Press.

Zilbovicius, M., R. Marx et al. (2002), 'A comprehensive study of the transformation of the Brazilian automotive industry', *International Journal of Automotive Technology and Management*, **2** (1), 10–23.

11. Platforms for the design of platforms: collaborating in the unknown

Pascal Le Masson, Benoit Weil and Armand Hatchuel

1. INTRODUCTION

This chapter explores how industry platforms can be designed using specific collaborative relationships that also take the form of platforms. In several sectors, the architecture of industry is tending to loosen or even disappear: 'smart grids' in electricity supply, biomaterials and home networking in telecommunications and consumer electronics are all examples of new industrial contexts in search of industry platforms. In such situations, who is the industrial architect? Who provides the industry platform? How do platforms emerge and how do companies contribute to the process? What are the different forms of collaboration for designing industry platforms? Are there different contexts? Can we specify the circumstances under which it will not be one entrepreneur, or a series of individual entrepreneurs, but rather a coalition of entrepreneurs, who will attempt to create a platform?

Despite its importance, surprisingly little research has been done on platform design and the collaborative relationships involved. Industry platforms, particularly in high-tech industries, have attracted considerable attention since they induce seemingly anomalous strategic behaviour, competitive positions or pricing policies. Successful platform strategies have been identified in a number of diversified situations: PC architectures (Intel), operating systems (Microsoft), computer games (Sony, Nintendo), Internet browsers (MS Explorer), Internet search (Google) etc. Issues regarding platform leadership management and platform wannabe strategies are today widely understood, thanks to empirical studies and theoretical models. The works on the subject underline the importance of platform design in successful platform leadership but have not really investigated the notion of platform design as such. All the empirical cases and the related models of strategic platform management are based on a given platform potential, provided by a platform entrepreneur who may become the platform leader. The literature insists on the importance of a platform 'core', performing one essential function or solving one essential problem of the system, but how can this core be identified or designed? The works also focus on optimal pricing, taking advantage of cross-sided networks effects. But how can these networks effects be identified or even designed?

Moreover, what if there is no platform entrepreneur providing the platform potential? Companies working in highly innovative fields – such as 'smart grids', home networking or new bio-materials – are currently looking for platforms to help them organize industry growth or industry renewal. They can rely on internal platform entrepreneurship but they are also keen to work with other companies to design industry platforms in a kind of collaborative entrepreneurship. However, the challenges of platform design by a platform entrepreneur might be compounded for the collaborative partners designing the platform. For instance, the issues of value appropriation and value sharing are more likely to block the collective design process. How can collaborative processes be organized and who should take part in them? What inputs, activities, phases and outputs are involved, and how can their performance be characterized?

It is interesting to note that these collaborative partnerships for platform design can share features with 'classic' industry platforms, in the sense that they support collective efforts around a collective core, organize networks of stakeholders and create value for all the members. However, contrary to the usual view of product platforms, they can *not* consist in the shared, core features of the future system since not only the components, but also the architectures, the customers, the partners, the performances and even the business models of the future systems are still to be explored.

We shall explore the issues raised by these collaborations for platform design using a multiple case study in four different industries: bio-materials, microelectronics, aeronautics and biotechnologies. In all four cases, we had the opportunity to follow a platform design process on a longitudinal basis.

The emergent theoretical framework suggests that the collaboration for platform design consists not only in delivering an industry platform but in positioning this platform potential into a strategic landscape, characterized by alternative platform strategies, the capabilities enabling these platform strategies and the values of these platform strategies for the partners. To achieve this objective, collaborations for platform design have to deal with three main processes:

1. Managing value creation, in order not only to identify a product platform for the industry but also to evaluate this platform compared to other alternatives and to integrate all the possible alternatives into a strategic mapping process.
2. Organizing knowledge production and learning, by involving partners, offering support for various experiments and providing specific knowledge production devices.
3. Managing the interests of each of the partners, by simultaneously creating value at the industry level and increasing the value of the partners' assets

This research suggests four research hypotheses: First, the platform design process is neither an aggregation of past experience (Moore et al., 1999) nor a functional, so-called 'top-down' design (Farrell and Simpson, 2003), nor an evolutionary adaptation of previous platforms (Gawer and Henderson, 2007; Meyer et al., 1997). On the contrary, the design process is a structured exploration of alternatives driven by common concepts, shared instruments for knowledge production and a clear set of shared procedures for managing the collaboration common purpose. Hence the collaboration itself appears as a platform, using a well-identified stable core, gathering networks of partners who all value the core. Therefore we propose to consider these collaborations as a platform for platform design (Hypothesis 1).

Second, platforms for platform design and platforms for product/system design share common attributes but require distinct types of strategic management (Hypothesis 2).

Third, platforms for platform design might perform better than platform entrepreneurs in situations with many unknowns (i.e. undecidability). This would reinforce the role of consortia, although they have often been considered as poor platform designers (Morris and Ferguson, 1993). It seems that conventional wisdom on the drawbacks of consortia (that they are complex, hence rigid and restrictive, and involve compromises) does not apply when the interests are unknown and discovered 'by walking' (Aggeri, 1999; Segrestin, 2005), and that the exploration and creation of interests can be enhanced through platforms for platform design (Le Masson et al., 2007) (Hypothesis 3).

Fourth, platforms for platform design have a strong impact on the evolution of platforms and open new horizons regarding classic issues of platform strategies: changing scope (Jacobides et al., 2006), avoiding envelopment by changing networks (Eisenmann et al., 2006), combining mobility and complementarity (Jacobides, 2006) (Hypothesis 4).

The rest of the chapter is organized as follows: Section 2 presents a short literature review of platform design and the issues raised by platforms for platform design; Section 3 gives the methods and the data; Section 4 presents the results of the multiple-case study; based on these results, Section 5 discusses the hypotheses, pointing out how they extend existing literature and offering some conclusions.

2. LITERATURE OVERVIEW: WHAT HAS TO BE DESIGNED? HOW?

The Main Features of an Industry Platform in the Literature

How can the process of designing an industry platform be organized? The literature on platform strategy and platform engineering has focused primarily on the advantages of platform leadership and the issues involved, and hence underlined what has to be designed for being a platform leader and/or for efficient platform management. We can identify three main dimensions that several authors have considered as essential features of an industry platform: (1) a set of fixed attributes that are always present in the final system; (2) networks of platform users; and (3) utility functions of the fixed attributes for the networks members.

In their definitions of platforms, several authors stress the importance of the first dimension, i.e. the set of fixed attributes that are shared by the systems built on the platform: Gawer and Cusumano (2002) and Gawer and Henderson (2007) define platforms as 'one component or subsystem of an evolving technological system, strongly functionally interdependent with most of the other components of the systems, and end-user demand is for the overall system' (Gawer and Henderson, 2007, p. 4). Bresnahan and Greenstein (1999) define platforms as 'a bundle of standard components around which buyers and sellers coordinate efforts'; West (2003) as an 'architecture of related standards' (p. 1260). With the concept of 'modularity' (Baldwin and Clark, 2000, 2006), the fixed set of attributes is represented by 'design rules' that ensure the compatibility of the modules. From an engineering standpoint, 'a platform design consists of a basic architecture, comprised of subsystems or modules and the interfaces between these modules' (Meyer et al., 1997, p. 91). Hence this basic core is not limited to a set of common components, technologies or subsystems but also includes compatibility rules that ensure that complements, modules and other systems are compatible with the platform. Note that in this perspective, the list of modules and complements is neither finished nor limited to 'standardized' components. Hence the process of designing a platform consists in first designing this core.

The literature provides insights into the interesting economic properties of the core. As stated by Gawer and Cusumano (2008, p. 29), it should bring value to the overall system ('it should perform at least one essential function within what can be described as a "system of use" or solve an essential problem within an industry') and enable innovation ('it should be easy to connect to or to build upon to expand the system of use as well as to allow new and even unintended end-uses'). It should also enable variety, low-cost development, fast adaptation to evolving markets and option strategies (Baldwin and Clark, 2000; Meyer and Dalal, 2002; Uzumeri and Sanderson, 1995).

The authors defining platforms insist on the importance of the second dimension of platforms, i.e. networks of platform users and their capacity to organize a 'collective endeavour' (see Gawer, Chapter 2 in this book). This aspect of platforms is particularly underlined in the economic approach to platforms (Rochet and Tirole, 2003, 2004), where platforms are defined as 'double-sided markets'. As explained by Eisenmann et al. (2006, p. 94), 'Products and services that bring together groups of users in two-sided networks are platforms. They provide infrastructure and rules that facilitate the two groups' transactions'. The definition of the networks can be more or less restrictive (Gawer and Henderson, 2007). The literature provides several cases where the platform user can be the owner itself (see Intel as a supplier of chipsets), suppliers (see the concept of modularity, the engineering platform perspective etc.), content providers (see cases of double-sided markets such as Adobe, computer games etc.), end users, complementors etc. Platform designing is obviously not limited to platform core design. The meaning of design is extended here to the design of all the attributes of the platform and is not restricted to *a priori* technical dimensions. Hence platform design also consists in identifying the actors that will be involved in the platform. Who are they and do they change over time?

The literature also provides insights into the 'good properties' of the networks to be designed. They should contribute to the development of innovative systems based on the platform; they should contribute to the platform financially, by buying the system or paying for using the platform; they should favour 'cross-sided network effects' which appear because 'the platform's value to any given user largely depends on the number of users on the network's other side' (Eisenmann et al., 2006, p. 94), hence creating increasing returns to scale for platforms. Another issue is to extend the size of each network (Morris and Ferguson, 1993). However, this extension should also be carefully tuned to control so-called 'same side negative network effects' (Eisenmann et al., 2006; Parker and Van Alstyne, 2005), i.e. situations where new entrants to a network reduce the value of the network and threaten the value of the overall platform. This question of tuning network extension is widely debated in the literature, with a view to deciding how open platforms should be (West, 2003) and how mobility on one side can favour the other side or the platform (or architecture) leader (Jacobides et al., 2006).

The dimensions concerning products and networks are both linked to a third dimension, the values of the platform. This is a key point from the perspective of industry architecture: according to Jacobides et al. (2006, p. 1205) 'industry architectures provide two templates, each comprising a set of rules: 1) a template defining value creation and 2) a template defining value appropriation'. As underlined by Gawer and Cusumano (2008, p. 30), platform leaders' 'balancing act' consists in ; 'protecting [their] source of profit while enabling complementors to make an adequate profit and protect their own proprietary knowledge'. This entails designing means of appropriation and incentives for commitment. For instance, Gawer and Cusumano mentioned that Google was able to create value through its search engine platform by inventing focused advertising. As underlined by Jacobides et al. (2006), IP, the control of complementary assets, but also the control of asset mobility (limiting mobility on one's own side and increasing mobility on the other side) must be designed by platform actors.

From this literature review we can infer that platform design aims to define:

- A set of fixed attributes F_i, $i = 1 \ldots n$, in which the attributes are subsystems, technology, system design rules etc., and the set is fully or partly used to design systems S defined by a list of attributes $S = \{F_j$, chosen in F_i, $i = 1 \ldots n$; $M_k\}$ where M_k can be modules, complements etc.
- A set of platform users U_j, who are members of one or several networks.
- A value function V_{Uj}, defined for each platform user, which defines the value that each user gives to the set of fixed attributes $\{F_i, i = 1 \ldots n\}$. Note that the value function is based on F_i and not on S: the value depends on the expectations on all potential systems S and not (only) on the realized or simply already-identified systems.

We have also identified the 'good properties' to be found in these elements: the economics of the design, innovation, increasing returns to scale through cross-sided network effects, industry leadership position, value creation at industry level etc.

Gaps in the Literature: How to Organize the Collective Design of a Platform?

How is platform design to be organized? Who can do it? What capabilities are required? The issue of how to design these three dimensions of platforms has been addressed in two different types of literature, the first on the design of industry platforms and the second on the design of enterprise platforms.

The latter, which considers platforms that are owned and managed mainly by a single firm, focuses on the platform core design. It identifies three different platform design processes.

The first is a so-called 'top-down' or functional approach (Farrell and Simpson, 2003; Simpson et al., 2001). The design process consists in pre-defined linear steps, beginning with market segmentation, then defining the scaling variables and ranges to cover the market, then aggregating product platform specifications to finally develop the product platform. The process requires being highly knowledgeable about the future product family and markets, the technologies and product design principles, the architectures and the components.

Second is a so-called 'bottom-up' (Farrell and Simpson, 2003; Moore et al., 1999) or product consolidation approach. The design process begins with a list of existing products that have to be consolidated to improve commonality and economies of scale. Moore et al. (1999) show how to use conjoint analysis for such a consolidation process.

A third approach assumes that the list of requirements, the architecture and technologies can change over time and are not fully predictable. Platform design is hence closer to a platform redesign process, where platforms are modified step by step over time (Meyer, 1997; Meyer and Dalal, 2002). For instance, the design can consist in a 'platform extension', i.e. in adding a new interface for a new module. It can also be a platform renewal when 'the product design is rearchitectured to incorporate major new subsystems and new subsystems interfaces. The new architecture may carry forward specific subsystems from older product platforms' (Meyer et al., 1997, p. 91–2). This platform renewal process is a kind of local search process (trial and error by limited modifications to an initial solution) guided by indicators of product family performance, so-called platform efficiency and effectiveness (Meyer and Dalal, 2002; Meyer et al., 1997). We can call it an 'evolutionary' model.

In the literature on industry platforms, we found very few models for the industry platform design process. Gawer and Cusumano (2008) evoke a model of platform design which we can call the model of the 'platform entrepreneur'. The design process is divided into two steps:

First, a platform entrepreneur identifies a 'platform potential' (p. 29), defined as follows: 'to have a platform potential, research suggests that a product (or a technology or a service) must satisfy two prerequisite conditions: 1 it should perform at least one essential function within what can be described as a "system of use" or solve an essential problem within an industry; 2 it should be easy to connect to or to build upon to expand the system of use as well as to allow new and even unintended end-uses' (ibid.). In the synthetic framework introduced above, this means that this first step consists in defining the platform core, relevant networks and value models.

Second, a would-be platform leader (platform leader wannabe) transforms the platform potential into an industry platform through 'technology actions' and 'business actions'. It consists in defining, in precise terms, the actors of the networks and the value appropriation policy, and occasionally in modifying the core.

This model is a good synthesis of all the examples found in the literature. More precisely, recent literature has made valuable contributions to understanding the second step of the model. For instance, authors provide rules to define optimal pricing and optimal openness (Parker and Van Alstyne, 2005; Rochet and Tirole, 2003) or insights to improve mobility and asset control (Jacobides et al., 2006). Gawer and Cusumano (2008) provide a further element for the second step: would-be platform leaders can be either in a platform 'coring' situation (no platform exists) or a platform 'tipping' situation (there is a platform war). The authors also point out that success in the second step largely depends on the first step (see Gawer and Cusumano, 2008). Several authors indicate that the obstacles encountered by a would-be platform leader might be overcome by redesigning the platform potential. For instance, the risk of platform envelopment (Eisenmann et al., 2006) was partially overcome by RealNetworks (Real), which managed to completely change the platform core and the networks, shifting from a media player software platform to an online subscription music service platform. The literature provides only very limited insights into the design process involved in this first step, i.e. the designing of a 'platform potential'.

The 'platform entrepreneur model' therefore raises two main questions that we shall discuss below: (1) what happens if the platform design process is not led by a platform entrepreneur? and (2) what is the design process for platform potential?

Gap 1: collaborative process for platform design

The first question appears to be a gap in the literature. Some authors (Morris and Ferguson, 1993) have proposed that the platforms resulting from a collective design process might be less efficient than those designed by platform entrepreneurs, since they 'settle on lowest-common denominator, compromise solutions' and are often hard to change. This raises the question of the efficiency of the resulting platform and the efficiency of the collective design process itself. A large number of authors have investigated the issues raised by organizational situations where actors have to collaborate to develop standards in consortia (Leiponen, 2008; Zhao et al., 2007), to initiate cooperation for industry-level innovations and to organize exploratory partnerships (Segrestin, 2005).

In this stream of research, a first approach studies a consortium as a decision-making process whose final decision and decision duration depend on networks externalities (Arthur, 1989; Axelrod et al., 1995), on the 'vested interests' of partners (Farrell and Simcoe, 1997), on the 'commercial pressure' and the 'tightness of Intellectual Property rights' (Simcoe, 2003). The decision also depends on whether the interest of users or that of developers is predominant in the consortia (Chiao et al., 2005). Zhao et al. (2007) show that the decision also depends on the potential conflicts between consortia participants, these conflicts being reduced when consortia begin early, i.e. before the formation of vested interests, or in situations such as e-business where the platform links firms 'which rarely compete directly with each other directly through standards' (Zhao et al., 2007, p. 251). This approach actually considers that there exists a proposed standard for well-identified networks (users, developers etc.). The value of the standards might be known or only uncertain but there exists one or several propositions on which the participants will decide. Moreover, participants know their interests. These interests might be more or less conflicting but each participant knows his own interest related to the proposals.

A second stream of research discusses precisely this hypothesis: the collaboration aims at creating new alternatives and the participants don't always know in advance what is in their interest (Aggeri, 1999; Segrestin, 1998). The authors provide strong insights into what has to be managed in such situations: Aggeri insists on the management of collective learning in situations of shared uncertainties. Segrestin underlines that in such situations, cooperating actors have to manage both 'cohesion', i.e. the emerging interests and possible common purposes, and 'coordination', i.e. the organization of the exploration process. This raises the question of the processes involved in managing coordination and cohesion in the collective design of platforms.

This literature review provides us with a useful framework for the analysis of collective aspects of platform design: (1) we shall consider whether this is more a collective decision-making process on known alternatives by known networks of participants with known interests; (2) if not, we shall pay attention to both coordination processes (phases, work divisions, resources etc.) and cohesion processes (involvement, property rights, type of commitment etc.).

Gap 2: platform design process?

The second question, the design process for the 'platform potential', is also a gap in the literature. It can be assumed that the designer of the platform potential, as an individual platform entrepreneur, uses processes described for enterprise platform design, namely 'bottom-up', 'top-down' and 'evolutionary'. However, such models are incomplete in the case of industry platforms since they do not address the issues of networks and values. Moreover, we have seen that bottom-up and top-down models cannot be applied in situations where future users, products and technologies are partially unknown. As a consequence, these models can be applied only in highly integrated, stabilized industries (one example is the historical IBM platform, as described in Bresnahan and Greenstein, 1999). However, in more dynamic industries, only an evolutionary model could be relevant. Baldwin and Clark (2000, 2006) provide certain elements for such a model at the industry level: they show that modular operators can apply at the lower levels of the design hierarchy; they also underline that these operators can only marginally change the platform architecture, 'the design rules of a modular system, once established, tend[ing] to be both rigid and long lasting' (Baldwin and Clark, 2006, p. 193). Hence the models of 'product platform design' seem to be able to describe only very limited industry platform innovation.

Gawer and Henderson (2007) help us to clarify this limit of industry platform innovation and the gap in literature. In their study of Intel platform extensions, they show that the process is driven by two critical issues: first, does the platform designer have the necessary capabilities; and, second, does the platform designer keep the existing architecture? Their study shows that platform design processes can cope with capability-building issues and can be driven by incomplete views of the future platform, to be completed at a later stage ('changing the platform/application interface without going into applications'). Hence there are two types of plaform design: using existing capability and existing architecture; or building new capabilities and exploring new architectures. Gawer and Henderson show that in the specific case of a platform entrepreneur such as Intel, the firm in question finally developed platforms where it already had the necessary capabilities and focused on platform extensions that kept the overall PC architecture, i.e. questioned neither the notion of application nor the notion of chipset. It is also shown that the design process is a trial-and-error process. But generally speaking this raises the question of whether it is possible to imagine a platform design process that actually favours capability building and broader explorations and occasionally revision of potential industry architectures. A process of this sort could then generate and select platform alternatives without necessarily following a trial-and-error process.

This literature review on platform design has enabled us to:

- clarify what has to be designed when designing a platform: platform core, platforms networks and platform values;
- raise questions regarding gaps in the literature on the industry platform design process.

Is there necessarily a platform entrepreneur or are there more collective forms of platform design? And, more precisely, in the case of a collaborative design, is it more like a negotiation on known alternatives, between known partners with known interests? Or do we find emerging alternatives, emerging partners and emerging interests? (Gap 1)

Do such platform designer(s) build new capabilities and explore wider changes in existing industry architectures? If yes, what could be the model of such a strong exploratory, collective process for platform design? (Gap 2)

3. RESEARCH METHODS AND DATA

Given the limited theory and the goal of exploring organizational phenomena in a new context, we adopted an exploratory approach based on grounded theory building (David and Hatchuel, 2007; Eisenhardt, 1989; Glaser and Strauss, 1967). The research method is an inductive, multiple-case study. Multiple cases enable a replication logic in which each case serves to confirm or disconfirm the inferences drawn from the others (Yin, 2003). A multiple-case study typically results in better-grounded and more general theory than single-case studies (Eisenhardt, 1989; Glaser and Strauss, 1967).

The sample is composed of four cases of collaboration in platform design. To enhance the generalization of the findings, the sample includes platform design in four different domains. Given the goal of understanding how platforms are designed through collaborative processes, this is a descriptive study requiring longitudinal research. The sampling focuses on collaborations that aimed at designing an industry platform, thus enabling us to study the early steps of the design process. We also checked whether

Table 11.1   Description of sample cases and case data

Case name	Hemp	ITRS	Cockpit	Biotech
Domain	Biomaterials	International Technological Roadmap for Semiconductors	New civil aircraft cockpits	Biotechnology research platforms
Resulting industry platform	Professional rules for building with hemp for home construction	Production template for the next semiconductor generation	Validation bench for cockpit instruments	Set of routine services for bio-analysis, made available to researchers
Interviews	23 (hemp producers, transformers, users, architects, building material experts)	12 (engineers and ITRS delegates of semiconductor companies)	23 (main experts in cockpit design and aircraft integration)	18 (instruments users, owners and designers)
Detailed design reasoning	Whole process	Focus on specific design issues (two sub-cases: patterning and radio frequency front end)	Whole process	Focus on specific design issue (two sub-cases: imaging small animals and bioinformatics)

these processes finally led to an industry platform, as defined by its core, its networks and values (see Table 11A.1 in the Appendix).

The study has two main sources of data: archives and interviews. The archives include sources from the main partners in the collaboration. The interviews were semi-structured and focused on the main actors in the collaboration (see details in Table 11.1).

In order to monitor the design process, we used the most recent models of design reasoning (Hatchuel and Weil, 2003, 2007, 2008), which generalize classic engineering design models (Pahl and Beitz, 2006) and search models (Hatchuel, 2002; Simon, 1969). This method helped us to rigorously identify the competencies used and created throughout the process and the various paths followed for different platform alternatives that emerged during the process. These representations of the collective design reasoning were built through archives and interviews and were validated by the main actors in the related design processes.

4.   RESULTS

Case Descriptions and Analyses

We briefly summarize each of the four design processes (detailed presentations of the design reasoning are given in the Appendix, Figures 11A.1 to 11A.3):

Building with Hemp: a hemp transformer became aware of several, uncoordinated initiatives to combine lime with hemp to obtain daub-like concrete. He organized an association, 'Building with Hemp' to bring together actors potentially interested in building with hemp, and architects, engineers, historians, lime experts, lead users and alternative associations defending sustainable development. Following the initial meeting, some of the actors met again to identify open questions on hemp building. A certain number of them realized that they could have long-term interests in such issues and decided to meet regularly. The central group of stakeholders decreased from several dozen at the first meeting to about ten after two years. However, this group met regularly, sharing learning on new experiments and updating the agenda of open questions. The process served to explore several forms of building with hemp (renovation of historical buildings, a substitute concrete for alternative home building, the do-it-yourself market etc.). In particular, the group applied for and obtained 'professional rules for building with hemp', which enable builders to use hemp and provide ten-year guarantees for insurance purposes. These professional rules are the (first?) industrial platform for 'Building with Hemp' (for a more detailed description, see Caron et al., 2008; Garnier et al., 2007).

ITRS: the International Technology Roadmap for Semiconductors is a worldwide consortium that organizes regular meetings (three per year) of the main players in the semiconductor industry. At these meetings, semiconductor manufacturers, process machine suppliers and semiconductor users discuss and update the technology roadmap for evolutions in semiconductor processes. They identify open questions and synthesize available knowledge on all the emerging technologies and regularly deduce the template for the next generation of semiconductor processes. One result of their work is therefore the continuous redesigning of the platform for semiconductor processes. Hence this is a sequence of industry platforms.

Cockpit: to innovate on civil aircraft cockpits, a cockpit supplier launched an in-house innovation process to design alternative cockpits. One of the alternatives gave birth to an original cockpit simulator that was used to work with aircraft integrator designers, aircraft companies and pilots. The partners worked together to explore and refine the cockpit concept by combining it with aircraft properties, innovative exploitation strategies and new ways of flying and 'governing' aircraft. The results of these simulations were discussed with the main actors (in particular the aircraft integrator) and gave birth to a new cockpit validation platform (first industry platform). The simulator was also used in a second step to design a platform for cockpit mass customization, developed jointly with a business jet manufacturer (second industry platform).

Biotech instruments: a group of scientists pioneering a new research field, and instrument managers in a research institute used a new instrument concept – devised by an instrument company – to design an original facility for their research experiment. After their first success, they offered the research community access to their facility for original research programmes. They selected projects that were relevant to the new research field and to the new instrument. The instrument maker was invited to follow and occasionally contribute to the experiments (free of charge). It helped him to develop a new instrument. The experiments finally led to the design of routinized measurement and analysis services, based on commercially available instruments. These services are a platform for the production of knowledge in biotechnologies (for a more detailed description, see Aggeri et al., 2007).

To analyse the design process in each of the four cases, we described each following the classic descriptors of a managerial process: input, outputs, actors, capability creation, phases, coordination mechanisms, resources and property rights. The results are synthesized in Table 11A.1 (see the Appendix).

Common Features in Collaborative Platform Design Process

In all cases we can distinguish three interrelated processes:

1. Value creation management (cognitive framing)
The collaboration begins by a shared question about a future industry platform. The process is then characterized by two concurrent moves. On the one hand, a refinement process shapes further details and builds further capabilities that appear to be useful for the final industry platform. On the other hand, the person or body in charge of managing the collaboration

also undertakes a 'divergence process' aimed at regularly identifying platform alternatives, close to or far from the dominating design path. This is done either by simply using any newly produced knowledge (discovery of deviant uses, of surprising technology performance etc.) or by launching specific investigations in new directions (organizing the exploration of blue-sky projects etc.). The process serves to explore different and occasionally surprising aspects of what will make value on the final platform, and for whom. For instance, in the case of Building with Hemp (see Figure 11A.1), three means of obtaining value were investigated: hemp for renovation (value for specialized builders and architects), hemp as a substitute for concrete in traditional building materials (potential value for a large number of builders); hemp for 'do-it-yourself' applications (value for retail stores, materials and process suppliers). At first view, the divergence process slows down the overall design process, as it disturbs, influences and criticizes the dominating path. However, it actually contributes in 'designing the value landscape' (Baldwin and Clark, 2000; Levinthal and Warglien, 1999; Thomke et al., 1998) on which the final platform will be based. It therefore increases the relative value of the final solution. Moreover, it paves the way for other platforms, exploiting other niches of the value landscape. The value management process takes the form of steering committees, which clarify the value landscape, the open questions and the platform alternatives. Note that it confirms the result of Levinthal (1997, p. 945): the process is organized to increase 'long jumps' on the fitness landscape to increase survival in the face of changing (or generally speaking: unknown) environment.

In a nutshell: the value management process is not only a decision process to lead people to agree to choose on a platform in a fixed set of well-identified platform alternatives; it is more a cognitive framing process, in which the actors are ready to explore several business conception alternatives and are free to rediscuss the established business architectures. This cognitive framing process contributes to value exploration and hence value creation. It actually mixes a development process ('exploitation') and an exploration process. It finally led to an industrial platform (with all three dimensions: core, networks and value) but also to other outputs: platform alternatives, a mapping of the related value landscape etc.

2. The organization of knowledge production (capability building)

One of the inputs of the collaboration is the identification of missing knowledge and capabilities (this identification actually takes place throughout the design process, as proved by the numerous steering committees listing open questions). In parallel, some of these questions are investigated. The results are synthesized and shared, at least partially, with the other players.

The investigations can be 'wild' and scattered, in particular when several players are interested in pursuing the explorations (see some phases in hemp and ITRS, see Figure 11A.1 and 11A.3). They can also be highly organized when no single actor is prepared to investigate, or when the investigations cannot be made by a single actor (see knowledge production on uses and ways of piloting in a new cockpit, which required the involvement of the cockpit designer, the aircraft integrator and some pilots), and/or when the investigations require specific collective investment in knowledge production instruments (see the experimental facility in biotech, or the simulator in the cockpit case). Note that knowledge produced in this process is not necessarily fully shared between all the participants. It can even be partially appropriated by the knowledge producer (see intellectual property policy). Note also that the knowledge produced is always restricted to some aspects of the final platform (a key technology, one user etc.); the new knowledge and capabilities have then to be integrated into one or several 'platform candidate(s)' (e.g. Cockpit designers will learn on pilot uses in specific context but the industry platform will also have to integrate some engineering constraints and so on). Hence knowledge production is divided between platform members; and this division, far from being a pure trial and error (where each partner would try one specific platform candidate in the hope that she will hit the winning one), requires a strong integration process that makes sense of all the knowledge provided by the participants. This is precisely the role of the value management process mentioned above.

In a nutshell, the knowledge management process is not (only) a knowledge sharing between the actors of the process but it is a capability creation process. The knowledge creation process mixes competitive knowledge production (competitors can concurrently and competitively explore technical alternatives, the results being shared with the other explorers), and collaborative knowledge creation (knowledge creation facilities enabling the actors to collaborate to produce knowledge together).

3. The organization of partners' involvement

Involvement is a key issue throughout the platform design process as the list of partners evolves constantly. Two types of partners can be identified: those taking part in the value management process and occasionally in the knowledge production process; and those who take part only in knowledge production (e.g. in the case of the biotech platform, the pioneering researchers and the instrument managers fall into the first category whereas the temporary users of the experimental facility fall into the second). The first have interests in the process and contribute to building the value landscape; the others may be interested only in one piece of knowledge resulting from the exploration or may contribute to only a very specific piece of knowledge. Their involvement in the value management process is impeded by the fact that they are specialized in one specific asset, thus leading to too restrictive an approach to the final industry platform (see technology suppliers in ITRS, component suppliers in cockpits, instrument suppliers in biotech). Although such actors could quite legitimately refuse to contribute when they are not involved in value management, why do they in fact take part (and even pay for doing so, as in the case of the instrument makers in the biotech case)? First, because knowledge production is a very strong way of influencing the process in situations where there is a general lack of knowledge; second, because the knowledge produced can be of direct interest to them, even if the final platform does not fully fit with their assets (e.g. the instrument maker was able to discover new needs for researchers and thus to adapt his offer accordingly).

In a nutshell, the involvement process is not limited to gathering the well-identified actors of a stabilized sector but it regularly changes the perimeter of the collaboration. The involvement process mixes aggregative process (add new members and new networks of members, occasionally far from the initial sector or 'deviant' from the main design path) and segregative processes (select preferably the members who are not stuck in one platform alternative but have interests in exploring several alternatives).

Fundamentally, this study provides results on our three main gaps in the literature:

1. It confirms that collaborative design of a platform is possible: the four cases show situations where collaborative design leads to the design of an industry platform; they also show that the design process doesn't consist in organizing negotiations on known alternatives, between known partners who know their interests (see Gap 1). Rather, alternatives, partners and interests emerge during the design process.
2. It implies strong capability building and wide exploration of platform alternatives, including severe revisions of existing industry platforms (Gap 2). It gives strong insight into the overall design process itself: the three processes (cognitive framing, capability building and people involvement) show that this is neither a bottom-up (synthesize known alternatives) nor a top-down process (optimize the fit between building blocks and functional requirements) nor a trial-and-error process (try platform alternatives to finally select the best one). Interestingly enough, we find a process that constantly balances the convergence towards an industrial platform and the regular opening of new divergence directions (emerging platform alternatives, blue-sky projects, involvement of new 'deviant' partners etc.).

5. THEORETICAL PROPOSITION AND DISCUSSION: THE NOTION OF A PLATFORM FOR PLATFORM DESIGN

These results lead us to present and discuss four hypotheses on collaborations for platform design.

Hypothesis 1: Collaborative Design of a Platform as an Original Form of Platform

A striking result is that the output of the process is not only one platform potential but several. Moreover, all these platforms are related to capabilities, networks and value proposition for the network members. Hence these platforms map a value landscape that was not present at the beginning of the process and is also a result of it.

These results lead us to consider that collaboration for platform design aims not only to deliver an industry platform but to position this platform potential into a strategic landscape, which results from the exploration and includes platform candidates, i.e. alternative platform strategies, with their related capabilities, core, networks and value functions. The collaboration designs several industry platform candidates and the related value landscape, and selects one of them in the short term but works on several of them in the longer term (see sequence of platforms in ITRS (Figure 11A.3) and in cockpit (Figure 11A.2). This design process involves a wide variety of actors who ultimately find an interest in the exploration process and not necessarily in the 'final' industry platform. Just as an industry platform doesn't aim at developing only one single system S but several, the collective platform design process doesn't aim at providing one single output (i.e. industry platform) but several (several industry platforms, capabilities, clearer picture of the industry value landscape etc.).

Hence we propose the following theoretical statement: a collaborative process of platform design can actually be itself a specific platform; we shall call it a 'platform for platform design'.

Hypothesis 2: Platform for Platform Design versus Platform for Product/ Service Development

For such a platform, we can describe what makes 'core', 'network' and 'value'. In each case we shall underline the similarities and differences with 'industry platform', i.e. platform for product/service development.

Core: the core of a platform for platform design relies on three main dimensions:

1. the structure of all the industry platform alternatives and the related value landscape that they embody (e.g. structure of alternatives in ITRS, in cockpit, in biomaterials etc.);
2. the knowledge production devices that are specific to the platform (see simulator, experimental facility etc.);
3. the collaboration protocols that support value management and knowledge creation (agenda, pace, organization and composition of steering committee; rules for exit and entry etc.).

This core contributes to the design of several platform candidates. It appears like a 'platform generator' just like the core of an industry platform appears as a product generator. This platform generator doesn't work only once but can be used several times.

Networks: the networks of a platform for platform design consist in all the contributors to the exploration. One feature is that only a limited number of actors in each network will contribute, but several heterogeneous networks can be represented. The number of networks involved can be far higher than the number of networks using the final industry platform (illustration: in Building with Hemp, architects were involved in the exploration process but are hardly interested in the professional rules; in ITRS a technology supplier can participate in the exploration but is excluded from the next-generation industry platform – and compete to be in the following one). The classic industry platform is segregative in the choice of participating networks (usually a 'buyer' network and a 'seller' network) and then aggregative (to a certain extent) in the involvement of the members of a chosen network to maximize network externalities. On the contrary, the platform for platform design is aggregative regarding the nature of the networks (seeking variety in committed networks) and segregative regarding the few people representing each network in the design process to keep only the members ready to produce and share knowledge between networks, to maximize learning externalities.

Value: the value delivered by a platform for platform design is not limited to the value of the final industry platform (i.e. the value created by all the products based on this platform). The first value created is the value landscape itself, i.e. all the potential sources of values, whether they are integrated into the final platform or not (strategic overview in ITRS, biomaterials, ITRS and cockpit). The second value created is the knowledge

Table 11.2   Platform for platform design versus industry platform

	Industry platform	Platform for platform design
Core	One core for multiple final systems Core = fixed attributes of the system Core = maximize the value of the resulting systems (max. profits)	One core for several industry platform candidates Core = value landscape + knowledge production devices + protocols Core = maximize the knowledge on the value of the resulting platforms, i.e. maximize the exploration of the value landscape
Networks	Segregative in the choice of networks (generally speaking two networks) Aggregative inside the networks (maximize network externalities)	Aggregative for the networks (many heterogeneous networks possibly interested in the future platform(s)) Segregative for the network representatives (only the most exploratory partners; maximize learning externalities)
Values	Platform users' externalities integrated by the platform Cross-sided network effects	Platform externalities integrated by the platform users Cross-sided learning effects

that will be useful for the actors, even if this knowledge is not used in the final industry platform (e.g. trials on cockpit revealed knowledge on piloting, on man–machine interfaces, on users, that will be used by industrial participants). Hence a platform for platform design creates externalities that are internalized by the platform partners (whereas an industry platform internalizes externalities generated by the networks). The third value concerns the specific knowledge that could not have been produced without the platform, i.e. through knowledge production processes resulting from the collaboration of two otherwise separate actors. Whereas an industry platform is characterized by a cross-sided network effect, a platform for platform design is characterized by a cross-sided learning effect, i.e. the learning on one side is considerably enhanced by the knowledge provided by the other side (and vice versa) (e.g. experience on cockpit with aircraft integrator, suppliers, aerial companies and even pilots).

These results and the comparison between industry platforms and platforms for platform design are summarized in Table 11.2 above. This new notion of platform for platform design opens two main areas of discussion: (1) why and when actors wishing to design a platform would favour a platform entrepreneur strategy or a platform for platform strategy? and (2) how does the platform design process influence the final industrial platform?

Hypothesis 3: Conditions for Choosing a Platform for Platform Design

As mentioned in the literature review, certain authors have underlined the limits of collective platform design (Morris and Ferguson, 1993) and others have underlined the difficulties in managing exploratory partnerships (Segrestin, 2005). One main reason to favour platforms for platform design is therefore simply that the platform entrepreneur strategy might be impossible! In this event, three conditions appear to favour platforms for platform design.

First, platforms for platform design are interesting in cases where the design is impossible without the contribution of a partner to provide new capabilities. For instance, in cases where the industry is changing drastically and the industry architectures are disappearing, the previous integrator can no longer manage the entire value chain and it is therefore interesting to spread the platform design capabilities between several partners. A first criterion is, therefore: platforms for platform design will emerge when individual actors lack some capabilities to design the platform and when none of the actors can create the missing capabilities without the collaboration of others (Criterion 1).

This first condition is necessary but not sufficient. In particular, if the value provided by the missing capability is clear to one actor, the latter could become platform entrepreneur and simply pay for the production of the missing capability (occasionally by sharing the related value). This situation is linked to issues such as complementary asset appropriation (Teece, 1986) and mobility enhancement (Jacobides et al., 2006): the platform entrepreneur strategy is possible in such cases (strong appropriation through integration or weak appropriation through mobility enhancement). However, the platform entrepreneur strategy is more difficult when the value of the missing capability is unknown. In this case, the debates on appropriation are weaker and collaboration becomes paradoxically easier. This is coherent with the studies of entrepreneurs in nascent markets (Santos and Eisenhardt, 2004) that show that entrepreneurs avoid 'ambiguity'. Hence platforms for platform design will appear in situations with 'unknown' value landscapes, where the ambiguity cannot be easily reduced by a platform entrepreneur (Criterion 2).

However, the situation with a lack of capability and a fuzzy value landscape may be very temporary, since the platform aims precisely to build capabilities and to design the value landscape. Consequently, a third condition of platforms for platform design is paradoxically to maintain the lack of capability and the unknownness of the landscape (Criterion 3). This is not contradictory with the main goal of the platform and the paradox can be easily overcome: in the design process, capabilities are built but new gaps appear simultaneously; the value landscape is designed and clarified in some areas but this process reveals fuzzy borders. This third condition echoes the divergence/convergence pattern noted in the value management process.

To summarize, platforms for platform design will emerge in situations where (1) each actor lacks some capabilities and is unable to produce them alone; (2) none of the actors has a clear view of the value landscape, meaning that the value landscape has to be designed; (3) the design process itself creates capabilities and explores the value; it also reveals missing competencies and unknown areas in the value landscape. It consists in balancing the realization (convergence) of a platform and the unavoidable conflicts of interests between the exploration members, with a constant level of unknownness that keep a promise of benefits for all collaboration members.

These propositions are in line with results in the literature: Morris and Ferguson (1993) as well as Farrell and Saloner (1988) posit that collaborative design of platforms is crippled by compromises made to find common agreements. Our work shows that platforms work precisely when the issue is not common agreement and compromise but the creation of common interests.

Gawer and Henderson (2007) showed that a platform entrepreneur such as Intel was able to design a platform where the firm had the relevant capabilities and the value of the platform extension was clear. Conversely, we found Intel involved in the ITRS consortium, in a situation where (1) capabilities were sorely lacking (what would be the processes and performances of the next generations of semiconductors?), (2) the value landscape was unknown in several cases (it was impossible for the company expert to compare the value of two immature processes yet to be developed), and (3) the uncertainty was never reduced. Note that the consortium recently faced great difficulties when the members debated on the opportunity to go for 450 mm process technologies: in this case, the value for the members was far clearer (Intel favouring mass production with 450 mm wafers, while other consortium members favoured more customized chipsets, with shorter batch sizes and smaller wafer diameters). The consortium resisted by opening alternative design paths to explore new areas of the value landscape (for instance, processes enabling 450 mm wafers with enhanced flexibility).

Lastly, these propositions also show that the conditions for platforms for platform design are very demanding. They are hardly ever met in stable industries. This could explain why such processes have rarely been observed until recently. However, new emerging competitive situations could lead to the multiplication of platforms for platform design.

Hypothesis 4: Specific Features of an Industrial Platform Resulting from a Platform for Platform Design

The second issue to be discussed concerns the impact of this particular platform design process on the resulting industry platforms. Do they differ greatly from platforms designed by platform entrepreneurs? We propose two main differences.

First, the resulting platform may be in a much better position to overcome the obstacles traditionally encountered by platforms: changing scope (Jacobides et al., 2006), avoid envelopment by changing networks (Eisenmann et al., 2006), combining mobility and complementarity (Jacobides, 2006) etc. When backed by the design platform, the industry platform can more easily develop new strategies on these classic issues. For instance, the first hemp platform based on professional rules for builders was able to change its scope by shifting to a platform for new 'do-it-yourself' business.

Second, the resulting platform shows more diversified forms of platform leadership. The platform entrepreneur model implies a strong link between the platform entrepreneur and the platform leader (see the Intel case). In our four cases, we found two types of industry platform leadership: a classic platform leader (cockpits) and platforms with collective leadership (ITRS, biotech, biomaterials). Strangely enough, the platform leader is not necessarily the main player in the platform for platform design: the cockpit designer had initiated and managed the platform for platform design but the company then gave the industry platform to the industry integrator (the aircraft integrator). This suggests that these platform design processes could pave the way for new platform leaderships: the platform leader might be the leader of the design platform, but the latter can also choose to delegate the industry platform leadership to one or several other actors.

ACKNOWLEDGEMENTS

This work was carried out with the financial support of the ANR – Agence Nationale de la Recherche – The French National Research Agency under the 'Programme Agriculture et Développement Durable', project ANR-05-PADD-015, PRODD (biomaterial case) and the 'Programme Entreprise', project RITE.

We are grateful to Annabelle Gawer for fruitful discussions on platform design and to the participants of the Platforms, Markets and Innovation Conference at Imperial College, London on 2 June 2008 for many thoughtful and productive comments. We thank Blanche Segrestin for her careful review and insightful suggestions.

REFERENCES

Aggeri, F. (1999), 'Environmental policies and innovation: a knowledge-based perspective on cooperative approaches', *Research Policy*, **28**, 699–717.

Aggeri, F., P. Le Masson, A. Branciard, C. Paradeise and A. Peerbaye (2007), 'Les plates-formes technologiques dans les sciences de la vie: politiques publiques, organisations et performances', *Revue d'Economie Industrielle*, 120 Numéro spécial biotechnologies (4ème trimestre), 21–40.

Arthur, W.B. (1989), 'Competing technologies, increasing returns, and lock-in by historical events', *The Economic Journal*, **99**, March, 116–31.

Axelrod, R., W. Mitchell, D.S. Bennet, and E. Bruderer (1995), 'Coalition formation in standard-setting alliances', *Management Science*, **41** (9), 1493–508.

Baldwin, C.Y. and K.B. Clark (2000), *Design Rules, Volume 1: The Power of Modularity*, Cambridge, MA: MIT Press.

Baldwin, C.Y. and K.B. Clark (2006), 'Modularity in the design of complex engineering systems', in D. Braha, A.A. Minai and Y. Bar-Yam (eds), *Complex Engineered Systems: Science Meets Technology*, New York: Springer, pp. 175–205.

Bresnahan, T.F. and S. Greenstein (1999), 'Technological competition and the structure of the computer industry', *Journal of Industrial Economics*, **47** (1), 1–40.

Caron, P., M. Barbier, P. Le Masson and F. Aggeri (2008), 'Elaboration de règles professionnelles et innovation dans les agro-matériaux de construction: le cas de l'association construire en chanvre', Paris: INRA-SADPT and Mines Paristech.

Chiao, B., J. Tirole and J. Lerner (2005), 'The rules of standard-setting organizations: an empirical Analysis', SSRN.

David, A. and A. Hatchuel (2007), 'From actionable knowledge to universal theory in management research', in A.B. Shani, S.A. Mohrman, W.A. Pasmore, B.A. Stymne and A. Niclas (eds), *Handbook of Collaborative Management Research*, Thousand Oaks, CA: Sage, pp. 33–48.

Eisenhardt, K.M. (1989), 'Building theories from case study research', *Academy of Management Review*, **14** (4), 532–50.

Eisenmann, T., G. Parker and M.W. Van Alstyne (2006), 'Strategies for two-sided markets', *Harvard Business Review*, **84** (10), 92–101.

Farrell, J. and G. Saloner (1988), 'Coordination through committees and markets', *The RAND Journal of Economics*, **19** (2), 235–52.

Farrell, J. and T. Simcoe (1997), 'Choosing the rules for formal standardization'. Mimeo, University of Toronto, last accessed December 2008 at http://www.rotman.utoronto.ca/timothy.simcoe/papers/formal.pdf.

Farrell, R.S. and T.W. Simpson (2003), 'Product platform design to improve commonality in custom products', *Journal of Intelligent Manufacturing*, **14**, 541–56.

Garnier, E., M. Nieddu, M. Barbier and B. Kurek (2007), 'The dynamics of the French hemp system and its stakeholders', *Journal of Industrial Hemp*, **12** (2), 67–85.

Gawer, A. and M.A. Cusumano (2002), *Platform Leadership: How Intel, Microsoft, and Cisco Drive Industry Innovation*, Boston, MA: Harvard Business School Press.

Gawer, A. and M.A. Cusumano (2008), 'How companies become platform leaders', *MIT Sloan Management Review*, **49** (2), 28–35.

Gawer, A. and R. Henderson (2007), 'Platform owner entry and innovation in complementary markets: evidence from Intel', *Journal of Economics and Management Strategy*, **16** (1), 1–34.

Glaser, B.G. and A.L. Strauss (1967), *The Discovery of Grounded Theory: Strategies for Qualitative Research*. Chicago, IL: Aldine Publishing Company.

Hatchuel, A. (2002), 'Towards design theory and expandable rationality: the unfinished program of Herbert Simon', *Journal of Management and Governance*, **5** (3–4), 260–73.

Hatchuel, A. and B. Weil (2003), 'A new approach of innovative design: an introduction to C–K theory', paper presented at the ICED'03, Stockholm, Sweden, August.

Hatchuel, A. and B. Weil (2007), 'Design as forcing: deepening the foundations of C–K theory', paper presented at the International Conference on Engineering Design, Paris.

Hatchuel, A. and B. Weil (2008), 'C–K design theory: an advanced formulation', in *Research in Engineering Design*, published online, 19 August.

Jacobides, M.G. (2006), 'The architecture and design of organizational capabilities', *Industrial and Corporate Change*, **15** (1), 151–71.

Jacobides, M.G., T. Knudsen and M. Augier (2006), 'Benefiting from innovation: value creation, value appropriation and the role of industry architectures', *Research Policy*, **35** (8), 1200–21.

Le Masson, P., Y. Morel and B. Weil (2007), 'Leveraging innovative design capabilities through open innovation', *Talent and Technology*, **1** (3), 13–16.

Leiponen, A.E. (2008), 'Competing through cooperation: the organization of standard setting in wireless telecommunications', *Management Science*, **54** (11), 1904–19.

Levinthal, D.A. (1997), 'Adaptation on rugged landscapes', *Management Science*, **43** (7), 934–51.

Levinthal, D.A. and M. Warglien (1999), 'Landscape design: designing for local action in a complex world', *Organization Science*, **10** (3), 342–57.

Meyer, M.H. (1997), 'Revitalize your product lines through continuous platform renewal', *Research Technology Management*, **40** (2), 17–28.

Meyer, M.H. and D. Dalal (2002), 'Managing platform architectures and manufacturing processes for nonassembled products', *Journal of Product Innovation Management*, **19**, 277–293.

Meyer, M.H., P. Tertzakian and J. M. Utterback (1997), 'Metrics for managing research and development in the context of product family', *Management Science*, **43** (1), 88–111.

Moore, W.L., J.J. Louviere and R. Verma (1999), 'Using conjoint analysis to help design product platforms', *Journal of Product Innovation Management*, **16**, 27–39.

Morris, C.R. and C.H. Ferguson (1993), 'How architecture wins technology wars', *Harvard Business Review*, **71** (2), 86–96.

Pahl, G. and W. Beitz (2006), *Engineering Design: A Systematic Approach* (K. Wallace, L. Blessing and F. Bauert, trans.), Berlin: Springer.

Parker, G.G. and M.W. Van Alstyne (2005), 'Two-sided networks effects: a theory of information product design', *Management Science*, **51** (10), 1494–504.

Rochet, J.-C. and J. Tirole (2003), 'Platform competition in two-sided markets', *Journal of the European Economic Association*, **1** (4), 990–1029.

Rochet, J.-C. and J. Tirole (2004), 'Two-sided markets: an overview', IDEI Working Paper, Toulouse, France: Institut d'Economie Industrielle.

Santos, F.M. and K.M. Eisenhardt (2004), 'Constructing markets and organizing boundaries: entrepreneurial action in nascent fields', Paper presented at the Academy of Management.

Segrestin, B. (1998), 'La naissance d'une politique multimodale entre la RATP et la SNCF. Vers de nouvelles formes de coopération inter-institutionnelle?', Paris: Mémoire de DEA, Organisation de l'Entreprise et de la Production, Ecole des Ponts et Chaussées, Université de Marne la Vallée.

Segrestin, B. (2005), 'Partnering to explore: the Renault–Nissan alliance as a fore-runner of new cooperative patterns', *Research Policy*, **34**, 657–72.

Simcoe, T. (2003), 'Committees and the creation of technical standards', mimeo, University of California at Berkeley, Haas School of Business.

Simon, H.A. (1969), *The Sciences of the Artificial*, Cambridge, MA: MIT Press.

Simpson, T.W., J.R. Maier and F. Mistree (2001), 'Product platform design: method and application', *Research in Engineering Design*, **13** (1), 2–22.

Teece, D.J. (1986), 'Profiting from technological innovation: implications for integration, collaboration, licensing and public policy', *Research Policy*, **15** (6), 285–305.

Thomke, S.H., E. von Hippel and R. Franke (1998), 'Modes of experimentation: an innovation process and competitive variable', *Research Policy*, **27**, 315–32.

West, J. (2003), 'How open is open enough? Melding proprietary and open source plaform strategies', *Research Policy*, **32**, 1259–85.

Yin, R.K. (2003), *Case Study Research: Design and Methods*, 3rd edn, Thousand Oaks, CA: Sage.

Zhao, K., M. Xia and M.J. Shaw (2007), 'An integrated model of consortium-based e-business standardization: collaborative development and adoption with network externalities', *Journal of Management Information Systems*, **23** (4), 247–71.

APPENDIX

C–K diagrams show the main elements of the design reasoning for the different cases. In C, note how the different platform alternatives emerged; in K, the capabilities used to design these alternatives. The text written in white on darker grey boxes on the right-hand K side of the figures shows the new capabilities built during the design process.

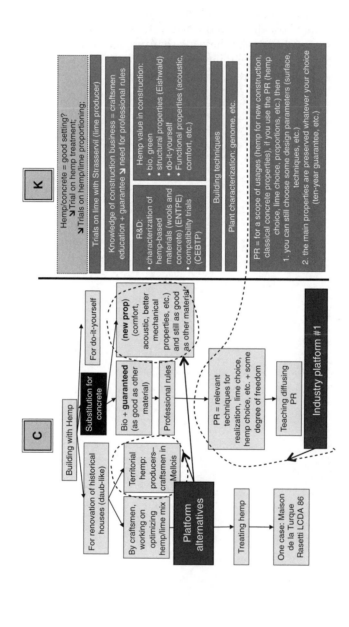

K

Hemp/concrete = good setting?
↘ Trial on hemp treatment;
↘ Trials on hemp/lime proportioning;

Trials on lime with Strasservil (lime producer)

Knowledge of construction business = craftsmen
education + guarantee ↘ need for professional rules

Hemp value in construction:
• bio, green
• structural properties (Eishwald)
• do-it-yourself
• Functional properties (acoustic, comfort, etc.)

R&D:
• characterization of hemp-based materials (wools and concrete) (ENTPE)
• compatibility trials (CEBTP)

Building techniques

Plant characterization: genome, etc.

PR = for a scope of usages (hemp for new construction, classical concrete properties), if you use the PR (hemp choice, lime choice, proportions, etc.) then
1. you can still choose some design parameters (surface, techniques, etc.)
2. the main properties are preserved whatever your choice (ten-year guarantee, etc.)

C

Building with Hemp

Substitution for concrete

For do-it-yourself

(new prop) (comfort, acoustic, better mechanical properties, etc.) and still as good as other material

Bio + **guaranteed** (as good as other material)

Professional rules

For renovation of historical houses (daub-like)

Territorial hemp: producers—craftsmen in Mellois

By craftsmen, working on optimizing hemp/lime mix

PR = relevant techniques for realization, lime choice, hemp choice, etc. + some degree of freedom

Teaching diffusing PR

Industry platform #1

Platform alternatives

Treating hemp

One case: Maison de la Turque Rasetti LCDA 86

Notes:

1. The industry platform 'professional rules for building with hemp' appears as a concept derived from the initial concept 'building with hemp', associated to new knowledge.

2. Platform alternatives appear beside the industry platform. They are candidates for future platforms.

Figure 11A.1 *'Building with Hemp' case*

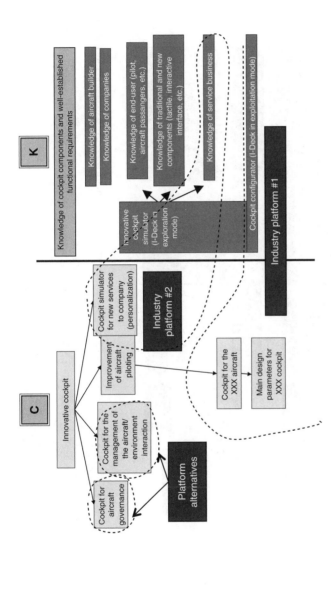

Notes:
1. The industry platform 'cockpit for the xxx aircraft' appears as a concept derived from the initial concept 'innovative cockpit', associated to new knowledge on cockpit configurations
2. A second industry platform appears beside the first one, on 'customized cockpit for new services', also using new knowledge. Other industry alternatives also emerge.

Figure 11A.2   The Cockpit case

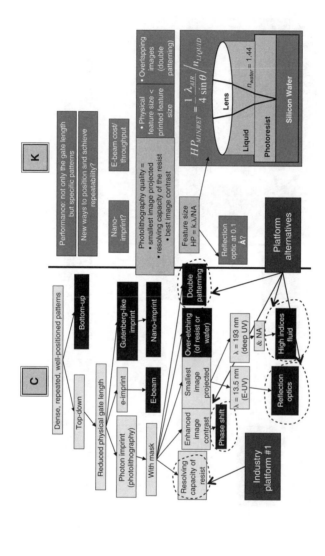

Notes:

1. The industry platform 'resist' appears as a concept derived from the initial concept 'patterning', associated to new knowledge on resists (material science, suppliers etc.)

2. Several platform alternatives are also listed, as candidate platforms for future generations.

3. Feature size is defined by the equation HP = k.λ/NA, where HP is the minimum half pitch, λ is the exposure wavelength and NA is the numerical aperture.

Figure 11A.3   The ITRS case, with a special focus on patterning

302

Table 11A.1 Main features of the design process

	Biomaterials	ITRS	Cockpit	Biotech
Goals	Build a new industry	Support industry growth	Industry growth through innovative cockpits	Build new research fields
Inputs	'Building with Hemp' + a list of potential partners + some isolated experiments	Several issues regarding concepts and processes in the non-competitive domain + main industry players (suppliers, manufacturers, users)	'Future cockpits'. A single player at the beginning: a cockpit supplier	New instrument concept (actionable phenomenon) + an original research question
New capabilities	Yes: characterization of materials, processes, usages, the construction business	Yes	Yes: on aircraft integrator utility and constraints, on aircraft companies, on pilots, on technologies etc.	Yes: on the research question (animals and pathologies, etc.), on the instruments underlying the phenomena, etc.
Phases	Subsets of one or a few partners conducting or financing experiments, research projects, validation projects, communication projects	Each partner conducts (or subcontracts) individual investigations on clear, well-identified technological issues	In-house exploration of conceptual alternatives for cockpits Design of cockpit simulators enabling collective explorations with aircraft integrator, companies and pilots	An original experiment with new instrument facility (+ publication) Other experiments with other researchers, based on the same instrument principle Improvement and innovation on the instrument principles
Coordination	Regular steering committee sharing results of the explorations,	Three conferences per year, with all ITRS group members. Working	Two levels: • inside company: gathering results,	Two levels: • device level: steering committee (instrument

303

Table 11A.1 (continued)

	Biomaterials	ITRS	Cockpit	Biotech
	listing open questions to be explored, discussing possible ways and collective facility for each related exploration	groups responsible for one process issue. Each group updates its related roadmap, identifies emerging solutions and pending questions	orienting explorations and choosing partners • simulator level: steering committee sharing results with main partners	manager + pioneer researchers) choosing relevant experiment to be accepted on the experimental device • experiment level: regular meetings between instrument manager and researcher
Resources	Classic association funding: partners pay for their own explorations	Members pay for their own explorations. Collective expenses (meeting) shared	Cockpit supplier provides the simulation bench	Initial fundraising through research contracts. Experimental devices then financed through public funding or foundations
Leading partners	Leading builders, architects, hemp transformers, lime suppliers, grouped in an association 'Building with Hemp'. Growing number of members in the association. Limited and varying number of members taking part in the association's steering committee (decreasing first and then increasing)	Main players of semiconductor industry (process suppliers, manufacturers, users such as cellphone manufacturers, PC integrators, etc.). Open participation ITRS groups are led by designers working for semiconductor manufacturers	Cockpit designer alone at the beginning. Then component suppliers, aircraft integrator, aircraft companies, pilots also participate (slow enlargement) Simulation level steering committee limited to aircraft integrator and cockpit supplier	Limited to one research pioneer and instrument pioneer at the beginning. Then extended to other researchers (in the same and in different fields), to the instrument manufacturer(s) etc. Selection of participants to use the exploratory device Steering committee limited to pioneers

Platform output	Industry platform = professional rules for new house building. Core = choice of materials, process parameters, etc. Networks = material providers + builders + architects + building owners. Value = new market (thanks to state guarantees for insurance purposes) + cross-sided network effects	Industry platform = production process platform for next semiconductor generation. Core = main technology process choices, performance level, etc. Networks = production process suppliers, manufacturers, users. Value = reduce investment risks for machines suppliers; direct semiconductor users' design efforts	Industry platform = validation bench for cockpit components. Core = bench, evaluation rules, etc. Networks = components supplier, cockpit integrator, aircraft integrator, aircraft companies, pilots etc. Value = leverage innovative technology in cockpit components, enable innovative cockpit with clear user value for companies and pilots	Research field platform = new services for measurement/ analysis to support efficient research in a new field. Core = routinized services, including self-service. Networks = research community, instrument makers. Value = easy access of researchers to a new research field, large market for new, routinized instruments
Other outputs	Strategic view of the field (other hemp building opportunities). Competencies	Strategic view of future, emerging platforms, at multiple time horizons	Representation of alternative cockpit concepts. Increase knowledge on user value	For pioneers: better understanding of the instrument potential applications and the possible research paths
Rights	No fees on professional rules. Patents obtained during the exploration process are owned by the explorers	ITRS roadmap is available for free. IP obtained during the exploration is the property of the explorer	Limited access to the simulator. IP for the explorers (either cockpit designer alone or cockpit designer + aircraft integrator)	Selective access to the experimental device. IP for explorers, shared with the instrument maker

305

12. Design rules for platform leaders

Stefano Brusoni and Andrea Prencipe

1. INTRODUCTION

The case illustrated in this chapter was explicitly chosen as an example of major strategic, and infrequent, decisions in the lifetime of the organization studied as it was engaged in the effort to develop a radically new platform. The aircraft engine industry case illustrates the introduction of a new platform architecture in a high-technology setting. The evidence describes radical changes that revolutionized the products and the manufacturing processes. This was a 'make-or-break' decision which implied the definition of a new 'way of doing things'. In choosing this type of empirical setting, this chapter focuses on phenomena that are likely to yield revealing observations about the distinct effects that products and knowledge bases have on organizations. On this basis, the aim of this chapter is not to question the robustness of the organizational implications found in the modularity literature. Such implications are reliable for understanding the behavior of organizations in 'normal' times. The objective of this chapter is instead to highlight the problems faced by organizations that (are forced to) choose to live in 'non-normal' times.

The chapter is structured as follows. Section 2 discusses the key building blocks of the multi-domain framework we propose. Section 3 provides a discussion of the case study that illustrates the complex dynamics of the relationship between product and organization. Section 4 discusses our framework and offers some thoughts on the implications for practice.

2. TOWARDS A MULTI-DOMAIN NETWORK APPROACH

In order to fully capture the complex dynamics that characterize the relationships between product and organization, we rely on the dynamic multiple networks approach proposed by Padgett and Powell (2003). This approach argues that social phenomena are the outcome of the interplay of multiple networks constituted by different domains. On the basis of

Table 12.1   Typology of ties

	Knowledge domain	Organization domain	Product domain
Constitutive ties	Co-authorship and collaborations	Contracts, projects, plans (programs)	Design rules
Relational ties	Citations, apprenticeships	Socialization and community-building processes	None
Transactional flows	Ideas, patents, advice, apprentices	Information, artifacts, young members	Information and materials – I/O relations among components

Source: Adapted from Padgett and Powell (2003).

previous studies (Brusoni et al., 2001), we consider three domains to be key to the argument of this chapter: knowledge, products and organizations.

Each of these domains is a network *per se* made up of elements connected through ties. Padgett and Powell (2003) identified three types of ties: constitutive ties, relational ties and transactional ties. Constitutive ties are the building blocks – often legally contractual – of the network. They are 'coherent and recognizable (though perhaps only by knowledgeable participants) categories' (ibid., p. 18). The actual content of such relations may of course change from domain to domain. The content of the constitutive ties is exchanged and/or transformed through transactional ties in order to 'enhance productivity' (ibid.). Relational social exchanges are based upon the transfer of gifts that people and organizations give to each other. This type of tie is 'more open-ended and embedded in professional relations or friendships' (ibid.). An example of such a tie is a citation to a paper written by a colleague, or a reference letter written for a student. This sort of relational tie underpins any kind of commercial, and contractually based, relationship. The key point is that it is 'crucial to keep these three types of ties distinct, so that we can chart whether these relationships combine in ways that are either reinforcing or degrading' (ibid.). Table 12.1 summarizes the typology of ties.

The network of firms that liaise to design the whole product, manufacture its components, and assemble and market it constitutes the organization domain. At the organizational domain level, constitutive ties are represented by those contracts and agreements that define ownership structures and governance mechanisms. They include plans, firm strategies and projects. They represent the formal elements that constitute an organization. Against this background, relational ties are represented by those activities that complement the formal organization. They include all those practices needed to establish and maintain reputation (within and between organizations); socialize new members into the organizational structure; become recognized members of sub-groups within the organization, and legitimate members of communities that cut across organizational boundaries.

Transactional flows relate to the exchange of information, artifacts and people. People can be exchanged through, for instance, temporary secondment and job rotation practices. This type of transactions is fundamental to socialize new members into the organization code (March, 1991), maintain relational ties and establish new ones, and support the development of new constitutive ties. Personal relationships play a role when selecting the human resources to be allocated to a specific project. Artifacts also play a key role in understanding the evolution of complex organizations. Recent research on boundary objects, for example, is highly relevant to our conceptualization of the organization as a network of heterogeneous units and communities (D'Adderio, 2001).

Product components constitute the product domain. A product is defined as an artifact comprising components and technologies. Components are the physically distinct portions of the product that perform specific functions and are linked to each other through a set of interfaces defined by the product architecture (Ulrich, 1995). Ulrich (ibid., p. 419) defined product architecture as 'the scheme by which the function of a product is allocated to physical components'. The product architecture defines the constitutive ties of the product domain. Two ideal typologies of product architecture, namely modular and integral, can be identified depending on the interaction of three dimensions: (a) the arrangement of functional elements, i.e. how the different functional requirements are structured in order to contribute to the total product performance; (b) the mapping between functional elements to physical components, i.e. which component implements which function; and (c) the specification of the physical component interfaces. In a modular architecture, there is a one-to-one mapping between physical components and functional elements, and the interfaces between components are de-coupled. In a modular architecture, product interfaces are governed by design rules (Baldwin and Clark, 2000), whereas an integral architecture is characterized by a complex mapping between physical components and functional elements, and tightly coupled interfaces between components.

The knowledge domain is constituted by the scientific and technological disciplines (in terms of the bodies of understanding and practice) that underpin product design and manufacturing (Pavitt, 1998). These disciplines on which organizations base their capabilities (combining them with organizational knowledge) form the basis of the coherent and recognizable categories embedded in the constitutive ties. The example of the invisible college put forward by Padgett and Powell (2003) well describes the type of constitutive ties that characterize the knowledge domain.[1] Co-publications, co-patenting and collaboration in research projects represent the key building blocks that define the knowledge domain. Similarly, membership of professional bodies, collaboration in research projects and technical evaluation committees play a key role in the development of the knowledge domain. Citations represent key elements of the relational ties of the knowledge domain. Apprenticeships within engineering communities play a similar role. Finally, ideas, patents, advice and excellence awards granted by professional associations are exchanged through participant activity to foster the functioning and productivity of the network.

Organizations need to act as catalysts of change as well as integrating devices to align the disjoint dynamics of products and knowledge (even in the presence of a modular product architecture). This role is key when innovation and change are the core of firm competitiveness (Grant, 1996).

3. DESIGN RULES FOR PLATFORM LEADERS

The case study of the Rolls-Royce RB211 aircraft engine project analyzed in this section looks at major changes in a high-technology setting and represents an illustrative example of cross-domain transformation. Three aspects are underlined. First, radical innovations entail changes across different domains so that without cross-domain rewiring innovations fail. Second, cross-domain changes rely on the presence of key individuals or organizations that give impetus to them. Third, even though all levels of the network are related and change in one entails changes in the others (for innovation to succeed), it is not necessarily true that all levels (product, organizations and knowledge) need to obey the same rules and exhibit the same topology.

Architectural innovations are not frequent events in the aircraft engine industry. Similar to other capital-good industries, product architectures in the aircraft engine industry are characterized by life cycles that can extend up to 50 years (Davies, 1999; Hobday, 1998). These long life cycles are due to the high development costs entailed by a variety of factors such as the complexity of the product and the technologies underlying it, and the thick regulation that imposes strict rules and procedures that manufacturers must comply with (Prencipe, 1997). This section argues that the development of a new aircraft engine architecture requires the development of new knowledge through specific organizational processes led by key individuals that act as vertical linkages across the knowledge, organization and product domains. Establishing new design rules is a demanding and painstaking process that requires manufacturers to invest heavily in new bodies of knowledge and practice.

Turbofan Engine Architectures

At the end of the 1960s, the aircraft manufacturers Boeing and Lockheed started developing larger aircraft. This move towards the development of larger aircraft called for more powerful engines. At the time, Pratt & Whitney (USA) virtually dominated the world market for large aircraft engines. General Electric (USA) and Rolls-Royce (UK) were considered to be market followers. Although they were competing in the same market, these three engine manufacturers adopted different technological solutions to respond to the new market demand. The two USA-based manufacturers responded by incrementally adjusting their existing engine architecture. Rolls-Royce, however, decided to develop a radically new engine.

The turbofan engine is characterized by two design architectures, the two-shaft and three-shaft. In the 1960s, the dominant aircraft engine architecture was the two-shaft. In a two-shaft architecture, a low-pressure turbine uses some of the hot gas energy from the high-pressure turbine to drive the fan via a shaft. A high-pressure turbine positioned downstream of the combustion chamber drives the high-pressure compressor via a shaft. In a two-shaft architecture, the low-pressure compressor and the fan run on the same shaft driven by the low-pressure turbine. The fan has to rotate relatively slowly in order to keep the fan blade tip speed within sensible mechanical limits. This restricts the speed of the low-pressure turbine and therefore the compression achievable by the low-pressure compressor. As a result, most of the compression duty is left to the high-pressure compressor. Therefore, in order to achieve higher thrust (and in turn a high-pressure ratio), the high-pressure compressor has to be composed of many stages. The number of stages increases the complexity of the engine design, and the length and weight of the engine (Baseley, 1992).

In a three-shaft architecture, the compression job is split across three compressors (low-pressure, intermediate-pressure and high-pressure). Each compressor can be driven by its own turbine to its optimum speed. The presence of an intermediate-pressure compressor (that runs on a third shaft at a higher speed) produces a higher-pressure ratio, so reducing the duty on the high-pressure compressor. As a result, the high-pressure compressor requires fewer stages and fewer variable stator vanes. Since all three compressors are shorter, they need shorter turbines. As a result, an engine based on a three-shaft architecture is lighter and shorter (Baseley, 1992). In addition, a three-shaft architecture is more modular than the two-shaft because the mapping between functions and physical structures tends to be more one-to-one (Ulrich, 1995).

Changes in the Product Domain

The two-shaft and the three-shaft architectures rely on the same scientific and technological fields (e.g. fluid dynamics, thermodynamics, combustion, tribology). The implementation of these fields into viable products is different. According to the multiple networks framework described above, a shift to a three-shaft architecture constitutes a variation in the topology of the product domain, which should affect, but not necessarily determine, the topology of the other two domains, and their relationships. The three-shaft architecture is in fact more modular than the two-shaft. The development of design rules for the three-shaft architecture required the acquisition of new knowledge by senior engineers, through specific organizational tools, namely the technology demonstrator programs.

Rolls-Royce had already decided to embark on the development of more powerful engines in the mid-1960s, when a study carried out at the time predicted an expanding future market for engines rated over 30 000 lb. At Rolls-Royce, the first program for a larger turbofan engine was based on the two-shaft architecture turbofan engine. The firm's view was that the fuel consumption benefits of a higher by-pass ratio would be more than offset by the fuel consumption costs attributable to the larger size of the fan, the greater weight of the engine, and the higher installed drag that a higher by-pass ratio would entail (Cownie, 1989; Pugh, 2001). This view had to change when 'tests in the US demonstrated that the installed drag penalty of the nacelle was less than half that assumed in European studies' (Ruffles 1992, p. 3). This led Rolls-Royce engineers to choose 'a three-shaft configuration as the best for both aerodynamic and mechanical reasons' (ibid., p. 4). The technological advances encompassed in the three-shaft architecture would result in an engine that was 'lighter, cheaper to run, simpler in construction (with 40 per cent fewer component parts) and easier to maintain than existing turbo-fan engines' (Gray, 1971, p. 84).

A technology demonstrator program was launched to test the new technological solution, with the first engine test run taking place in July 1966 (Cownie, 1989). The tests revealed a number of mechanical defects related to the innovative character of the three-shaft architecture. Lack of finance resulted in the demonstrator program being abandoned. Meanwhile, Rolls-Royce started a smaller three-shaft engine program, the Trent, which permitted the firm to gain some experience on a lower-rated version of a three-shaft engine. The Trent program, however, was cancelled in 1968.

Rolls-Royce engineers strongly believed in the potential of the three-shaft architecture. At the end of the 1960s, Rolls-Royce had in place two large three-shaft engine projects, namely the RB207 and the RB211. In 1968, after a long negotiation, the firm secured a large order for the three-shaft RB211 from Lockheed. Due to the numerous problems and ensuing escalating costs entailed by the development of the new architectures at the end of 1969, Rolls-Royce's financial situation deteriorated. Notwithstanding changes in management, redundancies and further augmented financial aid from the British government, in 1971 Rolls-Royce went into receivership (Cownie, 1989).[2]

Unsuccessful Rewirings

Rolls-Royce's decision to adopt a three-shaft architecture to develop engines for the larger aircraft being developed at the end of the 1960s is an example of (temporarily) unsuccessful rewiring. The development of the RB211 was unique for Rolls-Royce. As Harker (1976, p. 176) summed it up: 'This was a mammoth task; the engine itself was much bigger in overall dimension than anything the company had produced before; it was a different shape and the diameter of the fan was eighty-six inches, which necessitated large machinery to cut metal and required new techniques in welding.' The task became even more complex when the design specifications of the engine were modified to accommodate changes in the design of the aircraft. By the time the engine was ordered, aircraft performance requirements had become stricter, with the thrust required from the RB211 rising to 40 600 lb. Later, the thrust requirement climbed again to 42 000 lb because of the increased weight of both aircraft and engine. This thrust was twice that of the largest engine that Rolls-Royce had ever produced.

The new architecture would have directly affected the topology of the product domain through a deep variation in the interfaces across components. These variations were not completely achieved, however, because of the absence of consistent accompanying variations in the organizational and knowledge domains. The topology of each domain maintained its *status quo ante* and therefore a mismatch across them occurred. Rolls-Royce's organizational domain revolved around the older two-shaft architecture. Changes did not occur in the knowledge domain either.

The technology demonstrator program that would have been instrumental for changes in both the organizational and knowledge domains was cancelled due to financial constraints.[3] The cancellation of the demonstrator program meant that the design team could neither acquire nor deepen knowledge in the new architecture and therefore had to depend on parametric studies of smaller turbofan engines. The abandonment of the program also impaired the development of new constitutional ties among engineers around the new architecture. People play a fundamental role in cross-domain rewirings. The premature death of Adrian Lombard deprived Rolls-Royce of one of the finest trouble-shooting engineers in the industry (Hayward, 1989) who could have been instrumental in the development of the new design rules. In addition, when Rolls-Royce went into receivership, numerous people (including engineers) were made redundant, and others retired.

Achieving Successful Rewirings: The RB211 Thrust Growth Capability

The nationalization of the company in 1971 injected new funding into the firm and gained board support for the RB211 program. A number of Rolls-Royce's most illustrious engineers came out of retirement and took control of the program. Among them was Sir Stanley Hooker, who, among other activities, had led the development of the engine used in Concorde while working at Bristol Aero Engines (Pugh, 2001). Hooker became both technical director and a member of the Rolls-Royce board of directors with the charge of getting the RB211 program back on track. Cyril Lovesey and Arthur Rubbra, both well over 70 years old, worked with Hooker on what he called 'a kind of Chiefs of Staff committee' (Pugh, 2001, p. 235, quoting from Hooker, 1984). The double appointment of Hooker as well as the return of other retired engineers constituted a turning point in the cross-domain rewirings. Hooker's knowledge spanned both the knowledge and the organization domains to create new linkages across them needed to rewire the networks and make the architectural innovation happen. In addition, the return of retired engineers gave impetus to the development of new constitutive and relational ties through the socialization process of apprenticeship.

Once the new design rules had been developed, the RB211 was able to display all its inherent strengths. In the mid-1980s, Rolls-Royce engineers discovered that, because of the modularity embedded in the three-shaft architecture, they could upgrade the RB211 for the larger engine market without increasing the fan diameter, making dramatic savings in development costs compared with the earlier estimates (Pugh, 2001). The RB211 demonstrated the highest growth capability compared to its competitors.[4]

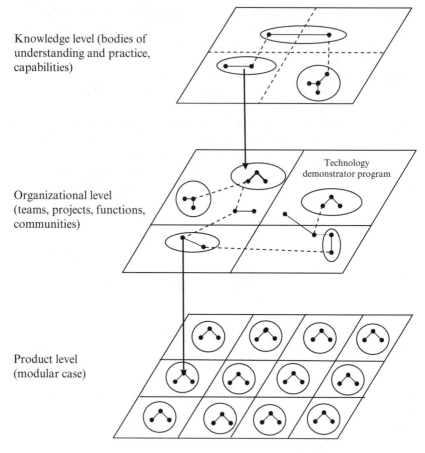

Knowledge level (bodies of
understanding and practice,
capabilities)

Organizational level
(teams, projects, functions,
communities)

Technology
demonstrator program

Product level
(modular case)

Figure 12.1   Cross-domain rewiring: failed

Modularity required the acquisition of new architectural know-how
through the learning processes of key people. These learning processes
facilitated the smoothing of the mismatches across the domains caused by
changes in the topology of the product domain.

4.   DISCUSSION AND IMPLICATIONS: DESIGNERS' RULES

Figures 12.1 and 12.2 summarize the results of the case study illustrated.
The case is an example of non-modular multi-domain networks, where the

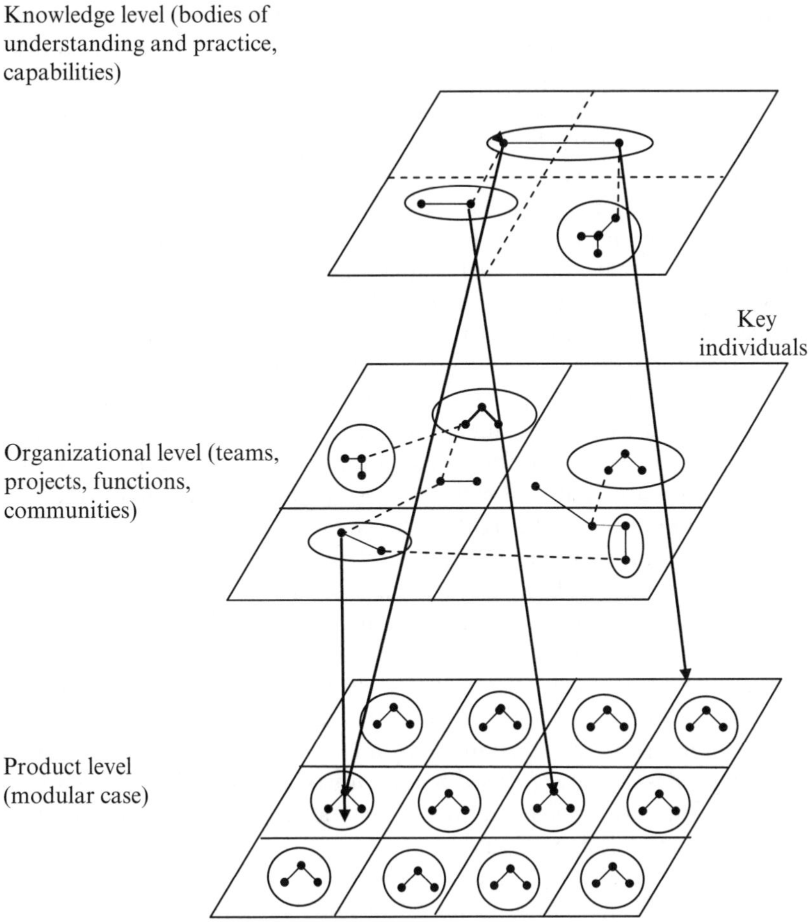

Knowledge level (bodies of
understanding and practice,
capabilities)

Key
individuals

Organizational level (teams,
projects, functions,
communities)

Product level
(modular case)

Figure 12.2   Cross-domain rewiring: achieved

topology of each domain does not map neatly – and automatically – onto
the others. In other words, design rules dominate the product domain, but
they do not define the characteristics of the other two domains. The one-
to-one mapping between product and organization design (on the basis
of modular design rules) is but one specific case of a more general situation where both knowledge and product dynamics play a role in shaping
organizations (Figure 12.1).

Organizations, however, take strategic decisions that affect the evolution
of product and knowledge. In order to be able to introduce radical innovations, organizations rely on a rich and complex set of ties (constitutive,

Platforms, markets and innovation

relational and transactional) that connect knowledge, organization and product domains (Figure 12.2). The key characteristic that sets networks apart is not the topology of each domain *per se*, but rather the nature, richness and variety of the ties that hold them together. The network described in Figure 12.2 is characterized by higher complexity, in terms of network topologies and variety of ties.

These findings support the results of previous research that found that the knowledge and product domains do not follow the same dynamics. Organizations that appear increasingly diversified in terms of bodies of knowledge on which they rely are at the same time increasingly specialized in terms of the range of products they market (Arora et al., 1998; Granstrand et al., 1997). Brusoni et al. (2001) found that when knowledge and product domains respond to different rules, a specific type of organization, labeled as systems integrating organization, acts as a catalyst of change across all domains for coordination purposes. Systems-integrating organizations are equipped with a set of capabilities that enable them to span the boundaries of different domains.

The case study provides micro-level evidence on the unfolding of systems integration. The aircraft engine case showed that systems integration relies on the presence of specific individuals who play a key role across all domains. They act as the channels of transmission of innovation across domains and thus facilitate the enactment of cross-domain rewiring: key individuals and their career paths constitute the fundamental linkages across domains. Whereas extant literature looked at situations dominated by design rules, we have focused on the efforts and problems related to the development and implementation of new design rules, therefore putting emphasis on the designers' rules.

Systems integration plays a fundamental role when the emergence of new disciplines and sub-disciplines triggers changes in the product and organization domains. The advent of digital electronics in the machine tool industry is a case in point. In the 1960s, rapid developments in electronics and software engineering led to the emergence of numeric control technologies that allowed the development of better and more reliable machine tools. Such developments had to be matched by parallel improvements in mechanical engineering to be embodied into the final product, however. Therefore machine tool manufacturers had to temporarily integrate with electronic firms specialized in numeric control techniques to learn how to integrate into the product domain the new functionalities enabled by the rapid development in the knowledge domain (Mazzoleni, 1999). The cross-domain rewirings occurred through the temporary integration (through joint ventures and alliances) between machine tools manufacturers and suppliers of numeric control technologies. Mazzoleni

(1999) showed that integration modified the organization domain in order to match the evolution of the knowledge domain with that of the product domain. Once the rewiring was achieved, the organization domain reverted to its disintegrated status.

The relevance of organizations as catalysts of change for the introduction of infrequent, discontinuous, radical innovations has also been suggested in recent management research. Gawer and Cusumano (2002) suggested platforms and not standalone products are the key locus of competition. Platforms are more than products since they encompass physical components, knowledge and capabilities, as well as organization design principles. It is when platforms are defined that relationships are established among people and units; new bodies of understanding and practice are generated and old ones discarded; information filters are implemented to selectively retain what is defined as relevant information. Definition of the appropriate product platform becomes fundamental to firms that need to introduce new products continuously and predictably (Brown and Eisenhardt, 1997). Modularity plays an important role since it allows the decoupling of complex products into less complex modules and establishes standardized components interfaces that in turn enable the introduction of new or upgraded modules (Baldwin and Clark, 2000). The very process of defining a new platform is, however, a major and highly risky undertaking in which firms engage very rarely. It is difficult to develop routines and heuristics capable of guiding such activities (exactly because they happen so rarely). Yet any wrong decision taken at this time will have long-lasting effects on firm profitability and eventual survival.

If Gawer and Cusumano (2002) are correct in stressing the increasing role that platform leadership is going to play in the future, then we need to understand better the very process through which new platforms are created and implemented. Looking at such a process is necessary to be able to advance research that has so far largely posited *ex post* the existence of systems-integrating organizations, but has not looked in detail at how systems integration actually happens.

Implications for Practice

The micro-level analysis of the development of new design rules for platform leaders has implications for practice. We have argued that key individuals play a fundamental role in enacting cross-domain rewirings. Leading figures that played a central role in the connection of the knowledge, organization and product domains were senior engineers with long careers in the industry – as in the case of the development of new design rules for tire manufacturing illustrated in Brusoni and Prencipe (2006).

Besides technical expertise, they also developed relevant relational ties that enabled them to maintain their central role when they came to assume senior positions at the corporate level. The double role of one senior engineer as member of the board and as a technical director gave impetus to the creation of new constitutive as well as relational ties in the organization.

This leads us to note that direct involvement in manufacturing activities was pivotal to the careers of engineers who led the process of development of new design rules. It was their involvement in the minutiae of everyday production that enabled them to cumulatively develop a systemic understanding of technologies, products and the overall industry. This is a major point to consider if one notes how easily manufacturing activities are now being outsourced to low-cost countries. While such a trend might be unstoppable, and completely justifiable in terms of cost reduction and access to fast-growing consumer markets, questions need to be asked about how the next generation of engineers of systems-integrating organizations will be trained.

In the 1990s, organizations such as NASA experienced dramatic problems engendered by extensive outsourcing policies. NASA is facing the problem that the cohort of engineers who were trained from the bottom during the *Apollo* years has now retired. After *Apollo*, NASA began to outsource the design, development and manufacture of subsystems and components to external suppliers. This was acceptable as long as NASA engineers had the systems knowledge to integrate the different components and subsystems in a coherent whole. This systems knowledge was largely developed in the 1960s through extensive involvement in design and manufacturing activities when most subsystems and components were developed in house (Bilbro, personal communication). Newly appointed systems engineers have been trained in the post-*Apollo* days when NASA had already outsourced the design and development of components and subsystems. Hands-on training in design and/or manufacturing activities did not take place. This may lead to the undesirable result that newly appointed engineers may well not be able – or at least find it more difficult – to develop systems skills needed to fully understand the large-scale consequences of seemingly minor problems. This might be one of the problems underlying the *Challenger* disaster.

If organizations such as NASA plan to act as integrators of somebody else's knowledge, activities, components and subsystems, and therefore make use of extensive outsourcing policies, then they ought to face the issue of developing and maintaining the in-house systems knowledge required to coordinate external organizations' activities as well as align changes across the product, organization and knowledge domains. Hands-on training and career paths thereby become strategic issues in order to develop such knowledge. The chief task of systems-integrating organizations is to act as catalysts of change between the evolution of bodies of scientific and technological knowledge on which they rely and the evolution of artifacts that ultimately determine their survival.

NOTES

1. It should be noted that firms rely on an invisible college that includes both scientific and technological disciplines.
2. For a detailed account of the troubled development of the RB211 and its consequences for Rolls-Royce see Lazonick and Prencipe (2004).
3. 'Many believed that some of the problems later experienced in RB211 development could have been solved earlier if running had continued with the RB178 demonstrator' Cownie (1989, p. 232).
4. The first variant was rated at 42 000 lb. The latest was rated 102 000 lb in April 2000. A company source claims that the Trent can be stretched up to 115 000 lb (Williams, 1995). These thrust requirements were unthinkable when the RB211 engine was first conceived. The growth capability of the Pratt & Whitney JT9D and the General Electric CF6 engine families was limited by their two-shaft configuration. Both engines show a long core that made it impracticable to add more stages to reach higher thrust ratings. Thrust improvements have been achieved through driving the core engine harder, and small increases to fan, compressor and turbine size. Due to the exhausted growth potential of the JT9D and CF6 engines and to increasing thrust requirements from airlines to power larger aircraft, Pratt & Whitney and GE Aircraft Engines have developed new engine families. At the beginning of the 1980s Pratt & Whitney started the development of the PW4000. To meet the thrust requirements in the band from 75 000 lb to 100 000 lb, GE Aircraft Engines developed an all-new engine labeled GE90 (Jane's Information Group, 1996).

REFERENCES

Arora, A., A. Gambardella and E. Rullani (1998), 'Division of labour and the locus of inventive activity', *Journal of Management and Governance*, **1**, 123–140.

Baldwin, C.Y. and K. Clark (2000), *Design Rules, Volume 1, The Power of Modularity*. Cambridge, MA: MIT Press.

Baseley, H.M. (1992), 'Advance three-shaft engines, configured for reliability, efficiency and growth', presented the 43rd AGM of the Aeronautical Society of India, February.

Brown, S.L. and K.M. Eisenhardt (1997), 'The art of continuous change: linking complexity theory and time-paced evolution in relentlessly shifting organizations', *Administrative Science Quarterly*, **41** (4), 1–34.

Brusoni, S. and A. Prencipe (2006), 'Making design rules', *Organization Science*, **17** (1), 179–89.

Brusoni, S., A. Prencipe and K. Pavitt (2001), 'Knowledge specialization, organizational coupling, and the boundaries of the firm: why do firms know more than they make?', *Administrative Science Quarterly*, **46** (4), 597–621.

Cownie, J. (1989), 'Success through perseverance: the Rolls-Royce RB211 engine', *The Putnam Aeronautical Review*, **4** (December), 230–38.

D'Adderio, L. (2001), 'Crafting the virtual prototype: how firms integrate knowledge and capabilities across organizational boundaries', *Research Policy*, **30**, 1409–24.

Davies, A. (1999), 'Innovation and competitiveness in complex product systems: the case of mobile phone systems', in S. Mitter and M. Bastos (eds), *Europe and Developing Countries in the Globalised Information Economy*, London: UNU Press, pp. 107–25.

Eisenhardt, K.M. (1989), 'Building theories from case study research', *Academy of Management Review*, **14**, 532–50.

Gawer, A. and M.A. Cusumano (2002), *Platform Leadership: How Intel, Microsoft, and Cisco Drive Industry Innovation*, Boston, MA: Harvard Business School Press.

Granstrand, O., P. Patel and K. Pavitt (1997), 'Multitechnology corporations: why they have "distributed" rather than "distinctive core" capabilities', *California Management Review*, **39**, 8–25.

Grant, R.M. (1996), 'Prospering in dynamically-competitive environments: organizational capability as knowledge integration', *Organization Science*, **7** (4), 375–87.

Gray, R. (1971), *Rolls on the Rocks: The Story of Rolls-Royce*, Salisbury, UK: Compton Press.

Harker, R.W. (1976), *Rolls-Royce from the Wings: Military Aviation, 1925–1971*, Oxford: Oxford Illustrated.

Hayward, Keith (1989), *The British Aircraft Industry*, Manchester: Manchester University Press.

Hobday, M. (1998), 'Product complexity, innovation and industrial organisation', *Research Policy*, **26**, 689–710.

Hooker, Sir Stanley (1984), *Not Much of an Engineer*, London: Airlife.

Jane's Information Group (1996), *Jane's Aero Engines*, Coulsdon, Surrey, UK: Sentinel House.

Lazonick, W. and A. Prencipe (2004), 'The governance of innovation: the case of Rolls-Royce Plc', in Anna Grandori (ed.), *Firms and Corporate Governance*, Oxford: Oxford University Press, pp. 246–75.

March, J.G. (1991), 'Exploration and exploitation in organizational learning', *Organization Science*, **2**, 71–87.

Mazzoleni, R. (1999), 'Innovation in the machine tools industry: a historical perspective on the dynamics of comparative advantage', in D. Mowery and R. Nelson (eds), *Sources of Industrial Leadership*, Cambridge, UK: Cambridge University Press, pp. 169–216.

Padgett, J. and W. Powell (2003), 'Economic transformation and trajectories: a dynamic multiple network approach', Working Paper, http://home.uchicago.edu/%7ejpadgett/papers/sfi/econ.trans.pdf, last accessed 6 October 2004.

Pavitt, K. (1998), 'Technologies, products and organization in the innovating firm: what Adam Smith tells us and Joseph Schumpeter doesn't', *Industrial and Corporate Change*, **7**, 433–52.

Prencipe, A. (1997), 'Technological capabilities and product evolutionary dynamics: a case study from the aero engine industry', *Research Policy*, **25**, 1261–76.

Pugh, P. (2001), *The Magic of a Name: The Rolls-Royce Story, Part Two: The Power Behind the Jets, 1945–1987*, Cambridge, UK: Icon Books.

Ruffles, P. (1992), 'The RB211: the first 25 years', 31st Short Brothers Commemorative Lecture.

Ulrich, K.T. (1995), 'The role of product architecture in the manufacturing firm', *Research Policy*, **24**, 419–40.

Williams, C. (1995), 'How the RB211's three-shaft have developed the largest engine family', *Aircraft Economics*, **21**, 4–7.

Yin, R.K. (1994), *Case Study Research: Design and Methods*, London: Sage.

APPENDIX: RESEARCH METHOD

The case study illustrated in this chapter was explicitly chosen as an example of major strategic, and infrequent, decisions in the lifetime of organizations. We chose a pragmatic approach, focused on a specific problem. In choosing this type of empirical setting, the chapter focuses on phenomena that are likely to yield revealing observations about the distinct effects that products and knowledge bases have on organizations. The key objective of the research method was to identify those factors that 'complicate' the relationship between product and organization design. Prior research and practice allowed us to predict that the evolution of knowledge will play a fundamental role. The objective was to highlight the centrality of one specific relationship (knowledge–organization–product) to one specific empirical phenomenon, i.e. the development of new design rules.

Two distinct types of data were employed in this study to establish construct validity (Yin, 1994). Multiple data sources enabled us to obtain stronger substantiation of constructs by triangulating evidence across cases. The first type of information was gathered from a systematic review of the technical literature, trade publications, specialized engineering journals, company annual reports and publications. These data were used to provide background information and to sketch an overall picture of the sectors analyzed.

The second type of information came from interviews. The aircraft engine case study is part of a larger research project designed to explore the distinction between the knowledge and production boundaries of firms that develop complex products such as aircraft engines. Within this research project, 27 semi-structured interviews had been carried out by one of the two authors with aircraft engine manufacturers. For the case study presented in this chapter, a further set of four interviews was carried out (one retired engineer, one company design engineer and two university professors of aircraft engine design technology).

Qualitative insights provided by interviewees proved to be fundamental for understanding the knowledge requirements underlying the patterns of relationships among the product, organization and knowledge domains. This stage has enabled us to identify, evaluate and match patterns as they emerged from within the case study (Eisenhardt, 1989, p. 540).

13. Detecting errors early: management of problem solving in product platform projects

Ramsin Yakob and Fredrik Tell

INTRODUCTION

The ability to speed up the product development process has been touted as one source of competitive advantage. Consequently a number of different approaches by which product development cycle times can be reduced have been suggested, often however with contrasting success depending on industry and product complexity (see Eisenhardt and Tabrizi, 1995; Kessler and Bierly, 2002). Product platforms has emerged as one approach towards the increased capability of firms to reduce development cycle times and provide a number of products at lower cost (Meyer and Lehnerd, 1997). Product platforms are often systems consisting of a complex architectural configuration of components and subsystems from which a number of derivative products can be produced. The higher and broader the architectural configuration of a system, the more independences between its parts. Subsequently the approach towards reducing product development cycle time needs to vary depending on the degree of complexity of the product being developed, since some systems have more complex architectural configurations than others (Clift and Vandenbosch, 1999).

In this chapter we take a problem-solving approach to product development (Clark and Fujimoto, 1991; Thomke and Fujimoto, 2000) whereby the ability to manage the problem-solving process is considered a key capability in reduced product development cycle time. The development of platforms is a complex endeavour requiring the organizing and utilization and involvement of a number of different functional areas of a firm and the inclusion of a variety of expertise, usually in cross-functional development projects. Problems and errors are an inherent part of any development work carried out in such projects (Vincenti, 1990; Lindkvist et al., 1998; Davis, 2006). As the complexity of the system increases due to the increasing number of components and interdependences, emerging problems and errors become gradually more difficult to solve. We thus envisage that the more complex the hierarchical configuration of product platforms, the more complex the problems and errors encountered in their development.

The study reported in this chapter investigates possible approaches to problem solving in product platform development. Previous research has distinguished between directional and heuristic problem-solving strategies (Nickerson and Zenger, 2004; Fleming and Sorensen, 2004). We discuss the appropriateness of these two strategies in product platform development projects. In particular, we are interested in the causes and consequences of emerging problems and errors in such projects. Our analysis is grounded theoretically as well as in an empirical study of two product platform projects: one in the telecommunications industry and one in the automotive industry. Our findings indicate that in developing capabilities for the complex problem-solving characteristic of product platform development projects, it is paramount to narrow the search process between errors identified and the problem underlying that error. The successful management of such compression increases the probability of finding remedies to errors, as it reduces the problem landscape in which solutions can be found. For this both heuristic and directional search processes are important.

Product and System Architectures and Platform Development

In common with complex derivative products and systems, product platforms consist of hierarchically ordered architectural structures of components, subsystems and systems. This architecture defines the functional requirements of the system, maps functional elements to physical elements, and defines interfaces among interacting elements of the system. Such architectures can broadly be defined as either modular or integral, reflecting the interdependence between the systems' constituent parts (Ulrich, 1995). It is the ordering of these parts, the systems' architectural configuration (Baldwin and Clark, 2000), that determines how the parts function together to carry out its desired functionality. Subsequently system parts can be configured in different ways to reach the same desired performance requirements.

By sharing elements of a single platform's architecture across several derivative products, benefits in terms of reduced development time and cost, and product development flexibility can be achieved. Such architectural commonality can exist at the level of individual components or subsystems, or at system level. The level at which this common architecture is to be found has implications for the application of the product platform. Component- or subsystem-level architectural commonality is warranted when a number of derivatives are produced within or between different firms. Such intra- or inter-firm platforms can be found in traditional manufacturing industries (Meyer and Lehnerd, 1997; Lundbäck, 2004). In other instances platforms have wider industry implications, such as within the computer industry (Gawer and Cusumano, 2002; Evans et al., 2006), where a platform is utilized at system level by external firms to produce complementary derivatives that work in conjunction with the existing platform.

Platforms also often use high degrees of interdependence and interaction between components and subsystems and product- and process-related technologies to form a coherent whole (i.e. a system) (Tatikonda, 1999). In addition to this, they draw on the maintenance of commonality of components, subsystems and interfaces with derivative products. Whilst commonality across derivatives is provided for by platform parts, derivative distinctiveness or uniqueness is often provided for by non-platform parts (Halman et al., 2003). Hence the platform part selection and maintenance process is important since it has implications for late derivative design decisions. Often development flexibility or increased planning capabilities are needed to include late design decisions. Such decisions often ferment the architectural configuration of the platform and put pressure on the commonality maintenance aspects of development work.

The architectural configuration and complexity of product platforms have a bearing on the degree of difficulty encountered in their development and the way in which encountered problems are managed. Configurative decisions must be taken throughout the development process as new input in the form of development obstacles, the inclusion of unplanned derivatives, commonality aspects, market requirements etc. poses challenges that need to be managed. Managing this process is, however, not a simple task, especially when dealing with a large number of system parts that are interdependent and configured in a complex way. The evolving interdependence between system parts can give rise to problems at all hierarchical levels within the system. Therefore problems are often dynamic and evolving, changing according to architectural decisions taken.

The Problem-solving Process

The broad construct of problem solving designates the entire process, i.e. action-oriented human thought, whereas the narrow construct denotes activities taking formulated problems as input and working towards their resolution as output (Smith, 1988). Whereas numerous factors influence the problem-solving approach of firms, problem solving as the synthesis of different knowledge pools explicitly links the problem-solving process to the creation of new knowledge capabilities (Henderson and Clark, 1990; Nickerson and Zenger, 2004; Fleming and Sorenson, 2004). By selecting which problems to resolve, firms can actively seek knowledge and capability development opportunities. This selection includes the choice of how to engage with that problem. Whereas the 'which' question is believed to be answered by the perceived returns of engaging with the problem and the assessment of the firm's capacity to reach high-value solutions (Nickerson and Zenger, 2004), the 'how' question is argued to be determined on basis of the character of the problem itself (Gavetti and Levinthal, 2000). How to organize the process, how to allocate resources for knowledge development, how to integrate knowledge and the choice between knowledge exchanges across specialized domains or focus on a few specialized domains also become important as complex problem solving often requires drawing upon the distributed knowledge of distributed/decentralized agents (Tsoukas, 1996; Dosi and Marengo, 1994).

We distinguish between directional search processes and heuristic search processes, seen as being located at opposite ends of the problem-solving search strategy continuum.[1] Directional search strategies rest on the assumption that a problem can be divided into constituent parts; each part worked on independently; and the contributing results to the solution observed independently (Nickerson and Zenger, 2004, Fleming and Sorenson, 2004). It can be portrayed as search guided solely by feedback or experience from prior trials, thus drawing upon previous activities carried out in finding a solution to a problem. Solutions are searched for incrementally and it is a warranted approach when problems are decomposable and involving limited knowledge interaction.

Heuristic search on the other hand has been defined as the attempts to define solutions based on experience or judgement without the ambition to guarantee an optimum (Foulds, 1983; Silver, 2004). Based on the cognitive representation of potential solutions to a problem, heuristic search builds on a 'forward-looking form of intelligence . . . premised on an actor's belief about the linkage between the choice of actions and the subsequent impact of those actions on outcomes' (Gavetti and Levinthal, 2000, p. 113). Heuristic search consists of attempts to cognitively evaluate probable consequences of choices taken (Nickerson and Zenger, 2004), thus 'identifying useless directions of search beforehand and [by] providing a glimpse of the possible' (Fleming and Sorenson, 2004, p. 912). Heuristic search processes are warranted when problems are complex, with high levels of interaction among knowledge sets and design choices.

Decomposing Complex Systems and Problems

From a decomposability perspective (Simon, 1969), problem solving can be comprehended as activities geared towards identifying interdependences between system parts. By increasing the knowledge of how system parts interrelate and interact, it is possible to come to better terms with the complexity faced. This involves increasing knowledge of the detailed linkage between alternative actions and possible outcomes of action, within the existing complexity faced (Gavetti and Levinthal, 2000; Nickerson and Zenger, 2004; Fleming and Sorenson, 2004). The measure of decomposability is a function of the degree to which activities influencing one part of a system can be carried out independent of or dependent on activities carried out on other parts of the system (Simon, 1962). This interdependence between various parts of a system is a function of the different kinds of interactions between parts, the complexity of each interaction, its frequency and its duration (Simon, 2000). When there is no interaction or interdependence between parts of a system it is rendered fully decomposable. In such a setting parts can be worked on independently with the expectation that the aggregation of independent efforts will contribute to the uncovering of valuable problem solutions (Nickerson and Zenger, 2004). Whereas full decomposability has been described as the isolation of system parts and problems into independent entities that can be developed and solved independently, non-decomposability implies that such decomposition is problematic. Within non-decomposable systems, the interactions between parts of the system are so extensive that separation between them becomes difficult. Non-decomposable systems are believed to give rise to high interaction problems, characterized by the need for high interaction among design choices and for extensive interaction among many knowledge sets to derive a solution (Nickerson and Zenger, 2004).

However, the majority of complex systems are neither fully decomposable nor non-decomposable, but are nearly decomposable (Brusoni et al., 2004; Marengo et al., 2005). Near-decomposability exists when some interaction is shared by all parts in a system and the interactions taking place within the subsystems are more frequent and tighter than those between subsystems (Simon, 1962). Thus problems themselves are often only nearly decomposable, reflecting the integral aspects of the majority of product and system architectures. However, problem solvers are often forced, due to their limited computational capacity, to decompose problems that are not fully decomposable. Faced with the challenge of understanding a problem, problem solvers often need to revert to finding good enough rather than optimized solutions (Foulds, 1983; Brusoni et al., 2004; Marengo et al., 2005).

At the same time, applying a heuristic problem-solving approach when dealing with complex systems offers only limited advantage (Fleming and Sorenson, 2004). Since interaction between all parts of the system cannot be predicted *a priori* through a cognitive exercise, directional search strategies fill an important function in identifying interdependences. This is because the application of a problem-solving strategy has implications for the degree of certainty, speed and clarity by which interdependences can be identified and understood. March (1991), for instance, argues that the feedback associated with exploitative (directional search) activities is better suited for tying consequences to activities whereas explorative (heuristic search) activities are subject to returns that are systematically less certain, more remote in time and organizationally more distant from the locus of action and adaptation. Thus the application of heuristics versus directional search activities is related to the ability and need to generate timely knowledge of a problem and its solution. This need in turn stems from the advantages provided by an early identification of discrepancies, where the ability to deal with problems increases, the earlier they are identified (Weick and Sutcliffe, 2007). However, the process of early discrepancy identification is harder than later identification. Viewing the product platform development process as primarily a problem-solving activity, we investigate the strategies applied to increase the speed by which product platforms are developed in two industrial firms.

THE TELECOMMUNICATIONS CASE

The telecommunications industry is a technology-intensive industry where a platform often takes the form of operating system software, where the software components determine the functionality of the platform and its physical features determine its overall capacity. This operating system software (i.e. the platform) provides the interfaces by which numerous internal and external applications, together making up the telecommunications network, are controlled (Yakob and Tell, 2007). The telecommunications platform denotes a specific technology and architecture consisting of a content and user application layer, a communications control layer, and a connectivity layer composed of hardware, an operating system and software applications on top. It furthermore serves as a technological and architectural base for the development and evolution of additional systems and applications. As such it can be categorized as an industry platform (Gawer and Cusumano, 2002; Evans et al., 2006).

We have studied an enhancement project of a post-3G telecommunications platform that ran for approximately three years, involving hundreds

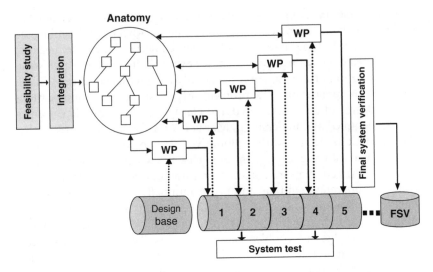

Figure 13.1   Development model: the telecommunications case

of engineers. Figure 13.1 illustrates the approach by which the telecommunications firm worked with the development of its platform. This way
of working arose from the need to address quality and delivery precision
failures that in previous development projects, had led to project delays.
Addressing failures and correcting system errors after final delivery was
a common aspect of the development process. Consequently a need for
sharper focus on more frequent and tighter technical integration of system
parts was identified as one approach by which quality, delivery precision
and flexibility could be increased in the development process. Central to
meeting these requirements were three fundamental development concepts: the project anatomy, work packages (WP), and latest system versions (LSV).

Decomposing the Anatomy

One central requirement of the development process was the early planning
of system technicalities and the creation of the anatomy, whose quality set
the path for the success of the development project. The anatomy was a visualization of development work to be carried out, broken down into work
packages (WP), the visualization of interdependences between WP, and
the grouping of WP into latest systems version (LSV). A WP represented a
functional entity to be integrated into the system and defined a small addition of verifiable system qualities. The anatomy also visualized internal

dependences between WP and subsystems within the final system, in effect mapping which WP within which subsystem required attention first in the development work. The visualized interdependences constrained the order of integration and verification of WP into LSV. An LSV was a number of WP integrated together to form a coherent whole. The LSV represented the latest version of the system, on which further development work was carried out. The anatomy thus visualized the system functionalities, and how functions were capsuled into WP, presented the interdependences between WP and between subsystems, showed how these were interconnected and presented their position in the anatomy. Responsibility for the creation of the anatomy was assigned to the product management team, who together with the receivers of the platform determined the initial functionality requirements and the specification of the system. Since the project ran for almost three years, it was deemed problematic to determine a specification that could hold for the whole period and hence the product management team was involved in continuously communicating changes made to the specification. A system management team had the responsibility of breaking down system requirements into technical requirements according to different subsystem and system areas.

Having a comprehensive understanding of the interdependences between different WP was crucial in the creation of the anatomy. This was because identifying new interdependences later on in the project could mean that the whole project had to be re-planned. This was pointed out as a deficiency in the development process that specified the preconditions for successfully creating the anatomy. When creating the anatomy it was important for all subsystem areas to consider what their task was. Establishing these tasks meant dividing the work into WP and subsequently creating WP teams (WPT). A WPT was a cross-functional development team with end-to-end responsibility for the development, analysis, testing and verification of a single system function. The function capsulation within one single WP had to be small enough to enable it to be easily removed if necessary due to changing prioritization or resource shortages. Working with WP was a flexible way of incorporating new requirements throughout the project's life cycle since they could be divided if they became too large or complex. These newly created WP could then be included somewhere else in the anatomy. Running large increments could be avoided, thereby reducing major effects on system structure. Thus it was important that WP had their own identity which furthermore would allow changes to the anatomy to be made. Important characteristics of a WP were its value-adding contribution, its independent integration into the system, and that it would ensure that the system worked after being integrated. Each WP was required to be verifiable independently, within the system as a whole, and also to be backward compatible. This would allow integration without interference with existing system functionalities or previously delivered and integrated WP.

However, establishing WP and determining the interdependences between them was a complex task requiring awareness of interdependences on a deep technical level. Complexity as a result of system size and number of subsystem and system areas involved required the involvement of several individuals in order to establish these interdependences. Although it was possible for a single individual to establish interdependences at a lower subsystem level, it required a group of knowledgeable people to understand these at the level of total system to carry out the feasibility study, encapsulate functionality in the form of WP, establish interdependences between WP and create the initial anatomy. Participation, interaction, communication and negotiation between numerous expert areas fed into the anatomy. Still, establishing all system interdependences at the outset of the project was not seen as a viable approach and consequently it was important to incorporate replanning flexibility. Restructuring and reordering the location of WP in the anatomy hence took place when required. Rigour to proceed with development activities, and provide flexibility to incorporate changes without interfering with existing development work, was required of the anatomy. Being considered a highly dynamic visualization of the system that could be updated and restructured whenever new interdependences were identified, the anatomy allowed the inclusion of new internal and external requirements throughout the project's life.

Encapsulating and Aggregating Functionality

WP development work took place in a local build environment separated from other development work. Testing and verification activities were carried out against a latest local version (LLV) of the aggregated system. An LLV was an exact copy of the LSV, which consisted of a number of finalized and integrated WP. Development, testing, verification and integration of a WP on an LLV prior to integration and creation of a new LSV was central since this reduced the need for later test and verification activities. Due to the difficulties of establishing all interdependences and determining system effects, some testing and verification were however still carried out centrally to ensure the successful integration of WP into LSV. Encapsulating functionality and thereby reducing interdependences between WP proved to be difficult since many WP built on each other to arrive at required functionality. This necessitated simultaneous testing of several WP, although planning WP carefully in order to avoid too many interdependences had been recognized as important.

Avoiding the case that too many WP were delivered for integration at the same time proved difficult. Despite the recognition that broad knowledge and tight cooperation between technical areas were important to ensure that WP were planned correctly, those involved in creating the anatomy were at times lacking this knowledge. Hence it was recognized that it would have been better to include resources with more technical expertise earlier in the planning process in order to identify interdependences. Newly identified interdependences late in the development process often led to delays and postponement of integration activities.

A central aspect of development work was hence the integration of WP into LSV. An LSV constituted a periodically created and functioning aggregation of the total system. It was created every two weeks, incorporating more functionality and system characteristics each time. The integration process, and the subsequent creation of an LSV, were carried out centrally by a verification and integration unit (VIU). Integration was also something that ran throughout the project from its initial point until final system verification. It took place at several levels within the project: at the WP level, between WP, and centrally though the VIU. After undergoing an extensive regression test and completing the integration process the latest version of the aggregated system was made public for remaining WPT. The LSV was then used at the local version of the system on which subsequent analysis, development, testing and verification activities were carried out, at the level of individual work packages. This process ensured that all WP development work across the firm was carried out on a similar and functioning LSV.

This procedure also meant that technical development limits were set by the functional capacity provided by each newly created LSV. For each LSV a predetermined degree of functionality was integrated, thereby setting the limits on the size of technical steps that could be taken by the following WPT. Stringent testing and verification demands for LSV and the exclusion of WP that adversely affected aggregated system performance ensured system qualities and the progression of development work. WP that had an adverse affect on system performance were not integrated into the LSV, but taken out and subjected to further development work and test, while remaining development continued as planned. Only after being determined not to have an adverse effect on the aggregated system were these WP considered for integration into the following LSV. Aimed at reducing negative effects on overall system performance, this process none the less had larger implications for the development work. The turn-around time for these types of problems increased since the rectified WP could be integrated only at the creation of the following LSV. Despite the instantaneous identification of errors at the time of integration tests, the correction process was slow. Correction responsibility had to be assigned, corrective development work carried out, integration and verification activities on LLV performed, and integration into LSV at predetermined time slots facilitated. Consequently it could take up to six weeks for a corrected WP to be integrated into an LSV, during which time functionality requirements and complexity could grow as development work proceeded. Initially the idea had been to keep WP small by reducing functionality contained within each and thereby facilitating the integration process when creating LSVs. However, since several weeks could pass before excluded WP could be slotted in for integration, they could become large and numerous. Hence situations occurred where several large WP were delivered at the same time, making the integration activity difficult. Despite the challenges involved, the project was deemed highly successful at its completion, meeting delivery requirements not only in terms of time but also in terms of specification.

THE AUTOMOTIVE CASE

The automotive industry has been illustrated as a mature, highly complex industry in terms of both organizational configuration and technological development (Lundbäck, 2004). An automotive platform can be depicted as consisting of a non-fixed number of components making up the underbody of a vehicle and take different forms within the industry (see, e.g., Simpson, 2004).

Within the automotive industry, a platform is usually used by a single firm to develop and manufacture a number of derivative products, although in recent years the notion of intra-firm platforms has emerged within the industry due to increased merger and acquisition activities (Lundbäck, 2004). None the less an automotive platform can be depicted primarily as an internal platform.

We have studied a development project of a multi-brand automotive platform with an anticipated life span of ten years, involving thousands of engineers, which needs to cater for the development and construction of approximately 15 derivative products. Figure 13.2 is a simplified illustration of the process by which the automotive firm worked with the development of its platform. This way of working attempted to cut development time and increase quality by reducing development uncertainty at the level of platform components. Consequently a focus on shared technology at the levels of subsystem and system was seen as one way to reduce development lead time, increase quality and facilitate flexibility.

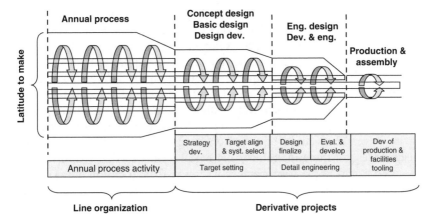

Figure 13.2   Development model: the automotive case

Central to meeting these requirements were concepts of shared technology, the determination of the platform tool-box, and the search for problems and errors.

Shared Technology Focus

Within the platform development process, the definition of technical solutions required for future derivatives was an activity carried out outside of the platform project. By creating system and knowledge libraries in an iterative annual process separate from the engineering design phase, knowledge of required technical solutions and the interrelationship between components could be gradually increased. This process was initiated several years before the application of the required technology and consequently knowledge up front was a driving force behind the platform development process. By creating knowledge of expected technical solutions and requirements prior to the initiation of the engineering design phase, the firm hoped to be in a better position to determine future development needs. The goal was to establish up to 80 per cent of the engineering design requirements in the annual process, and to reduce the uncertainty surrounding how long it would take to develop a component and regarding final component quality. Through this approach it was believed that requirements to reloop the engineering design phase, reduce product requirements or redo initial specifications in order to reach delivery targets could be avoided. By reducing the innovative aspects of engineering design taking place within the project, it was believed that the output of the engineering design phase could be determined more accurately. In doing so, integration and verification no longer focused on individual component level but rather on system levels. Product strategy decisions could be taken earlier since system selection could be made earlier. Being able to decide earlier the technical requirements of different derivatives and technical solutions was believed to increase engineering design stability. The possibilities of joint virtual development processes, synchronized data between R&D units, enhanced manufacturing and sales, reuse of components, and augmented commonality were believed to improve. Time could be saved on later development phases by, for instance, establishing manufacturing requirements earlier. However, this required a shift in platform perspective, away from focus on the platform as being made up of a number of different components of the undercarriage (i.e. the chassis) to include more strategic decisions. More business thinking with regard to the platform was required, rather than a focus solely on product and geometry.

Thus the new way to think about the platform was in terms of system solutions that together made up its architecture and framework. Commonality aspects focused on system levels rather than on the level of individual platform components. Differences between derivatives at the level of individual platform components were thus accepted as long as engineering work proceeded from the same platform base architecture. Application of concept solutions became an important aspect of engineering work and individual platform commonality requirements across derivatives had become replaced by focus on 'shared technology'. Responsibility for ensuring shared technology focus in the development of the platform was assigned to a platform development organization, with coordination, compilation and managerial responsibility. The role of this organization was to ensure the delivery of a number of platform components and the maintenance of commonality across a number of different brand derivatives. Within this organization the platform was understood as a shared technology set up with a life-cycle responsibility for the platform's components and systems. This perception of the platform was well established at higher managerial levels within the derivative projects but not so at lower levels. Important roles within the platform organization were the launch manager, part vehicle team leader, program module team leader and the program module sub team leader. These had various management coordination responsibilities for different technical areas (for instance instrument panel, climate system). Engineering design work for a component was led by an assignment leader. This resource was predominantly activated in the engineering design phase, assigned to a specific derivative project, furthermore carrying out work as part of the project organization.

Determining the Platform Tool-box

Determining the platform component tool-box was deemed a challenge since a number of derivatives were to be developed at intervals of several years. Consequently, up to ten years of planning foresight had to be incorporated in the initial conception of the platform. For this, future derivative projects were required to provide input into the conception and development of the platform. However, due to project resourcing aspects this was not a viable approach. Consequently the platform tool-box was to a large part determined by the early derivative projects, whereas later projects influenced the platform tool-box to a lesser extent. Determining how many components should be part of the platform and how many different derivative models and sizes it should accommodate constituted other difficulties. The challenge thus resided in securing the required knowledge early on, when setting platform requirements and deciding its content. In reality this meant that a prediction or approximation of future platform requirements had to be made.

One approach to overcome this deficiency in required knowledge was to incorporate flexibility in the engineering design work. By focusing on commonality at system levels (through system solutions), engineers had the opportunity to make required alterations at the level of individual platform components, as long as the principal solution and base architecture remained the same.

In the engineering design phase, the understanding of how design solutions affected other components, both platform and non-platform, became important. This included derivatives in production, derivatives under development and future derivatives. Here the launch manager and the part vehicle team manager fulfilled important roles by being involved in the analysis work required to understand how design solutions affected commonality aspects, and by propagating the selection of design solutions that contributed to the maintenance of commonality.

This procedure created an increased challenge for engineers involved in engineering design work. More attention to carry-forward and carry-back effects had to be given as the number of derivatives in production grew and the requirements of future derivatives became better known. Thus, as consideration of existing derivatives and the knowledge of future derivatives grew, so did engineering design complexity. Substantial differences in derivative product characteristics and the inability to receive early input from all development projects made it difficult to fully determine the platform component tool-box at its initial conception. Other requirements had to be added throughout the life cycle of the platform, thereby contributing to the growth of complexity. In this way, the early inclusion of system solutions and concept development work acted as boundaries in the engineering design work.

Searching for Problems and Errors

A central aspect of the development process was the ability to reduce the overall number of late engineering design errors. Increased understanding of technology requirements, recognition of insufficient technical knowledge to warrant a technical solution, and better understanding of when there was substantial technical uncertainty was required. The firm attempted to move away from the identification of errors at the stage of physical testing at the level of individual components, subsystem and system levels, and final product level. These had traditionally been recognized as an easy way to find errors but also an extremely expensive procedure since the possibility to make changes at later stages was limited. Hence the firm tried to reverse this perspective so that errors could be found earlier in the development process. By realizing the potential of system solutions and new technology, understanding knowledge limitations, and evaluating uncertainty in proposed technical solutions, the firm believed it could reduce late-emerging errors. This involved increasing knowledge of how, why, when and where errors were likely to occur, and taking corrective action. Thus central to the engineering work was the early identification of potential and existing errors and the work towards their resolution. This process was made difficult because problems and errors encountered in the different development phases differed and the manoeuvrability to make large changes decreased as the project progressed. This was due to increased interdependences within and between platform and non-platform component subsystems. Large changes would give rise to effects affecting a larger number of components and subsystems. Searching for and reporting existing and potential problems and errors was thus an essential theme of the development process, particularly in the engineering design phase. The work became problem-driven and solution-driven. Problems and errors, commonly referred to as 'issues' within the company, were registered in a database when encountered. Responsibility for deeper investigation into an issue was then assigned to an assignment leader (connected to a specific component) through collective agreement by the part module team leaders, who were also expected by the assignment leader to propose a solution if required. This person in turn was expected to provide information with regard to the technical source of the reported issue, if the component had been manufactured according to specifications, if the supplier had fulfilled their commitment, or whether there was something wrong with the specification and hence the construction of the component itself.

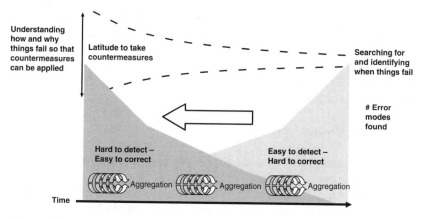

Figure 13.3   Detecting error modes early

In the work towards finding a solution, the assignment leader had to rely on the knowledge of many others in order to understand how potential solutions would influence other derivatives, thereby avoiding implementing solutions that would resolve one issue but create others further on in the engineering design phase. Thus changes of a technical character that affected platform components needed to be understood and agreed across many different areas. Feeding information from and to a large number of different resources made the work towards a solution visible for many different resources. The platform development project has to date accommodated the need of several derivative products in production and is still used in the development of future derivatives.

ANALYSIS: DETECTING ERRORS EARLY

We illustrate the problem-and-error-finding logics within the two cases in Figure 13.3. The problem-solving strategy applied is one where efforts towards finding error modes earlier in the engineering design phase of the development process are in focus. By such a process, the latitude to take countermeasures can be increased since more time is available and the complexity arising from having integrated many components and subsystems in the latter stage of the design engineering phase can be avoided. Such an approach recognizes the increasing complexity the further into the engineering design phase the process is, since the degree of decomposability diminishes the further in the process the engineers are (in essence the system moves along the perfect–non-decomposable continuum). The process is also characterized by a shift from searching for, and identifying when, errors have occurred, to a process where comprehension of how and why things fail so that countermeasures can be applied is in focus. One important aspect of this is the ability to draw wisdom from aggregated system performance. Yet such an approach is not non-trivial and the application of this problem-solving logic is applied to differing success in the two case studies presented.

In Search of Problems and Errors

The existence of problems and errors in product development is not new, but the conceptual difference between the two is often overlooked. We submit that this distinction is valuable when analysing approaches to problem solving in complex systems, such as product platforms. A number of different concepts have been used to refer to errors, including failures, bugs, defects or even incidents (Carroll, 1998; Reason, 2000: Davis, 2006; Weick and Sutcliffe, 2007), often referring to the same phenomenon. Reason (2000) argues that an error can occur as a result of aberrant human behaviour but also be of a systemic character. In the system approach to errors, errors are an inherent part of any organizational process. They are seen as consequences of problems rather than the cause of them, with their origin in systemic factors. An error can be understood as being closely related to the lack of correlation between the intended consequences of an action and its actual consequences. When dealing with complex systems, the complex hierarchical configuration of components, subsystems and systems often obscures the impact of particular actions and gives rise to the invisibility of latent errors (Carroll, 1998; Reason, 2000). Another salient characteristic of an error is that it can be known for sure only after the event has occurred (Nightingale, 1998) and needs to be found and fixed only once (Davis, 2006). Another way to understand errors is as weak signals of discrepancies or failures given by problems (Weick and Sutcliffe, 2007).

Although there is an arguable lack of a coherent and agreed definition of what a problem is and what it is not (see Volkema, 1983; Smith, 1988), several contributions have aimed to develop the concept. A problem has been explained as being concerned with the divergence between a desired and an actual condition (Smith, 1988). It is an undesirable situation that is significant to and may be solvable by an agent and concerns the remedying of the gap between preferences and reality and the expected difficulty of doing so (Smith, 1989). Due to the dynamic nature of problems, they often give rise to the identification of new problems or sub-problems as knowledge of them increases (Volkema, 1983). It is an obstacle that makes it difficult to achieve a desired goal, objective or purpose, and refers to a situation, condition or issue that is as yet unresolved and dynamic in character.

Whereas problems are often manifested in physical attributes, they are themselves not physical in nature. They have been described as a construct of intrinsic subjectivity, whereby the understanding of a problem and the way it is understood defines the problem domain (Smith, 1988). Consequently, problem solving has been argued to be the process of thinking done in advance of acting (Smith, 1988). Such a perspective mirrors the cognitive aspect of intelligence, argued to be a forward-looking form premised on an actor's beliefs about the linkage between the choice of actions and the subsequent impact of those actions on outcomes (Gavetti and Levinthal, 2000, p. 113). Such a definition mirrors closely a cognitive theory of knowledge whereby knowledge is considered as a capacity to extrapolate patterns (Nightingale, 1998).

Drawing on the case illustrations provided, we suggest that a solitary focus on errors within the problem-solving process does not accurately reflect the focus of attention on the development aspects of the platforms. Addressing the consequences of a problem, i.e. an error, is likely only to reduce the signals of a problem rather than addressing its underlying cause. The case illustrations show that problem solving draws on multiple resources and knowledge bases. The occurrence of errors requires a distinctive kind of approach: an error-solving approach. The process of problem solving frequently starts with the perception of stimuli, often in the form of an error, which arouses a concern that needs to be addressed (Weick and Sutcliffe, 2007). This implies that numerous problem-solving occasions must be allowed for within the development process. Problem-solving activities without the existence of errors are a central requirement for successful product development. Such activities often take their form in the heuristic evaluation and design of product, visible through conceptual drawings, designs and product specifications. The conceptual distinction between a problem and an error suggests two different approaches in the reduction of errors in product platform development. One is concerned with the proper search, identification and correction of errors, whereas the other is concerned with the understanding of why and how errors emerge and the consequent resolution of their underlying cause, i.e. the problem. In such a perspective successful problem and error solving in product development is a matter of reducing the knowledge gap between an error (effect) and the underlying problem giving rise to that error (cause). In this process, there is a need to (1) translate or migrate an error, conceived, anticipated or materialized, into a problem, and (2) resolve the identified problem, thereby avoiding the error in the first place. The characteristic of problems and errors respectively none the less has implications for the ability of agents to identify and understand problems once errors are encountered. Being subject to intrinsic evaluation by individuals, a problem can take many forms and have different meaning and implications for different agents. Identifying, understanding and agreeing on a problem definition thus becomes a delicate process drawing upon the integration of many agents' perception of what constitutes a problem, how it is to be understood, and what action to take in response to it.

The distinction between problems and errors furthermore highlights the relationship between the representation of a problem and the domain of solutions that the representation can produce (Volkema, 1983). Carroll (1998) has made a distinction between design logic and operating logic, where the first builds on cognitive efforts of design and the latter includes learning by doing. Cognitive efforts towards problem solving need to be complemented by more direct efforts of trial in order to reduce the scope of the problem and its possible solutions since 'engineers often derive the required knowledge from the internal needs of design itself' (Vincenti, 1990, p. 11), reverting to directional search activities that draw upon more easily accessible and existing knowledge. Local search is required to identify interactions since these cannot be predicted *a priori* through a cognitive exercise, especially when dealing with a highly coupled set of components (Fleming and Sorenson, 2004). Thus engineering design as illustrated in the cases focuses predominantly on the identification, understanding and resolution of errors – a directional search process. Dealing with problems through directional search, drawing extensively upon feedback information, does not contribute to learning if this knowledge is not fed forward into future design decisions. In attempts to shift the focus from outcomes (errors) towards a focus on variables that will give rise to desired outcomes, a move from backward-looking wisdom (Gavetti & Levinthal, 2000) to attempts to establish forward-looking wisdom is warranted. Such wisdom requires the ability to enhance the knowledge arising from corrective activities (to identify errors) towards the increasing reliance on such knowledge so as to avoid future problems (the source giving rise to errors). Proactively addressing potential problems thus becomes a more viable way of reducing errors than reactive adjustment of identified errors ever can be. For this purpose heuristic search and feed-forward information and knowledge and directional search and feedback information and knowledge is required.

CONCLUSION

In this chapter we have discussed platform development in a complex problem-solving perspective. Based on the distinction between heuristic and directional search processes, problems and errors, and the concept of system architecture, we analysed two product platform development projects. Our study suggests that there is a need for a more profound understanding of problem solving. This implies a shift from general problem-solving perspectives where all deviations from expected or desired outcomes are considered to be a problem to a perspective where a distinction between problems and errors is made and different search strategies applied for their identification and rectification. We find that problem solving should be understood as a matter of reducing the search space between errors identified and the underlying reason for their existence, i.e. the problem. Such a perspective has implications for the way in which the traditional 'problem-solving' process is to be understood and managed. By early identification of errors, a reduction of the search space for finding a solution to them, and efforts to implant such solutions at the beginning of the development project, development cycle time can be reduced.

By mentally converting future errors into current problems, it becomes possible to better evaluate suggested solutions and increase their impact factor. This in turn implies a conversion from a non- or nearly decomposable perspective into a fully decomposable perspective of the system, albeit recognizing that all interdependences are difficult to identify, and in the process requiring a change of problem-solving approach.

In particular this implies not only a conversion (or inclusion) of directional search strategies but also increasing application of heuristic search processes. The requirement of both heuristic and directional search processes in the development of complex products stems from their distinct contribution to the discovery of solution landscapes and the subsequent exploration of these regions (e.g. Nickerson and Zenger, 2004). The process of establishing and understanding the input–output relationship in terms of solutions chosen cannot be catered for by heuristic search processes since the large numbers of interdependences makes this impossible. Rather a conversion towards directional search strategies (trial-and-error) is required in order to identify interdependences and the implications of chosen solutions. The determination of a problem and its degree of decomposability, in combination with the ability or degree of understanding of the interlinkages between solutions and possible outcomes, should influence the organization of the product platform development process.

On this view, problem solving becomes a matter of reducing the search space between errors and problems. It is also a process of trying to increase knowledge of errors in order to increase the understanding of how to resolve problems. By engaging in efforts to reduce the discrepancy between errors and problems, by increasing knowledge, the search process can be facilitated. However, since the activity of dealing with problems and errors is not a straightforward endeavour and organizations must be able to cope with and manage ambiguity and complexity in various forms (especially when dealing with complex platform products), learning and retention of problem-related and error-related activities become important. Finding ways for employees to manage complexity, by reducing the search space for problem- and error-solving activities in the product development process, should be an important endeavour for many companies.

In general, our study indicates that understanding a problem is a process of identifying and understanding interdependences between components, subsystems and systems. However, understanding the interlinkages is only one aspect of problem solving. Equally important is the need to understand the detailed linkage between possible alternative actions and possible outcomes of that action, not only focusing on the content of the problem, but also understanding the implications of a chosen solution. We suggest that future managers and students of product platform development need to take these issues into account, and hope that our study has paved the way for future developments in this direction.

NOTE

1. Similar concepts discussing directional search strategies include: exploitation (March, 1991), experiential search (Hsieh et al., 2007), trial and error (see, e.g., Cyert and March, 1963; March and Simon, 1958; Nelson and Winter, 1982), and online learning (Lippman and McCall, 1976). Similar concepts discussing heuristic search strategies include: exploration (March, 1991), scientific search (Fleming and Sorenson, 2004), offline learning (Lippman and McCall, 1976), and approximation method (Foulds, 1983).

REFERENCES

Baldwin, C.Y. and K.B. Clark (2000), *Design Rules: The Power of Modularity*, Cambridge, MA: MIT Press.

Brusoni, S., L. Marengo, A. Prencipe and M. Valente (2004), 'The value and costs of modularity: a cognitive perspective', Brighton: SPRU (SPRU Electronic Working Papers Series, No. 123), p. 22.

Carroll, J.S. (1998), 'Organizational learning activities in high-hazard industries: the logics underlying self-analysis', *Journal of Management Studies*, **35** (6), 699–717.

Clark, K. and T. Fujimoto (1991) *Product Development Performance: Strategy, Organization, and Management in the World Auto Industry*, Boston, MA: Harvard Business School Press.

Clift, T.B. and M.B. Vandenbosch (1999), 'Project complexity and efforts to reduce product development cycle time', *Journal of Business Research*, **45**, 187–98.

Cyert, R. and J.G. March (1963), *A Behavioral Theory of the Firm*, Englewood Cliffs, NJ: Prentice-Hall.

Davis, T.P. (2006) 'Science, engineering, and statistics', *Applied Stochastic Models in Business and Industry*, **20**, 401–30.

Dosi, G. and L. Marengo (1994) 'Some elements of an evolutionary theory of organizational competences', in R.W. England (ed.), *Evolutionary Concepts in Contemporary Economics*, Ann Arbor, MI: University of Michigan Press, pp. 157–78.

Eisenhardt, K.M. and B.N. Tabrizi (1995), 'Accelerating adaptive processes: product innovation in the global computer industry', *Administrative Science Quarterly*, **40** (1), 84–110.

Evans, D.S., A. Hagiu and R. Schmalensee (2006), *Invisible Engines: How Software Platforms Drive Innovation and Transform Industries*, Cambridge, MA: The MIT Press.

Fleming, L. and O. Sorenson (2004), 'Science as a map in technological search', *Strategic Management Journal*, **25**, 909–28.

Foulds, L.R. (1983), 'The heuristic problem solving approach', *Journal of the Operations Research Society*, **34** (10), 927–34.

Gavetti, G. and D. Levinthal (2000), 'Looking forward and looking backward: cognitive and experiential search', *Administrative Science Quarterly*, **45** (1), 113–37.

Gawer, A. and M.A. Cusumano (2002), *Platform Leadership: How Intel, Microsoft and Cisco Drive Industry Innovation*, Boston, MA: Harvard Business School Press.

Halman, J.I.M., A.P. Hofer and W. van Vuuren (2003), 'Platform-driven development of product families: linking theory with practice', *Journal of Product Innovation Management*, **20**, 149–62.

Henderson, R.M. and K.B. Clark (1990), 'Architectural innovation: the reconfiguration of existing product technologies and the failure of established firms', *Administrative Science Quarterly*, **35** (1), Special Issue: Technology, Organizations, and Innovation, 9–30.

Hsieh, C., J.A. Nickerson and T.R. Zenger (2007), 'Opportunity discovery, problem solving, and a theory of the entrepreneurial firm', *Journal of Management Studies*, **44** (7), 1255–77.

Kessler, E.H. and P.E. Bierly (2002), 'Is faster really better? An empirical test of the implications of innovation speed', *IEEE Transactions on Engineering Management*, **49** (1), 2–12.

Lindkvist, L., J. Söderlund and F. Tell (1998) 'Managing product development projects: on the significance of fountains and deadlines', *Organization Studies*, **19** (6), 931–51.

Lippman, S. and J. McCall (1976), 'The economics of job search: a survey', *Economic Inquiry*, **14**, 155–87.

Lundbäck, M. (2004), 'Managing the R&D integration process after an acquisition: Ford Motor Company's acquisition of Volvo Cars', doctoral thesis, Luleå Tekniska Universitet.

March, J.G. (1991) 'Exploration and exploitation in organizational learning', *Organization Science*, **2** (1), 71–87.

March, J. and H.A. Simon (1958), *Organizations*, New York: Wiley.

Marengo, L., C. Pasquali and M. Valente (2005), 'Decomposability and modularity of economic interactions', in W. Callebaut and D. Rasskin-Gutman (eds), *Modularity: Understanding the Development and Evolution of Complex Natural Systems*, Cambridge, MA: MIT Press, pp. 835–97.

Meyer, M.H. and A. Lehnerd (1997), *The Power of Product Platforms: Building Value and Cost Leadership*, New York: Free Press.

Nelson, R.R. and S.G. Winter (1982), *An Evolutionary Theory of Economic Change*, Cambridge, MA: Belknap Press of Harvard University Press.

Nickerson, J.A. and T.R. Zenger (2004), 'A knowledge-based theory of the firm – the problem-solving perspective', *Organization Science*, **15** (6), 617–32

Nightingale, P. (1998), 'A cognitive model of innovation', *Research Policy*, **27**, 689–709.

Reason, J. (2000), 'Human error: models and management', *British Medical Journal*, **320**, 768–70.

Silver, E.A. (2004), 'An overview of heuristic solution methods', *Journal of the Operations Research Society*, **55** (9), 936–56.

Simon, H. (1962), 'The architecture of complexity', *Proceedings of the American Philosophical Society*, **106** (6), 467–82.

Simon, H.A. (1969), *The Sciences of the Artificial*, Cambridge, MA: MIT Press.

Simon, H.A. (2000), 'Can there be a science of complex systems?', *Proceedings from the International Conference on Unifying Themes in Complex Systems*, Cambridge, MA: Perseus Books, pp. 3–14.

Simpson, T.W. (2004), 'Product platform design and customization: status and promise', *Artificial Intelligence for Engineering Design, Analysis and Manufacturing*, **18**, 3–20.

Smith, G.F. (1988) 'Towards a heuristic theory of problem structuring', *Management Science*, **34** (12), 1489–506.

Tatikonda, V.M. (1999), 'An empirical study of platform and derivative product development projects', *Journal of Product Innovation Management*, **16**, 3–26.

Thomke, S. and T. Fujimoto (2000) 'The effect of front loading problem solving on product development performance', *Journal of Product Innovation Management*, **17**, 128–42.

Tsoukas, H. (1996), 'The firm as a distributed knowledge system: a constructionist approach', *Strategic Management Journal*, **17** (Winter Special Issue), 11–25.

Ulrich, K. (1995), 'The role of product architecture in the manufacturing firm', *Research Policy*, **24**, 419–40.

Vincenti, W.G. (1990), *What Engineers Know and How They Know it*, London: The Johns Hopkins University Press.

Volkema, R.J. (1983), 'Problem formulation in planning and design', *Management Science*, **29** (6), 639–52.

Weick, K.E. and K.M. Sutcliffe (2007), *Managing the Unexpected: Resilient Performance in an Age of Uncertainty*, 2nd edn, New York: John Wiley and Sons.

Yakob, R. and F. Tell (2007), 'Managing near decomposability in complex platform development projects', *International Journal of Technology Intelligence and Planning*, **3** (4), 387–407.

14. The effect of technological platforms on the international division of labor: a case study of Intel's platform business in the PC industry

Hirofumi Tatsumoto, Koichi Ogawa and Takahiro Fujimoto

INTRODUCTION

In this chapter we examine the diffusion process of platforms, focusing on the product architecture of platforms, and the acceleration of technological innovation transfer from developed countries to developing countries. These two factors have led, ultimately, to a change in the form of the international division of labor.

The effect of product architecture on innovation is one of the central questions in existing research on technical innovation (Abernathy and Utterback, 1978; Henderson and Clark, 1990; Christensen, 1992; Ulrich, 1995; Baldwin and Clark, 2000).

Product architecture is the basic concept used to describe how the functions of a product are allocated to components, and is classified into modular and integral architecture (Ulrich, 1995). A modular architecture involves a one-to-one mapping from functions to components, and uses decoupled and clear interfaces between components (Ulrich, 1995; Baldwin and Clark, 2000; Fujimoto, 2007). By contrast, an integral architecture involves a complex mapping from functions to components, and uses coupled and rough interfaces between components (Ulrich, 1995; Fujimoto, 2007).

The growing use of modular architecture has led to an increase in the importance of innovations in modular cluster industries (Langlois and Robertson, 1992; Sanchez and Mahoney, 1996; Baldwin and Clark, 2000). The rise of the computer industry in Silicon Valley is the most typical and successful case of modular cluster innovations (Baldwin and Clark, 2000).

The platform, meaning a system made of interdependent products or components, has played a key role in modular cluster innovations (Gawer and Cusumano, 2002; Iansiti and Levien, 2004). Under modular architecture, the platform is a special module that provides a means for mixing and matching other modules and for constructing numerous combinations to achieve the most valuable design. The platform promotes the development of an ecosystem of complementors and leads modular cluster innovations (Baldwin and Clark, 2000; Cusumano and Gawer, 2002; Iansiti and Levien, 2004).

However, little is known about the mechanism by which platforms are diffused before the establishment of the ecosystem and modular cluster innovations. Early studies on platforms focused on the management of the self-sustaining process in modular cluster innovations after the achievement of critical mass for the adoption (Gawer and Cusumano, 2002; Iansiti and Levien, 2004), with network externalities fueling further growth (Rogers, 2003; Shapiro and Varian, 1998).

The explanation of the diffusion process using the analogy of an ecosystem has produced important insights, but it is fundamentally incomplete. The ecosystem model has elucidated the diffusion process after the achievement of critical mass, but the diffusion mechanism before the achievement of critical mass remains unclear.

In other words, the aim of the ecosystem model is to answer the question why the platform encourages the innovations after the achievement of critical mass. However, the question of how the platform obtains sufficient shipment volume to create the ecosystem before the achievement of critical mass remains unanswered.

Furthermore, a viewpoint incorporating the international division of labor seems necessary for understanding the diffusion mechanism of platforms because the platforms are often used in products produced by developing-country firms. Recent researches on the international division of labor suggest that platforms have provided turnkey solutions for the establishment of new global production networks (Sturgeon, 2002; Berger et al., 2005; Shintaku et al., 2006). They emphasize platform-based production networks such as contract manufacturing in value chain modularity.

In this chapter, we develop and apply a new model that grew out of a case study on Intel's platform business in Taiwan in the 1990s. This helps to give a detailed understanding of the characteristics of the platform, the diffusion mechanism into developing-country firms, and the effect on the international division of labor.

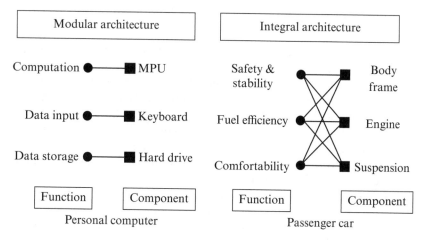

Figure 14.1   Product architecture

LITERATURE REVIEW AND CONCEPTUAL FRAMEWORK

Two Types of Product Architecture

Systems are generally classified, based on their characteristics, into two types of product architecture: modular architecture and integral architecture (Figure 14.1).

This typology is based on the interdependence of the elements that compose the system. A system consists of many components, and each set of components has interdependence with others. A system with a simple and one-to-one mapping from functions to components is called a modular system, while a system with complex and one-to-many mapping from functions to components is called an integral system.

The typical example of integral architecture is the passenger car. When improving the fuel efficiency of a car, you also need to lighten the body frame and to redesign the suspension in order to maintain comfort and safety/stability. However, in the case of a modular architecture such as the personal computer (PC), upgrading the hard drive from 10 GB to 100 GB does not require redesign of the keyboard or the microprocessor.

Two Types of Technology

With modular architecture, it is not necessary to make a complete and detailed design of the overall system at the early stage of the design process. Designers can mix and match modules to find the most valuable design. We define technologies where designers individually vary the designs and evaluate them with mix-and-match flexibility as modular technology.

In contrast, integral architecture requires the designers to make a complete and detailed design at an early stage. We define technology where designers jointly organize and adjust designs with coordinate-and-fit optimization as integral technology.

In terms of the speed of technological diffusion, there are considerable differences between the two forms of technology, because they are based on different background knowledge: codified knowledge and tacit knowledge (Teece, 2006).

Modular technology is based on codified interfaces specified by a modular architecture. Designers can make choices without consulting other designers within the limits set under the design rules. This codified knowledge is clear, and can be easily transferred among designers (Baldwin and Clark, 2000; Teece, 2006). On the contrary, integral technology is based on the sharing of tacit knowledge among the designers. This tacit knowledge is not easily transferred to others because it is difficult to articulate and explain (Teece, 1986, 2006; Nonaka and Toyama, 2004).

Consequently, modular technology diffuses at a very high speed as it is adopted by new organizations, while integral technology often remains constrained within particular organizations and diffuses at a very low speed.

The Hierarchy of Modular Architecture

Ideally, modular architecture should be fully modular. However, this is not always the case in the real world. Strictly speaking, modular architecture products must form a completely decomposable system. But they actually often form a system that is nearly decomposable (Simon, 1996). In this case, the coordination of knowledge and organization cannot be achieved purely by mix-and-match methods based on design rules. Rather, the achievement of knowledge and organizational coordination requires interactive management of the actors and activities involved (Brusoni and Prencipe, 2001). This suggests that quasi-modular architecture products require both modular and integral technology.

The concept of the hierarchy of architecture can help us to understand this complex phenomenon (Alexander, 1964; Clark, 1985; Ulrich, 1995;

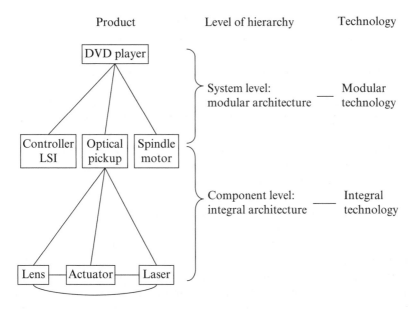

Figure 14.2   Hierarchy of architecture with two types of technology

Eppinger et al., 1990; Simon, 1996). Product architecture is hierarchical, and different layers can make use of different technologies. Ideally, fully modular architecture should adopt modular technology for all the layers. In reality, however, architectures that are said to be modular often consist of both modular technology layers and integral technology layers, because they are not completely decomposable systems but only nearly decomposable ones.

For example, a DVD player shows the modular architecture product consisting of several layers with different technologies (Figure 14.2). Manufacturers mix and match DVD player modules such as optical pickup, spindle motor and controller LSI, and bring new DVD players promptly onto the market. This demonstrates that at the system level, the DVD player is based on modular technology. However, the core components such as the optical pickup consist of an integral technology layer. The optical pickup is made of lenses, holograms and lasers, which require mutual adjustment.

The Separation Effect of Platforms

As a consequence of the hierarchy of architecture, a product with quasi-modular architecture can be based on one of two patterns of coordination, depending on the technology layer. The first pattern is automatic coordination with mix-and-match flexibility realized by sharing codified interface information. The second involves interactive coordination based on the sharing of tacit knowledge among designers through deep and long-term communication.

The second pattern of coordination takes place when there are special companies whose capabilities span technological fields wider than the range of activities that they actually perform in house. These firms are defined as system integrators (Brusoni and Prencipe, 2001) or platform leaders (Gawer and Cusumano, 2002). Both are essentially equivalent with respect to the pattern of coordination. In this chapter, we shall focus on the latter pattern.

As explained above, platforms are special components provided by actors who have wider capability or knowledge than what they actually perform in house (Cusumano and Gawer, 2002; Iansiti and Levien, 2004). The platform is not equivalent to the other modules in a modular architecture because it incorporates the coordination within itself and converts the product architecture from a nearly decomposable system to a completely decomposable one. The conversion leads to a clear separation of the mixture of two technologies used in the modular architecture into modular and integral technology. We define this conversion as the separation effect of platforms.

This 'separation effect' of platforms leads to a change of the quasi-modular architecture into completely modular architecture, which allows modules to evolve freely within the limits set by design rules, and allows designers to vary their design and seek the best design of the whole system based on modular technology. This change leads to a remarkable increase in the importance of design rules, and in turn to a powerful ecosystem of complementors with increasing mix-and-match flexibility. As a result, the separation effect of platforms rapidly and steadily accelerates modular cluster innovations based on the platform.

The Effect of Platforms on the International Division of Labor

As mentioned above, the separation effect of platforms encourages modular cluster innovations. At the same, it deeply affects the international division of labor in modular architecture products.

The speed of diffusion of technology for quasi-modular architecture products is moderate since the two technologies are mixed and inseparable. However, the existence of a platform splits the technologies into two streams, and converts the quasi-modular product into a completely modular product consisting of modular layers at the system level and integral layers at the platform level. Separating the two technologies of the quasi-modular architecture product affects the technology diffusion speeds of the finished products and the platform differently.

As shown schematically in Figure 14.3, the technologies used in the finished products diffuse rapidly into firms located in developing countries because they are based on completely modular technology, which has a high diffusion speed. By contrast, the platform technology remains in the original firm, which tends to be located in a developed country, because the platform uses integral technology, which has a low diffusion speed.

The separation leads to a loss of the advantages of the manufacturers of finished products in the developed country. After the establishment of the platform, the system level comes to require modular technologies rather than the integral technologies that traditional firms in a developed country foster. New firms in developing countries may be able to adopt modular technology more quickly than their counterparts in developed countries.

Consequently, the separation effect of platforms leads to a shift in the production of the finished products from the developed country to developing countries while keeping the platform in the developed country.

We explore the validity of this framework through a brief summary of the competitive and technical history of the PC industry. Using the case study of Intel's platform business in Taiwan, we attempt to explain the characteristics and influences of the platform. Since the 1990s, the growth of the Taiwanese economy has had a major influence on the electronics industry. Cooperation between a US CPU (central processing unit) vendor and Taiwanese motherboard or notebook PC manufacturers is a typical case of a successful platform. This chapter focuses on the collaborative economic development process between Intel and Taiwanese firms.

METHOD

Research Approach

Intel's platform business is a well-known case of a technological platform. However, few researchers have explained it from the viewpoint of both product architecture and the international division of labor. Therefore, in this chapter we examine the relationship between the architecture and the international division of labor.

Data on PC product architecture were gathered from various technical documents and discussions with developers of PCs. These data provide necessary information for the analysis, including the interdependence among components and the mapping information from functions to components.

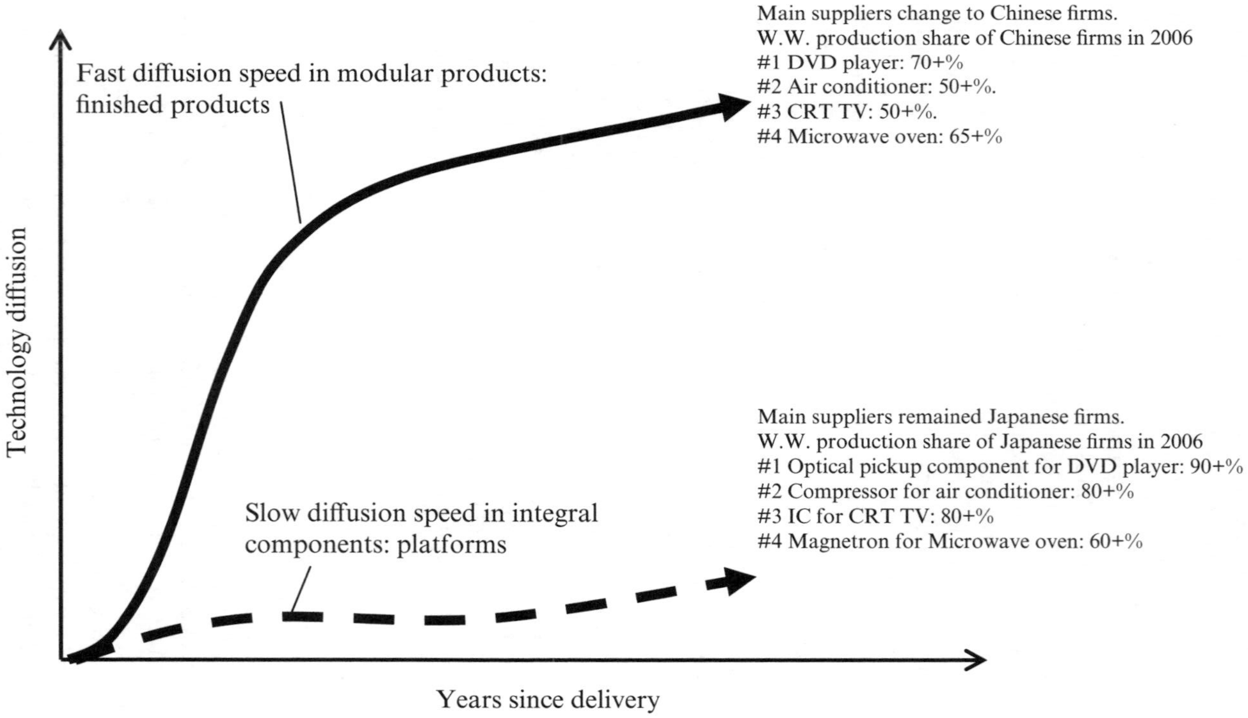
Technology diffusion
Fast diffusion speed in modular products:
finished products
Slow diffusion speed in integral
components: platforms
Years since delivery
Main suppliers change to Chinese firms.
W.W. production share of Chinese firms in 2006
#1 DVD player: 70+%
#2 Air conditioner: 50+%.
#3 CRT TV: 50+%.
#4 Microwave oven: 65+%
Main suppliers remained Japanese firms.
W.W. production share of Japanese firms in 2006
#1 Optical pickup component for DVD player: 90+%
#2 Compressor for air conditioner: 80+%
#3 IC for CRT TV: 80+%
#4 Magnetron for Microwave oven: 60+%

Figure 14.3 Difference in technology diffusion of modular and integral architecture observed in Chinese and Japanese firms, 1997–2005

In addition to these data, we gathered interview data and time trend data on prices and shipments of PCs. The data include many interviews with US, Taiwanese and Japanese people in the PC industry. The interviewees included managers of Intel's design center in Taiwan and Taiwanese motherboard and notebook PC manufacturers. Today, 90 percent of the worldwide demand for motherboards and notebook PCs is filled by products made in Taiwan, while Intel supplies both the CPUs and chipsets for these Taiwanese companies. To gain an understanding of the effect of the existence of a platform on the international division of labor, we analyzed the time trend data on prices and shipment volumes of PCs.

Research Design

The research questions can be broken down into the two following operational questions.

Research Question 1

What architectural change takes place with the technological platform in the view of the indicator 'integral–modular'?

To elucidate this architectural change, we used a PC bus structure map including the main components. Electrical signals run through the bus, and each semiconductor chip communicates and works with the others. Thus the bus enables these components to link to each other logically and functionally. The PC architecture is considered to be integral when significant coordination is required in the bus. On the contrary, the architecture is regarded to be modular when each item works individually.

Research Question 2

What effect does the existence of a platform have on industries in developing countries?

It is assumed that the existence of a platform affects the international division of labor and encourages production in the developed country. To examine this effect of the platform, we focus on the growth of the Taiwanese PC industry in the 1990s.

We used two trend data sets to examine the relationships between the platform and the expansion of Taiwanese production. The first data set shows market share trends for Intel's chipsets, which is an indicator of the presence of Intel's platform. The second data set shows trends in Taiwanese production of motherboards and notebook PCs using Intel's platform. The relationship between the two data sets can explain the effect of the platform on the international division of labor.

CASE STUDY AND FINDINGS

Industrial Environment: The Background of Intel's Platform Strategy

Intel's CPU business was facing a critical threat in the early 1990s. Some CPU companies, including Cyrix and AMD, began to compete with Intel, supplying compatible CPUs. Moreover, there were new entries into the PC CPU market by companies developing CPU for minicomputers and workstations.

Intel's basic strategy was 'If we supply the latest CPUs more quickly and on a larger production scale than our competitors, we can get further scales of economy and attain market dominance.' A large supply would allow Intel to sell the latest CPUs at a low price, even if it had made enormous investments into development and manufacturing. Moreover, its CPU products would dominate the market, and complementors would provide software and hardware for this market. These complementary goods would increase the value of Intel's CPUs. As a result, it would be able to achieve market dominance.

This strategy sounds simple but was difficult to execute in the early 1990s because the development lead time for CPUs was much longer then than it is today. Furthermore, the speed of market penetration for the latest CPUs was slow, since traditional PC makers often hesitated to adopt the latest CPUs. They preferred to profit from existing CPUs rather than adopt the latest ones. From the standpoint of Intel, a rapid and extensive spread of the latest CPU was desirable. However, at the time, Intel was supplying a limited number of traditional PC manufacturers. It needed to find new manufacturers. This is why Intel decided to adopt the new way of business.

The Platform and the Change in PC Architecture

Intel needed to open new markets and gain new customers in order to supply a large number of the latest CPUs. It decided to target new ventures and no-brand companies. However, such new companies were generally young and lacked adequate technologies to handle Intel's novel products.

In order to ensure that it could supply the latest CPUs to them, Intel planned to provide CPUs and chipsets simultaneously. Previously, chipsets were provided by specialized companies, and were not fully adjusted to CPUs. PC manufacturers had to make great efforts to make sure that the latest CPUs and chipsets would work together.

In the motherboard development process, compatibility problems were often caused by a lack of mutual coordination among the developers of CPUs and the chipsets. It often took a significant amount of time to clear up the problem. Intel had to wait a long time to see PCs in the stores after finishing the latest CPU. To resolve this, Intel decided to provide CPUs and adjusted chipsets simultaneously as a single platform. This strategy led to the architectural change as illustrated in Figure 14.4.

Before the advent of the platform, PCs were composed of a CPU and three controllers (DRAM controller, I/O bus controller, IDE controller). The CPU and controllers were supplied by different companies, and the chips were not fully coordinated.

After the introduction of the platform, the three controllers were integrated into two (the north bridge and south bridge) and fully fitted with the CPU. In addition, the two controllers were designed to have good mutual connections. The CPU and controllers became the large components later known as the platform. The PC came to be composed of one large chunk, the platform, and many small components.

What is important is that the platform-based PC does not require enormous efforts to coordinate among the components, because the platform is already adjusted with the chipset. Since the platform eliminates problems caused by interdependence among components, the PC was converted from quasi-modular architecture to completely modular architecture.

It was 1993 when Intel began to plan to incorporate its latest CPUs, such as the Pentium CPU, and the chipset into a single platform based on the same roadmap. Figure 14.5 shows how Intel gained market share. It began to offer chipsets on the market as a platform in 1993. Its market share began to grow rapidly. In 1995, Intel grabbed the top share with 34 percent of the market and completed the platform.

The Standardization of the PC

Intel's strategy was not just to supply the chipset. It standardized everything in the PC, including the internal bus, size of the components, and various interfaces connected to the external peripherals. Figure 14.6 illustrates what parts of the PC are standardized. In some cases, Intel initiated the standardization on its own, and in other cases worked with other companies.

As Figure 14.6 shows, the interfaces of the PC are classified into three categories: standardized interfaces, closed interfaces and licensing

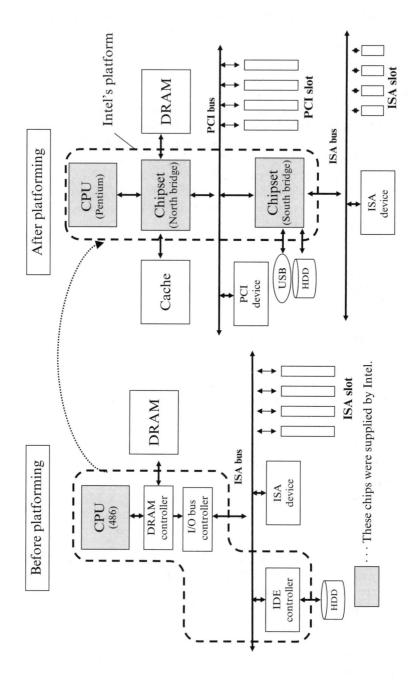

Figure 14.4   The Intel architecture before and after platforming

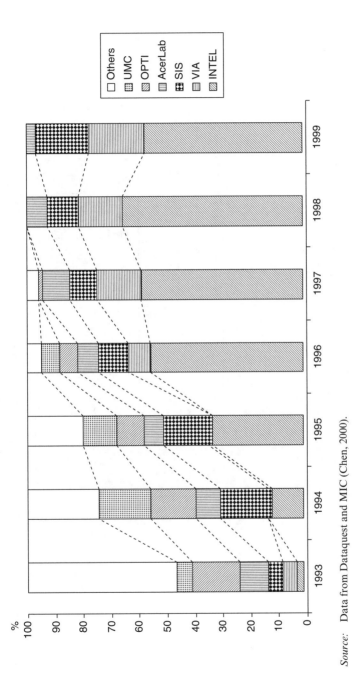

Source: Data from Dataquest and MIC (Chen, 2000).

Figure 14.5 Trends in chipset share

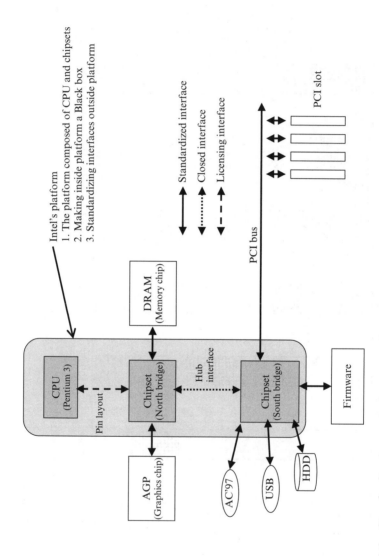

Figure 14.6　Standardized areas in the personal computer

interfaces. The standardized interfaces are accessible and open to the public. The closed interfaces are available only to Intel. The licensing interfaces are also restricted, but some specific firms licensed by Intel can access them. Nearly everything except the inside of the platform was standardized.

PC manufacturers use Intel's chipset, and then add various standardized devices, components and peripherals. The standardized interfaces are desirable for complementors, who can prepare their products for a single interface and then sell them to various customers. This standardization attracted a number of complementors, and led to the development of a huge ecosystem.

Another effect of the standardization was consumer confidence. Consumers assumed that this standardization would guarantee function and interoperability. When a PC has standardized interfaces such as USB and PCI, the consumer gains a feeling of confidence, even if it is a no-brand PC. On the other hand, however, the standardization makes product differentiation difficult in terms of function or quality.

The development of large chipsets with standardized interfaces promoted a rapid conversion of the PC into a completely modular product. The standardization has taken place in the notebook PC as well as desktop PC.

The Expansion of Taiwanese Production

The change in the architecture of the PC prompted many new companies to enter the market. These new companies included many in developing countries.

Figure 14.7 shows that Taiwanese production of motherboards and notebook PCs has been growing since 1995, the year that Intel completed the platform. This suggests that Intel established the platform with the partnership of Taiwanese manufacturers. Further, Intel's chipsets contributed to the rise of motherboard and notebook PC assembly in Taiwan. Taiwanese companies quickly extended their production with Intel's platform, as shown in Figure 14.7.

In the early 1990s, Taiwanese PC manufacturers were already producing motherboards and notebook PCs. However, their production was limited, as they could not produce the latest PCs based on the latest CPUs and chipsets. They did not have their own brands, and built PCs under outsourcing contracts from the major US OEMs (original equipment manufacturers). The US OEMs did not outsource the latest high-end PCs, but produced them themselves. Thus the Taiwanese manufacturers provided mainly the economy versions of motherboards and notebook PCs that were functionally obsolete.

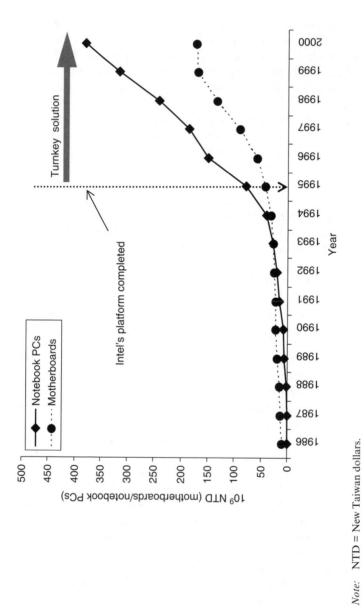

Note: NTD = New Taiwan dollars.

Source: The internet information search system, Department of Statistics, Ministry of Economic Affairs, ROC.

Figure 14.7   Trends of Intel's chipset market share and production of motherboards and notebook PCs in Taiwan

For the Taiwanese companies, who were shut out from the high-end market, being able to produce the latest motherboards was an attractive prospect. Their gross margin ratio climbed above 60 percent when they began to provide the latest high-end motherboards for PCs based on Intel's platform in 1995. Figure 14.7 shows that Intel's chipset enabled them to enter this market, and they extended their production quickly with the platform.

Intel offered not only the platform but also a turnkey solution, composed of the chipset, evaluation kit, materials list, reference design and design know-how. It even contained the data necessary for production. The chipset and other offerings were provided as a turnkey solution for motherboard and notebook PC manufacturing. This complete solution stimulated the Taiwanese PC industry. Taiwanese firms achieved great success in the field of motherboards, and subsequently in notebook PCs.

Formerly, traditional notebook PC firms had a competitive advantage, because they had the overall system knowledge required for development and manufacturing. This knowledge included heat design, power consumption design and so on, which are controlled by the chipset. At that time, Taiwanese companies could not buy the latest chipsets for notebooks, because they were developed in house by the traditional firms. Therefore it was difficult for Taiwanese manufacturers to gain a foothold in the latest notebook market.

Taiwanese firms had begun production of notebook PCs in the early 1990s, but on a limited scale. They were able to produce only obsolete economy versions of notebook PCs since they did not have sufficient knowledge of the entire system. Their production share was only 20 percent or so in 1995. By 2005, after the change, it had risen to 80 percent.

The Taiwanese notebook PC industry faced a substantial change in the mid-1990s. After 1995, Intel began to provide chipsets for the latest notebook PCs. Before that time, the chipset market for notebook computers had been regarded as a niche market. However, Intel began to supply chipsets for this market, with Taiwanese manufacturers as the main target.

The chipset for notebook PCs was carefully designed with respect to power consumption and heat radiation. This chipset helped to extend battery life by standardizing the power-saving control function under a specification known as ACPI. Before the change, resolving such problems required an overall system knowledge of the notebook PC. However, the introduction of the chipset for notebook PCs gave Taiwanese manufacturers the ability to develop and produce notebook PCs, even the latest ones, without such knowledge. With the growing production of Taiwanese manufacturers, Intel's platform spread all over the world.

Price Erosion of the Standardized Components and Stability of the Platform

The technological platform led to a conversion of the PC to a completely open modular product. In addition, the turnkey solution accelerated the expansion of Taiwanese production. This change had a dramatic effect on the PC market.

Severe price competition began in the open market, resulting from the standardization. Standardized components such as hard drives and DRAM suffered a sharp price drop. Figure 14.8 shows trends in the average sales price of key components of the PC. It shows that the price of hard drives and DRAM kept dropping at a serious pace. However, Intel was able to maintain the price of CPUs.

This split of the market into a dual structure resulted from the architectural position. Intel's platform continued to be based on integral architecture. Moreover, Intel made its platform into a black box. On the contrary, hard drives and DRAM came to be based on open modular architecture because they connected with the standardized interfaces of Intel's platform. The standardization accelerated the openness of the market. This means that the platform divides the market into two segments: one is the closed, integral architecture inside the platform; and the other the open, modular architecture outside of the platform.

By 2003, the average sales price of HDDs had fallen to about 40 percent of its price in 1995. DRAM suffered from an even more rapid drop: the average sales price hit 40 percent of the price in 1995 by 2000, just five years later.

Figure 14.9 shows trends in the price of DRAM per megabit rather than per module. In 1995, the year that Intel's platform was completed, there was severe price erosion. The price per megabit, which was $3 in 1995, plunged to just $0.08 in 2000. This amounts to a fall to 1/30 of the original price in just five years.

The architectural conversion of the PC had a major influence on the competition in the HDD and DRAM market. Seagate rapidly gained market share in the HDD market after 1995, and Samsung did the same in the DRAM market. A strategic change took place in the market for standardized components such as DRAM and HDDs. Large-scale production and cost leadership became the key factors to success.

As main components prices fell, the price of the final product declined as well. Moreover, product differentiation decreased as almost all areas of the PC were standardized, and the popularization of the PC increased. Cheap PCs spread all over the world. Consumers who could not afford them before could now buy one.

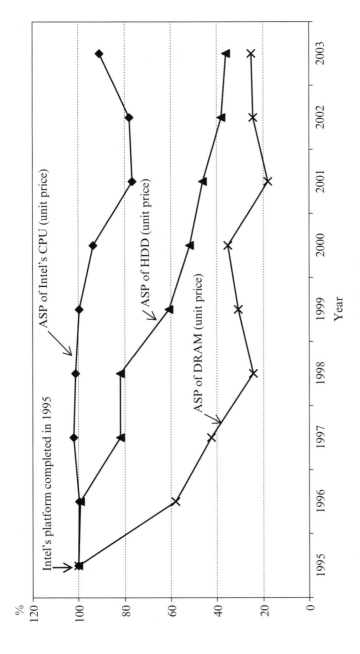

Source: All ASPs have been originally calculated by the authors based on the data on CPUs from Microprocessor Design Report, HDDs from Techno System Research, DRAMs from iSuppli and various other information.

Figure 14.8 Trends in average sales prices of key PC components

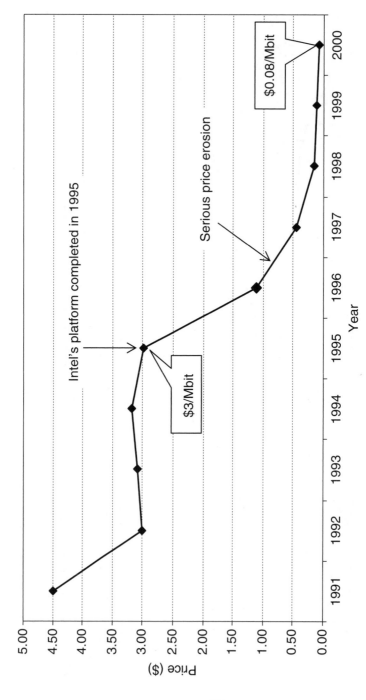

Source: Data from iSuppli.

Figure 14.9 Trends in DRAM price per Mbit

The architectural conversion of the PC also affected competitiveness strategy. Companies that tried to achieve product differentiation through technology faced a difficult situation. Those that focused on circulation channels, such as Dell, gained a greater competitive advantage.

DISCUSSION

Results from Findings

The purpose of this study was to examine the characteristics of the technological platform and the effect of the technological platform on the international division of labor.

For Research Question 1, we established two facts:

1. Intel began to supply CPUs and chipsets as a single platform. The CPU and chipset were combined into a large chunk of elements that are fully adjusted to one another. Intel's platform is classified as integral architecture.
2. The platform has fully standardized interfaces towards the outside. Intel strongly promoted this standardization. As a result, many complementors can supply products to fit the standardized interfaces.

The platform has two kinds of characteristic: the closed, integral architecture inside the platform; and the completely open modular architecture outside the platform. Because of this dual nature, the more the platform is diffused, the more completely modular the PC becomes. Consequently, the PC has come to be composed of one large chunk, the platform, and many small standardized components. The prices of the standardized components have dropped sharply along with the price of PCs themselves. By contrast, Intel has been able to maintain the price of the platform because the platform remains the integral architecture and the black box inside.

For Research Question 2, we established two facts:

1. Taiwanese motherboard and notebook PC manufacturers expanded their production quickly with the spread of the platform. Formerly, they were able to access only a limited market, but the platform enabled them to access the latest high-end market.
2. Intel provided not only the platform but also a turnkey solution, which includes the technological platform, design know-how and useful information for production. This complete solution stimulated the Taiwanese PC industry.

The platform and complete turnkey solution affected the international division of labor in the PC industry. This led to an acceleration of production in developing countries, although the platform has remained in the developed country. The growth of production in developing countries allowed the rapid development of a huge global market for PCs. From Intel's perspective, these finished products allowed its integral products, such as CPUs, to reach the worldwide market at lightning speed.

After the platform was established, firms in developed countries expanded their production of finished products quickly and intensively. They found the platform very attractive, because it enabled them to enter not only the market for obsolete PCs but also the advanced market. In addition, firms in developing countries were able to offer much lower prices than their counterparts in developed countries. Thanks to their vigorous efforts at cost reduction, PCs became affordable for consumers in the BRIC (Brazil, Russian, India and China) economies, and a huge global PC market began to emerge. It would have remained limited and small without the platform. However, the platform itself remained in the developed country because it was based on integral technology.

CONCLUSION

The adoption of the platform enabled an architectural conversion of the PC to a completely modular product. This architectural change stimulated the industry in developing countries and established a new model of economic collaboration.

The root cause of this new model of collaboration is the separation effect of the platform. Figure 14.10 illustrates this separation and its effect on the international division of labor. The adoption of the platform leads to a decoupling of technologies in the finished products into modular technology and integral technology. The modular technology has rapid technology diffusion speed while integral technology has slow technology diffusion speed.

The separation effect is derived from the dual nature of the platform. The platform has two kinds of characteristics: the completely integral architecture inside the platform and the completely modular architecture outside it.

With the rapid diffusion of technology, the adoption of a platform leads to a quick expansion of production in developing-country firms. The cost reductions in developing-country firms allow affordable prices and help to create a huge global market, such as the BRIC market. The growing platform led to a radical production shift from developed to developing

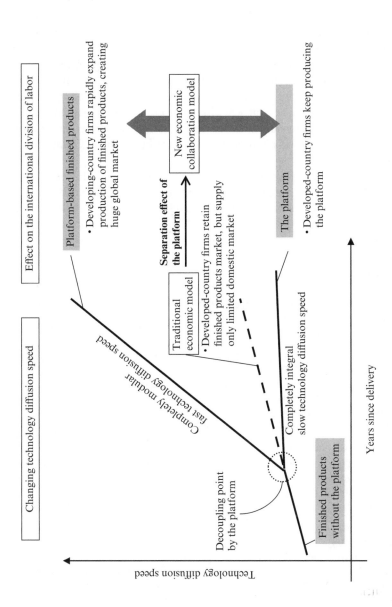

Figure 14.10 Changing technology diffusion speeds by the platform and effect on the international division of labor

367

countries. As a result, the platform fundamentally changes the international division of labor by noticeably strengthening the new model of economic collaboration between the developing and developed countries.

This model will become increasingly important in the future, as it can be applied to many products, including cellphones, DVD players, and even LCD and photovoltaic panels. The growth of developing countries is stimulated by platforms, and at the same time, the developed country that supplies the platform is given access to the huge global market in partnership with the developing countries. This collaboration has an intense effect on the international division of labor. In this sense, this new collaboration model based on platforms is important both for business and for academic studies.

In this study we examined the issue of technological platforms using a case study. For further generalization, future research should be carried out based on case studies in another product segment or using cross-sectional statistical data.

REFERENCES

Abernathy, W.J. and J.M. Utterback (1978), 'Patterns of industrial innovation', *Technological Review*, **50**, 40–47.

Alexander, C. (1964), *Notes of the Synthesis of Form*, Cambridge, MA: Harvard University Press.

Baldwin, C.Y. and K.B. Clark (2000), *Design Rules: The Power of Modularity*, Cambridge, MA: MIT Press.

Berger, S. and the MIT Industrial Performance Center (2005), *How We Compete: What Companies Around the World Are Doing to Make It in Today's Global Economy*, New York: Currency/Doubleday.

Brusoni, S. and A. Prencipe (2001), 'Unpacking the black box of modularity: technologies, products and organizations', *Industrial and Corporate Change*, **10** (1), 179–205.

Chen, W. (2000), 'Shuanlong Qiangzhu de Jingpianzu Shichan' ('Competition between two dragons in the chipset market') (in Chinese), Securities Research Report, Taiwan, KGI Securities Co., Ltd.

Christensen, C.M. (1992), 'Exploring the limits of the technology S-curve, Part 1: Component technologies', *Production and Operations Management Journal*, **1**, 334–57.

Clark, K.B. (1985), 'The interaction of design hierarchies and market concepts in technological evolution', *Research Policy*, **4** (5), 235–51.

Eppinger, S.D., D.E. Whitney, R.P. Smith and D. Gebala (1990), 'Organizing the tasks in complex design projects', *ASME Conference on Design Theory and Methodology*, Chicago, IL, September, pp. 39–46.

Fujimoto, T. (2007), 'Architecture-based comparative advantage: a design information view of manufacturing', *Evolutionary and Institutional Economics Review*, **4** (1), 55–112.

Gawer, A. and M.A. Cusumano (2002), *Platform Leadership: How Intel, Microsoft, and Cisco Drive Industry Innovation*, Boston, MA: Harvard Business School Press.

Henderson, R.M. and K.B. Clark (1990), 'Architectural innovation – the configuration of existing product technologies and the failure of established firms', *Administrative Science Quarterly*, **35** (1), 9–30.

Iansiti, M. and R. Levien (2004), *The Keystone Advantage: What the New Business Ecosystems Mean for Strategy, Innovation, and Sustainability*, Boston, MA: Harvard Business School Press.

Langlois, N.L. and P.L. Robertson (1992), 'Networks and innovation in a modular system: lessons from the microcomputer and stereo component industries', *Research Policy*, **21** (4), 297–313.

Nonaka, I. and R. Toyama (2004), 'Knowledge creation as a synthesizing process', in H. Takeuchi and I. Nonaka (eds), *Hitotsubashi on Knowledge Management*, New York: John Wiley & Sons, pp. 91–124.

Rogers, E.M. (2003), *Diffusion of Innovations*, 5th edn, New York: Free Press.

Sanchez, R. and J. Mahoney (1996), 'Modularity, flexibility, and knowledge management in product and organization design', *Strategic Management Journal*, **17** (Winter Special Issue), 63–76.

Shapiro, C. and H.R. Varian (1998), *Information Rules: A Strategic Guide to the Network Economy*, Boston, MA: Harvard Business School Press.

Shintaku, J., K. Ogawa and T. Yoshimoto (2006), 'Architecture-based approaches to international standardization and evolution of business models', 21COE, University of Tokyo MMRC Discussion Paper No. 96.

Simon, H.A. (1996), *The Sciences of the Artificial*, 3rd edn, Cambridge, MA: MIT Press.

Sturgeon, T.J. (2002), 'Modular production networks: a new American model of industrial organization', *Industrial and Corporate Change*, **11** (3), 451–96.

Teece, T.J. (1986), 'Profiting from technological innovation: implications for integration, collaboration, licensing and public policy', *Research Policy*, **15** (6), 285–305.

Teece, D.J. (2006), 'Reflections on "profiting from innovation"', *Research Policy*, **35** (8), 1131–46.

Ulrich, K. (1995), 'The role of product architecture in the manufacturing firm', *Research Policy*, **24** (3), 419–40.

Index